W9-AAF-972

# HUMAN SEXUALITY

# HUMAN SEXUALITY

## An All-Embracing Gift

GERALD D. COLEMAN, SS

ALBA · HOUSE    NEW · YORK

SOCIETY OF ST. PAUL, 2187 VICTORY BLVD., STATEN ISLAND, NY 10314

Library of Congress Cataloging-in-Publication Data

Coleman, Gerald D.
    Human sexuality: an all-embracing gift / Gerald D. Coleman.
        p.   cm.
    Includes bibliographical references (p.      ).
    ISBN 0-8189-0643-X
    1. Sexual ethics — United States.   2. Sex — Religious aspects
— Catholic Church.     I. Title.
    HQ32.C65      1992
    241'.66 — dc20                                      92-20661
                                                              CIP


Nihil Obstat:
Rev. Robert W. McElroy, S.T.D., Ph.D.
Censor Librorum

Imprimatur:
✠ Most Rev. John R. Quinn, DD
Archbishop of San Francisco
February 17, 1992

The Nihil Obstat and Imprimatur are official declarations
that a book or pamphlet is free of doctrinal or moral
error. No implication is contained therein that those
who have granted the Nihil Obstat and Imprimatur agree
with the contents, opinions or statements expressed.


Produced and designed in the United States of America by the
Fathers and Brothers of the Society of St. Paul,
2187 Victory Boulevard, Staten Island, New York 10314,
as part of their communications apostolate.

ISBN: 0-8189-0643-X

© Copyright 1992 by the Society of St. Paul

**Printing Information:**

Current Printing - first digit        2    3    4    5    6    7    8    9    10

Year of Current Printing - first year shown

                                 1995              1996              1997

# In Gratitude

I would like to dedicate this book to the many men and women I have had the privilege of working with in pastoral ministry and especially those seminarians who have been a constant challenge and encouragement to me in refining my ideas about human sexuality.

I am profoundly grateful to so many people who have shared their own lives with me and have helped me to see the importance of love and friendship: especially my mom, dad and brother; along with Father David Pettingill, Sister Patrick Curran, S.M., Sister Grayce Ross, S.N.J.M., and Mrs. Jeanne Robles; and the Carmelite Nuns of Carmel, California, and in Espoo, Finland, without whose spiritual support and encouragement this work would not have been completed. I am indebted to these extremely fine people in ways too deep to express in words.

# TABLE OF CONTENTS

# INTRODUCTION

Judith Viorst writes:

Infatuation is when you think that he's as sexy as Robert Redford, as smart as Henry Kissinger, as noble as Ralph Nader, as funny as Woody Allen, and as athletic as Jimmy Connors. Love is when you realize that he's as sexy as Woody Allen, as smart as Jimmy Connors, as funny as Ralph Nader, as athletic as Henry Kissinger and nothing like Robert Redford in any category — but you'll take him anyway.[1]

Viorst's quip about the love-versus-infatuation question is one that certainly plagues contemporary society. This book roots itself in this problem with the hope of articulating clearly the Church's teachings, presuppositions and viewpoints regarding love and the question of human sexuality.

It is necessary to specifically highlight this love-versus-infatuation problematic: i.e., in the Church's understanding and teachings, infatuation is not love and love is no mere *obiter dictum* (an incidental reality). Love is rooted in God and finds its most profound meaning in relationship to the mystery of God. Love is not banal and love is simply not an attitude or action that has no human link or consequence.

Lisa Sowle Cahill concludes her book *Between the Sexes*[2] with these words:

Sexual morality is a difficult subject, one that impinges in a most intimate and often painful way on the consciences, identities, anxieties, and hopes of those who address it. In the churches, as in the wider culture, sexuality has been a source of division, exclusion, suffering, and even hatred... Various theological and moral perceptions of sexuality still need to be formulated with an appropriate degree of humility as well as honesty... How, for instance, shall the charisma of celibacy be understood in an age in which the end time (*eschaton*) has receded and it has become dubious that sexual abstinence is a precondition of thoroughgoing religious commitment? How shall marriage be understood in a society whose basic organization no longer depends on kinship, and in a world where unlimited procreation would be an evil not a good? How shall the sexual identity of the single adult be understood in a culture in which marital and familial ties no longer define social identity in roles, in which the assumption that all adults shall wed has become problematic, and in which the expressive, pleasurable, and companionable potentials of sex receive widespread appreciation and even promotion? How shall the homosexual's situation be understood after empirical studies have indicated the relative uncontrolability of sexual orientation, along with the fundamental relation of sexuality to identity and personality?[3]

This present work attempts to approach the question of sexual morality aware of all of these complicated questions, rooted in a humility which appreciates that not all questions have clear and immediate responses, but also conscious of the fact that over the centuries the Church has taught and still teaches extremely important parameters that help color the landscape of human sexuality. As Cahill has rightfully remarked, "The horizon against which all moral activity is to be evaluated is the communal life as body of Christ in the world."[4]

This book stresses that one's sexual identity is a gift and is a part of God's creation. Human sexuality is thus good. Many people view the gift of sexuality with great ambivalence and some even understand their sexuality as a liability. Such responses may be manifested in ignorance of basic aspects of sexuality, anxieties regarding sexual expression, inability to enter into intimate relationships, and uncertainty about the limits of sexual expression.[5] In light of this vast possibility of responses, this book deals not only with fundamental moral questions regarding human sexuality; but also in many instances draws out as fully as possible the physiological and biological aspects of our sexuality. It is indeed a fact that oftentimes ignorance about one's body may inhibit the capacity to find and enjoy intimacy and love as God intends. Since our capacity to know what we are feeling and to experience those feelings is rooted in bodily experiences, to be ambivalent about or alienated from our bodies is to be estranged from ourselves.[6] Our sexuality is basic to who we are and affects our thoughts, feelings and actions.

This book also hopes to encourage its readers to acknowledge fully their own sexuality, despite any discomfort that such an awareness might create. Within a faith perspective, it is very important to discover ourselves as sexual beings. We ought not to call "bad" what God has called "good."

The Church is a setting in which two important responsibilities can take place. First, the Church is responsible for the life and nurture of its own members; our faith and unity will be known to the world by our love for one another. Second, the Church may never forget its prophetic nature. In this light, the Church has a responsibility to teach clearly important norms regarding human sexual behavior. In addition, the Church cannot stand aloof on public issues, since all of us bear a responsibility to address issues that affect people's lives and welfare.

In 1987 Archbishop John R. Quinn addressed Pope John Paul II in Los Angeles when the Pope met with the bishops of the United States.[7] Archbishop Quinn's presentation helps situate properly our discussion here of human sexuality, for the morality of sex must be placed within the context of moral theology itself. Moral theology, Archbishop Quinn pointed out, is an example of human wisdom struggling to understand God's revelation about how we live. This struggle is dramatically portrayed in the opening sections of *Gaudium et Spes*[8] and is unavoidable for several reasons:

1. We are limited human creatures wrestling with the word the infinite God has spoken.
2. We are affected by the reality of sin.
3. We are profoundly affected by rapid and pervasive change.

Archbishop Quinn incorporated into his presentation the insights of the distinguished American theologian, Father John Courtney

Murray, S.J. Murray captured well this struggle between human wisdom and God's revelation:

> (H)istory... does change... the human reality. It evokes situations that never happened before. It calls into being relationships that have not existed. It involves human life in an increasing multitude of institutions of all kinds, which proliferate in response to new human needs and desires as well as in consequence of the creative possibilities that are inexhaustibly resident in human freedom... History continually changes the community of mankind and alters the modes of communication between man and man as these take form 'through external acts.' In this sense, the nature of man changes in history, for better or for worse, at the same time that the fundamental structure of human nature, and the essential destinies of the human person, remain untouched and intact.
>
> As all this happens, continually new problems are being put to the wisdom of the wise at the same time that the same old problems are being put to every man, wise or not.[9]

There are, then, "new human needs and desires," new realities, which confront non-believers, believers and the Church in a community of moral discourse. The Church and we as believers meet these new human realities with a critical posture. *Gaudium et Spes* teaches, "Faith throws new light on everything, manifests God's design for man's total vocation and thus directs the mind to solutions which are fully human."[10] This perspective of faith affirms the supernatural dignity of the human person and of human sexuality and thus we must scrutinize and interpret the signs of the times always in the light of the Gospel.

Archbishop Quinn points out that as the Church encounters these new and changing realities, moral theology confronts the dual task of the conversion of the mind and the conversion of the heart. In the United States, conversion of the mind necessitates the need to convey to American Catholics and to all of society that the revolutionary changes which have occurred in personal and societal life are not grounds for dismissing Church teaching as outmoded, but rather that these changes point all the more strongly to the value of the Church's tradition in interpreting new human realities.

The conversion of the heart challenges us to convey to Catholics and to all people of good will the reality that the Christian moral life is challenging, but not onerous: that it is a call to holiness by a God who understands our weaknesses and walks with us in our struggle to live out the values of the Gospel. Moral theology and its specific reflection in sexual morality is not a set of abstract rules designed to constrict our lives, but a call to pilgrimage and conversion that can enrich our lives.

Archbishop Quinn then outlined some of the critical new realities which face the Church in this country:

1.  The fact that the United States is a major military power in the world.
2.  Pervasive divorce and family instability, which so greatly harm the ability of the family to be the basic transmission belt of civilization and religion.
3.  The immensely high standard of living enjoyed by a great part of American society and the responsibilities as well as the human problems this standard of living creates.
4.  The development of new medical technologies which aid both in the generation and prolongation of life, and the shocking paradox that the noble profession of medicine, the servant of human life and well-being, has also become a destroyer of human life through widespread abortion.
5.  The constantly developing insights of the psychological and sociological sciences into the nature of human sexuality and of the human emotional life.
6.  The sexual revolution, which has created a pervasive climate in which sexual activity is declared to have a value independent of other human responsibilities and moral exigencies.
7.  The dramatically altered and changing social status of women, with its concomitant impact on personal meaning and social identity.
8.  The increased, widespread high level of education among American Catholics and its impact on their understanding of and expectations about their role in the Church.

Archbishop Quinn, commenting on these various "new realities" presents a point of view that greatly influences the thread which
guides the discussions of this book:

> Rooted in the mystery of Christ, guided by the teaching of the
> Church and calling to a life of authentic discipleship, moral theology
> must respond to these new human realities in a manner which at once
> reflects what newness there is in these issues, the legitimate devel-
> opment of the human sciences, the enduring nature of the human
> person, the tradition of moral wisdom in the Church and the absolute
> claims of the Gospel.

This perspective, this landscape of faith, is not an easy road to
traverse, especially because the Church's teachings in the area of
sexual morality are at times subjected to severe negative criticism.
Archbishop Quinn comments that such criticism can, in some instances, be ascribed to the permissive, narcissistic and consumer
qualities of our society. In such a setting, people's sensitivity to these
kinds of difficult and challenging moral teachings can be dulled and
their ability to hear and their willingness to listen reduced. It is thus
necessary to always search for more careful and effective ways of
translating the Church's teachings into more attractive language so
that "in language intelligible to each generation, [the Church] can
respond to the perennial questions which men ask."[11]

In 1991 the Presbyterian Church in the U.S. issued a controversial Committee document for discussion, *Keeping Body and Soul
Together*.[12] While this document was extremely problematic and
erroneous in many ways, especially in its methodological sugges-
tions, it did present well the upheavals which we have experienced on
the "sexual landscape" of our culture:[13]

1.  Family patterns continue to undergo remarkable changes.
    There is no longer a statistical norm of the American family
    and this diversity of families characterizes the social
    landscape that touches our lives. By the year 2000, half of
    all families in the U.S. will be headed by a single parent,
    and 90% of these parents will be women.
2.  Both women and men are acknowledging the limitations of

traditional gender roles and are currently struggling to find
more egalitarian modes of social and sexual relating.

3.  Medical developments have dramatically altered the context
    in which individuals live as sexual persons. Inexpensive
    means of birth control have become available and abortion
    is often considered another means of birth regulation.
    Because of unprecedented freedom in this area, dramatic
    changes in sexual practice have followed.

4.  The average life-span has dramatically increased. A mar-
    riage, e.g., now has the potential for lasting longer than ever
    before in history. Better health and increased longevity also
    mean that people have more active years, including sexu-
    ally active lives, than previous generations. The ability to
    control the process of procreation raises issues about life,
    sexuality, and human intimacy to new levels of concern.

5.  New genetic developments in reproductive technologies
    also affect the sexual context. *In vitro* fertilization, embryo
    transfer, and surrogate motherhood raise troubling ques-
    tions about the meaning of reproduction and the meaning of
    human sexuality.

6.  The HIV/AIDS pandemic has generated intense debate
    about health, disease, and their relation to sexuality. This
    crisis has also given rise to virulent hostility toward persons
    and groups affected by this disease, and many people have
    been stigmatized.

7.  The commercialization and exploitation of sexuality in the
    economic market, and the linkage of sexuality with vio-
    lence and brutality in the mass media, are very apparent
    realities on the contemporary scene. Pornography is big
    business in the U.S. and sexual tourism is an international
    problem, one in which poor women, women of color, and
    children are often outrageously exploited.

8.  There is increased awareness that patterns of sexual abuse
    and violence are great problems in our American families
    and in our sexual relationships and this violence takes place
    across the socio-economic spectrum.

9.  A body-spirit dualism contributes greatly to an attitude that

XX                                        HUMAN SEXUALITY

regards human sexuality with distortion and generates either a fear of or a fixation with sex and the body.

10. Sexism is a problem present in a great deal of our society, a problem which contributes to injustice and damages profoundly the relationship between male and female.

11. We live in a very violent society where nearly every newscast and paper is filled with stories of murder, assault, racially motivated hate crimes, gay bashing, spousal battering, rape and child abuse. This type of violence is often eroticized and glorified in our culture, with consequent sexual undertones pervading many of our cultural images and activities, especially seen in the lucrative market of pornographic materials.

These types of "new realities" color the landscape that must be walked when dealing with basic issues of human sexuality. In its nine chapters, this book intends to address many of these issues, with the hope of accomplishing several tasks: (a) naming problems clearly; (b) articulating presuppositions and moral assumptions unambiguously; (c) presenting the Church's teachings with humility but with a desire for accuracy in order to highlight not only the normative character of the Church's teaching on sexual matters, but also the authentic human values which the Church desires to protect and safeguard by these teachings; (d) describing current biological, behavioral and sociological information about human sexuality; (e) offering pertinent pastoral perspectives; (f) respecting human sexuality as a good creation of God; and (g) enunciating all of this within a perspective of faith.

Bishop Donald W. Wuerl's introductory remarks to John Paul II's *The Theology of Marriage and Celibacy*[14] provide a good bridge to this book:

Nothing, perhaps, more clearly points out the prophetic nature of the Gospel message and its countercultural force than matters of human sexuality. The radical, primordial nature of human sexuality brings with it atavistic responses. The urges and drives that sexuality evoke are capable of sanctified human union as well as violent dehumanizing degradation. What separates the two responses in either poll and the vast range of area in between is our understanding of what is the nature of the human body. For the believer this necessarily takes into account as normative, God's revelation...

Human sexuality is one area most visible and most contested in the present struggle to make present the Word of God. It is no secret that the Gospel value of enduring human love, self-giving love and other-serving love is out of step with the brand of love that sells on TV, whether during the program or the commercial break. Part of the conflict is that there are definitely two or more views about the purposes of sex. To some extent the physical dimension of sex has so dominated the scene that even minimal interpersonal and spiritual aspects of this basic human reality are so clouded over as to be lost.

Consequently, sexual love is always an *embodied* love; and a loving intention is not the sole or sufficient criterion of even a revised sexual morality. "Love" and "freedom" alone cannot be given exclusive control of decisions in sexual morality, for this only leads to a false and destructive dualism.[15]

## CHAPTER ONE

# PRINCIPLES AND PRESUPPOSITIONS

## 1. THE GIFT OF SEXUALITY

In his 1935 book *In Defense of Purity*, Dietrich von Hildebrand wrote:

> Sex... as contrasted with the other departments of bodily experience, is *essentially* deep. Every manifestation of sex produces an effect which transcends the physical sphere and, in a fashion quite unlike the other bodily desires, involves the soul deeply in its passion... It is a characteristic of sex that in virtue of its very significance and nature it tends to become incorporated with experiences of a higher order, purely psychological and spiritual. Nothing in the domain of sex is so self-contained as the other bodily experiences: for example, eating and drinking. The unique profundity of sex... is sufficiently shown by the simple fact that a man's attitude towards it is of incomparably greater moral significance than his attitude to the other bodily appetites. Surrender to sexual desire for its own sake defiles a man in a way that gluttony, for example, can never do. It wounds him to the core of his being... It represents a factor in human nature which essentially seeks to play a decisive part in man's life. Sex can keep silence, but when it speaks it is no mere *obiter dictum*, but a voice from the depths, the utterance of something central and of utmost significance. In and with sex, man, in a special sense, gives himself.[1]

As dated as this work is, von Hildebrand touches on significant views regarding human sexuality: i.e., sexuality is profoundly human and should never be considered accidental to the meaning of the human person; in addition, sexuality is not merely physical but also profoundly psychological and spiritual. As von Hildebrand claims, sexuality plays a decisive role in a person's life.

The purpose of the gift of sexuality is life: a life of love, fully expressed in Jesus who is the way, the truth and the life. Seen in this light, sexuality has a role which goes beyond the transmission of life to encompass the very being of God:

> Beloved, let us love one another; for love is of God, and he who loves is born of God and knows God. He who does not love does not know God; for God is love.[2]

This is the point emphasized by von Hildebrand when he writes that "Every manifestation of sex produces an effect which transcends the physical sphere..." This life is expressed whenever persons relate to one another, but particularly in friendship and marriage, which in turn both point to the inner life of God. The life which sexual intercourse produces goes far beyond biology. Through it spouses recurrently affirm their meaning for each other as they recognize, want and appreciate each other's lives, and through the sexual act sustain, heal and help one another to grow. These life-giving characteristics participate in the very mystery of God, which as St. John reiterates in his Gospel is essentially linked to life and love. Sexual intercourse helps us glimpse something of the meaning of this mystery. At its height, two persons who keep their identity fuse, and this is a pivotal example of simultaneous unity and distinction. This significance is highlighted by St. Paul who makes the analogy with Christ and the Church in Ephesians 5:31-32.

If sexual activity is so intimately linked with the divine, why did Jesus exclude it from his life? How does the single state fit into such a perspective of the theology of sexuality? The Gospel of John shows that in his life Jesus was already in full relationship with his Father and the Spirit in and through love. He had already attained completion. The "I am" passages in John testify to his wholeness and fullness. Furthermore, Jesus teaches that in the resurrection there will be no marriage inasmuch as marriage is a relationship of this world.[3]

The Judaeo-Christian tradition, then, points to a mystery of God as three persons in a relationship of love through which they realize the plenitude of life. Insofar as humankind has been created in the image of God, then we must assume that sexuality points to the very heart of the divine as a principle way for humanity to attain divine fullness. As such, therefore, its nature is sacred and holy.[4]

In the introduction to the first Kinsey volume in 1948, Alan Gregg also emphasizes the unique nature of human sexuality:

> Certainly no aspect of human biology in our current civilization stands in more need of scientific knowledge and courageous humility than that of sex. The history of medicine proves that insofar as man seeks to know himself and face his whole nature, he has become free from bewildered fear, despondent shame or arrant hypocrisy. As long as sex is dealt with in the current confusion of ignorance and sophistication, denial and indulgence, suppression and stimulation, punishment and exploitation, secrecy and display, it will be associated with a duplicity and indecency that lead neither to intellectual honesty nor human dignity.[5]

Human dignity requires us to view sexuality in its unique and transcendental character. When this perspective is enhanced by faith, sexuality's meaning becomes even more dynamic and clear. Genesis reveals, for example, that at the dawn of creation, humanity was created in the image and likeness of God. And God saw all creation, including sexually differentiated human beings, as "very good."[6] Therefore, our gender, our sexual identity as male or female persons, is an intimate part of the original and divine plan of creation. The mystery of what it means to be human — incarnate, embodied and therefore sexual — is bound up in the mystery and purpose of God, who is the author of all life, and love itself.[7]

From the outset, we want to be clear that human sexuality is a divine gift, a gift which must be approached with a deep and abiding sense of appreciation, wonder and respect. Human sexuality is a primal dimension of each person, a mysterious blend of spirit and body, which shares in God's own creative love and life.

We are proposing here, then, a theological view of sexuality, one that affirms that we are authentically human to the extent in which we stand consciously in the presence of God. This book is written with the conviction that in all areas of human life there are some ways of acting which are helpful in attaining the ends and goals of human life; and there are other ways or patterns of acting which violate the meaning of human life. From this perspective, John C. Dwyer draws two important conclusions in his book *Human Sexuality: A Christian View.*[8]

(1) Sex is not to be confused with God: i.e., our sexual powers are not of *absolute* value. Pansexualism, or the divinization of sex, is not genuinely human, and it does not reflect a real understanding of the place of sexuality in our lives. This divinizing of sex leads to an unnecessary preoccupation with maximizing sexual pleasure. To call our sexuality the "gift of God" is to say something extremely positive about it, but it is also to deny both divinity and ultimacy to sexuality and sexual activity *per se.*
(2) Sex is not demonic: i.e., our sexuality is not the place in our lives where evil forces are manifest. Sex is not dirty, shameful, or impure.

The most important conclusion to be drawn from these two points is that we need to accept our sexuality and rejoice in it as the gift of God which it is. We ought to do this without anxiety and with great inner peace, because in accepting this gift we honor the God who gives it.

As von Hildebrand has indicated, human sexuality is all-embracing. It is *total* in every sense of the word: it affects the whole human being. Our sexuality is not something which we simply *have* or *possess*. It is impossible to distance ourselves from our sexuality; it is part of our existence.

We can never separate ourselves from our sexuality and the attempt to do so is extremely destructive. Attempts to distance ourselves from our sexuality will leave us fragmented and no longer whole. One form of such distancing is that of the sexual ascetic, who is repelled by sex and is determined to live as a non-sexed being. This person is disgusted by sex and rejects it, thereby denying a fundamental structure of his or her personality; and denying a fundamental gift of God. Our sexuality is the means chosen by God to reveal the truth that it is not good for the human being to be alone. The existence of two sexes is a fundamental structure of human life; it is not simply a biological fact, but is rather the most basic way in which human beings are related to each other.

There is another way in which we may try to separate ourselves from our sexuality: the way of the libertine: i.e., the playboy or playgirl approach. A sole concern of this approach is to avoid all personal involvement. This approach strips sexuality of its personal dimension: as Dwyer points out, "The attitude of the sexual athlete toward sex is just as negative as that of the sexual ascetic, although his approach is superficially different. His motto is 'I can have it, but I can remain untarnished by it, because it has nothing whatsoever to do with the real me.'"

We must keep in mind as well that since sexuality touches every aspect of the personality, there are distinctive manly and womanly ways of understanding, feeling and acting; there are distinctive manly and womanly forms of imagination, reason and decision. There is strong evidence from electroencephalography, e.g., which indicates that men are more capable of tapping the resources of the left side of the brain, and women are most successful in tapping the resources of the right side. This means that men and women *think* somewhat differently. Neither is more intelligent than the other, but intelligence functions differently in men and women, and in women intelligence is more thoroughly integrated into the affective life.

In other words, such qualities and abilities as intelligence, sensitivity to personal values, courage, intuition, and responsibility, should be found in both men and women, but they will be present in the two sexes in slightly different ways, in different "styles." These differences reflect the fact that the sexes represent two fundamentally different ways of being related to the world and of understanding ourselves. These two different ways are constituted by the fact that in men and women, different character traits, different symbols, and different values are dominant in the conscious and unconscious cells respectively. The same character traits are present in men and in women, but they are divided differently between the conscious and the unconscious. Jung maintained that it is possible to make some statements about the fundamentally different ways in which men and women possess their personal existence — statements which are quite general in nature, but which are at the same time important. As we will see, even the physical structures of human sexuality and of sexual intercourse are the sign, the symbol, and the expression of the fundamental differences in the nature of manly and womanly existence. These points lead to several conclusions:

(1) We are called to accept our dependence on the other sex in order to discover ourselves and to find our own identity.

(2) We are called to accept responsibility for the other sex and for the task of helping those of the other sex achieve a healthy sexual identity and true sexual maturity.

(3) We are called to understand that securing full and universal equality for the other sex is an essential part of this responsibility.

(4) We are called to affirm the total complementarity of the sexes. Stephen B. Clark thus points out in *Man and Woman in Christ: An Examination of the Roles of Men and Women in Light of Scripture and the Social Sciences* (1980) that there is a complementarity of the male and female psyche which constitutes the true possibility for self-giving in human sexuality.

(5) We are called to accept all of these tasks in the conviction that to be a human being is to be one who is made in the image and likeness of God.

Because of these tasks, our sexuality is not simply a *given*, a datum of existence, but is rather a *challenge* and an *achievement*. Our basic vocation is to achieve personhood, to love with a truly human love, and this means to love *as sexed beings* and not apart from or aside from this most fundamental characteristic of our personal existence.

Lisa Sowle Cahill treats the differences in our womanly and manly existence in *Women and Sexuality*[9] by tracing the special prominence of intimacy and committed friendship in the writings of women about sexuality. She convincingly demonstrates that the female sexual experience is different than the male "...to a degree which would make its repercussions in our affective, emotional, social, and even cognitive lives fairly profound."[10]

Citing the writings of Carol Gilligan and the Whiteheads, Cahill explains that women tend to find close relationships essential, satisfying, and even a source of security. On the other hand, mens' emotional security comes from independence; and relationships can be threatening to their sense of self. Cahill comments:

> In friendships, women tend to seek self-disclosure, while men seek camaraderie, and this spills over into their sexual expectations. Women respond to friendship first at the emotional level, and "look forward to connecting with" another person "in experiences of empathy, care, and companionship." Only subsequently are women open to the possibility of sexual intimacy in certain friendships. Hence, "for most women, emotional closeness comes before and opens the way for genital love." But men often "experience these two aspects of eros in the reverse order: for them sexual attraction comes before and opens the way to a deeper emotional connection."[11]

This entire question becomes much more complicated when we consider recent social, scientific and anthropological studies which suggest that culture is at least as influential as biology in determining social conceptions of appropriate traits and behavior for men and women.[12]

Our sexuality is not naturally integrated. Integration is a possibility; but so is disintegration. We can be, and often are, selfish and self-centered. The integration of sexuality is a challenge because love and the physical expression of our sexuality are not the same, are not identical. No sexual relationship leaves the partners untouched because every attempt to make love reveals feelings toward the other person, even when those feelings are destructive, victimizing and negative. Ideally, the sexual relationship is an expression of our love and our trust. But the sexual relationship often falls short of this ideal and thus may become an expression of fear and even of hatred and violence. Facile optimism about sex is just as ungrounded as is the cynical pessimism which sees sex as basically selfish and self-centered.

In his book *Motivation and Personality*,[13] Abraham Maslow points out that the sex-life of psychologically healthy people is quite distinctive. In his interviews with happily married people, he found that love and the physical expression of sex were very frequently joined or fused. Maslow was quite aware that love and sexual expression were conceptually distinct, but at the same time he noted that in the lives of healthy people they tended to become less separate, and they even tended to merge. Maslow affirmed that psychologically healthy people will not seek sexual expression for its own sake, and they will never be satisfied by it, unless it is part of love.

Authentic sexual love, therefore, is a total personal response to another individual. It is a feeling of a special kind. It is not self-contained. It is a feeling which does not have its term and center in the one who experiences it, but rather in another. It is a feeling which *intends*, reaches out toward another. In this respect, it resembles the feelings of awe and wonder, a feeling inspired by the mystery inherent in another person. Sexual love is a way of *being there*, of existing, for another as a person. Authentic sexual love desires union with the other, and this union is seen as something right and proper and good. This union is not genital sexuality, but rather a *communio* which touches another's life in its entirety: we want to be with this other person, close to him or her, sharing as much of the other person's life as possible. At its deepest level, this union is a *knowing* of the other person and an authentic act of acceptance. In *The Road Less Travelled*, M. Scott Peck describes well the meaning of authentic love:

> ...a major characteristic of genuine love is that the distinction between oneself and the other is always maintained and preserved. The genuine lover always perceives the beloved as someone who has a totally separate identity. Moreover, the genuine lover always respects and even encourages this separateness and the unique individuality of the beloved. Failure to perceive and respect this separateness is extremely common, however, and the cause of much mental illness and unnecessary suffering... In its most extreme form the failure to perceive the separateness of the other is called narcissism.[14]

The tenderness and affection of sexual love is a manifestation of caring for the other person, of assuming responsibility for another, and of wanting to foster and promote another's life as far as it is within

our power to do so. Maslow, Fromm[15] and others have all pointed out that authentic sexual love for another engenders cheerfulness, joy and play: i.e., true psychological intimacy. The two persons want to know and be known by each other. Secrets are shared, and in many areas of life something like a code language develops. When two people are truly in love, then, there is a union of wants and needs and desires. Each feels the other's needs as though they were his or her own. Love is the active striving for the growth and happiness of the loved person.
There are different dimensions to this love:[16]

(1) The first dimension is that of *libido*, the vital level on which physical union is sought. This level is not merely physiological but has important psychological components as well. It is on this level that we experience the build up of sexual energy and tension. The attempt to live on this level alone is destructive, not because there is something wrong with libido, but because libido, in order to be true to itself, needs the other dimensions of love.

(2) The second dimension is that of *eros*, the level of tenderness, affection and passion. It is the level on which the total complementarity of the sexes is felt, sensed and experienced. This level also, if sought entirely for its own sake, is destructive, not because there is anything wrong with it, but because of the fact that, of its very own nature, it calls for fulfillment within the multi-dimensional unity of love.

(3) The third dimension is *agape*, the unselfish desire of simply *being there* for the other. This is the essential human love, the love which makes us fully personal. We become genuine persons to the extent to which agape reaches into all levels of our existence. Agape is genuine love.

Dwyer concludes in his *Human Sexuality: A Christian View* that agape is the soul of sexual love, while eros and libido are its body. Libido and eros need agape in order to be fully human. When they are integrated by agape, they become ways of being there for the other on all dimensions of our being — the spiritual, the emotional and the physical.
In *Familiaris Consortio*,[17] John Paul II also speaks of each

person "as an incarnate spirit, i.e., a soul which expresses itself in a body informed by an immortal spirit" (n 11). Acknowledging that love is "the fundamental and innate vocation of every human being," the Pope goes on to say that "love includes the human body, and the body is made a sharer in spiritual love."[18] We are created not as angels or pure spirits but as human beings, embodied and sexual. We make incarnate God's own goodness, love and vitality in our frail human efforts to love.

Sexuality is a relational power, not merely a capacity for performing specific sexual acts. Masters and Johnson capture this point well:

> Nothing good is going to happen in bed between a husband and wife unless good things have been happening between them before they got into bed... There is no way for a good sexual technique to remedy a poor emotional relationship.[19]

The Congregation for Catholic Education speaks of sexuality as "a fundamental component of personality, one of its modes of being, of manifestation, of communicating with others, of feeling, of expressing and of living human love."[20] Sexuality prompts each of us from within, calling us to personal as well as spiritual growth and drawing us out from self to interpersonal bonds and commitments with others, both women and men. It includes the qualities of sensitivity, understanding, intimacy, openness to others, compassion, and mutual support. Sexuality is a dimension of one's restless heart, which continually yearns for interpersonal communion, glimpsed and experienced to varying degrees in this life, ultimately finding full oneness only in God.

It is important, then, to distinguish between the more inclusive and relational term sexuality and the more restrictive act-specific term sex:

> *Sexuality* refers to a fundamental component of personality in and through which we, as male or female, experience our relatedness to self, others, the world, and even God.
>
> *Sex* refers *either* to the biological aspects of being male or female (i.e., a synonym for one's gender) *or* to the expressions of sexuality, which have physical, emotional, and spiritual dimen-

sions, particularly genital actions resulting in sexual intercourse and/or orgasm.[21]

Lest we approach the question of human sexuality from an overly romantic perspective, it is critical to recall that the reality of original sin remains an inevitable counterpoint to all our efforts to promote a healthy, holistic, and Christian approach to life. While we are called to incarnate the image of God in the way we live and love, the gift of human sexuality also can be abused, sometimes intentionally, sometimes through immaturity, ignorance or addiction. Given how important sexuality is to one's self-concept and interpersonal attractions, such errors in judgment frequently have a profound impact for ill on one's psyche, human commitments, and relationship with God. [22]

Aware of these points and counterpoints, the United States Catholic Conference's document *Human Sexuality* underlines these three Christian convictions:

*First*, human sexuality, a core dimension of the human need to love and to be loved, is a gift from God, which commands appreciation, wonder and respect.

*Second*, being sexual, like being intelligent or athletic or gifted in any other way, is a two-edged experience. We can respectfully direct this gift in a manner reflective of our human dignity and God's gracious design, or we can misuse or even abuse ourselves and others by irresponsible sexual actions.

*Third*, the incarnation and redemptive life, death, resurrection, and promised return of Jesus Christ make available the inspiration and grace to respond more fully to God's invitation to live a sexually responsible life.[23]

The Congregation for the Doctrine of the Faith's document *Declaration on Sexual Ethics* also affirms these three basic characteristics:

(T)he human person is so profoundly affected by sexuality that it must be considered as one of the factors which give to each

individual's life the principal traits that distinguish it. In fact, it is
from sex that the human person receives the characteristics which,
on the biological, psychological and spiritual levels make that
person a man or a woman, and thereby largely condition his or her
progress towards maturity and insertion into society.[24]

Other documents from the Church underline the lofty nature of
human sexuality. The 1977 *National Catechetical Directory for
Catholics of the United States* emphasizes, for example, that "Sexuality is an important element of the human personality, an integral part
of one's overall consciousness. It is both a central aspect of one's self-
understanding (i.e., as male or female) and a crucial factor in one's
relationship with others."[25]

*Educational Guidance in Human Love* of the Congregation for
Catholic Education also teaches that "Sexuality is a fundamental
component of personality, one of its modes of being, of manifestation,
of communicating with others, of feeling, of expressing and of living
human love. Therefore it is an integral part of the development of the
personality and of its educative process."[26]

St. Thomas' vision in the *Summa Theologiae* was set forth in the
architectonic notion of all things (beings, *entia*) proceeding from and
returning to God (the *exitus-reditus* schema). This organizing framework gave expression to Thomas' pivotal theological affirmation, the
doctrine of providence, as well as his major philosophical affirmations
of finality and intentionality.[27] Human sexuality must be seen within
this organizing framework. Vatican Council II's *Declaration on
Religious Freedom* certainly makes this point when it teaches that
"God orders, directs and governs the entire universe and all the ways
of the human community, by a plan conceived in wisdom and love."[28]

## 2. THE MORAL LIFE AND JESUS

The main quest of moral theology is to understand the Jesus who
reveals the truth about God, who gives us new hearts and leads us to
the fullness of life. While the New Testament attributes to Jesus no
systematic ethical teaching, it does suggest the moral imperative of
imitating Jesus and with him testifying to the presence of the King-

dom of God. Jesus exhibits the virtues of the Kingdom: trust and obedience, boundless compassion, forgiveness, and refusal to hate even one's persecutors. His followers are to do likewise.[29]

Leading an authentically Christian moral life means taking to heart the message of Jesus regarding the meaning of his cross. In *Be Blessed In What You Do*, Michael K. Duffey carefully explains:

> The resurrection revealed to them [Jesus' followers] that Jesus had been raised to incomparably "new" life — and had given them reason to hope for such life — by submitting to the cross as the final chapter in a life of boundless compassion. As Jesus' dedication to others had no limits, now his glorification by the Father was total. Mark's Gospel draws the intimate link between Jesus' glorification and his passion, underscoring the proleptic presence of God's reign in the darkest hours of Jesus' life. The kingly imagery of Jesus being "crowned" with thorns, robed in royal purple, and 'thrown' between two thieves all anticipate his full glorification. Together Jesus' death and resurrection affirm God's dominion over sin and its fruit, death... Jesus' death and resurrection give Christians new courage. Jesus' submission to sin singles God's binding up of brokenness in the very midst of Jesus being broken.[30]

In faith, then, the Christian moral life announces with St. Paul: "We preach Christ crucified, a stumbling block to Jews and folly to Gentiles, but to those who are called, both Jews and Greeks, Christ the power of God and the wisdom of God."[31] Thomas Merton reminds us that "It is useless to study truths about God and lead a life that has nothing in it of the Cross of Christ. No one can do such a thing without, in fact, displaying complete ignorance of the meaning of Christianity."[32]

Jesus is the grounding of our moral and spiritual lives. James Gustafson writes that the moral life of the Christian community "is in its fullest sense a way and a pattern of life for those whose faith in God has Jesus Christ at its center. It is not first of all a universally valid objective model of morality. This it may provide, but only as an expression of God's ways to man in Jesus Christ."[33]

Jesus is, then, normative precisely because he embodies the ways of God. In *The Peaceable Kingdom*, Stanley Hauerwas sees disclosed in the Christian profession of Jesus the essence of the Christian moral life:

> We are called to be like God: perfect as God is perfect, like this man whom God sent to be our forerunner in the Kingdom. That is why Christian ethics is not first of all an ethics of principles, laws, or values, but an ethic that demands we attend to the life of a particular individual — Jesus of Nazareth. It is only from him that we can learn perfection — which is at the very least nothing less than forgiving our enemies.[34]

The Christian moral life is a call to be Jesus' disciples, a call which challenges us out of our present state of self-awareness in order to follow him. This calling forth is the center of our spiritual and moral journeying. Responding to the call to come out of ourselves and be possessed by God is the general form of our obedience to Jesus' commands. It is the first movement necessary for God to possess us and bear fruit in us.

The Christian journey to others and to self is the journey with Jesus toward entry into the reign of God. Baptism, symbolizing our willingness to go with him into the ultimate unknown, death, reminds us that we cannot stay where we are but must venture into the unknown with him. He whom we thought we knew when we assented to being his disciples is revealed more fully to us on the journey. We know him in the love of neighbor. We know him when we take up his cross. We know him most especially when we celebrate the Eucharist. Discipleship is, then, both the fruit of conversion and the way of deepening conversion. Coming to know Jesus Christ is at the center of the Christian moral and spiritual life.

William E. May speaks well to this point:

> (D)eep down, we know that we have the freedom to choose, to make ourselves to be ourselves (*sui iuris*). Moreover, we know that in our struggle to come to know what we are to do if we are to be fully the beings we are meant to be, and to choose to do what we come to know we are to do if we are to be fully the beings we are meant to be, there is someone to help us. For Jesus is our best and greatest friend (cf. St. Thomas, *ST*, 1-2, 108, 4), and he has not left us orphans. He has

given us his Church... to remind us who we are and what we are called to be: God's children, summoned to walk worthy of the vocation to which we have been called and to participate in Christ's redemptive work.[35]

Nowhere in the New Testament is there a fuller description of the "ethic of the Kingdom" than in the Sermon on the Mount (Matthew 5-7 and Luke 6). Here Jesus urges his hearers to be compassionate, to love their enemies, to forgive, to be peacemakers: in short, to be transformed by trusting in the goodness of the Father.

The fifth chapter of Matthew ends with Jesus declaring, "You, therefore, must be perfect, as your heavenly Father is perfect."[36] The perfection to which human beings are called involves a completion which cannot be either fully known or attained in the present life. However, it is not warranted to interpret what Jesus taught as a future reality present now only as an ideal. The call to perfection after the manner of God's perfection is a call to present movement toward fullness of life. Once again, Duffey's summary is helpful:

> Jesus' call to "be perfect" recalls the Holiness Code of ancient Israel, in which the purpose of observing the law is summarized repeatedly in the refrain, "You shall be holy, for I the Lord your God am holy" (Lv 19:2). If indeed perfection and holiness take us to the heart of the Christian moral life, what do they require of us? To be perfect cannot mean to become God, since God is, was and will be "other" than we are. Yet the divine attribute of holiness is not meant to inspire such awe and fear that we dare not approach God. Human perfection and holiness must mean in some way the penetration of divine reality into ours.[37]

In other words, the moral teachings of Jesus in the New Testament are eschatological: i.e., they call us to "be perfect." Jesus always displayed compassion, understanding and forgiveness. At the same time, however, he held fast to strong and clear principles: for example, his teachings on divorce.[38]

St. Thomas Aquinas speaks of charity (*caritas*) as the divine love which God gives to human beings in order that their friendship with God may be possible. He teaches that charity directs "the acts of all other virtues to the last end... giv(ing) the form to all other acts of virtue."[39] All of the virtues have, then, as their goal preparing human beings for divine friendship. This is an extremely important point lest we forget that all of our virtues come from God and serve the end of bringing us to God. The danger of an "ethic of virtue" is that we will think of the acquisition of virtue as a self-sculpting process in which we create and perfect ourselves. The holiness to which Christians are called is a divine gift. It is not earned — least of all when we are tempted to think we are earning it. The importance of centering one's moral life in Jesus is stated clearly by Duffey:

> *Caritas* is fully present in Jesus, who expresses the fullness of divine love in dying in order to save us. The stories of his acts of compassion culminate in his act of self-sacrifice on the cross. In him we witness the divine love as a costly act of self-spending. The New Testament writers use the word *agape* to describe Jesus' sacrificial love. In his own teachings about love Jesus commands his listeners: "Love your enemies, pray for those who persecute you" (Mt 5:44). In answer to a pious Jew's question about how he might possess eternal life Jesus taught: "You must love the Lord your God with all your heart, with all your soul, with all your strength, and with all your mind, and your neighbor as yourself. Do this and life is yours" (Lk 10:27-28). When the questioner persisted by asking, "And who is my neighbor?" Jesus described the apathy of the priest and the Levite toward the one in need and the compassion of the Samaritan. Jesus concluded the parable with *the* significant question: "Which of these three, do you think, proved neighbor to the man who fell among robbers?" It is no longer a question of *whom* we shall regard as neighbor but rather what is required of us *as neighbor*. The parable makes clear that we are to help anyone in need, heedless of whether or not they are "one of our own kind."[40]

In *Free and Faithful in Christ*, Bernard Haering puts all of this in wonderful perspective:

> One of the main concerns of all great theologians of our time, and especially of Karl Rahner and Dietrich Bonhoeffer, is to assert adoration in its own right. While one may, like Immanuel Kant, come to faith in God through a deep understanding of the ethical

dimension, one should never subordinate adoration to morals. James Gustafson puts this clearly: "One is not a religious person in order to have reasons of mind and heart to be moral; rather, one is religious as a consequence of experience of the reality of God, and this experience requires that one be moral."[41]

The more thoroughly we are open to the religious dimension — to adoration in its own right — the more will the fruitfulness of esteem for the moral life be insured. If our whole being proclaims the greatness of God and rejoices in the wonderful privilege we share with Jesus, to call God "Father," then we shall be led into the covenant morality with all those dispositions that befit the daughters and sons of God. Clearly, religious conversion engenders moral renewal. Consequently, whenever we synthesize our moral value system in categories unrelated to a faith-response, we cause a split between religion and our everyday life. Moral responsibility, seen in a distinctively Christian way, is our God-given capacity to make all of our moral aspirations and decisions, indeed, all of our conscious life, a response to God, and thus to integrate it within the obedience of faith.

## 3. A CALL TO CHASTITY

We have seen thus far that human sexuality is a gift of profound meaning. In addition, this gift is fully understood only in its relationship to the meaning of the moral life in general and to Jesus in particular. In the 1989 statement *Called to Compassion and Responsibility: A Response to the HIV/AIDS Crisis*, the United States bishops specifically addressed the question of chastity in light of the gift of sexuality.[42] The bishops maintained that human integrity requires the practice of authentic chastity. Chastity is understood as the virtue by which one integrates one's sexuality according to the moral demands of one's state in life. It presupposes both self-control and openness to life and interpersonal love which goes beyond the mere desire for physical pleasure. In particular, desire for union with another must not degenerate into a craving to possess and dominate. Chastity calls us to affirm and respect the value of the person in every situation.

While chastity has special meaning for Christians, the bishops taught, it is not a value only for them. All men and women are meant to live authentically integral human lives. Chastity is an expression of this moral goodness in the sexual sphere. It is also a source of that spiritual energy by which, overcoming selfishness and aggressiveness, we are able to act lovingly under the pressure of sexual emotion. Chastity makes a basic contribution to an authentic appreciation of human dignity.

The bishops go on to say that there are many factors which militate against the practice of chastity today. Our culture tends to tolerate and even foster the exploitation of the human person. People are pressured to seek power and domination, especially over other persons, or else to escape into self-gratification. Television, movies and popular music spread the message that "everybody's doing it." One can scarcely exaggerate the impact this has. Casual sexual encounters and temporary relationships are treated on a par with permanent commitment in marriage. It is taken for granted that fidelity and permanence are not to be expected and may even be undesirable. Sin is made easy because the reality of sinfulness is denied. The bishops then state:

> What is sin? It is an act motivated by the deliberate refusal to live according to God's plan. It is a destruction, more or less serious, of the order which should prevail in our relationship with God and with one another. It is the root cause of alienation and disintegration in individual and social life. It is a practical denial of God's presence in oneself and one's neighbor.[43]

In his November 1989 address in Rome to the International Conference on AIDS sponsored by the Pontifical Council for Pastoral Assistance to Health-Care Workers, Pope John Paul II emphasized this same point. He said, "(T)he Church... is concerned not only with stating a series of nos to particular behavior patterns, but above all with proposing a completely meaningful lifestyle for the person. She marks out with vigor and joy a positive ideal, in whose perspective moral behavior codes are understood and lived."[44]

Chastity is, then, an expression of moral goodness in the sexual sphere. As we have seen, each of us is a sexual being, embodied with a gender, influenced by hormones and sexual stimuli, called to channel and direct this dimension of ourselves toward love and life and holiness. Married persons experience their sexuality in a variety of ways, including conjugal love and genital intercourse. Infants, children and adolescents are also sexual persons. So, too, are single adults, divorced and widowed people, and homosexual women and men. Vowed and professed celibates likewise remain sexual beings, for they achieve sexual maturity, in part, because of their commitment to an intense, exclusive relationship to God and God's world in nongenital ways. Since sexuality is a fuller, more pervasive reality within humanity than its genital expressions, dealing creatively with one's own sexuality — gender, sexual feelings and desires — becomes a fundamental challenge in every person's quest for spiritual integrity and psychological well-being.

Woven through every search for genuine love, for personal maturity, and for interpersonal commitments is a call to be chaste, sexually responsible, and to be and to act in accord with one's commitments.

Citing the Congregation for Catholic Education's document *Educational Guidance in Human Love*, the U.S.C.C. document *Human Sexuality* teaches:

> Chastity "consists in self-control, in the capacity of guiding the sexual instinct to the service of love and of integrating it in the development of the person." Chastity is often misunderstood as simply a suppression or deliberate inhibition of sexual thoughts, feelings, and actions. However, chastity truly consists in the long-term integration of one's thoughts, feelings and actions in a way that values, esteems, and respects the dignity of oneself and others. Chastity frees us from the tendency to act in a manipulative or exploitative manner in our relationships and enables us to show true love and kindness always.[45]

This document goes on to say that it is certainly not easy to be chaste in contemporary American society. A natural curiosity about sex and a sincere desire for intimacy are given greater license by peer pressure and a culture that romanticizes and trivializes all things sexual. A person seeking maturity and balance, someone striving to live Christian love, "practices the virtue of chastity by cultivating modesty in behavior, dress, and speech, resisting lustful desires and temptations, rejecting masturbation, avoiding pornography and indecent entertainment of every kind, and encouraging responsible social and legal policies which accord respect for human sexuality."[46] Chastity requires us, then, to authentically learn self-control, a characteristic which presupposes such virtues as modesty, temperance, and respect for one's life and the life of others. It is not prudish but sensible to maintain that modesty and temperance both involve a sense of balance, an ability to dress and act appropriately in given situations. As *Human Sexuality* indicates:

> The old adage "moderation in all things" captures, to some degree, the spirit of these two related virtues or good patterns for living one's vocation responsibly. Underlying and grounding the practice of modesty and temperance is a deep and abiding respect for life, one's own and that of others...[47]

Whatever vocation or way of life one is called to live, there can certainly be failures in the areas of modesty and temperance. There will always be a need, then, for repentance and mutual forgiveness. Frequent recourse to the Church's sacrament of reconciliation serves both as a source of healing grace and as an impetus to incorporate humility, mercy, magnanimity, and an ability to forgive into one's daily life.

It is also important to stress here that chastity is not synonymous with an interior calling to celibacy. Controlling one's desires for sexual intimacy can be particularly difficult. Being single in a largely couples' society is not an easy calling, whether it be temporary or permanent. Societal stereotypes regarding the single life abound. Some presume that single people are sadly incomplete and unfulfilled without a mate or spouse. Others stereotype the single lifestyle as carefree. As *Human Sexuality* states:

> Thus single adults are sometimes imposed upon to carry more than their fair share of family or social burdens. A mature single person seeks a careful balance between a healthy independence, with a reasonable degree of privacy and freedom, and the need for love, including genuine intimacy and community "belonging."[48]

Those who choose single life or who find themselves living a single life, open to whatever the future may bring, can surely find a model *par excellence* in Jesus. During his life on earth, he was a single person. Single people testify to the fact that our God-given purpose and destiny incorporate but are not synonymous with one's marital status. Single women and men can, and many do, live deeply happy, whole, and holy lives.

In *Women and Sexuality*, Cahill notes that single persons understand *themselves* not in relation to matrimony but in relation to other roles: e.g., roles created by friendships, family, and vocational choices. Single persons thus identify themselves by what they are, rather than what they are not (i.e., unmarried):

> A single woman may see herself as a woman, a Christian, a sister or daughter, a teacher or lawyer, ... and so on. But if she sees "unmarried woman" as part of her core identity, it is at least in part because a set of social categories have marginalized the importance of her own experience of positive role-fulfillment even in her own self-understanding.[49]

It is important in this context to say something about the realities of loneliness and intimacy that every human being must strive to balance. Oftentimes, despite a variety of relationships and commitments, there are lonely times that perhaps touch the life of single people more profoundly. Sometimes, these are moments of uncertainty, of pain, of a sense of isolation. No bromide immediately erases such feelings, but it is equally vital to recall that moments of loneliness can be potentially fruitful times, even if not particularly happy times. In these moments of loneliness one can encounter God, face to face as it were, if one learns to "let go," trusting that God is there. While God is tangibly present in life's moments of intimacy, God also can be experienced powerfully in life's moments of loneliness.[50]

In 1 Thessalonians 4:1-8, St. Paul exhorts his hearers to make progress in their Christian life. Being holy includes abstaining from sexual immorality or "fornication." It seems that "fornication" is used here in a broad sense, because in verse 6 the attraction is to the wife of another Christian. The Gentiles may be lustful, but they do not "know" God. To "know" God is to recognize what God is really like, to acknowledge God's authority, even to accept God's friendship. To "know" God is to draw near to God and hence to draw away from certain forms of sexual behavior. The holiness of any shrine demands a certain ritual purity of the worshipper. The holiness of God demands chastity of whomever would approach God.[51]

Chastity is best understood within the context of the freedom a Christian enjoys by virtue of Christ's resurrection. In 1 Corinthians 5, Paul clearly teaches that the body of a Christian is part of the body of Christ. To have intercourse with a prostitute is, for example, to become "one body" with her. Hence, this makes Christ "one body" with the prostitute. If she is a ritual prostitute, intercourse would unite her so-called god with the true God. Even if she is a commercial prostitute, intercourse would be offensive.

Even more basically, "the fornicator sins against his own body" (1 Cor 6:18). Although Paul does not elaborate on this point, perhaps it might be accurate to conclude that even in a permissive city like Corinth, going to prostitutes was considered disreputable for honorable citizens. Whatever ethical norms come into play, Paul is interested in giving specifically Christian motives for chastity: "Do you not know that your body is a temple of the Holy Spirit within you, which you have from God? You are not your own; you were bought with a price. So glorify God in your body."[52]

In short, however the pagans may behave, the baptized person stands in a special relationship to God, to Christ, and to the Spirit, and this relationship calls for chastity. The Christian is a member of Christ's body, one in spirit with Christ and called to imitate the earthly Jesus. The body of the Christian is a holy place where God dwells. It is a thing of great value in God's eyes.

In Colossians 3, Paul writes that the Christian should "seek the things that are above, where Christ is, seated at the right hand of God."[53] He goes on to state: "Set your minds on things that are above, not on things that are on earth. For you have died, and your life is hid with Christ in God."[54] The basic reason for chastity in Paul is, then, the new status of the Christian: already holy, already one of the saints, already a child of light. This special relationship with God is ennobling, and this new dignity calls for a new standard of self-discipline above and beyond what any natural sense of personal dignity might demand. When one has been made a peer of the Kingdom, one has to act accordingly. The scriptural appeal of chastity is, therefore: act in accord with what you really are, transformed people who were once in darkness, but now are in the light of the Lord.

## 4. BASIC MORAL PRINCIPLES

### A. *Natural and Unnatural Sins*

In his teaching on sexuality, St. Thomas Aquinas made a distinction between sexual sins "against nature" (*contra naturam*) and "according to nature" (*secundum naturam*).[55]

Thomas explains this distinction:

(a) In sins according to nature (*peccata secundum naturam*), the sin is determined as being "contrary to right reason": for example, fornication, rape, incest, adultery, sacrilege.

This lack of conformity to right reason is common to all sexual sins.

(b) In sins against nature (*peccata contra naturam*), the sin contains an *additional* aspect: it is not only against reason but it is also inconsistent with the end of the venereal act, i.e., the begetting of children: for example, masturbation, bestiality, homosexual activity, contraception.

In this teaching, it is important to keep in mind that Thomas did not determine the gravity of sin simply according to its external consequences, but rather by the inner disharmony which sin brings to a person: i.e., the ontological disharmony, rather than the psychological effects it may produce. For Thomas, then, unnatural sexual sins are unreasonable because they attack a fundamental ontological order. These acts always violate an intelligible good: for example, homosexual activity is a generic act which is always forbidden, and needs no further specification. The *act* involves a will hostile to the goods of procreation and the authentic giving of self. For Thomas, therefore, certain acts are always forbidden, no matter what the circumstances.

In his 1984 "Apostolic Exhortation on Reconciliation and Penance," Pope John Paul II revisits this Thomistic teaching:

> (S)ome sins are intrinsically grave and mortal by reason of their matter. That is, there exist acts which, *per se* and in themselves, independently of circumstances, are always seriously wrong by reason of their object. These acts, if carried out with sufficient awareness and freedom, are always gravely sinful.[56]

This area of teaching is very controverted and needs careful attention. It is part of the Catholic tradition that there are certain acts that are intrinsically evil (*intrinsece malum*) and therefore can never be done. Traditional manuals of moral theology tended to list these categories for such acts:

(a) Lying: The purpose of the human faculty of speech is to communicate truth and it is never right to contribute actively to either error or ignorance. Consequently, lying is always wrong; it is always intrinsically evil.

(b) Suicide: Human life is a gift from God and human beings have the use of human life, but not control over it. To take one's life is therefore an act of presumption, a taking over of a divine prerogative. The prohibition of suicide is thus without exception, an intrinsically evil act.

(c) Destroying the marriage contract: In the case of sacramental and consummated marriage, remarriage was absolutely forbidden.

(d) Sex outside the marriage contract: The free exercise of the sexual faculty, apart from normal sexual intercourse within a marriage relationship, and indeed intercourse essentially open to the possibility of procreation, was prohibited, no matter what the intention or the situation.

(e) The direct taking of innocent life: To directly take innocent life is always prohibited and admits of no exceptions.[57]

Intrinsic evil denotes a specific act which is universally and necessarily evil.[58] In Kant's terminology, such acts can be formalized in the synthetic *a priori* judgments, in which case the act becomes a principle: for example, "slavery is immoral or evil." Thus, although "absolute" and "intrinsic" are the same in terms of universality and necessity, there are two important differences between them. First, absolute is a primary or fundamental concept: it is the basis for all acts and principles which are either intrinsic or *prima facie*. On the other hand, intrinsic is a derivative or secondary concept; it derives its moral character precisely from the community. Secondly, since the ethical — *absolute* — implicitly covers, or is coextensive with, the whole moral order, it is somewhat indeterminate. On the other hand, intrinsic refers to a specific or determinate act or principle.

*Prima facie* evil denotes a specific act or principle which is significantly evil and therefore evil in general, or evil in the ordinary run of situations, but not universally and necessarily evil, not evil in so-called extraordinary or exceptional situations. In Kant's terminology, *prima facie* evil acts or principles can be formulated in synthetic *a posteriori* judgments.

Of central importance to *prima facie* evil is a distinction between the "common" and "particular" features of an act. The former denotes those features shared by all instances of a class of acts in virtue of which they are members of that class: for example, any individual wars included within the class "war" because of certain common features which apply to all wars without which they could not be so classified. The common features of an act constitute the definition of that act, or its "essential core."

On the other hand, the particular features of an act denote the individuating circumstances of a singular concrete act within a given class of acts, which circumstances make it *that* act and none other. For example, the Vietnam War has certain unique and individuating circumstances — i.e., particular features — which make it different from all other wars. The particular features of a singular act are excluded from the definition or essential core of the class of acts of which it is a member.

From a moral viewpoint, then, any individual act is a combination of two kinds of features: its common features which constitute and define a given class of acts; and its particular features, which distinguish an individual act from every other one within that class.

The notion of *prima facie* evil applies to the common features, the essential core, of an act. It is the evilness of this essential core which makes a given class of acts evil in general, or evil in the ordinary run of situations. However, since *prima facie* evil as such does not apply to the particular features of an act, we cannot say that the evilness of the common features makes every instance of that act evil. It is quite possible, for example, for the particular features of some of these instances to possess less than the evil contained in its common features. Such instances, however, constitute so-called extraordinary situations; they are the exception rather than the rule. For the essential core, precisely as essential core, tends to override or outweigh the particular features. Therefore, a general bias or attitude ought to be established against the performance of *prima facie* evil acts.

The concept of intrinsic evil applies to the act *as a whole* — to both its particular and common features. And since such an act is evil as a whole, it is universally and necessarily evil, or evil in all actual and possible instances. An act is intrinsically evil when its essential core is so gravely evil that no actual or possible set of circumstances, whatever goodness they may contain could render an instance of that act good in the concrete; that it is impossible for any individual act's particular features to possess sufficient goodness to outweigh or even equal the evil of its common features; therefore, the act *as a concrete whole* always possesses more evil than good. In other words, the essential core is so evil that its evilness diffuses and corrodes the act as a whole, and overrides whatever goodness the particular features may have, notwithstanding that a particular feature considered in isolation from the whole act may have more good than evil.

Walter G. Jeffko gives this example:

> In my judgment, "slavery" — either on an individual or institutional level — is intrinsically evil. Slavery here is defined as an established or settled type of interpersonal relatedness — a *modus vivendi*, if you will — in which the self treats the other solely as a means and not as an end, or treats him merely as an object, thing or function and not as a person. As so defined, slavery so gravely violates the constituent values of community — equality, freedom and justice — that I cannot conceive of a situation in which it would be morally justifiable.[59]

In *The Making of Moral Theology*, John Mahoney devotes an entire chapter in an attempt to explain carefully the meaning of objective morality.[60] He explains that while subjective morality refers to the moral goodness or badness of an individual's behavior as it actually appears to her or him, objective morality refers to the moral goodness or badness of a piece of behavior *considered in itself*, whatever the individual subject may think of it. In the *Sentences*, for example, Peter Lombard viewed some actions as containing an intrinsic morality which made them evil in themselves, and no intention, however good, could make up for this inherent interior badness. Some actions are bad "of their type," while others are inherently good, although they can become bad through a bad intention. Lombard's successors were to follow this line of analysis of actions being good or bad in their own right, and it was Philip the Chancellor who defined "good of its kind" as good on account of the "material" out of which it is made, or by reason of its material object. Thus, in every moral act what was considered was not just the intention or the motive with which it was produced, but, as it were, the raw material from which the act was fashioned. It was this raw material which Thomas was to describe as the "object" of any action: "Any act has a double purpose: the purpose at hand, which is the object, and the further purpose at which the agent is aiming."[61]

In the philosophical analysis to which Thomas subjected every moral action, he viewed the moral agent as choosing from a range of types, or species, of actions and as choosing one of these types in order to clothe and bring about the intention which the person has in mind. The individual's action is therefore necessarily colored or shaped by the qualities inherent in the type of action which has been chosen. Hence, the moral evaluation of any individual action must take into account not only the *purpose of the agent* in acting, and the *circumstances* in which he or she acts, but also the material out of which the action is fashioned, its *object*, with the conclusion that for any act to be morally good it must satisfy the criterion of goodness in *each* of these three elements.[62]

This analysis by Thomas of the moral act into its three components was to become the dominant view in the thirteenth century and eventually to be accepted as definitive in classical moral theology. The balanced relationship which Thomas appeared to have secured

between objectivity and subjectivity was radically upset and undermined in the centuries immediately following his. Moral theology
entered the age of Occam and nominalism which was to shake the
hold on objectivity which Thomas had seemed to secure in the century
following Abelard. For Occam and nominalism the idea of what is
good or bad is not to be concluded from a close examination of the
natures of things, there being none such, nor is it even to be analyzed
rationally from the order of God's creation. God is absolutely free,
and since he could, strictly speaking, have made everything entirely
different, the only ultimately secure basis of morality must lie in the
free decision of God's will, who commands exactly as he wills. The
stress on the will, or voluntarism, was to result in a positivist morality
of commands and of resulting obligations to obey such commands,
which even then could not guarantee absolute security or certainty.

This view introduced into moral theology a provisional and
questioning note concerning the moral commandments and laws
which God has issued. Morality did not issue from within reality, but
was painted on to it from outside.

In a very different mode, Thomas taught that the human person
sustains the habit of conscience: i.e., an habitual, intuitive grasp of the
first principles for action, the precepts of the law of nature, which
"prompts us to good and complains at what is bad."[63] The human
person has an habitual grasp of the basic rules of morality. And
conscience "in the strict sense" is the action of applying such
knowledge to our past or contemplated actions. The action of conscience is, then, no more and no less than an ordinary act of human
reason applying the various principles of morality to individual
situations. Conscience is the medium or "image" of God's eternal
reason, or eternal law, which is the primary and supreme rule of
human behavior.

In light of our discussion here, the following long quotation
from Mahoney is of extreme importance:

> Two aspects of conscience to which Aquinas gave particular consid-
> eration and which were to play a significant part in the making of
> moral theology were the deductive manner in which increasingly
> detailed objective moral principles are derived from more general
> principles, and the consequences for man of error in his subjective

grasp and application of such principles. Objectively speaking, the conclusions of natural law principles are not all universally applicable, since the more one descends in reasoning from the general to the particular, and the more qualifications one builds into the principles, then the more circumstances and counter-qualifications will also enter into consideration and affect the reaching of particular conclusions. Thus Aquinas argued that although the first principles of natural law cannot change, the secondary precepts, which have the nature of conclusions drawn from these principles, are subject to change in a minority of practical applications according to circumstances. This flexibility of conclusion and application, which later moral theology was not to accept in any wholehearted manner, is also expressed in definitional terms by Aquinas in his statements that underlying moral principles always make such actions as murder, theft, or adultery unalterably wrong as a matter of natural law, but that what will vary according to circumstances is whether individual situations really satisfy the definition of what constitutes such actions.[64]

At this point, it would be helpful to formulate a concept of conscience. The medieval tradition accorded two levels to the concept of conscience. These levels, though they can be well distinguished, must be continually referred to each other.[65] Mainstream scholasticism expressed these two levels in the concepts *synderesis* and *conscientia*.

The word *synderesis* sustains a complicated history of interpretation and thus can be more clearly defined by the Platonic concept of *anamnesis*. This word *anamnesis* should be taken to mean exactly that which St. Paul expressed in the second chapter of his Letter to the Romans: "When Gentiles who have not the law do by nature what the law requires, they are a law to themselves, even though they do not have the law. They show that what the law requires is written on their hearts, while their conscience also bears witness..." (Rm 2:14-15).

This *anamnesis* consists in the fact that something like an original memory of the good and true has been implanted in us: i.e., there is an inner ontological tendency within the human person. From its origin, our being resonates with some things and clashes with others. This *anamnesis* of the origin, which results from the Godlike

constitution of our being is not a conceptually articulated knowing, a
store of retrievable contents. It is rather an inner sense, a capacity to
recall.

This *anamnesis* instilled in our being needs assistance from
without so that it can become aware of itself. But this "from without"
is not something set in opposition to *anamnesis* but ordered to it. It has
a maieutic function, imposing nothing foreign, but bringing to frui-
tion what is proper to *anamnesis*, namely, its interior openness to the
truth.

The first, essentially ontological level of the concept of conscience is, then, *anamnesis*. The second level is that of judgment and
decision, the level which the medieval tradition designates with the
simple word *conscientia*. St. Thomas described *anamnesis* (*synderesis*)
as the inner repugnance to evil, and an attraction to the good. The act
of conscience (*conscientia*) applies this basic knowledge to the
particular situation.

The act of conscience is divided according to Thomas into three
elements: recognizing (*recognoscere*); bearing witness (*testificari*);
and finally, judging (*iudicare*). Thomas understands this sequence
according to the Aristotelian tradition's model of deductive reasoning. But Thomas is careful to emphasize what is peculiar to this
knowledge of moral actions whose conclusions do not come from
mere knowing or thinking. Whether something is recognized or not,
depends too on the will which can block the way to recognition or lead
to it. It is dependent, that is to say, on an already formed moral
character which can either continue to deform or be further purified.

On this level, the level of judgment (*conscientia* in the narrower
sense), it can be said that even the erroneous conscience binds. This
statement is completely intelligible from the rational tradition of
scholasticism. No one may act against his or her convictions, as St.
Paul writes in Romans 14:23. But the fact that the conviction a person
has come to certainly binds in the moment of acting, does not signify
a canonization of subjectivity.

It is never wrong to follow the convictions one has arrived at.
But it can very well be wrong to have come to such askew convictions
in the first place by having stifled the protest of the *anamnesis* of
being. The guilt lies then in a different place: not in the present act, not

in the present judgment of conscience, but in the neglect of one's being which made a person deaf to the internal promptings of truth.

This distinction between *anamnesis* and *conscientia* illuminates the teaching in number 16 of the Vatican Council's *Pastoral Constitution on the Church in the Modern World*:

> In the depths of his conscience, man detects a law which he does not impose upon himself, but which holds him to obedience. Always summoning him to love good and avoid evil, the voice of conscience can when necessary speak to his heart more specifically: do this, shun that. For man has in his heart a law written by God. To obey it is the very dignity of man; according to it he will be judged.
>
> Conscience is the most secret core and sanctuary of a man. There he is alone with God, whose voice echoes in his depths... Hence the more that a correct conscience holds sway, the more persons and groups turn aside from blind choice and strive to be guided by objective norms of morality.

In 1952 and 1956 Pope Pius XII strongly reaffirmed the claims of objectivity in his strong reactions against "situation ethics":

> The writers who followed this system consider that the decisive and ultimate norm for action is not the objective right order, which is determined by the law of nature and known with certainty from this law, but some interior mental judgment of each individual, a light by which he knows what he should do in the concrete situation. According to them, this final decision is not the application of the objective law to the particular case with due attention and weight to the particular features of the "situation" according to the laws of prudence, as is taught by the tradition of objective ethics followed by more important authors, but it is an immediate inner illumination and judgment. In many matters at least, this judgment is ultimately not measured or measurable or to be measured in its objective rightness and truth by an objective norm outside man and independent of his subjective conviction. It is fully self-sufficient.[66]

In *The Making of Moral Theology*, John Mahoney exegetes this whole matter of objectivity in morality by concluding:

The objective... considers every moral action... as potentially a step towards, or away from, one's final goal in life and in eternity. And every step counts. Morality is basically a matter of how each step fits into that movement. If it carries one forward it is morally good and if it takes one down a side-road or even backwards then it is disordered and morally bad. Everything depends... on where the person puts his/her feet in one's moral odyssey. And individual acts in the abstract are to be viewed as so many stepping-stones surrounding the human person... (W)hatever takes one a step closer to God is by definition a morally good act, and whatever causes one to waiver or falter on the way is venial sin, in contrast to mortal sin, which is a deliberate striking out in a new direction, objectively away from God. What is more, God... has mapped out the way ahead for us, and leads us along "the right path."[67]

The *Pastoral Constitution on the Church in the Modern World* of Vatican Council II also reaffirmed that Christian morality is determined by *objective standards*: "These, based on the nature of the human person and his or her acts," are not intended to preempt human evaluation and discernment, but neither are they reducible solely to sincere intentions or an evaluation of motives.[68] On this point, the U.S.C.C. document *Human Sexuality* explains:

(T)he inherent and abiding worth of such basic values as life, love, and truth are indisputable. Each is a constitutive dimension of human well-being to be preserved and fostered if one is to be a responsible and virtuous person... In some instances, the linkage between a core value and the subsequent positive or negative norm derived from it is so self-evident that the prescription or proscription shares the absoluteness of the value itself. For example, if one accepts that human life is a value, that a certain dignity adheres innately to all living members of the human species, then certain actions, particularly if specified carefully, would in all cases be right or wrong. Thus, the Church holds that the direct killing of the innocent (e.g., abortion, euthanasia, murder, bombing aimed at noncombatants) as well as all directly intended bodily harm to innocent persons (e.g., rape, child or spouse abuse, and torture) are always and everywhere morally wrong.[69]

William May also speaks to this point:

> The moral teachings of the Church, as Pope John Paul II has ceaselessly sought to show, are rooted in a profound respect, indeed, reverence for the human person and the true goods of human persons.[70]

## B. Parvity of Matter

In the manuals of moral theology prior to Vatican II, sin is generally defined as the free transgression of the divine law. Three elements are listed for every sin: the transgression of a law; knowledge of the transgression; and free consent to the act.[71]

Every sin was considered from two different aspects: objectively: the act itself; and subjectively: the act as it appears imputable in the consciousness of the individual who performs the act.[72] The performance of an objectively evil act apart from the imputable elements is called "material" sin. Sin is considered "formal" when the conditions necessary for subjective imputability, namely knowledge of the transgression and free consent, are present. The manualists taught that the determination of the objective sinfulness of an action is made on the basis of divine revelation as interpreted by the magisterium of the Church and on the basis of the rational analysis of the nature of the act.

There is no question that the manualists considered the matter of sin as the font of morality separate from the fonts of circumstance and intention. Considered abstractly, the matter consists of the act itself. More specifically, however, in moral manuals and in magisterial teaching, matter included both the act and the object of the act. Thus, the matter in the act of stealing is the taking of another person's money. The manualists further taught that the matter of sin can admit a moral evil in itself apart from the consideration of circumstance and intention. In addition, this sinful matter can be quantified as either serious or light.[73]

The manualists classified sin according to the seriousness of the matter. Mortal sins *ex toto genere suo* are sins whose matter is so evil that there is no possible situation in which the gravity of the evil can be lessened: i.e., the matter is intrinsically evil. Mortal sins *ex genere suo* are sins whose matter can be either serious or light depending upon the circumstances which specify the act. In this category sins within the same species may be mortal or venial depending upon the seriousness of the matter. For example, the degree of malice of the sin of theft depends not only on whether something valuable or something petty is taken, but more precisely on the person from whom the object is stolen. If a petty amount is taken from a rich person, then the matter is considered light; on the other hand, the same amount if taken from a pauper is considered serious matter. Venial sins *ex toto genere suo* are sins whose matter is always light as long as there are no added circumstances that might change the species of the act.[74]

It is the long established teaching in classical moral theology that the matter in every sexual sin falls into the *ex toto genere suo* category. For centuries moral theologians and the papal magisterium have taught that there can be no parvity of matter in sins against the sixth and ninth commandments.

In 1975, the Congregation for the Doctrine of the Faith published *Persona Humana*, the "Declaration on Certain Questions Concerning Sexual Ethics." This document states that, according to the Christian tradition, right reason, and the Church's teaching, every direct violation of the moral order of sexuality is objectively serious because in the moral order of sexuality such high values of human life are involved.[75]

There is a long history regarding the question of parvity of matter but the turning point specifically in regard to the sixth and ninth commandments occurred in 1612 with the proclamation of the decree of Claude Acquaviva, S.J., the General of the Society of Jesus. Up until that time the Holy See had not as yet addressed the question of parvity of matter in sexual sins directly. After 1612, with few exceptions, it was more or less a closed question. In 1612, Fr. Acquaviva issued a decree aimed at those who taught that some slight pleasure in venereal matters (*in re venerea*) deliberately sought could be excused from mortal sin. His decree forbade all the members of the Society of Jesus from teaching this doctrine in any form. It forbade Jesuits from showing themselves in any way supportive toward it or from counselling according to it.[76]

Father Acquaviva issued the decree for two reasons. The first was that the opinion in favor of parvity of matter in his mind was harmful to the reputation of the Society. He also believed that the purity of life which the Society demanded of its members and its externs required such a teaching. His second reason for promulgating the decree was that the learned and authoritative fathers of the Society with whom he had consulted in this matter considered it in practice to be a teaching totally false and very much opposed to the virtue of chastity. These authoritative and learned fathers arrived at this conclusion because of the inherent danger in holding the contrary doctrine and because of the impossibility of distinguishing in practice between light and grave matter.

Father Acquaviva was so insistent on the prohibition that he attached severe censures to the violation of the decree. The decree bound all members of the Society under the vow of holy obedience and its violators were subject to a number of penalties including excommunication. It also imposed upon all Jesuits by virtue of holy obedience the obligation of revealing the names of those Jesuits who failed to observe the decree. In his letter to the whole Society, Father Acquaviva wrote that he knew how offensive the teaching of parvity of matter was to Pope Paul V and that the doctrine he put forth in the decree was actually the teaching of the Holy See.[77]

Although some non-Jesuits continued to argue this point, by the middle of the eighteenth century the teaching of no parvity of matter in sins against the sixth and ninth commandments was firmly established and the theological reasons fairly well developed. Two prominent manualists, Noldin and Schmitt taught, for example, that directly willed venereal pleasure outside of marriage is serious matter. They cite four reasons in support of this statement:

(1) The enjoyment of venereal pleasure illicitly is against the order of nature. All venereal experiences are ordered to one specific act, namely, that act which promotes generation. This unique act is the conjugal act, exercised properly only in marriage.

(2) It is a great disorder to subject something which is intended for the good of the species and for the propagation of the human race to one's own private convenience. This is

precisely what happens when one seeks venereal pleasure
outside the marriage state. It is subordinating one's reason
in a matter of the greatest importance.

(3) The seeking of venereal pleasure outside marriage would
cause very great harm to the human race. Men and women
would avoid the "burden" of the marital state if they could
enjoy venereal pleasure free from all moral sanctions. Such
a situation would be greatly detrimental to the human race
and would greatly hinder its propagation.

(4) In Scripture, God has prohibited all kinds of sins of impurity which exclude one from the Kingdom of God.[78]

Noldin and Schmitt, as well as other manualists, argued that the
sixth and ninth commandments are unique among the ten commandments in not allowing parvity of matter, whereas the majority of the
other commandments allow for degrees of seriousness. They cite two
reasons for this:

(1) In sins against the majority of the other commandments the
matter is able to be light since the total disorder is not fully
present in each degree as it is in venereal pleasure.

(2) The inclination to further acts of sin is not present in sins
against the other commandments as it is in the sixth and
ninth commandments.

This teaching regarding parvity of matter in the sixth and ninth
commandments has received a great deal of critique among many
contemporary moral theologians. The approach of *parvitas materiae
in sexto* has been profoundly challenged in a revisionist method of
moral theology which views evil in its premoral and moral aspects.
For example, Fr. Joseph Fuchs writes that there is a real distinction
between premoral and moral evil. Killing, wounding, lying, steriliz-
ing are premoral evils, not necessarily moral evils in themselves. A
premoral evil becomes a moral evil when it is taken up as an evil in
one's intention. This occurs when there is no proportionate reason for
causing the premoral evil. According to Fr. Fuchs, the moral quality
of an act cannot be determined from the action in itself.[79] He writes
that a moral judgment of an action may not be made in anticipation of

the agent's intention since it would not be the judgment of a human act. The object must be considered simultaneously with the intention of the agent and circumstances before the true meaning of the action, its true moral character, can be stated.[80]

However, Fuchs does not abandon the material content of an action. In his opinion, material content contributes something toward the judgment of an act's morality. To say the contrary is just as wrong as to say the human person is the only determinant. In other words, an individual cannot give to each action the meaning that appeals to him or her. The proper assessment of an act's morality depends on both the objective content of an action as well as the possible meaning for the person whether speaking of that objective content generally or in its concrete specific situation.

Thus, for Fuchs, the morality of sexual activity cannot be judged from the biological or psychological reality of sexuality alone (what has come to be called the "physicalist" approach).[81] Nor can it be judged from one's personal experience alone. The morality of an act can be judged only from *both* aspects: the meaningfulness of one's self-realization through a definitive type of behavior in the sphere of biological and psychological sexuality.

Patrick J. Boyle concludes his study of *Parvitas Materiae in Sexto* by stating:

> Throughout the many centuries of its existence, the magisterium of the Church has not hesitated to call certain moral acts evil in themselves. In recent times Vatican II has reiterated many of these morally evil acts. Such acts as infanticide, euthanasia, genocide, suicide, and devastation of entire cities with their inhabitants were considered by the council fathers as intrinsically evil acts. Pope Pius XII, John XXIII, Paul VI taught that abortion was intrinsically evil. Paul VI stated that all means of artificial birth control were objectively evil. Fornication, adultery and sodomy were condemned by the Sacred Congregation for the Doctrine of the Faith. Thus, the magisterium has consistently asserted its competency in designating certain acts intrinsically evil, even though others have questioned this competency.[82]

Boyle indicates that this traditional teaching on parvity of matter has certain positive benefits for the pastoral life of the Church:

> If understood correctly, it could generate a respect for the importance of sex. It could show that sex should not be used at one's whim. Another advantage in the traditional teaching is the security of knowing which acts are bad and to be avoided by the faithful. A third advantage consists in the uniformity in counselling which the traditional teaching provided. In other words, such acts as masturbation and fornication are evil for all irrespective of circumstance or proportionate reason... It is evident that the traditional teaching on the gravity of matter in sexual sins separated sins against chastity from most of the other sins. This separation had the positive effect of engendering a certain fear of unchastity. It marked the virtue out as something special. This positive attitude is created in much the same way that the prohibitions against the taking of one's own life and against abortion implicitly create the positive attitude in an individual of a great respect for life. Even in wartime, soldiers who have witnessed death or who have been forced to take a life often grow in this respect for life because they see the finality of death.[83]

Fr. Gerald Kelly's 1941 *Modern Youth and Chastity* represents a widely-used example of its time which forcefully approached matters of sexuality in terms of no parvity of matter.[84] He taught, for example, that *directly venereal acts* are those which of their very nature are so closely connected with the sexual appetite that they serve the single purpose of stimulating or promoting the generative function: for example, passionate embracing and kissing. Kelly argued that the direct and exclusive effect of such acts is to stimulate or further venereal passion. He concludes that such actions are always immoral and no "good intention" can make them right.

He thus enunciates these principles:

(1) Every directly venereal action outside the context of marriage is against the law of God and thus a serious sin of impurity.

(2) Any action is a serious sin against chastity when it is performed with the intention of stimulating or promoting

venereal pleasure. Care must thus be exercised in regard to impure intentions; dangerous occasions; and obscenity.

(3) It is a mortal sin for one to expose oneself freely and knowingly to the proximate danger of performing a directly venereal action or of consenting to venereal pleasure.

(4) It is a venial sin to perform an indirectly venereal action (i.e., those actions which frequently stimulate the sexual appetite but which *also* serve another purpose entirely distinct from venereal stimulation: for example, the study of physiology or medicine) without a relatively sufficient reason. Indirectly venereal actions are not sinful if one has a good and sufficient reason for beginning or continuing such actions.[85]

This teaching of the Church on no parvity of matter in the sixth and ninth commandments emphasizes that sexuality is not at the periphery of human personality. On the contrary, sexual expression manifests the *self*, the total person, in a peculiarly intense way. Sexuality is an essential aspect of our human condition, and it engages the center of the personality in a way that the other spheres of life do not. This is the strength of the traditional teaching about "no parvity of matter." The modern adage to the effect that our sexual activities have nothing to do with the kind of persons we are is profoundly untrue and represents a trivializing of sex which leads to a trivializing of the self.

## Conclusions

Because of the significance of the Church's teaching on parvity of matter, it is important to reiterate here the main points of this teaching. We have seen that for centuries moral theologians and the papal magisterium have taught that there can be no parvity of matter in sins against the sixth and ninth commandments. The 1975 document from the Congregation for the Doctrine of the Faith *Persona Humana* reaffirms this tradition that every direct violation of the moral order of sexuality is objectively serious because such high values of human life are involved. Prominent manualists of moral

theology have offered several reasons why there can be no parvity of
matter in sins against the sixth and ninth commandments:

(1)  The enjoyment of venereal pleasure illicitly is against the
     order of nature. All venereal experiences are ordered to one
     specific act, namely, that act which promotes generation
     and this act is the conjugal act, exercised properly only in
     marriage.
(2)  It is a great disorder to subject something which is intended
     for the good of the species and for the propagation of the
     human race to one's own private convenience.
(3)  The seeking of venereal pleasure outside marriage would
     cause great harm to the human race in that men and women
     would avoid the marital state if they were able to enjoy
     venereal pleasure free from all moral responsibilities.
(4)  In Scripture, God prohibits all kinds of sins of impurity.
(5)  In sins against the sixth and ninth commandments, the total
     disorder is totally present in each venereal act outside the
     context of marriage.
(6)  The inclination to further acts of sin is present in sins
     against the sixth and ninth commandments.

In recent times, *Gaudium et Spes* has reiterated many of these
morally evil acts and has included as intrinsically evil infanticide,
euthanasia, genocide, suicide, and the devastation of entire cities with
their inhabitants.[86] As we shall see in Chapter Eight, abortion is also
included in this series of intrinsically evil acts. These and other
examples lead clearly to the conclusion that the magisterium has
consistently asserted its competency in designating certain acts as
intrinsically evil.

In matters of sexuality, the strength of the teaching about no
parvity of matter lies in the Church's emphasis that sexuality is not at
the periphery of human personality and that sexuality is an essential
aspect of our human condition, an aspect which engages the center of
our personality in a manner that other spheres of life often do not.

In his treatment of "The Absoluteness of Moral Terms,"[87]
Joseph Fuchs makes reference to Karl Rahner's teaching on "a moral
faith-instinct."[88] Fuchs points out that Rahner means by this term that

it is possible, especially for a believer, to draw "an objective picture of revealed reality" on the basis of the content of revelation. Fuchs thus concludes: "(T)his ethic is 'human' ethics... projected by the believer as an imperative of a Christian theology which, in turn, depends... on an 'objective picture of revealed reality...' (T)he imperatives of a Christian theology... represent the attempt to be as objectively relevant as possible to given realities through man's reflection in light of the Gospel...; they are not to be arbitrary precepts, therefore, but the most objective possible, and in this reduced sense, absolutes."[89]

Fuchs goes on to explain that the Holy Spirit assists the whole process of teaching and leading in the Church: i.e., comprehending, discovering, evaluating, mutual listening and deciding. The Spirit thus guarantees that error, which in human comprehension-discovery-evaluation-listening-deciding, can never be absolutely excluded, will not become in the end an essential component of the Church. Hence, a certain "presumption" of truth must be granted to the teaching and leading in the Church. Fuchs thus comments:

> Declarations by the Church *in rebus morum* [in moral matters] can be understood in all cases as an attempt to formulate 'absolute,' i.e., non-arbitrary, but objective imperatives, properly conformed to a concrete human reality and expressed in terms of a presumptively valid ecclesial orientation.[90]

Fuchs then summarizes well a viable pastoral understanding of that which is intrinsically evil (*intrinsece malum*). He demonstrates that from a practical point of view, these norms have their worth on several counts:

(1) Such norms, insofar as they are based on true perception, indicate a value or a non-value: negative norms are to be avoided and, in particular, as evil, they may never serve as intentions for human action.

(2) There can be norms stated as universals, including, i.e., a precise delineation of the action, to which we cannot conceive of any kind of exception.

(3) Norms can be stated as universals corresponding to human and social situations that have been actually experienced.

(4)  These norms present a point of reference: i.e., every action that is objectively — *secundum rectam rationem* — not justified in the concrete human situation is intrinsically evil (*intrinsece malum*) and therefore absolutely to be avoided.
(5)  The function of these norms serve as guides to right actualization and are thus indispensably important, because no one who is incorporated into the community of the Church is without norms.[91]

## 5.  BIBLICAL PERSPECTIVES

Vatican II gave a clear-cut perspective for our present efforts in moral theology when it said:

> Theological disciplines should be renewed by livelier contact with the mystery of Christ and the history of salvation. Special attention needs to be given to the renewal of moral theology. Its scientific exposition should be thoroughly nourished by scriptural teaching. It should show the loftiness of the calling of the faithful in Christ, and their mission to bring forth fruit and love for the life of the world.[92]

Moral theology has much to learn from the great and all-pervading perspectives of the Scriptures. Here, the great themes that are particularly fruitful for ethics overlap and integrate each other. In his work *Free and Faithful in Christ*,[93] Bernard Haering has carefully outlined a number of these over-arching perspectives.

### A.  God's Word and Calling

The Bible does not present God in a perspective of causality as, e.g., the prime mover of humanity. Mainly, the Bible presents God in a perspective of his creative word and call to fellowship: "God spoke and it was." This is the great vision of the book of Genesis and, indeed, of the entire Old and New Testaments.

The theme of God's creative word becomes solemn when it is a matter of people made in his image and likeness: "Then God said, 'Let us make man in our image, after our likeness; and let them have dominion over the fish of the sea, and over the birds of the air, and over the cattle, and over all the earth, and over every creeping thing that creeps upon the earth.' So God created man in his own image, in the image of God he created him; male and female he created them."[94]

God's creative word is a calling, for we are to be not only images of our Creator by freedom in shaping the earth, but also and above all, to be with God in freedom. God calls us to himself and thus offers us repose and peace. The great theme of the Sabbath introduces the vision of adoration and liberty. We can be free only as an adorer, finding God's peace.

### B. God's Call to Repentance and Salvation

Out of a sinful world, God calls Noah to fidelity and trust. Indeed, God calls all people to repentance and thus to salvation. The story of Noah symbolizes God's abiding concern for the salvation of humankind: salvation through an exodus of repentance and trust. God's call and the gift of his covenant are infinitely merciful, but those who refuse to respond with faith and repentance are warring against themselves, condemning themselves to perdition.[95]

### C. God's Call: Election and Promise

God calls Abraham to another exodus: "Go from your country and your kindred and your father's house to the land that I will show you."[96] God's call for an exodus is election and promise. It is blessing for Abraham and for all his descendants insofar as they put their faith in God as pilgrims, responding trustfully and faithfully to God's calling.

The great theme becomes more perceptible here. History is understood as the history of God with his people. God calls them to shape their history by courageous faith, by fidelity to God's calling, which is always election and promise for those who walk with him.

### D. God's Calling: Liberation and Covenant

God calls Moses and manifests his saving fidelity. He calls Moses into the desert to live the exodus personally, and there to experience God's powerful presence, to know him, the Holy One, the Liberator. The story of Moses embodies the prophet's and the people's trustful response to God. It also manifests the history of distrust and its terrifying consequences.

God's saving and liberating action becomes the main motif for life. God makes a new covenant with Moses and the people, and all of Israel's morality is covenant morality, a shared response in gratitude and fidelity. Israel's liberty will always depend upon her gratitude for God's liberating action and on his fidelity to the covenant. Again, God manifests himself as the Lord of history. History's events depend, however, also upon our response.

### E. The People's Repentance and God's Calling of Charismatic Leaders

Whenever people forget God and become unfaithful to the covenant, they are in distress and hopelessly embattled with their enemies. But when they repent and call upon him, responding to his promise of mercy, God intervenes by calling and sending charismatic leaders.

This is one of the great themes of the Old Testament, especially of the book of Judges and the two books of Samuel. God has called humankind by his word. He graciously listens to his people when they sincerely turn to him and call upon his help. The charismatic leader, who puts all trust in the Lord and responds creatively to God's calling, configures the history of Israel. Liberation happens only in the realm of conversion and of God's undeserved mercy.

### F. God Elects and Rejects Kings

A perspective that is all-pervasive in the Old Testament is the value and ambiguity of authority. Already in Genesis 3:16, the abuse of power — male domineering over female — becomes the chief symbol and reality of the fall away from God. When people do not adore God, they will yield to the lust for power which is the cause of destructiveness and disunity. The charismatic leaders directly sent by God such as Moses, Gideon and Samuel serve the good of the people without looking for power and dynasties. They are the real symbols of God's gracious reign. A healthy charismatic authority is a great blessing, coming from God.

The Old Testament presents then the whole history of kings as a striking symbol of the ambiguity of earthly kingdoms and power. Involved is not just the sin of the kings themselves but also the sin of the people who want a king to serve as symbol and cause of their own power among nations. This makes the institution of monarchy a constant source of curse.[97]

Even so, God's intentions are for peace and salvation. He gives to Saul, David, and to so many other kings, a chance to be a sign of his gracious election, to be anointed by his Spirit if they abide in the covenant and call their people to covenant fidelity. But again and again, Israel's kings and their priests acted just like the kings of sinful nations who did not know God.

God is with the kings when they listen to the prophets and are zealous in preserving faith in the one true God. He blesses kings if they trust in him and manifest concern for justice, unity and peace.

### G.  God Calls Prophets and They Respond

The summit of the Old Testament is the history of the prophets. They are characterized as men of vision, seized by God, who calls them and sends them. They are given a profound experience of God, which, however, is never severed from history, from the joys and sorrows, the needs, hopes and anguish of the people and their times.

The history of ethical prophetism gives a unique vision of the ever-present perspectives, "the sacred and the good." The prophets experience at the same time God's holiness and his mercy. By their discernment and boldness, they restore the synthesis between the vertical and the horizontal, between the experience of God's holiness and the people's commitment to justice, mercy and peace.

Mary synthesizes the history of ethical religious prophetism when her life-song spells out, "Holy is his name; his mercy sure from generation to generation towards those who fear him."[98] Those who do not show mercy toward the widow, the orphan, the immigrant worker, the disadvantaged and persecuted, manifest their hidden atheism. They do not know the holy God.

The prophets are not authorities for the sake of their own

prestige; they are called and sent by God. Their whole life proclaims, "Lord, here I am, call me; Lord, here I am, send me." The prophet receives neither salary nor honors. The prophet is totally at the service of God and his or her fellows; and for this the prophet has frequently to suffer and to die.

### H. The Servant of Yahweh

The summit of the Old Testament, and especially of the history of ethical and religious prophetism, is Second Isaiah, who presents the "Servant of Yahweh."[99] Israel is clearly called to be a servant among the nations. Only thus will Israel herself be saved, and all nations will be blessed in the name of the God of Israel. When she puts her faith and trust in the Lord and accepts the role of humble servant, as witness among the nations, Israel is a sign of God's blessing and gracious presence. This is the heart of the prophetic message: that God will finally call and send One who is fully, faithfully and creatively the Servant of God and men and women. This is the messianic hope.

### I. The Covenant and the Law

God's call to Noah, to Abraham, to Jacob, Moses and all of Israel issues in a covenant. God commits himself to his saving covenant. By the very gift of the covenant and the saving action that brings it forth, God grants Israel the gift of the Law. But the Law is not something externally added to the covenant; it flows from it. If Israel gratefully and humbly accepts and celebrates the covenant, she will respond in fidelity, observing the statutes by which God wants to protect her on the road of her history. The law is not an imposition or a burden to make life hard for Israel. As much as the covenant, and with the covenant and through it, the law is a gracious gift of God. Therefore the true Israelite rejoices in observing the law of the covenant.

### J. Christ is the New Covenant

At the very heart of the New Testament is Christ. When Christ chose to be baptized with others in a general baptism in the Jordan, he revealed his will to bear the sin-burden of all in saving solidarity. Then the Spirit came visibly upon him and the voice was heard saying, "This is my Son, my beloved, on whom my favor rests."[100] This solemn word of the theophany evidently refers to the first song of the Servant of Yahweh, in which the Messiah is foretold as the covenant of the people. It is in view of this covenant morality that St. Paul speaks of the "law of Christ": "Bear the burden of each other, and in this way you will fulfill the law of Christ."[101] In and with Christ, in a solidarity of liberating love, we fulfill his law.

In addition, Christ is not "one of the prophets," but the Prophet, filled with the Spirit, driven by the Spirit and anointed by the Spirit, he makes visible by his life and death the synthesis of love of God and love of neighbor. On the cross he entrusts himself to the Father and, at the same time, gives himself to his brothers and sisters, so that we too may have life in the Spirit.

Jesus alone knows the Father and can make him known to those whom he baptizes by the Holy Spirit. By all that he says and does, and especially by the Paschal Mystery, he makes the Father visible as holiness and mercy. It is Jesus who brings the history of the prophets to its summit. Jesus teaches us to adore the Father in spirit and truth: "God is Spirit, and those who worship him must worship him in spirit and truth."[102] Thus does Jesus set us free from alienation and estrangement.

Jesus is driven by the Spirit to give himself totally for his brothers and sisters, to be the living Gospel for the poor, and the liberator of the oppressed. By baptism in the Holy Spirit his call to discipleship becomes truth in liberation. Those who are in Jesus Christ, believe in him, and are baptized by the Spirit, are known by their harvest of the spirit: "love, joy, peace, patience, kindness, goodness, fidelity, gentleness and self-control."[103] Those who are baptized by the Spirit and "belong to Christ Jesus have crucified their selfishness with its passions and desires. If the Spirit is the source of our life, let the Spirit also direct our course."[104]

By his whole life, and especially his death and resurrection, and the mission of the Holy Spirit, Jesus reveals to us the saving justice of the Father. Justification by grace and faith, and peace as the gift of the risen Lord, set us free to live fully in Christ Jesus. Christ thus calls us to be his disciples. He calls each by name and bestows special gifts on each of us.

We will now invite these general biblical themes to inform our attitudes about sexuality:[105]

## a. The Old Testament

In Israelite religion there was a firm conviction of God as "Other": God is radically different in nature from his own creation. This factor is very different from ancient Israel's neighbors where fertility religions celebrated creation as the result of the union of male and female deities: i.e., creation-as-procreation. In these religions, there tended to be a prevailing attitude that human sexuality was divine and to be used in the worship of the gods as imitative of their own mysterious creativity. In Israel, however, there was no sexuality associated with God — and no divine begetting of offspring. To become a child of God was thus not the result simply of a physical relationship, but rather a spiritual one. We find here, then, the demythologizing of fertility. By his will alone, God has created in the natural order the processes by which fertility was assured, and agricultural success could not be coerced or stimulated by imitating the supposed divine fertility.

This paradigm has profound implications. Sexuality was placed totally within the realm of creatures because the archetypal sexual partnership was no longer divine but human. The prototypal couple were no longer a god and his consort but two created beings. The distinction of the sexes is thus seen as a creation of God. Thus, the plurality of the sexes belongs to the created order and this distinction becomes one of the major differences between man and God.

Human sexuality is also removed from the realm of the demonic and impersonal forces which are to be placated through ritual activities. Sexuality is thus an element in human life over which men and women have control, however difficult that may be at times. Men and women are thus held responsible for how they use their sexuality.[106]

In Genesis 1 through 3, men and women are viewed as a psychophysical unity. The Hebrews did not view "man" in terms of a body-mind dualism but rather as a psycho-physical unity: "spirit," "flesh" and "soul" are not considered as coincidentally or unfortunately linked. The soul (*nephesh*) is rather the life-principle, an individual's vitality — that which is alive; and the mental and physical activities of men and women are seen simply as different manifestations of this same underlying "living being."[107] For the Hebrews, "man" was both an "animated body" and an "incarnate soul."

The Priestly Account (Genesis 1:1-2:4a) was written about 500 B.C.. In this account, we read that God created man in his own image, in his own likeness, in his own reflection. In other words, humanity's creation is not to be seen in an overly material way: i.e., man is not created in God's *physical* image but rather possesses the capacity to think, to communicate, to act self-consciously, and preeminently to *respond* to God's will. Thus does "man" reflect God's nature: humankind possesses qualities similar to God's and thus the strong condemnation of graven images. It is therefore logical to conclude that "man's" body is an *inseparable* part of one's total unity. Man's *whole person* is seen to be in God's image and likeness, and it is all "very good."

Man (*adam*) is a generic term referring to a sense of humankind as distinct from the animals. *Adam* does not refer to man as a biological creature. When "man" is referred to in this category — as distinct from "woman," the word used is *ish*: thus, the first human was not a male/female who was later separated as the result of some type of sin. Man and woman are created simultaneously with no hint of temporal or ontological superiority. The blessing of fruitfulness and dominion is given to both male and female together, and the "image of God" refers to *both* Adam and Eve *together*. Thus was God's creation of humankind not complete until *both* man and woman were created and the two had been brought together in a sexual relationship. Sexuality is thus understood as an intended part of creation. Therefore, sexuality is presented as fundamental to what it means to be human, and therefore it must be taken seriously.

God commands the male and female to exercise their sexuality and this is seen as both a command and a blessing.[108] Thus, the desirability of procreation did not arise as punishment for human sin; rather is procreation a normal and intended part of God's good creation.

The Jahwist Account (Genesis 2:4b-3:24) was written about

950 B.C. In this account we see that the creation of the woman is understood as the profound summit of creation — in marked contrast to the creation of the animals. The woman is created "alongside him" and "corresponding to him," with the notion of similarity as well as supplementation. The woman is the last and the most mysterious of God's creations. The woman is clearly the equal and the partner of man (the *una vita*): i.e., *until* the woman is created, the man is incomplete and "alone," without suitable companionship. True humanity thus exists only in community and the fundamental form of community is the relationship between man and woman. Consequently, only in relationship with someone does "man" enter into a fully human existence.

Cahill comments:

> This story reveals the sexual "one flesh" unity of man and woman as the immediate meaning of sexual differentiation. But while the story associates both woman and man as companions and partners in the task "to till and keep" the garden of Eden (Gn 2:15), it mentions neither the institution of marriage, nor parenthood as the meaning of sexuality or the determinant of gender roles. And the mission of parenthood is charged to two partners, stamped equally with the divine likeness in Genesis 1.[109]

It is generally not a tenable position that the "knowledge of good and evil" refers to sexual experience or consciousness, since it also is referred to as a specific possession of God (the very point used by the serpent). The first sin was thus of over-stepping one's limits, of trying to be as God was, having a knowledge of all things. The result of sin was therefore a disordered relationship and also *shame*: i.e., their weakness was exposed, their vulnerability before a powerful and righteous authority.

The Jahwist author could be interpreted as stating that sexuality is a knowledge of entering into a relationship with that which is known: an opportunity for the most complete and accurate availability to another.[110] In coitus, man for the first time came to really know what it meant to be a man.

In the Old Testament, marriage is often used as an analogy for the relationship between Yahweh and his people.[111] In Hosea, e.g.,

God is related to his people as a husband to his wife or as a father to his son: i.e., a relationship of undeniable sexual elements. Hosea thus *adds* the notion that sexuality is to be seen as a genuine relationship. Hosea even adds that a man could take back his unfaithful wife.[112] In other words, a new relationship has been established based upon the impulse of the heart.[113]

The Song of Songs stresses the praise of human love: i.e., a simple extolling of love between the sexes. Since God created everything, all things speak of his love for his creatures if used as God intended. Therefore, sexuality is a gift to humankind that is to be used and enjoyed rationally and responsibly. There is in the Song of Songs an inseparable relationship between love and emotion, between sensuality and love.

There are, however, limits to human love, seen in the many laws. These indicate the extreme seriousness about sexuality that the Hebrews held. But these laws never indicate a condemnation of sexuality or an idea that sexuality is evil.

Reproductive power was always upheld as ultimately significant.[114] Relations which did not protect this power were thus seen as unnatural.[115] Man was thus to be involved in sexual relations with the human female and any deviation was forbidden, especially in the early period when survival was at stake. Also, human seed was not to be wasted, as it was to be used to propagate descendants of Abraham and to fulfill God's command and blessing. Propagation was thus seen as a *religious* duty meant to meet *relational* demands of one's covenant with God and with others.

Man was seen to have complete possession of his wife and thus was adultery seen as a transgression of another man's property. Thus could a man sin against the marriage of another man. But the biblical law here *also* considered adultery a moral crime, and just not a personal injury to a husband. The emphasis was clearly on a happy married life together.[116]

## b. The New Testament

As we have seen, Jesus saw himself as inaugurating God's earthly reign.[117] Jesus' ethical demands thus take on a unique note. Jesus repeatedly appealed, e.g., to God's primordial will as originally intended in creation. God's will was thus not accomplished by an inordinate attention to minor precepts,[118] but is accomplished by a human righteousness that must exceed that of the scribes and the Pharisees.[119] It is the "extra measure" that came about by the correct orientation of one's heart — and not by ritual and cultic observance. The right inner disposition was essential and thus the external act is important only insofar as it is the fruit of the internal disposition.[120] At the same time, however, religious piety is empty without moral authentication through action.

Central for Jesus is, then, the union between *religion* and *morality*. Thus, the standard against which any question of human interpretation of the law must be judged is the divine purpose in promulgating the law. Jesus understood the law only in terms of the will of God, and not the will of God in terms of the law. In Mark 10:2-9 and Matthew 19:39, Jesus goes *behind* the law of Moses (which was a concession to selfishness and hardness of heart), and he appeals to God's original intention in creation.

Jesus thus taught that a *real* union occurs in marriage and this union is further perfected by physical intercourse, a bond that could not be eliminated by a bill of divorce. Jesus teaches that this union is permanent. Jesus' prohibition of divorce thus places a high regard on the sexual union between husband and wife. He cites Genesis 2:24 as his "definition" of marriage and clearly stresses the unitive element of marriage, the mutual companionship of the couple. Because of this teaching, women could no longer be regarded as mere chattel, a possession that could be put away for "some indecency." Jesus himself does not speak of submission of wives to their husbands.

In Jesus' treatment of the adulterous woman in John 8:1-11, he clearly teaches that the penalty is not to be inflicted on the woman alone, as would be the case for the Pharisees.[121] Rather, Jesus indicates to the woman's accusers that her sin was no worse and thus no more deserving of punishment than their more subtle sins of pride and hypocrisy. This attitude is repeated in Matthew 5:17-18: What matters is one's inner motivation. As we have seen, in lust the person becomes an object to be used to gain the self's own satisfaction without regard for the other. Here, then, the decisive factor is not the act but the will. For Jesus, then, sex is much more than the physical merging of bodies, as the wrong desire is as open to condemnation as the wrong act itself.

St. Paul would have learned Diaspora Judaism which was influenced by Hellenistic thought and language. But his Jewish background must have led him to interpret these ideas from his Hebraic point of view. He would have witnessed, then, an attitude toward sexuality and marriage developing which was not at all in keeping with his Judaic assumptions. Paul's most extended treatment of sexual matters is found in 1 Corinthians 5-7. Here Paul indicates that God's will can be found and discerned by observing "nature" — even though man's vision is now blurred because of sin. Paul clearly felt in this regard that the "new creation" in Christ was once again in harmony with God's original intention. God's world is thus seen as unquestionably good and is to be accepted with gratitude and enjoyed through proper use.

It is important to note, e.g., in 1 Corinthians 5 that Paul did not advocate other-worldly asceticism. Thus he talks about the leaven. Paul's concern is only about the misuse of sexuality, and not sexuality *per se*. For Paul, the evil of the misuse of sex was its effect upon others, specifically on the community of believers.

Consequently in 1 Corinthians 6 he urged the *right use* of sexuality, which is God's gift. Here he lists vices that prevent entrance into God's kingdom. Paul is teaching that all things are not helpful and it is possible to become enslaved by anything. Sexuality should thus not become a preoccupation and ruling force in one's life. For Paul, therefore, it is simply not true that what a person does has no effect upon who that person is.[122] Sexual expression must thus involve the whole person and just not sexual organs. One's behavior must have an effect upon the "self."[123] The body is our means of manifesting praise to God. The "flesh" becomes sinful only when humans set it up as their ultimate value and concern and regulate their life according to its values and desires. Life "in the spirit" is thus one's life regulated by faith in God's act through Christ rather than in one's own standards. Paul thus felt that a transitory, commercial sexual encounter joins two people and thus did he advocate a heightening view of the sexual act itself. The body is to be used to glorify God. It is thus unthinkable to join it to a prostitute.

Finally, in 1 Corinthians 7 Paul expresses a preference for the single life. In other words, for Paul everything becomes relative to the eschaton. Christians are to be totally free to serve the Lord. Here Paul also indicates the absolute equality and mutuality of the partners in conjugal relations. Marriage was not merely a physical genital relationship designed to satisfy passions. Nor was it an evil. The couple, rather, is consecrated by being set apart for God's service. They are thus made holy. The one-flesh is so complete, in fact, that the unbeliever is sanctified by the believer. Here Paul clearly includes the bodies in the process of sanctification. In verses 3-5 Paul made clear that marriage necessarily includes coitus and therefore this consecration takes place through physical proximity. Therefore, Paul clearly recognizes coitus, and thus human sexuality, as "sacramental": a channel through which the material is used to bring spiritual results.

## CHAPTER TWO

# SEXUALITY AND THE NEED
# FOR INTEGRATION

Bernard Haering has suggested that sexuality is a language,[1] and he points out that learning a language necessarily involves making mistakes. Over-reaction to mispronunciations and grammatical errors serves only to inhibit the learning process.[2] Haering argues that in the case of sexual development the situation is very much like this: "The sexual language has to be learned gradually and dramatizing the imperfections and mistakes of childhood and adolescence leads to alienation of sexuality."[3] In interpreting Haering's remark, Vincent J. Genovesi argues in *In Pursuit of Love* that "Nonetheless, the mastery of sexual integration and the perfection of chastity are expected somewhat unrealistically... At the same time, it stands to reason that mistakes we can tolerate in children and the ones we can expect, however unhappily, in adolescents, are less easily understood and acceptable when they occur in the lives of adults."[4] In *Reflections on Humanae Vitae*, Pope John Paul II also adopts the "sex as language" metaphor: sex is "the language of the body" which has "an important interpersonal meaning, especially in reciprocal relationships between man and woman."[5]

By employing the paradigm of sexuality-as-language, it is obviously critical to ask about the basic meaning of our sexual language: i.e., What is human sexuality saying and what does it tell us about ourselves? As we have seen in Chapter One, the meaning of human sexuality is not haphazard but is rather derived from the meaning of our lives as spiritual human beings. As Genovesi rightly remarks:

As a people of faith... we realize that we have been loved into being. We live because God loves us, and insofar as we live with his life we are enabled to love even as he has first loved us. At its deepest and truest level, Christian living is an extension of the Incarnation; in other words, it is a continuation of Christ's embodiment of God's love for us. By professing to be Christians, we commit ourselves to giving an affirmative response to God's expectation of us that we will have love become flesh in our attitudes and actions. Our sexuality plays a crucial role in our ability to answer this call to love.[6]

As we have already seen, our sexuality is essential both to our becoming fully human and to our human becoming.[7] As a reality that not only symbolizes our call to communication and communion, but also encourages and facilitates our response to this invitation, human sexuality expresses concretely God's intention that we find our authentic humanness in relationship. It is important, then, to carefully study the various components that constitute human sexuality as a language, and which ingredients contribute to a disintegration of human sexuality as a language.

## 1. THE MEANING OF INTIMACY

The *Declaration on Sexual Ethics* emphasizes that the human person is so profoundly affected by his or her sexuality that it must be considered one of the factors which give to each individual's life the principal traits that distinguish it.[8] Sexuality is thus integral to the human enterprise and the capacity for intimacy creates the possibility for sexuality to be authentically human. In other words, intimacy gives to sexuality part of its human meaning. In *Out of the Shadows*,[9] Patrick Carnes demonstrates how a lack of intimacy demeans human sexuality, thus limiting and in some cases demolishing any authentic human meaning: e.g., a person who comes to orgasm only when beaten; a person who is erotically excited only through voyeurism; or a person who has intercourse only in a violent situation such as rape.

Sexuality is not authentically human if the possibility for intimacy is lacking or deficient, and this capacity is absent in the presence of these non-values: hatred, despair, violence, isolation, manipulation, injustice, sadness, coldness, chauvinism, rejection, constraint, or deceit. Cardinal Joseph Bernardin's intervention at the 1980 World Synod of Bishops is relevant to this discussion:

> (I)ntimacy is a complex phenomenon with both psychological and physical dimensions. It involves a loving sharing of one's being with another and openness to similar sharing by the other. It is part of God's plan for human beings, precisely because we are created in God's image and likeness and human intimacy reflects the intimacy of the Trinity itself.
>
> Although there is a universal human need for intimacy, the enriching experience of intimacy can be elusive. People become lonely and embittered, couples separate and divorce — all because they are unable to experience intimacy or because they experience it in frustrating and disappointing ways.
>
> The latter experience is particularly worth the Church's attention in fostering a spirituality of marital intimacy. The phases of intimacy in married life are not uniformly gratifying and fulfilling. Unless they are properly prepared and supported by the Church, the discovery by married people that this is so, especially in the crucial early years of marriage, can lead to marital discord and the collapse of marriages.
>
> It is important therefore to help people understand their experience of intimacy in the light of the Paschal Mystery. An asceticism which is based on the nuptial meaning of the body and takes into account the difficult virtues and skills required to realize this meaningfully, will thus strive to assist man and woman in all phases of the recurring cycles of their intimacy — in good times and in bad.
>
> It will concentrate especially on the point at which they must die to the "old" person in themselves and in their relationship in order to be born again as "new" persons with a new and deeper love.
>
> Rich resources for a spirituality of intimacy exist in the Old and New Testaments, in the images and symbols of the Christian tradition, and especially in the Easter story.

In the context of the Sermon on the Mount (Matthew 5), Jesus says, "You have heard that it was said, 'You shall not commit adultery.' But I say to you that everyone who looks at a woman lustfully has already committed adultery with her in his heart."[10] The moral meaning of intimacy can be enlightened by a careful understanding of its opposite, lust, which Christ calls "adultery committed in the heart."

The lust of the flesh is a permanent element in our sinfulness (*status naturae lapsae*). The interior act of lust, which springs from this basis, changes the very interiority of another's existence, reducing the riches of the perennial call to the communion of persons, the riches of the deep attractiveness of masculinity and femininity, to mere satisfaction of the sexual "need" of the body. As a result of this reduction, a person becomes for the other person the object of the potential satisfaction of one's own sexual "needs." In this way, the mutual "for another" is distorted, losing its character of communion of persons in favor of the utilitarian function. Lust thus destroys a capacity for intimacy and consequently destroys the human language of sexuality. For example, a man who "looks" in this way at a woman "uses" the woman and her femininity to satisfy his own "instinct." Although he does not do so with any exterior act, he has already assumed this attitude deep down, inwardly deciding in this way with regard to a given woman. This is what adultery "committed in the heart" truly consists of.

Understood in this fashion, then, lust attacks human unity and consequently a capacity for intimacy. Jesus calls us to a "purity of heart,"[11] and thus to a liberation from lust. With this understanding in mind, "purity of heart" gives a new meaning to human intimacy and to the virtue of chastity, of which we have already spoken. In other words, chastity is not simply confined to avoiding faults but rather is aimed at attaining higher and more positive goals. It is a virtue which concerns the whole personality, both interior and outward behavior. Outward behavior, however, presupposes an interior purity of heart, a consistent refusal to fall into the sin of reductionism.[12]

## 2. THE NEED FOR INTEGRATION

In his *Contributions to the Psychology of Love*,[13] Sigmund Freud maintains that a fully normal love cannot be insured without the union of "the affectionate and the sensual..." In other words, as we have seen already, human sexuality is more than a simple, biological function. This same union is referred to by Paul Ricoeur in his analysis of "eroticism" and "tenderness" and in Rollo May's caring-wisdom, in which he ponders the mystery of the "daimonic" and the "tender."

These authors certainly do not translate sensuality in any pejorative way: i.e., by such terms as lust, lewdness, lechery, lasciviousness, salaciousness. On the contrary, sensuality is properly the whole complex of instinctual and organic impressions, needs and drives which tend to excite the body and, more specifically, the genital centers. Sensuality refers both to the cognitive and the appetitive functions of the senses.

To be fully human, however, sexuality must have another constitutive element: tenderness. Because of tenderness, human sexuality becomes a relationship between two persons. The spiritual dimensions of the tender affections produce a new quality of human presence. Tenderness, unlike sensuality, expresses togetherness in the mode of "being." It is a principle of identification rather than one of possession.

Neither sensuality nor tenderness exist independently. Rollo May is correct when he endows "feelings" with a certain "intentionality": "A pointing toward something," "An impetus for forming something," "A call to mould the situation."[14] May's insight is important because he is emphasizing that human feelings are merely not sensuous but are impregnated with direction. Sensual emotions normally have at least some possibility of giving shape to tender concern and so participate in the meaningful goals which human subjects pursue.

Another way of looking at this same point is to appreciate the fact that the body itself has a memory. The human body is a privileged point of access and exchange between the spirit and its environment. How we act sexually is always significant because of the deep reverberations which sexuality has in the body and in the spirit. Established patterns have a way of settling in deeply and leaving traces. Hence the body remembers in a pre-conscious way that is deeper and different than the conscious mind. One's body has a memory for the good life and a rebellious spirit, once in charge, has a way of worming itself into the bone.[15]

The human goal is an attempt to *integrate* sensuality and tenderness into a truly human conversation. Tenderness includes the whole host of capacities such as caring, hoping, patience, attentiveness; and sensuality includes all of these expressions as they are grounded in our sexuality, genital sexuality being only one of many human expressions. In light of what has been said above, lust isolates the physical, sensual side of sexuality and disavows its important connection with tenderness.

## 3. GENDER ASSESSMENT

The integration of sensuality and tenderness does not exist in a vacuum but finds its originality in each one of us. Each of us experiences our sexual lives within certain limitations, mainly rooted in our gender self-assessment. This gender self-assessment moves along three separate dimensions: gender identity, sexual orientation, and sexual intention.[16]

These three dimensions, separately or together, are basically parts of a subjective, psychological, intrapsychic phenomenon. As one facet of a many-faceted sense of the self, sexual identity exists with other identities, such as political, ethnic, religious, generational, vocational. Although there are important objective, behavioral aspects of sexual identity, its uniqueness can be more clearly perceived from its subjective aspects.

### A. Gender Identity

Gender identity is the first aspect of sexual identity to form. The child develops a sense of being a boy or girl early in the second year of life, probably based upon an inconspicuous, repetitive, labelling process underway since birth. The child is taught its gender and subtly steered into various directions by the family. Simone de Beauvoir insightfully remarks, "No one is born a woman."[17] In other words, one is born female, but in order to become fully a woman, she has the task of learning and living her femininity. She does this by taking into account, often unconsciously, the models and images provided by one's family and cultural settings.

Families have many conventional, and some very unique, attitudes about appropriate behaviors for boys and girls. By accepting their labels and the early steering, most children "choose" to be further influenced in a masculine or feminine direction. Normal children, between the ages of one and a half and three, show many subtle signs of temporary gender confusion and envy of the opposite sex. Perhaps as many as ninety percent of children develop what is known as a core gender identity, consonant with their biologic sex, by the middle or end of the third year of life.

In recalling early childhood, most parents and children seem to completely forget the instances of cross-gender identifications, curiosities, envy, and fantasy that are often part of the "cuteness" of early life. This forgetting or inattention to cross-gender preoccupations misleads many into thinking that gender sense is solely a biological phenomenon that merely unfolds, rather than a feeling that the child acquires and elaborates on. The establishment of core gender identity is based on identifications with others, particularly those with whom the child has a trusting relationship. As a consequence of establishing core gender identity at the usual time, boys and girls will maintain a relatively consistent sense of themselves as boys or girls, and become preoccupied with behaving in an acceptable masculine or feminine fashion. Because of this vital consequence, core gender identity can be considered the psychological foundation of sexuality.

Once comfortably and inconspicuously established, gender identity continues to evolve and be influenced by a person's subsequent identifications in an ever widening world. At any stage of life, the unique sense of the self as a certain type of male or female can be considered a reflection of gender identity. It becomes progressively harder, however, to define the limits of normal gender identity as humans progress from the rudimentary boy versus girl identification stage to adult styles of masculinity and femininity. Cultural forces — e.g., television, playmates, educational systems, adolescent subcultures, impact on the child to shape the evolution of gender self-images. It is especially difficult to be certain of gender identity development during adolescence. Beyond adolescence, "normal" generally refers to the absence of concern about masculinity or femininity. Clearly, then, an individual is normally born with a given sex (male or female) but one's gender (masculine or feminine) is a learned phenomenon.

The gender identity of others can be inferred from their behaviors. As one author indicates:

"The rough and tumble play of a four-year-old boy, e.g., often reassures parents that their son is 'all boy.' The preference for playing with dolls similarly reassures some parents that their daughter is feminine. Play, clothing style, mannerisms, and interest pattern may be considered gender role behaviors to the extent that they are indicative of a person's gender identity."[18]

Gender role behavior can never be completely relied on to indicate the subjective, psychologic sense of gender identity. Conventional gender role behaviors are often seen in adults with unconventional gender identities. Some adolescents try out many gender roles in the process of consolidating a stable gender identity. As we shall see, adult gender identity disorders represent the failures to comfortably resolve the problem every toddler faces: "Am I a boy or girl? Is that all right with me?"

### B. Sexual Orientation

The second dimension of sexual identity is sexual orientation, which also has subjective and objective aspects. Adult subjective orientation refers to the sex of people or mental images of people that attract and provoke sexual arousal. Adults can be considered heteroerotic if the great majority of images, fantasies, and attractions associated with sexual arousal concern members of the opposite sex. Homoerotic adults think about, are attracted to, or aroused by images of persons of the same sex. Bierotic individuals have the ability to become sexually aroused by images of both sexes. Sexual orientation is also reflected in adult behavior. Adults are generally classified as heterosexual, homosexual, or bisexual, depending on the biologic sex of their partners and their own set of images and attractions. The two aspects of sexual orientation are not always consistent: a homoerotic woman may behave heterosexually; a man who behaves bisexually may be entirely homoerotic; a heteroerotic man may engage in homosexual behavior. The homoerotic nature of male orientation is usually consciously manifested several years before heteroerotic orientation. Onset of partner sexual behavior and masturbation also tends to be earlier in homoerotic grade school and junior high students. The opposite patterns tend to be true for homoerotic and heteroerotic girls — i.e., female homoerotic orientation tends to manifest itself later than female heteroeroticism.[19]

Despite many assumptions, homosexuality, heterosexuality, and bisexuality are not *preferences*. Each is a sexuoerotic orientation or status.[20] They are no more chosen than a native language is. The roots of sexuoerotic status are complex. According to one common view, the labeling or social-construction theory of development, erotic orientation depends only on social learning and is independent of genetic or prenatal influence. This view assumes a dichotomy of nature and nurture. Other schools of thought draw a more persistent line between nature and nurture and conclude that heterosexuality, homosexuality, and bisexuality all have both prenatal and later causes, which interact during critical periods of development to create a long-lasting and probably immutable sexuoerotic status or orientation.

It is not correct to regard prenatal influences as biological and postnatal ones as non-biological. Influences that reach the brain through the senses during social communication and learning are just as much biological as those that reach the brain through hormones circulating in the bloodstream of a fetus. A unified theory must explain how erotic orientation becomes masculine or feminine. The theory should eventually account for both heterosexuality and homosexuality, as well as andromimesis (man-miming) in females and effeminacy or gynemimesis (woman-miming) in males. It might also account for transvestism and transsexualism. We will discuss these points in further detail later.

In mammals, including human beings, it is clear that prenatal influences help to determine an individual's masculinity/femininity ratio. Genes determine directly whether the primitive gonadal cells in the embryo will become testicles or ovaries. After that the sex hormones take over; they govern the sexual differentiation of the fetal brain by determining whether its sexual pathways will be masculinized or not. This process is mainly prenatal but in human beings extends for some time past birth.

In the absence of special hormonal conditions, the brain is feminized. A fetus with neither ovaries nor testicles will ordinarily develop as sexuoerotically female. Masculine differentiation requires testicular hormones supplied either directly from the fetus' own testicles or from a substitute source; brain cells change testosterone into a metabolite which can be used as a masculinizing agent. The fetal brain may be demasculinized without feminization or defeminized without masculinization. Both processes may also coexist to varying degrees, causing both masculine and feminine behavior in the same person. In other words, sexuoeroticism may be bisexual.

## C. Sexual Intention

Sexual intention — what a person actually wants to do with his or her sexual partner — constitutes the final dimension of sexual identity. Conventional sexual intentions include a wide range of behaviors, such as kissing, caressing, genital union, which are mutually pleasurable to consenting persons. Conventional intentions involve giving and receiving pleasure. While the behavioral repertoire of conventional intention is usually wide, the fantasy repertoire may be much wider. Unconventional sexual intentions involve raw or disguised aggression toward a victim, rather than mutual pleasure (tenderness). The victim may be the self or another person. In addition, they are often relatively limited to a few behaviors that provoke arousal. Sadism, masochistic degradation, exhibitionism, voyeurism, rape, and pedophilia are examples of unconventional developmental outcomes of intention. Erotic intention refers to the intrapsychic fantasy aspects. Behavioral intention refers to what is actually acted out.

Unconventional erotic intentions, generally referred to as paraphilias, are far more common than unconventional behavioral intentions. Unconventional intentions are probably first manifested with clarity for most individuals in adolescence. However, careful review of individual fantasy evolution often demonstrates the presence of precursors for many years.

What conclusions might be reached regarding this treatment of gender self-assessment? Each of the three dimensions of sexual identity can be thought of as structures of the mind created through the processes of development. The structures remain relatively fixed throughout adulthood. In general, gender identity is more fixed than sexual orientation, which, in turn, is more enduring than sexual intention. The constancy of the structures is not absolute, however. Dramatic shifts in each dimension of sexual identity have been reported, and many unreported shifts have been observed clinically. Nonetheless, the relative stability of these structures should be emphasized. The following description summarizes the identity structure of the conventional mind:

|  | MALE | FEMALE |
|---|---|---|
| gender identity | masculine | feminine |
| gender role | masculine | feminine |
| erotic orientation | heteroerotic | heteroerotic |
| sexual orientation | heterosexual | heterosexual |
| erotic intention | peaceable mutuality | peaceable mutuality |
| behavioral intention | peaceable mutuality | peaceable mutuality |

Sexual identity structures are clinically manifested in reports of attractions, fantasies, partner behavior and dreams. The clarity of the conventional person's classification is often subtly obscured during intensive psychotherapy. The intimacy of the therapeutic process often reveals unconventional elements embedded in conventional structures. A clinician who has this experience is better able to accept the unverifiable idea that few, if any, people are entirely conventional in their attractions, fantasies, dreams or behavior over a lifetime. It is, then, less shocking to realize that a "normal" feminine, heteroerotic, heterosexual woman with peaceable intentions may, e.g., occasionally experience homoerotic images, have fantasies of victimizing her partner, or have a sense of being masculine. In other words, the subjective side of sexual identity is quite private and generally denied to scientists who probe with questionnaires and rating scales.

### Summary

We have focused thus far on the paradigm of sexuality-as-language; and before we study various ways where this "language" becomes disturbed, confused or even falsified, it is critical to recall the *positive* elements of our human sexuality when viewed from the eye of language. Only in this way are we enabled better to critique the various forms of aberrant sexuality. In this light, Bernard Haering has pointed out that even when the sexual language unmasks a lack of liberty and fidelity and even speaks in plain lies, its very misery is crying out for the liberating truth, for communication in true love.[21]

When we view sexuality as a "language," we are reminded that authentic sexuality manifests its purpose in a truly human way only to those who look first for its meaning. And its meaning is truthful love. *Gaudium et Spes* wisely remarks, "This love is an immensely human one since it is directed from one person to another through an affection of the will. It involves the good of the whole person. Therefore it can enrich the expression of body and mind with a unique dignity, ennobling these expressions as special ingredients and signs of the friendship distinctive of marriage."[22] Human sexuality comes to its summit, then, when one person speaks out himself or herself for the other in a covenant of love.[23] Authentic human sexuality seeks the word that endorses its meaning. It comes to its full truth only when one person communicates with another in all one's reality, and so communicates in such a way which bespeaks belonging to one another and being for one another. Only an integrated person can bring sexuality fully home into the dimension of communication of the full truth of love. To bring human sexuality home into this dimension is a part of our ongoing redemption.

As we have suggested above, James B. Nelson has suggested several characteristics of human language which can provide insights into authentic sexuality:[24]

First, speech is culturally determined. The physical potentiality to talk is, of course, generically given. But our own actualization of the physical potential for speech depends on culture. Simply put, it takes a human environment to develop speech. The same is true for sexuality. Our sexuality is never simply biological. Rather, it is the way in which we relate to God and to the world as male or as female beings. As with speech, it takes a human environment to develop human sexuality, precisely because our sexuality is a pattern of meanings.

Second, words are symbols, and the sounds which make up words have in themselves no particular meaning or validity, but rather acquire meanings by social consensus. In some ways, the same is true of the "sounds" in sexual expression. For example, a mouth-to-mouth kiss has an erotic meaning, although there is nothing intrinsic about a kiss which determines that sexual meaning. This does not mean that sexuality is up for grabs; but it does mean that we must always search for the authentic meaning of sexual expression.

Third, human language as distinguished from animal communication is propositional in character and structure. For example, the same physical act can have a whole range of different meanings, depending on the context of those acts. Genital intercourse in one setting can be immensely pleasurable for both partners and may also bear the richest meaning of covenantal love in marriage. In a different context, genital intercourse can be exploitive and dehumanizing. The physical act is the same, but the propositional or syntactical setting is different.

Fourth, while animal communication is basically an instrument of biological survival and need-reduction, human speech regularly and usually transcends survival needs — even in the process of meeting those needs. The same is true of sexual expression. For example, when a husband and wife have intercourse with the intent of conceiving a child, the meaning they bring to the sex act surely transcends this felt need to be procreative. In other words, the procreative intent is lifted into a unitive dimension.

The concept of sexuality-as-language reminds us, therefore, that while our sexuality has a biological foundation, it also, and especially, elicits patterns of meaning which are socially constructed and transcend mere biological needs. This concept presses us to try to understand every sexual act as an expression of or the limitation of the human search for meaning and belonging. Sexual acts which limit and bereft human life of meaning and belonging have no moral justification.

Genovesi wisely comments:

The meaning of sexuality is not up for grabs; rather, the meaning of sexuality is something derived from the meaning of our lives as human beings. As a people of faith, moreover, we realize that we have been loved into being. We live because God loves us, and insofar as we live with his life we are enabled to love even as he has first loved us. At its deepest and truest level, Christian living is an extension of the Incarnation; in other words, it is a continuation of Christ's embodiment of God's love for us... Our sexuality plays a crucial role in our ability to answer this call to love. We say this because human sexuality is 'both the physiological and psychological grounding of our capacity to love.' It is 'a basic way in which we profess both our incompleteness and our relatedness. It is God's ingenious way of calling us into communion with others through our need to reach out and touch and embrace — emotionally, intellectually and physically.' Our sexuality is simply essential both to our becoming fully human and to our human becoming.[25]

Mindful of these notions of sexuality-as-language, we are now better positioned to critique various forms of aberrant sexuality.

## 4. ABERRANT SEXUALITY

What is the cause of paraphilias? Peculiar erotic interests have their roots in early childhood, when the first links between love and sex are forged.[26] Dr. John Money has coined the word *lovemap* to represent the seemingly indelible brain traces that ultimately help determine what arouses people sexually and enables them to fall in love. A lovemap depicts an idealized lover, love scene, and program of erotic activities. Lovemap patterns develop similarly in both heterosexuals and homosexuals.

Aberrant erotic development is often fostered by traumatic family and social experiences and becomes solidified in fantasy, dreams, and sometimes sex acts during adolescence, when a floodtide of sexual feelings naturally emerge. These distortions, long called sexual perversions, are known medically as paraphilias.

There is no evidence that paraphilias are biologically determined, although hormonal factors may influence a child's susceptibility to developing a paraphilia. Many psychoanalysts see paraphilias growing from unresolved and misdirected hostility, while behaviorists claim paraphilias are learned behaviors. But both psychodynamic and behavioral explanations emphasize the importance of traumatic events that sidetrack the development of eroticism and result in deviant sexual excitement.

Many paraphilias are both personally and socially devastating and preclude any semblance of normalcy. Men with vandalized lovemaps may ultimately be aroused and able to perform sexually only when surreptitiously watching women undress, or by frightening them through a public display of genitals, or by taking women by force or killing them. Or they may be able to attain sexual excitement or fulfillment only with prostitutes or children, or only when they are being strangled or restrained and beaten, or when they are inflicting intense pain on their partners. Dr. Money explains that people with such paraphilias typically describe themselves as periodically over-come by an irresistible compulsion to perform their aberrant sexual acts. They often relax into a trance-like state that temporarily blocks rational thoughts and acts.

To obtain a clear perspective on the nature and origin of paraphilias, Dr. Money has grouped the forty or so of them that are known into six major categories, or strategies:[27]

(1) Sacrifice and expiation: these allow for the expression of "sinful lust" on condition that the person atone for the irrevocable defilement of "saintly love." Attempts at atonement may take the form of penance, e.g., by self-administered asphyxiation, or the form of sacrifice of the partner through sadistic acts or lust murder.

(2) Marauding and privation: sinful lust is permitted into the lovemap on the condition that it be stolen, abducted or imposed by force. A person with a predatory lovemap may be either predator or prey.

(3) Mercantile and denial strategies: here lust is granted expression on the condition that it is traded, bartered or purchased, not freely exchanged, e.g., by buying sex from a prostitute or hustler or by exchanging play money with a spouse.

(4) Fetishes and talismans: lust is given expression through a token, fetish or talisman that is a substitute for the lover, such as certain odors or tactile sensations, as in fetishes involving rubber, leather, fur or silk fabrics or garments.

(5) Stigmata and eligibility strategies: lust can be expressed without defying the lover by having a partner who is not part of the person's social set and would evoke disapproval from the family. Such partners include children, people with missing limbs and those of another race or religion.

(6) Solicitation and allure: exhibitionism, voyeurism and the
    dependence on pornography for sexual excitement are the
    best known examples of this paraphiliac strategy, in which
    a kind of foreplay is substituted for the actual act of copula-
    tion.

In his book *Human Sexuality: A Christian View*,[28] John C.
Dwyer rightfully describes pornography as "an industry." In addition,
pornography should not be thought of as a victimless crime. Sexual
perversion is not an entirely private matter. We are all affected by
what we see and what we read, and then we proceed to affect others
as a result of it. Education is built on the principle that exposure to
intellectually and aesthetically sound material will foster the development of the human person. The obvious correlative to this is that
exposure to distorted and warped material interferes with the development of the person and is likely to produce a warped and distorted
human being.

Dwyer points out that pornography is often opposed for the
wrong reasons. In the proper sense of the word, the sexualization of
life is a very good thing, and anything which impedes the authentic
sexualization of life should be opposed. Indeed, pornography must be
distinguished from legitimate art which may have an erotic aspect.
This underlines the real problem with pornography: it works *against*
the healthy sexualization of life, and this is the only valid and safe
reason for opposing it. An effective long-term answer to the problem
of pornography is an ethos which sees the healthy sexualization of life
as an ideal, and which has learned to express and embody this ideal
in all of the arts — in music, sculpture, painting, dance, in the novel,
in poetry, in drama and in film. An essential task of art is to promote
the healthy sexualization of life, and a society which is successful in
this respect will have no really serious pornography problem. Healthy
sexuality is incomparably more intriguing and infinitely more fulfilling than sick sexuality.

Finally, pornography involves elements other than the overtly
sexual. Much of the "sex" on TV is not pornographic in any serious
way, although it is often quite silly and poses a threat to authentic
sexuality for precisely that reason. In fact, most of the "sex" on TV
really seems designed to titillate excessively naive adolescents, and

the real problem with the so-called suggestive lines and scenes of contemporary mass entertainment is that they trivialize or banalize human sexuality and are therefore not authentically sexual. Sexuality is a wonderful gift and deserves better treatment than this.

## A. *Transsexualism*

Leslie M. Lothstein begins his treatment of transsexualism by indicating:

> Although transsexualism is recognized as "*un mal ancien*," which has historical, mythological, cultural and anthropological roots, it was not until 1980 that it was formally recognized by the American Psychiatric Association as a serious emotional disorder. In fact, the term, "transsexual" only appears in the literature in 1949 and it was not until 1966 that it was accorded clinical status by Benjamin whose pioneering work, *The Transsexual Phenomenon*, provided the first textbook on transsexualism. In this sense, one must regard the clinical disorder of transsexualism as a recent phenomenon.[29]

It is important to distinguish transsexualism from hermaphroditism. In medical terminology, a true hermaphrodite (*hermaphroditus verus*) is an individual who has both ovarian and testicular tissue. The condition is extremely rare. Only 60 cases have been reported in the entire world medical literature of the twentieth century. Such an individual may have one ovary and one testicle or sex glands that contain mixtures of ovarian and testicular tissues. This combination of tissues and hormones is usually accompanied by a mixture of masculine and feminine characteristics, but hermaphrodites usually have masculine genitals and feminine breasts. There often is some sort of vaginal opening beneath the penis, and many hermaphrodites menstruate. Development of the uterus is often incomplete — with, for instance, only one fallopian tube present. True hermaphrodites are usually genetic females (XX). They can be raised as males or females and the decision is often made based on their appearance at birth.

In addition to true hermaphrodites, there are also male and female pseudohermaphrodites. Unlike the true hermaphrodite, the pseudohermaphrodite does not have both ovarian and testicular tissue. But pseudohermaphrodites do have some sex organs that resemble the organs of the opposite sex. The development of both male and female sex organs is caused by the simultaneous presence, in significant amounts, of male and female sex hormones during embryological development.[30] Over the past two decades, the phenomenon of transsexualism has attracted widespread interest. As a result of converging evidence on transsexualism from many disciplines our understanding of the etiology, pathogenesis, and phenomenological and theoretical aspects of male and female transsexualism have undergone considerable revision. Moreover, as a consequence of large numbers of surgically sex-changed individuals entering the mainstream of society (between 3,000 to 6,000 worldwide), serious questions have been raised about the meaning and implication of sex reassignment surgery insofar as it may lead to dramatic changes in such traditional social phenomena as the family, marriage, ritual, religion and legal definitions of sex.

Over the past decade a number of theories of transsexualism have been proposed that challenge some of the classical views of the disorder. We will here briefly overview these theories, placing them within the context of the so-called classical theories of transsexualism.

During the nineteenth century physicians, neuropsychiatrists, and sexologists documented case histories of individuals who wished to change their sex. These patients, males and females, were viewed as bisexualists who shared many common features: from early childhood on they wished to become the opposite sex; complained that they were a "man/woman trapped in a woman/man's body"; exhibited a compulsive desire to cross dress and live and work in the cross gender role; desired to attract same-sex partners in a love relationship, but denied they were homosexual and viewed the ensuing relationship as a "heterosexual" one; and were generally viewed as non-psychotic: i.e., they were not delusional about their sexual status; and they knew that they were a male or female but wished to become the opposite sex. Patients who exhibited these core features of a gender identity disturbance were initially labeled according to current standards of psychiatric nomenclature.

Over the course of the last 100 years these gender disturbed patients have been variously diagnosed as having contrary sexual feelings; being sexual inverts; transvestites; contrasexists; having *psychopathia transsexualis*; eonism; psychosexual inverts; and as being gender dysphoric. However, all of these patients shared certain commonalities: they had a core belief about being the opposite gender, and an obsessive and relentless drive to change their body to match their mind through sexual surgery.

According to the American Psychiatric Association's *Diagnostic and Statistical Manual of Mental Disorders III*, the following criteria must be present for a diagnosis of transsexualism to be made:

(1) A sense of discomfort and inappropriateness about one's anatomic sex;

(2) A wish to be rid of one's own genitals and to live as a member of the other sex;

(3) The disturbance has been continuous (not limited to periods of stress) for at least two years;

(4) The absence of physical intersex or genetic abnormality; and

(5) Not due to another mental disorder such as schizophrenia.

The DSM III criteria for diagnosing transsexualism were based solely on descriptive criteria that were unrelated to the possible etiology of the disorder, a diagnosis that many psychodynamically oriented clinicians felt uncomfortable making since it relied on behaviorally oriented criteria alone. While the DSM III diagnostic enterprise may have aimed at methodological consistency, it ignored the wealth of clinical studies linking transsexualism to unconscious fantasies, psychodynamic precursors, a variety of character problems, and, more recently, to borderline pathology. Moreover, the DSM III diagnosis of transsexualism implied that sex reassignment surgery was the treatment of choice and artificially created a number of serious social, psychological, and bioethical dilemmas.

In their book *Man and Woman/Boy and Girl*, Money and Ehrhardt[31] attempted to shed light on the effect of all of the above variables on typical gender identity development. The book summarizes the research of the effects of all types of biological conditions on the formation of gender role and identity. What about the evidence? Is transsexualism a biological disorder? Indeed, there is evidence that some transsexuals are motivated because of underlying cerebral pathology, specifically temporal lobe disorders. However, only a small number of transsexuals have actually been diagnosed as having a temporal lobe disorder. In summary, the EEG findings, while suggestive of a link between cerebral pathology and transsexualism, are inconclusive, especially since EEG abnormalities have been associated with non-organic personality disorders which many transsexuals have.

Another biological hypothesis has focused on the possible chromosomal defects in transsexuals. Again the evidence is inconclusive. Some transsexuals have been diagnosed as having a serious hormonal disorder: e.g., progestin induced hermaphroditism; adrenogenital syndrome; testicular feminizing syndrome; Turner's and Kleinfelter's syndrome. However, the number of transsexuals who have these disorders are so few, and their symptomology so diverse, that it seems improbable that transsexualism could be explained by those disorders.

The most promising research area linking transsexualism with hormonal causes is in fetal behavioral neuroendocrinological research, focusing on the effects of prenatal hormones on childhood and adult behavior. Ehrhardt and Meyer-Bahlburg, summarizing the findings on the effects of prenatal hormones on gender-related behavior, concluded that: "The evidence accumulated so far suggests that human psychosexual differentiation is influenced by prenatal hormones, albeit to a degree... The development of gender identity seems to depend largely on the sex of rearing."[32] In conclusion, the evidence from all areas of investigation suggests that while any or all of the suspected biological factors may play a facilitating role in the establishment of transsexualism, there is no hard evidence that transsexualism is caused by organic pathology. However, as new insights are gained into the micromolecular structure and functioning of the endocrine system, we will probably have to modify some of our assumptions about how gender identity and role are formed. The best evidence to date, however, suggests that the development of gender identity depends largely on the sex of rearing.

Respected psychoanalysts writing in this area generally view transsexualism as arising within the context of a pathological family structure, even though there is disagreement as to how precisely this takes place. For some, the patient is a target of the family's intense gender conflicts in which trauma defense, ambivalence, and conflict play pivotal roles in the transsexual-to-be's evolving gender identifications. The disorder of transsexualism is viewed by most psychoanalysts as a maladjustment, interfering with the child's separation and individuation and leading to structural ego defects, impairment incognition, specifically a defect in symbol formation, and profound impairment in ego functioning. For example, the family lives of transsexual patients were characterized by disorganization, chaos, and over stimulation, with violence, physical and sexual abuse, incest, and abandonments evident in the majority of families. The pattern was anything but "stable."

Most clinicians have noted that there are a wide variety of clinical variants who identify as transsexuals. What these patients seem to have in common, in addition to their transsexual ideazation, is serious emotional conflict of a preoedipal nature and severe character pathology. Until recently, most of the transsexuals' symptoms and pathological character structure were explained as a result of their transsexualism. However, as a result of clinical evidence suggesting that transsexuals have profound psychological problems, a developmental arrest, and primitive mental functioning, many clinicians have speculated about the possible relationship between transsexualism and borderline pathology. Indeed, from a clinical standpoint transsexuals resemble borderlines. Like the borderline patients they appear to have a "stable instability" to their personality organization and are usually described as quite intact and stable on clinical interview, but disorganized and unstable on prolonged evaluation and psychological testing.

In addition, transsexuals have a defective narcissism, in which the goals of the transsexual's self system are magically transformed into the admired omnipotent cross-gender object, bolstering their self-esteem. In this light, transsexuals are involved in three tasks: attempting to prove stability and cohesion in their precarious gender self-representation; trying to repair their defective ego mechanisms regulating gender-self constancy; and finally, trying to structuralize and consolidate their core gender identity. The reparative fantasy is meant to restore some sense of cohesion to a perceived fragmented self-system and ward off either psychosis or personality decompensation. The transsexual fantasy thus serves both a mirroring and idealizing function: providing the self with a solution to the perceived sense of narcissistic depletion by simultaneously gratifying exhibitionistic, voyeuristic, perfectionistic needs through a fusion with the mirroring and idealizing object. Of course, this solution must fail since it has not been adequately internalized and structuralized as part of the total self system. This may explain why many transsexuals continue to request further surgery in order to activate a state of perfection.

There is, then, increasing clinical evidence that the majority of transsexuals suffer from some type of pathology. While a few transsexuals may have a biological substrate that organizes their transsexualism, the disorder is primarily psychological. It would appear, therefore, that a psychological disorder deserves to be treated by psychological, not surgical methods. Essentially, the transsexual wish represents the unconscious fantasy for wholeness and integrity of the self system; a defense against annihilation anxiety; an expression of the transsexual's defect in symbol formation; and an overvalued idea that was highly encapsulated and rigidly adhered to, providing a barrier to conscious awareness of and integration of their profound separation/individuation conflicts and their underlying sadomasochistic fantasies that threatened to engulf and destroy their fragmented self system.

## B. Transvestism

Transvestism is a difficult problem.[33] Transvestites must be seen in relationship to their family setting which, according to many observers, determines the nature and course of cross-dressing. One must be ready and able to sense the attitudes of family members who may be dynamically involved in the origin and reinforcement of cross-dressing behavior. If such family members are part of the problem they must be included in the concern and in the responses. Transvestism is a phenomenon which affects both males and females. For purposes of brevity here, we will concentrate on the question of male transvestism, although many of the factors mentioned are applicable to both sexes.

It is not the most surprising thing in the world to find very young boys trying on the clothes of the opposite sex, especially in homes in which girls seem to get preferential treatment. Over-reaction to this kind of experimental behavior is not called for. Commonsense tells us that if such behavior persists it needs a cautious and even-handed investigation by persons not ready to find the worst. Generally speaking, such experimental behavior is reported in small children as a temporary phenomenon.

Cross-dressing and related behavior reported at adult levels is clearly rooted in early life experiences. Adults report frequently that their problem with such behavior began as early as two years of age.

The research of psychiatrists James Spensley and James T. Barber underscores the significance of cross-dressing.[34] On the basis of their experience, Spensley and Barber feel that such behavior in adolescents "should be clearly evaluated since cross-dressing is not a part of the normal adolescent identity struggle." They also suggest that the entire family be evaluated as well because they are convinced that cross-dressing behavior is "initiated, encouraged and sustained directly and indirectly by other members of the family." They do not perceive this problem as having one explanation or one, single, dynamic meaning. Interviewing the whole family together provides some insight into its members' expectations about male or female behavior in their children and helps one to make prudent judgments about the individual involved with cross-dressing or transvestism. They believe, moreover, that many mistakes are made by categorizing all cross-dressing behavior under the notion of transvestism, a term which may have certain implications about the presence of homosexuality, which are not verified in each situation. They offer several classifications and counsel that each type has distinctive features related to the style of the family dynamics and that, although there is some overlap, the nature of the family is extremely relevant to understanding the particular difficulty in question. In speaking of the transvestite population which they studied, Spensley and Barber describe family factors which they felt were significant in the shaping of the cross-dressing behavior. The mother proved to be a dominant figure while the father is reported as distant and passive.

The mother is related in a close and then hostile fashion to the young man in one of the examples which they cite. In this particular instance the boy's cross-dressing started when the mother began caring for her sister's two daughters during the day. The boy engaged in vandalism of the houses along his paper route which he knew were empty. He would dress in girl's clothes and tear the house up, finally destroying the clothes he had worn during this activity.

Although anti-social actions are not ordinarily associated with transvestism, the researchers felt that the other family factors were and that two-thirds of the cases they studied fell into this classification. The family dynamics pivoted on the nature of the mother's relationship toward the son who was clearly in a less preferred status than his own sister or the infant female cousins in his mother's care. The mother was hostile toward masculinity in general and toward her son's efforts to achieve masculinity in particular. The father's failure to play a supportive role or to provide a figure of identification is also significant. In other words, the cross-dressing behavior was an effort to become like the girls who in his family experience were the desired and preferred children. In the place of fetishism, the individual uses female underclothing in pursuit of sexual satisfaction principally through masturbation. Although female underclothing is frequently used as a fetish object, a wide variety of clothing and other objects may also be used.

In the clinical examples cited by Spensley and Barber, there is evidence of a seductive quality in the mother's relationship to the boy involved. His defensive response was an increased hostility that included aggressive sexuality. It is the interpretation of these researchers that boys who employ fetishes for sexual purposes do not wish to appear as girls. They are, in fact, already strongly favored by their mothers and so are quite different from those in category one. Their sexual behavior is a reaction to the seductive nature of the mother's relationship to them. Mothers can transmit seductive impulses without any overt word or gesture. The attitude, even when unmeasurable, is extraordinarily powerful in shaping the psychological atmosphere of the home. The son's response is highly symbolic even though he has no direct insight into it. His acting-out sexual behavior constitutes a hostile form of defense against the mother's overwhelming sexual approach. This kind of response is highly specific and should not be confused with any of the other classifications.

Thirdly, transsexual cross-dressing differs from the two previous examples in that the young boy involved clearly wishes to be a girl, not just by dressing like one, but by becoming one as much as possible. These boys exhibit extremely effeminate behavior with very self-dramatizing gestures and mannerisms and a highly volatile emotional life.

There are also individuals who may believe themselves to be women trapped inside of male bodies. Such persons often request transsexual operations in an effort to harmonize their feelings of femininity with their overall sense of themselves. Kennedy's comment here is similar to the data presented above in our treatment of transsexualism: "Typically the involved families do not offer a setting in which the young person can develop a disciplined sense of self and so the individual is left with little power to control internal urges that may become overwhelming."[35]

Although cross-dressing is associated in the popular mind with homosexuality, Spensley and Barber feel that this is a dangerous and unfortunate generalization. It is a mistake immediately to identify cross-dressing with homosexuality in early adolescence. Adolescents who are homosexuals may dress in women's clothing but the symbolic significance is not the same as it is in the situations previously described. Young homosexuals dress in women's clothing to attract males for overtly homosexual activity. This problem may on the surface resemble the other cited classifications, but a sensitivity to the possibilities of difference — and their relationship to differing family backgrounds — is a major responsibility of counselors who are consulted in these circumstances.

## C. Pedophilia and Ephebophilia

Stephen J. Rossetti has edited *Slayer of the Soul*,[36] a book on child sexual abuse. In this section, we will follow the outline of the chapter on "Psychological Theories of Pedophilia and Ephebophilia" by L. M. Lothstein.[37]

The clinical evaluation of pedophiles reveals them to be a diverse group. They differ educationally, vocationally, religiously, and socio-economically. They vary in the amount of force or aggression used in their pedophilic acts. They may be involved in a wide variety of other variant sexual behaviors, such as exhibitionism, voyeurism, frotteurism [sexually touching or fondling an unwilling person], masochism or sadism. Also, they vary in the many different causes that led to the development of their sexual problems.[38]

For some child molesters, their sexual acting out can be explained by the presence of a psychosis or an organic brain deficit. Individuals with a history of closed or open head injuries and individuals with a diagnosis of schizophrenia may become sexually aggressive because of their unique mental disorder or because of their brain injuries. Their pedophilic behavior is not the result of a primary sexual disorder but of an organic disorder.

Therefore, no single explanation can account for all the different pathways leading toward pedophilia. Any theory of pedophilia must be multifaceted and account for the wide range of behaviors, fantasies, and organic factors that may play a role in the development of this disorder. A comprehensive theory of pedophilia must refer to psychological, familial, environmental, social, genetic, hormonal, organic and biological factors.

Any discussion of the causes of the sexual abuse of children should distinguish between *pedophilia* and *ephebophilia*. A *pedophile* is an adult who has recurrent, intense, sexual urges and sexually arousing fantasies involving a prepubescent child. The age of the child is arbitrarily set at 13 years or younger and the adult is at least 5 years older than the child. An *ephebophile* is an adult who has recurrent, intense sexual urges and sexually arousing fantasies toward an adolescent. The age of the child is arbitrarily set at 14 through 17 years. Again, the adult is at least 5 years older than is the child.

In their article "The Child Molester: Clinical Observations,"[39] Groth, Hobson and Gary divide pedophiles into two groups, *regressed* and *fixated*. *Regressed* pedophiles are described as individuals with a primary sexual orientation toward adults of the opposite sex. Under conditions of extreme stress, the regressed pedophile may psychologically regress to an earlier psychosexual age and engage in sex with children. The typical case is a male whose wife is emotionally unavailable to him and who thus turns to his daughter for sex. *Fixated* pedophiles/ephebophiles have a primary sexual interest in children or teens; they rarely, if ever, engage in sex with peers. In most cases, they are described as exclusively interested in children or teenagers.

In a review of the research, Araji and Finkelhor[40] raise several critical questions that must be answered:

1. Why does the adult have an emotional need to relate to children?
2. Why does the adult become sexually aroused by children?
3. Why are alternative sources of sexual and emotional gratification not available?
4. Why can the adult not inhibit arousal toward children/teens based on normal prohibitions against sexual behavior with minors?

Their review suggested that:

1. Children have a special meaning to pedophiles because of the children's lack of dominance (emotional congruence).
2. Pedophiles have an "unusual pattern of sexual arousal toward children" (deviant sexual arousal).
3. Pedophiles seem "blocked in their social and heterosexual relationships" (blockage).
4. Many pedophiles were sexually abused as children, and use alcohol or other drugs to lower their inhibitions prior to offending with children (disinhibition).

Araji and Finkelhor then view the theories of pedophilia as organized into these four basic categories: emotional congruence; sexual arousal; blockage; and disinhibition. Any perspective on pedophilia/ephebophilia will have to address this four factor approach, as well as the regressed/fixated typology mentioned above.

Psychological theories of pedophilia/ephebophilia address only those aspects of the emotional congruence, sexual arousal, blockage, and disinhibition that are independent of organic causes. These theories include such diverse perspectives as psychoanalysis, social learning theory, and family systems.

Psychoanalytic theories look at deviant sexual behavior as stemming from early childhood trauma during ages 2 to 5. This trauma, which may take the form of sexual or physical abuse, leaves the child in a state of over stimulation, confusion, separation anxiety, and rage. Feeling helpless, out of control, and powerless, this victim may, in turn, sexually act out as a way of re-creating the original trauma and attempting to master the anxiety associated with it. This psychic mechanism is called a repetition compulsion.

Or this victim may identify with the aggressor, i.e., he or she may identify with the abusing adult and then act out sexually with a younger child. Identifying with the aggressor would enable the person to defend against the unwanted feelings of helplessness and powerlessness. The sexual acting out with children or adolescents makes the individual feel alive and vital; it reestablishes a feeling of control, dominance and power, and allays the anxiety associated with the childhood trauma.

However, this is only an illusory feeling of having solved an earlier childhood conflict. The feelings of dominance, control, power, and being alive soon dissipate and re-enactment (i.e., the molestation) has to be repeated. Because the molester's attempts at mastery and problem-solving are illusory, he or she must molest over and over again.

*Psychoanalytic theories* regard pedophilia as resulting from arrested emotional development between the ages of 2 to 5 years old. Because of the unresolved feelings associated with childhood trauma, he or she may eventually become the offending adult who compulsively repeats the pedophilic act with others in an attempt to master the original anxiety. This compulsion to repeat has come to be known as the addictive process in pedophilia.

*Family system theories* stress the role of unresolved intergenerational family dynamics on specific family members. Some researchers[41] have argued that deviant sexuality is learned within the family. It first arises within the nuclear family and then is unconsciously transmitted along family lines. Thus, individual members can be "targeted" to act out family conflicts. For example, an unconscious conflict which is unacceptable to a parent may be encouraged in a child. A parent's unconscious wish to act out sexually with children may be repressed or pushed out of consciousness because of the fear of punishment. These unresolved wishes may be projected onto a child who is vulnerable. In the context of subtle family communications, the child may be passively or actively encouraged to act out those parental wishes. In this way, parents can both repress the forbidden sexual impulse and act it out through their child's behavior.

*Behaviorism and social learning theories* stress the importance of learning our behavior. For example, a child may have had same-sex experiences with other children or adults which were prolonged. Sexual excitement, even when it is the result of abuse, is pleasurable. Pleasure is a strong, positive reinforcer of behavior and, thus, such sexual experiences have a high probability of becoming learned behavior and/or of becoming generalized to other sexual behavior.

At the same time, a child who has been sexually assaulted by an adult or another child may experience a tremendous guilt over these early sexual experiences. This guilt is likely to be associated in the child's mind with sexual pleasure. The child is thus vulnerable to distressing symptoms because of the internal conflict of guilt versus pleasure associated with normal sexuality. When the child becomes an adult, this internal conflict, and the resulting ambivalence, may take the form of sexual acting out with children. This psychological approach, stressing the psychic, social and environmental factors that give rise to child sexual molestation, must never lose sight, however, of the importance of biological factors. These factors acknowledge the importance of organic issues, especially brain pathology.

The search for a biological explanation of pedophilia/ephebophilia is compelling and has attracted many researchers. The central question is: What effect does the brain have on perverse sexual behavior? Can deviant sexual arousal be attributed to brain illness or damage? This is an important question, the answer to which may link sexually deviant behavior to a brain disease. Research in this area has taken several paths, linking certain kinds of brain damage and hormonal problems to sexual deviants.

Psychologists have shown that the male sex drive and male aggression are mostly related to the male hormone testosterone. Researchers have inquired: Does too much of this male hormone lead to violence or chaotic and deviant sexuality? Many have suggested that there is a direct relationship between male hormone levels and aggression/sexuality, although this relationship is not a simple one.

Some studies have even shown that a fetus can be adversely affected by its mother's stress or by the specific drugs she took during pregnancy. These events may alter the testosterone levels of the fetus *in utero*. Researchers have speculated that specific brain pathways are created *in utero* by hormonal changes in the mother. Thus, the mother's hormones may have a profound effect on her fetus by organizing such diverse behavioral patterns as sexual identity and sexual orientation which are not manifested until years after birth.

Is there a relationship between hormones and pedophilia? Berlin and Coyle[42] did find significantly elevated testosterone levels in pedophiles. Other researchers have found unusually elevated levels in pedophiles of another hormone called "luteinizing hormone" when they were given injections of a related hormone LHRH (luteinizing hormone-releasing hormone). Like testosterone, luteinizing hormone and LHRH have been connected with human sexual behavior. The researchers concluded that there is a specific hormonal abnormality in many pedophiles.[43]

Another line of research has focused on naturally occurring "experiments." Some researchers have reported on four cases of men whose pedophilia began after the onset of some kind of brain injury.[44] These men also showed cognitive impairment: their thinking was disorganized and confused. Researchers have reported on patients in whom hypersexuality or altered sexual preference (homosexuality and/or pedophilia) occurred after brain injury such as head trauma or injuries resulting from a stroke.

Other studies have tested groups of pedophiles using newer medical technologies that can "image" the brain (PET scans, MRI, brain imaging) and reveal specific brain abnormalities. Moreover, using neuropsychological tests, psychologists have correlated the paraphile's brain abnormality with behavioral problems. We can not only document that there is brain abnormality using sophisticated medical technology, we can also relate specific behavioral problems to specific brain deficits. Almost all of these studies have found some kind of brain abnormality or damage in pedophiles. Whatever the abnormality is, it is not due to the toxic effects of alcohol or drugs alone.[45]

There is a relationship between alcohol, substance abuse, and the paraphilias that needs to be explored fully. Most sexually deviant men report using alcohol excessively prior to acting out sexually. The alcohol or drugs seemed to lower their inhibitions while increasing their level of impulsivity. However, not all sex offenders use alcohol or drugs prior to their sexual encounters. Moreover, the use of alcohol does not explain the content, aim, and direction of a child molester's sexuality. Clearly, alcohol may fuel the fires of a pedophile's sexual desires and increase the dangers of acting out, but it does not cause pedophilia/ephebophilia. An individual with brain pathology who drinks excessively may, however, be increasing the likelihood of some kind of deviant sexual behavior occurring.

In attempting to explain why an individual expresses his or her sexual drive toward children or adolescents, the distinction between *fixated* and *regressed* is useful. Fixated sexual offenders direct their sexual drives only toward children or adolescents. They are not aroused by adults under any condition. In many cases, there is an exclusive interest in one sex or the other, or with a certain kind of child (e.g., blue-eyed, brown hair). Sexual offenders who indiscriminately choose children of either sex or from a variety of age groups are less likely to benefit from treatment.

Fixated pedophiles typically are:

- developmentally arrested
- psychosexually immature
- non-assertive
- heterosexually inhibited
- lacking in social skills
- without a basic knowledge of sexuality

Fixated child molesters talk about their need for control over others and how the child can be a wonderfully pliant object to control and manipulate. Fixated child molesters are dangerous because they may become chronic sexual predators, ferociously incorporating children into their sexual lives. On the other hand, regressed child molesters may be able to control their sexual impulses once their coping skills are rehabilitated, the stimulus cues for sexually acting out are understood, and a prevention program is initiated. This is not the case for fixated child molesters.

For a pedophile, the emotional congruence factor is critical. The perpetrator is developmentally arrested and may be at the same psychosexual age as his victims. Thus, the pedophile emotionally and sexually identifies with the child who becomes his or her victim. Pedophiles may even engage in sexual acts appropriate to their arrested psychosexual age such as showing or touching. For example, the pedophile might say to the child, "Let me see what you have and I will show you what I have." Pedophiles often state that, in order to be aroused, their victim must lack pubic hair and have a smooth body. Some pedophiles become hyperaroused by the slightest hint of a child's presence. In this sense, it is not a particular child who is arousing but the sight, smell or sounds of a child. For example, some pedophiles can only be aroused by girls with blonde hair and blue eyes.

Power and control are critical factors for the pedophile. The child is pliant and yielding, unlike an adult who may be rigid and unyielding. The child can be coerced and brought under control through simple requests and demands; the child will yield to the adult's power and control because he or she still lacks autonomy and self-initiative. If the adult is employed in a high status/powerful role (e.g., teacher, coach), the child is particularly vulnerable.

The pedophile desires a sexual object that is safe and non-threatening; thus it cannot be an adult. The child is perceived as unthreatening, unaggressive, and lacking the ability to retaliate because of his or her small size and lack of power. In this sense, the child is not viewed by the pedophile as a real person with real needs and power.

A child is also submissive and used to bending to parental authority. By offering bribes and favors, the pedophile exercises control over the child's inner needs. In a sense, the child molester does what the adult does with the prostitute: i.e., bypasses personal autonomy and bargains via primitive economic systems. It is perhaps not a coincidence that a high percentage of prostitutes were themselves sexually abused as children.

In the pedophilic act, a sexual "game" is enacted between the perpetrator and the victim. This game may take many forms and follow the model of the "doctor" game of childhood sexual exploration. One child molester initiated contact by "wrestling" with his victim; another played a "tickling" game. A more sophisticated game involved enlisting teenage boys to complete a "sexual survey" which was then used to stimulate and excite the boys prior to the actual seduction.

Most pedophiles, with the exception of the rare sadist, deny malevolent intent. They do not see themselves as aggressive or wishing to harm the child. Many of them say that they are afraid of the child and distort the size of the child, viewing the child as potentially dangerous. Some offenders are genuinely hurt when their aggressiveness is confronted. They view themselves as being unfairly treated and accused. For many pedophiles, such cognitive impairment or denial is a critical part of their dysfunctional sexual patterns.

The ephebophile's attraction to older children reflects a higher level of social and psychosexual development than does the pedophile's attraction to younger, prepubescent children. If the ephebophile chooses girls as victims, the attraction may be to their virginity and lack of sexual experience. Having sex with a virgin means not having to worry about how she compares you sexually to other men. If boys are victimized, the focus is on genital sex.

The sexual abuse of male teenagers by women is thought to be underreported owing to social and cultural forces. When an older woman coerces a teenage boy, it is unlikely that a report will be filed, although sexual exploitation has taken place. Society may look upon it as acceptable and call it an initiation of the boy into sexuality. In addition, if the teenage boy reports the molestation and it is publicized, he may become the target of ridicule and suffer more from the social ostracism than from the original abuse.

The ephebophile is often unaware that sexual coercion has taken place. He or she may say that the teen was not a victim and enjoyed both the sex act and the attention. A common argument by the perpetrator is that the teenager can choose to engage in sexual relationships. This argument not only denies social and legal standards, but also fails to appreciate the power of adult roles.

Pedophiles and ephebophiles differ in many respects but they share certain characteristics:

- cognitive distortions
- deviant sexual fantasies
- distorted sexual arousal pattern
- interpersonal dependence
- low self-esteem
- low victim empathy
- planning of the sexual offense

- deficient sexual knowledge
- lack of social skills

The sexual offense is often precipitated by the perpetrator's inability to cope associated with increased stress, workaholism, alcohol abuse, profound feelings of loneliness and emptiness and a feeling of despair about his lack of connectedness to others. The sexual acting out results in a more pleasant emotional state (e.g., sexual excitement instead of depression) and provides the psyche with an internal experience of integration instead of disintegration.

Pedophilia or ephebophilia is always an aggressive act. The perpetrator's lack of awareness of this aggressive component in the relationship is akin to disavowal or denial and is a delusional suspension of reality. Such persons may rationalize their molestation as serving in a caretaker or parental role, performing an educational function, or providing friendship, even though there may be a 30-year age difference.

The establishment of an aggressive relationship gives the perpetrator power, control and dominance over the child and provides a connection to a real individual in order to overcome feelings of isolation and loneliness. During the "courtship" phase, the perpetrator disguises the aggression in order to manipulate the child and coerce him or her into participating in the "game" or "play."

The child's adoring or admiring attitude, or the teenager's idealization, is critical to the deception. This adoration and admiration feeds the narcissistic grandiosity of the perpetrator, provides him with a modicum of self-esteem, and confirms his self-image as loving and caring. Essentially, the victim unwittingly provides the pedophile/ ephebophile with an important narcissistic balance to an otherwise depleted and depressed personality. The sexual encounter provides a feeling of cohesion to a psyche which is in danger of disintegrating.

Given the perpetrator's lack of self-assertion, psychosexual and psychosocial immaturity, and inability to form gratifying peer relationships, the child/teenager is an ideal object for sexual exploitation. Because the abuser lacks genuine empathy and connectedness to others, the child or teenager is viewed as a pliable object that can be persuaded to relate sexually to the adult.

During the sexual molestation, the aggressor's thinking is

disturbed. Many sex offenders speak of the molestation as taking place in a hypnotic-like trance from which they awaken only after an orgasm. This trance is the mind's way of separating the rage from consciousness. Some researchers might argue that this results from damage to the frontal and temporal lobes of their brains, leading to poor judgment, blunted anxiety, and impulsivity. Moreover, the disappearance of sexually motivating fantasies in the post-ejaculatory phase suggests a biological link between the body's hormone system and human cognition.

In all cases, an attempt is made to engage the child/teenager in a relationship, what some have called a "technique of intimacy," in which sexual excitement and altered ego states are played out in games and scenarios that substitute an intense sexual feeling for genuine intimacy. The true nature of the relationship is kept secret to maintain the fiction and to avoid confrontation. The "game of pretend" allows both parties to pretend that what is happening is not really happening.

The child too may be in a "dream-like" state induced by the aggressor. When the child awakens from the "trance" and recognizes the betrayal, there is a need to cleanse the self, to confess the "game," and to break the conspiracy of silence. The molester may feel victimized when a report is made and not understand why the child/ teen has betrayed him. The destruction of the perpetrator's delusion that a genuine friendship has taken place may lead to a suicidal crisis.

### D. Sexual Addiction

A number of books deal well with the question of sexual addiction[46] but perhaps Patrick Carnes' *Out of the Shadows*[47] describes most succinctly this whole question and problem. Carnes explains that a common definition of alcoholism or drug dependency is that a person has a pathological relationship with a mood-altering chemical.[48] The alcoholic's relationship with alcohol becomes more important than family, friends and work. The relationship progresses to the point where alcohol is necessary to feel normal. To feel "normal" for the alcoholic is also to feel isolated and lonely since the primary relationship he or she depends upon to feel adequate is with a chemical, not other people.

The sexual addiction is parallel. The addict substitutes a sick relationship to an event or process for a healthy relationship with others. The addict's relationship with a mood-altering "experience" becomes central to his or her life.

The addict's belief system contains certain core beliefs which are faulty or inaccurate and, consequently, which provide a fundamental momentum for the addiction. Generally, addicts do not perceive themselves as worthwhile persons. Nor do they believe other people would care for them or meet their needs if everything was known about them, including the addiction. Finally, they believe that sex is their most important need. Sex is what makes isolation bearable. Their core beliefs are the anchor points of the sexual addiction.

As Carnes describes, for a sexual addict an addictive experience progresses through a four-step cycle which intensifies with each repetition:

1.  *Preoccupation* — the trance or mood wherein the addict's mind is completely engrossed with thoughts of sex. This mental state creates an obsessive search for sexual stimulation.
2.  *Ritualization* — the addict's own special routines which lead up to the sexual behavior. The ritual intensifies the preoccupation, adding arousal and excitement.
3.  *Compulsive sexual behavior* — the actual sexual act, which is the end-goal of the pre-occupation and ritualization. Sexual addicts are unable to control or stop this behavior.
4.  *Despair* — the feeling of utter hopelessness addicts have about their behavior and their powerlessness.

Sexual addicts are hostages of their own preoccupation. Every passerby, every relationship, and every introduction to someone passes through the sexually obsessive filter. More than merely noticing sexually attractive people, there is a quality of desperation which interferes with work, relaxation, and even sleep. People become objects to be scrutinized. A walk through a crowded downtown area is translated into a veritable shopping list of "possibilities."

Carnes points out, e.g., that visual addiction does not always have obvious consequences. It is common to see men straining their necks as they drive to watch an attractive woman walk down a street on a summer day. The addict, however, will turn around to go by her a second time — perhaps nearly causing an accident — in an effort to watch her again. Endless hours go by browsing in a porno bookstore, sitting in the beach parking lot, driving around college campuses, tennis courts, and shopping malls, stopping every night at the topless bar. Soon time takes its toll. Work does not get done and excuses are made. Lies are told to the family about the long work hours. Addiction is, then, a relationship, a pathological relationship in which sexual obsession replaces people. The ultimate core belief of the addict emerges clearly: Sex is my most important need. Absolute terror of life without sex combines with feelings of unworthiness for having such intense sexual desires. In addition, sexual activity never meets the need for love and care, but it continues to be seen as the only avenue. The addict has a high need to control all situations in an effort to guarantee sex. Yet there is a secret fear of being sexually out of control. Addicts promise themselves to stop or limit sexual behavior because of this fear.

Carnes suggests the following formula as a guideline: Signs of compulsive sexuality are when the behavior can be described as follows:

1.  It is a *Secret.* Anything that cannot pass public scrutiny will create the shame of a double life.
2.  It is *Abusive* to self or others. Anything that is exploitive or harmful to others or degrades oneself will activate the addictive system.
3.  It is used to avoid (or is a source of) painful *Feelings.* If sexuality is used to alter moods or results in painful mood shifts, it is clearly part of the addictive process.
4.  It is *Empty* of a caring, committed relationship. Fundamental to the whole concept of addiction and recovery is the healthy dimension of human relationships. The addict runs a great risk of being sexual outside of a committed relationship.

The advantage of this SAFE (Secret, Abusive, Feelings, Empty) formula is that it is built on the basic concept of addiction and is in the spirit of the Twelve Steps.[49] It requires a ruthless honesty given that the addict's sanity is at stake. Using a group or a sponsor as an ongoing reality check can help keep the addict "safe."

## CHAPTER THREE

# THE QUESTION
# OF BIRTH REGULATION

## 1. THE CONTEXT OF THE QUESTION

In his book *Human Sexuality: A Christian View*,[1] John C. Dwyer summarizes the magisterial teaching on contraception in these propositions:

1. Sexual intercourse is a natural, biological process. Here the word "natural" refers to a way of acting which has its own inherent purpose; i.e., its purpose is "given" in the nature of the case and it is not up to us to determine it. To call the process "biological" is simply to assert that its purpose is determined by the need to propagate or protect life, physical life. Magisterial teaching does not deny that intercourse is, or at least should be, *more* than a merely biological process. It simply asserts that whatever else sexual intercourse may be on some occasions, or ought to be on all occasions, of its very nature it is always, and at least, a biological process.
2. This process is obviously designed to move to a certain term and to achieve a certain purpose. The whole reproductive mechanism is designed to bring two cells, the ovum and the sperm, together. Sexual excitement adapts the organs themselves for intercourse, in the process of which the sperm is given a path to seek out the ovum. To summarize, sexual intercourse is designed periodically to secure fertilization of the ovum by a sperm cell.

3. It is possible to interfere with this process. This can be
done, e.g., by mechanical means (e.g., condoms; diaphragms; IUDs), by pharmaceutical means (e.g.,
spermicidal jellies and sprays), by oral contraceptives (e.g.,
the Pill), by withdrawal of the penis before the ejaculation
of sperm, or by surgical sterilization (e.g., a tubal ligation;
or a vasectomy). Since it seems clear that fertilization
normally occurs in the fallopian tubes, it may be that some
of the methods actually function by preventing *implantation*
of the already fertilized ovum, and not by preventing
fertilization itself. In all cases, interference with this process
is illicit.

4. It is seriously wrong to frustrate a fundamental process
which is part of our nature. To violate a life-process is to
violate human life itself and to destroy the finality, the
purposiveness of sexual intercourse. This is the case
because the awakening of new life is deliberately blocked.
The magisterial tradition has consistently taught that
contraception is a *serious matter* because reproduction is a
fundamental necessity and the passing on of life is a sacred
duty. In this teaching, it is precisely the *interference* from
the outside which is wrong. If sexual intercourse fails to
result in fertilization because of some "natural" fact or
event (e.g., if intercourse occurs after menopause or during
that time when the ovum is not correctly placed for fertilization), there is no moral problem. In fact, assuming that
there is a valid reason for not desiring a child at a particular
time, Catholic teaching allows couples to take advantage of
the wife's infertile period and to have intercourse during
that time.

In his treatment of "Marital Sexuality: Contraception and Beyond,"[2] Vincent Genovesi gives a helpful overview of the official
Roman Catholic teaching on contraception that helps us to understand
these four propositions. As a preliminary remark, Genovesi makes a
helpful distinction:

(W)e must first make note of the fact that contraception itself is a narrower reality than birth-control, for this latter concept has unfortunately come to be understood as including any means employed to limit the number of live births; even abortion is frequently regarded as a last-ditch method of contraception, which, of course, it is not. Contraception, even when it takes the permanent or quasi-permanent form of sterilization, comprises any and every action undertaken to prevent conception or fertilization..., whereas abortion is an action initiated after conception has in fact taken place. As distinct realities, contraception and abortion involve different moral issues and questions.[3]

In December of 1930, Pope Pius XI issued the encyclical *Casti Connubii* (On Chaste Marriage). This encyclical was issued at least in part in reaction to the revised teaching of the Anglican Church on contraception. It is thus important to recall that well into the twentieth century, the Christian churches were *generally agreed* that contraception was a threat to the institution of marriage.[4] In 1930, however, after failed attempts to do so in 1908 and 1920, the Lambeth Conference of Anglican Bishops gave qualified and cautious approval to contraception. In a resolution adopted in August, these bishops while abandoning the absolute prohibition of contraception, nonetheless called for restraint and Christian sensitivity:

Where there is a clearly felt moral obligation to limit or avoid parenthood, the method must be decided on Christian principles. The primary and obvious method is complete abstinence from intercourse (as far as may be necessary) in a life of discipline and self-control lived in the power of the Holy Spirit. Nevertheless, in those cases where there is such a clearly felt moral obligation to limit or avoid parenthood, and where there is a morally sound reason for avoiding complete abstinence, the Conference agrees that other methods may be used, provided this is done in the light of the same Christian principles. The Conference records its strong condemnation of the use of any methods of conception-control for motives of selfishness, luxury, or mere convenience.[5]

In *Casti Connubii* Pope Pius XI made these points: He defended the institution of marriage against the abuses of the popular doctrine of "free love," and he argued against the notion that women needed to be freed from the "slavery" of children, for implicit in this idea is the perception of children as constituting a burden in life rather than a blessing. Specifically, the following paragraph from *Casti Connubii* is important:

> Since, therefore, openly departing from the uninterrupted Christian tradition, some recently have judged it possible solemnly to declare another doctrine regarding this question, the Catholic Church, to whom God has entrusted the defense of the integrity and purity of morals, standing erect in the midst of the moral ruin which surrounds her, in order that she may preserve the chastity of the nuptial union from being defiled by this foul stain, raises her voice in token of Divine ambassadorship and through Our mouth proclaims anew: Any use whatsoever of matrimony exercised in such a way that the act is deliberately frustrated in its natural power to generate life is an offense against the law of God and of nature, and those who indulge in such are branded with the guilt of a grave sin.[6]

*Casti Connubii* also understands intercourse as having two purposes, one of which is primary, while the other is secondary: "...the conjugal act is destined primarily by nature for the begetting of children... [but] in the use of the matrimonial rights there are also secondary ends, such as mutual aid, the cultivating of mutual love, and the quieting of concupiscence which husband and wife are not forbidden to consider so long as they are subordinated to the primary end and so long as the intrinsic nature of the act is preserved."[7]

At the close of its fourth and final session in 1965, the Second Vatican Council promulgated the *Pastoral Constitution on the Church in the Modern World (Gaudium et Spes)*. This Constitution contains a number of important points about Christian marriage which are critical for a complete understanding of the Church's teaching on the meaning of family life and contraception.[8] We note here seven points:

1. As a "community of love" (n 47) and as an "intimate partnership of life and love" (n 48), marriage both reflects and shares in the loving covenant which unites Christ with the Church. The beauty and significance of the Christian family lie in the expectation that "by the mutual love of the

spouses, by their generous fruitfulness, their solidarity and faithfulness, and by the loving way in which all members of the family work together," the living presence of Christ in the world will be made manifest to all (n 48).

2. Coital expressions of conjugal love are regarded as having a substantial value independent of procreation. Marital acts of love are titled "noble" and "worthy," and in their truly human expression, they "signify and promote the mutual self-giving by which spouses enrich each other with a joyful and thankful will" (n 49).

It is helpful here to recall St. Augustine's teaching about the "three goods of marriage": the *bonum prolis*, the *bonum fidei* and the *bonum sacramenti*. These three goods can be translated as the:

(1) Good of procreation and education.
(2) Good of reciprocal faithfulness and assistance.
(3) Good of indissoluble sacramental union.

Largely because of the anti-Manichean context in which Augustine was writing, he dealt with *fides* in a juridical manner: i.e., the only reason that justified the good of reciprocal faithfulness and assistance was the *bonum prolis*. In other words, procreation was the only legitimate motivation for sexual intercourse. It is thus important to see this background in order to appreciate more fully the context of *Gaudium et Spes*, especially numbers 47 through 50.

3. At the same time, however, conjugal love is not unrelated to the procreation and education of children. Both matrimony itself and conjugal love "are ordained for the procreation and education of children, and find in them their ultimate crown" (n 48). Moreover, precisely as "the supreme gift of marriage," children "contribute very substantially to the welfare of their parents" (n 50).

4. When married couples fruitfully exercise their procreative power, they come to enjoy a certain special participation in God's own creative work. In elaborating upon the place of children in married life, *Gaudium et Spes* urges that, "While

not making the other purposes of matrimony of less account... parents should regard as their proper mission the
task of transmitting human life and educating those to
whom it has been transmitted" (n 50).

It is important to note here that *Gaudium et Spes* does not
employ the traditional terminology of a "hierarchy of goals or ends"
whereby the procreation and education of children is referred to as the
primary purpose of marriage and conjugal sexuality, while the expression and fostering of love between spouses is designated as the
secondary purpose of marital sex. In other words, both "goals or ends"
are of equal and significant value. On this point, Genovesi's words are
important:

> According to the official legislative history of the Council, various
> amendments to this text were proposed, calling for a re-assertion of
> the idea of a "hierarchy of ends," i.e., the distinction between
> primary and secondary purposes or goals. Nonetheless, all of these
> amendments, one of which stated explicitly that "conjugal love is
> ordained to the primary end of marriage, which is offspring," were
> rejected. Thus, marriage and conjugal sexuality are seen as having
> dual purposes, but the Council Fathers refused to render a judgment
> on the relative importance of these purposes by ranking them first
> and second.[9]

The 1917 Code of Canon Law taught that "The primary end of
marriage is the procreation and education of children; its secondary
end is mutual help and the allaying of concupiscence" (canon 1013:1).
It is important to understand something of the history that contributed
to this distinction of the primary and secondary purposes of marriage.
Ulpian was a Roman lawyer who died in 228 A.D. Ulpian defined the
natural law as that which teaches all the animals. He distinguished the
natural law from the *ius gentium*. The *ius naturale* is that which is
common to all animals, whereas the *ius gentium* is that which is proper
to humans.[10] Laws that were, then, common *ad animalia* (to all
animals) were of *primary* significance; and those which were *ad
homines* (proper to men) were of *secondary* significance. Albert the
Great rejected Ulpian's definition of the natural law, but St. Thomas

accepted it, and even showed a preference for Ulpian's definition. In his *Commentary on the Sentences*, e.g., Thomas maintains that the most strict definition of natural law is the one proposed by Ulpian: *ius naturae est quod natura omnia animalia docuit*.[11]

In his *Commentary on the Nichomachean Ethics*, Thomas again shows a preference for Ulpian's definition.[12] Aristotle had proposed a two-fold division of *iustum naturale* and *iustum legale*, but Ulpian proposed the three-fold distinction of *ius naturale, ius gentium* and *ius civile*. St. Thomas solves the apparent dilemma by saying that the Roman law concepts of *ius naturale* and *ius gentium* both belong under the Aristotelian category of *iustum naturale*. In other words, "man" has a double nature. The *ius naturale* rules that which is proper to both humanity and the animals, such as the union of the sexes and the education of offspring; whereas the *ius gentium* governs the rational part of the human person which is proper to humanity alone, and embraces such things as fidelity to contracts.[13]

In the *Summa Theologiae* St. Thomas cites Ulpian's definition on a number of occasions.[14] In the classification of natural law, Thomas again shows a preference for Ulpian's definition. Thomas accepts the division proposed by Isidore of Seville, according to which the *ius gentium* belongs to the category of human law and not to the category of divine law. Thomas uses Ulpian's definition to explain Isidore's division. The natural law pertains to the divine law because it is common to humanity and to all the animals.[15] In a sense, the *ius gentium* does pertain to the category of human law because the human person uses his or her reason to deduce the conclusions of the *ius gentium*.

Thomas thus employs Ulpian's definition of natural law as opposed to what reason deduces (the *ius gentium*) to defend the division of law proposed by Isidore. The same question receives somewhat the same treatment later in the *Summa*.[16] The texts definitely show that Thomas knew and even accepted the definition of natural law proposed by Ulpian.

Qestion 94 in the *Summa* (I-II, a. 4) thus states,

> Wherefore according to the order of natural inclinations, is the order of precepts of the natural law... (T)here is in man an inclination to things that pertain to him more specifically, according to that nature

which he has in common with other animals; and in virtue of this
inclination, those things are said to belong to the natural law, which
nature has taught to all animals, such as sexual intercourse, education of offspring and so forth.

This is a long digression from an appreciation of number 50 of
*Gaudium et Spes*, but it is very critical to appreciate Ulpian's influence on natural law morality. As we have seen, the natural law for
Ulpian is defined in terms of those actions which are common to
humanity and all the animals. There results from this the problem of
identifying the human action with mere animal or biological processes. This is the root of the "physicalist critique" which we dealt
with in Chapter One. In other words, "nature" and "natural" in
Ulpian's meaning are distinguished from that which is specifically
human and derived by reason. Traditional moral theology has tended
to use the words "natural" and "nature" as synonymous with animal
or biological processes and not as denoting sufficiently human actions
in accord with the rational nature of man.

As we noted in Chapter One, the manuals of moral theology
generally divided the sins against the sixth commandment into two
categories — the sins against nature (*peccata contra naturam*) and
sins in accord with nature (*peccata secundum naturam*). "Nature" is
used in Ulpian's sense, as that which is common to humanity and all
the animals. In matters of sexuality — and Ulpian himself uses the
example of the sexual union as an illustration of the natural law — the
human person shares with the animal world the fact of the sexual
union whereby male seed is deposited in the vas of the female. Sins
against nature, therefore, are those acts in which the animal or
biological process is not observed: masturbation, sodomy, bestiality,
and contraception. Sins according to nature are those acts in which the
proper biological process is observed but something is lacking in the
sphere which belongs only to rational people: fornication, adultery,
incest, rape, and sacrilege.[17]

Ulpian's understanding of the natural law led to a problematic
anthropological understanding of the human person. The distinction
between two parts in the human person — that which is common to
the human person and all the animals, and that which is proper to the
human person — results in a two-layer version of the human person.

A top layer of rationality is added to an already constituted bottom layer of animality. The union between the two layers was seen as merely extrinsic, the one lying on top of the other. The animal layer retains its own finalities and tendencies, independent of the demands of rationality. Thus was the human person not to interfere in the animal processes and finalities. This anthropology has led Charles E. Curran to note:

> Ulpian's notion of nature easily leads to a morality based on the finality of a faculty independently of any considerations of the total human person or the total human community. One must, of course, avoid the opposite danger of paying no attention to the physical structure of the act or to external actions in themselves. However, Catholic theology in the area of medical morality has suffered from an oversimple identification of the human action with an animal process or finality.[18]

5. Married couples are to carry on the task of procreating and educating children "with human and Christian responsibility." In planning their families, Christian spouses should "thoughtfully take into account both their own welfare and that of their children, those already born and those which may be foreseen." Responsible parenting means that married couples "will reckon with both the material and spiritual conditions of the times as well as of their state of life;" spouses will, in addition, "consult the interests of the family group, of temporal society, and of the Church herself." Parents who raise a relatively large family are accorded special mention, and they are reminded of their duty to raise their children "suitably," and it is expected that the decision to have a large family entails "wise and common deliberation" (n 50). Here again, Vincent Genovesi's words are significant:

> (T)he Catholic Church is not opposed to responsible or planned parenthood. *Gaudium et Spes* does not glorify uncontrolled procreation, nor does it offer any praise for the procreation of children without reminding us of their need to be educated. For Christian

spouses, then, responsible parenting would seem to entail three things: they must be open to procreation, and they must properly care for children already born; finally, when and as necessary, spouses must establish appropriate limitations to their power to conceive.[19]

6. Regarding the decision to transmit human life, "the parents themselves should ultimately make this judgment, in the sight of God," but they are to realize "that they cannot proceed arbitrarily." Rather, Christian spouses must come to their decision in a responsible or conscientious way, which is to say, that "they must always be governed according to a conscience dutifully conformed to the divine law itself, and [they] should be submissive toward the Church's teaching office, which authentically interprets that law in the light of the Gospel" (n 50).

7. Finally, it is recognized that married couples often "find themselves in circumstances where at least temporarily the size of their families should not be increased." Thus parental responsibility to avoid procreation comes into conflict with the desire to express conjugal love in a physical way. In such circumstances, spouses feel pulled in two different directions: responsibility requires both that they avoid conception and that they maintain the "faithful exercise of love and the full intimacy of their lives." Failure to preserve "the intimacy of married life" is clearly a threat to the spouses' mutual fidelity, but it may also endanger the welfare of their children already born and undermine parental courage and generosity to accept new ones (n 51).

It is important to note here that in offering guidance to spouses as they attempt to "harmonize conjugal love with the responsible transmission of life," *Gaudium et Spes* warns against "dishonorable solutions" and advises married couples that the moral propriety of their conjugal expressions of love is determined by objective standards which are based on the nature of human persons and their actions and which "preserve the full sense of mutual self-giving and human procreation in the context of true love" (n 51). Genovesi remarks:

What is most significant in this statement is the fact that acts of conjugal love are not to be judged simply with reference to their biological dimension, but rather by their relationship to the whole human person. Quite simply, the document chooses to move away from the oft-repeated argument against contraception which looks only to the biological structure of the coital act considered in isolation from the persons performing the act. The norm of morality is seen rather as rooted in the nature of human persons, not in the isolated purposes of specific actions.[20]

*Gaudium et Spes* ends its discussion on marriage and family life by encouraging spouses to the practice of conjugal chastity (see Chapter One), which means, in part, that in attempting to regulate birth, married couples are to avoid those methods "found blameworthy by the teaching authority of the Church in its unfolding of the divine law" (n 51). No more specific guidance is given here on this question, but a footnote in the text is explanatory: "Certain questions which need further and more careful investigation have been handed over, at the command of the Supreme Pontiff, to a commission for the study of population, family, and births, in order that, after it fulfills its function, the Supreme Pontiff may pass judgment. With the doctrine of the magisterium in this state, this holy Synod does not intend to propose immediately concrete solutions."[21]

## 2. *HUMANAE VITAE*

A special papal commission on the study of population, family, and births was initiated in 1963 by Pope John XXIII. In 1964, Pope Paul VI appointed a large number of additional members to the commission. Both laity and clerics compromised the 60 to 70 members of the group, and their number included physicians, social scientists, married couples, priests, bishops and cardinals. At the conclusion of the commission's deliberations in June of 1966, two separate reports were submitted to Pope Paul VI. In the minority opinion, the traditional prohibition of all forms of artificial contraception was maintained. The majority opinion recommended a change in the Church's official teaching on methods of contraception.

In February of 1966, prior to having received the papal commission's report, Pope Paul VI addressed the National Congress of the Italian Women's Center. In this speech, the Pope referred to the complexity and delicacy of the issues being considered by the commission which had been set up specifically "with the task of going into these problems more deeply from all points of view — scientific, historical, sociological and doctrinal — while making abundant use of the advice of bishops and experts."[22] In urging his audience "to await the results of these studies and to accompany them with... prayers," the Pope noted the Church's need for caution and careful study in its attempt to teach the people of God:

> The magisterium of the Church cannot propose moral norms unless it is sure that it is interpreting God's will. In reaching this certitude, the Church is not excused from carrying out research nor from examining all the many questions proposed for its consideration from every corner of the world. Sometimes these operations take a long time and are anything but easy.[23]

Pope Paul VI's response to the commission's reports came two years later in his encyclical letter, *Humanae Vitae*, in July of 1968.

In the opening section of this letter (n 5), the Pope thanks the commission for its work but indicates that its conclusions could not be considered as definitive, nor do those conclusions dispense him from a personal examination of the questions at hand. The Pope remarks that the papal commission had reached "no full concordance of judgments concerning the moral norms to be proposed"; furthermore, he indicates that in the commission's report, certain criteria for solutions to the question of contraception had indeed emerged "which departed from the moral teaching on marriage proposed with constant firmness by the teaching authority of the Church." Finally, with the assurance that he has "attentively sifted the documentation" presented to him, the Pope, "after mature reflection and assiduous prayers," maintains that there can be no change in the Church's opposition to the use of artificial contraceptives (n 6).

*Humanae Vitae* offers the following rationale: "Each and every marriage act must remain open to the transmission of life" (n 11), because God has willed "the inseparable connection... between the two meanings of the conjugal act: the unitive meaning and the procreative meaning." By virtue of its intimate structure, "the conjugal act, while most closely uniting husband and wife, capacitates them for the generation of new lives, according to laws inscribed in the very being of man and of woman" (n 12). Thus, it is "intrinsically dishonest" (n 14) and "always illicit" (n 16) for spouses to engage in sexual intercourse while at the same time attempting deliberately and positively to frustrate the act's procreative potential.

The teaching of *Humanae Vitae* in numbers 11 through 16 clearly asserts that sexual intercourse is a single act with two aspects or meanings (*significationes*): the unitive and the procreative. These two meanings are inseparable and thus anyone who deliberately attempts to render the act of intercourse sterile attacks its very meaning as an expression of mutual self-giving. Richard A. McCormick interprets this understanding by stating that "by excluding the child as the permanent sign of the love to be expressed in coitus, one introduced a reservation into coitus and therefore robbed it of that which makes it objectively unitive."[24]

Accordingly, then, *Humanae Vitae* teaches that the unitive and procreative meanings of sexual intercourse are so intimately joined as to be inseparable. This means that any deliberate interference with one of these meanings must necessarily have a disruptive or destructive influence upon the other, so that the moral significance of the sexual act as a whole is undermined. Thus the inseparability of the unitive and procreative dimensions of conjugal love lies at the root of the Church's prohibition against any use of sexual intercourse which involves the positive attempt to prevent the act from resulting in the possibility of procreation. This point is of such significance, the Latin text of the encyclical needs to be carefully understood:

> *Verumtamen Ecclesia, dum homines commonet de observandis praeceptis legis naturalis, quam constanti sua doctrina interpretatur, id docet necessarium esse ut quilibet matrimonii usus ad vitam humanam procreandam per se destinatus permaneat.*[25]

This sentence translates literally as, "But the Church, calling men back to the observance of the norms of the natural law, interpreted by her constant teaching, teaches that each and every marriage act must remain open to the transmission of life." We have noted clearly that *Humanae Vitae* teaches the inseparable link between the unitive and procreative dimensions of the act of intercourse. We know at the same time, of course, that not every act of sexual intercourse (*quilibet matrimonii usus*) is *de facto* biologically procreative: e.g., during the infertile periods of a woman's menstrual cycle. This realization would seem to indicate that the point of this particular teaching in *Humanae Vitae* is to stress that whenever a couple uses their sexual activity at a time when procreation is indeed possible, that procreative possibility must be respected. In other words, the word-by-word translation of this sentence gives some people the impression that *Humanae Vitae* is teaching that a couple must intend each and every marriage act to be open to children. This is not the point of the teaching. Rather, should sexual intercourse (*matrimonii usus*) take place at a time when procreation is indeed possible, then the couple must sustain a respect for this procreative possibility: they must not frustrate it.

Six days after the publication of *Humanae Vitae*, at his weekly audience at Castel Gandolfo, Pope Paul VI reflected on his encyclical and disclosed his own tortured feelings in the course of its preparation and in the making of his final decision. First and foremost was the continual awareness of the weight of his enormous responsibility, which had caused him great spiritual suffering, to respond to the Church and to all humanity against the background of tradition and the teaching of his immediate predecessors, as well as of the Council itself. He seemed predisposed to accept so far as he could the conclusions and the consultative nature of the papal commission,[26] but at the same time to act prudently. He was fully aware of the impassioned discussions going on, of the media and of public opinion, and of the appeals of countless individuals. He had frequently felt submerged in a sea of documents, and humanly overwhelmed at the apostolic duty of pronouncing on them all. Often he had trembled before the dilemma of simply yielding to current opinion or of delivering a judgment which would be ill received by contemporary society or might be of arbitrary imposition on married couples.[27] The words of the Pope at his Audience at Castel Gandolfo on 31 July 1968 are of importance:

*Humanae Vitae...* is above all the positive presentation of conjugal morality concerning its mission of love and fecundity... but it is not a complete treatment regarding man in this sphere of marriage, of the family and of moral probity. This is an immense field to which the magisterium of the Church could and perhaps should return with a fuller, more organic and more synthetic exposition.

In this talk, the Pope specifically referred to an article by Father Martelet that would help enlighten a proper interpretation of the encyclical. He then goes on to say that he had sustained a feeling of "very grave responsibility" and that this feeling caused him "much spiritual suffering."[28]

An official commentary on the Encyclical had been presented by Monsignor Lambruschini on the occasion of *Humanae Vitae*'s publication. Monsignor Lambruschini was professor of moral theology at Rome's Lateran University, and was also an official spokesman of the Vatican on this occasion. In addition, he had been a member of the papal commission. The most important point which Monsignor Lambruschini made concerned the status of the encyclical as a teaching document of the papal magisterium. After observing that study of the encyclical did not suggest that it was an infallible statement, but that nevertheless its authenticity was reinforced by its continuing the teaching of the Church's magisterium, he made the following statement:

The pronouncement has come. It is not infallible, but it does not leave the questions concerning birth regulation in a condition of vague problematics. Assent of theological faith is due only to the definitions properly so-called, but there is owed also loyal and full assent, interior and not only exterior, to noninfallible pronouncement of the magisterium, in proportion to the level of the authority from which it emanates — which in this case is the supreme authority of the Supreme Pontiff — and to its object, which is most weighty, since it is a matter of the tormented question of the regulation of birth. In particular, it can and must be said that the authentic pronouncement of the *Humanae Vitae* encyclical prevents the forming of a probable opinion, that is to say an opinion acting on the moral plane in contrast with the pronouncement itself, whatever

the number and the hierarchical, scientific, and theological authority
of those considered in the past few years that they could form it for
themselves. The pretext of presumed doubt in the Church because of
the Pope's long silence has no substance and is in conflict with the
renewed pontifical and conciliar appeals to observe previous and
always valid directives of the magisterium.[29]

On 16 February 1989, *L'Osservatore Romano* printed a commentary entitled "The Moral Norms of *Humanae Vitae* and Their
Pastoral Obligation."[30] In light of Monsignor Lambruschini's comment, some specific points raised in this 1989 commentary are of
significance:

1. "The affirmation that the moral norms set forth in *Humanae
   Vitae* concerning contraception is part of this precise
   obligation ["The duty to call good and evil by name within
   the ambit of responsible procreation..."], in that it prohibits
   an act that is by its very nature disordered, and admits of no
   exceptions. Such an affirmation is by no means a rigid and
   intransigent interpretation of moral law. It is simply Paul
   VI's clear and explicit teaching, which has been taken up
   and re-proposed time and again by the present Pope." (n 2)
2. *Humanae Vitae* states, "In truth if it is sometimes licit to
   tolerate a lesser evil in order to avoid a greater evil or to
   promote a greater good, it is not licit, even for the gravest
   reasons, to do evil so that good may follow therefrom; i.e.,
   to make into the object of a positive act of the will something which is intrinsically disordered, and hence unworthy
   of the human person, even when the intention is to safeguard or promote individual, family or social well-being" (n
   14 of *Humanae Vitae*).
       This 1989 commentary notes: "This is not a theological
   opinion open to free discussion; as John Paul II said June 5,
   1987, 'Whatever the Church teaches concerning contraception is not open to deliberation among theologians. To teach
   the contrary would be equivalent to leading the moral
   conscience of the married couple into error.'" (n 2)
3. "The Christian moral tradition has always distinguished

between 'positive norms' (which are a mandate to do something) and 'negative norms' (which prohibit an action). Furthermore, it has always clearly and consistently maintained that the negative norms, those which prohibit acts intrinsically disordered, admit of no exceptions: Such acts, in fact, from the moral standpoint are disordered because of their very structure, therefore of and in themselves, ... they contradict the human dignity of the person. For this very reason such acts, from the point of view of morality, cannot be made 'ordered' by any intentions or subjective circumstances, because these are unable to change their structure.

"Contraception is just such an act: In and of itself, it is always morally disordered, because objectively and intrinsically (independent of intentions, motives or subjective circumstances) it contradicts 'the innate language that expresses the total reciprocal self-giving of husband and wife.'" (n 3)

How might we understand the teaching of *Humanae Vitae* from a pastoral point of view? I would propose that the authentic meaning of *Humanae Vitae* must still be fully discovered. [31] In view of Pope Paul's actions in the Council regarding marriage and the birth control question, his issuance of *Humanae Vitae* represents a spiritual act of discernment, a prophetic gesture, with all of the problems which such a gesture carries. In other words, part of the meaning of the encyclical is the sense in which it was written; and this "sense" is rooted in a prophetic, discerning gesture. Pope John Paul II has described *Humanae Vitae* as "a truly prophetic proclamation."[32] By this statement, however, Pope John Paul II does not mean to suggest that *Humanae Vitae* should be read in such a way that its ideal is something to work toward. Pope John Paul firmly rejects this type of "prophetic-ideal" approach when he observed that married people "cannot look on the law as merely an ideal to be achieved in the future: they must consider it as a command of Christ the Lord to overcome difficulties with constancy."[33]

Mahoney interprets Pope John Paul II's reference to *Humanae Vitae* as "a truly prophetic proclamation" to mean that Pope Paul VI was calling our attention to an aspect of conjugal love that "should never be lost sight of in the whole."[34] Within this understanding of "prophecy," the teaching of the Church on contraception becomes a "vocation," an invitation which aims at stressing certain values which are in danger of being submerged or overlooked in the many complex problems of married life:

> Trust in God and his foresight, which is a central insight of all biblical prophecy; the incomparable dignity of being selected by God to collaborate in his creation at its peak — the emergence of a new human person; the sacrificial element which is central to all genuine love: these and other values may be considered the prophetic dimension in the Church's traditional refusal to permit married couples to express their love for each other in ways which systematically block off that expression from one of its normal consequences. To insist that this consequence should never be impeded in order to highlight the values which such insistence betokens can be seen as prophetic, as a... trumpet call from within an orchestral score containing many other melodies.[35]

Pope John Paul II's reference to *Humanae Vitae* as a prophetic document means, then, that we have in this encyclical an instance of an insight in search of fuller explanation and articulation, a moral truth which the mind can reach but which it cannot, or not yet, fully grasp. This apparently intuitive element of Christian experience is one which Karl Rahner has referred to as "a moral instinct of faith," a Christian capacity to form moral judgments, whether in particular instances or on more general topics, which cannot be adequately expressed or justified by purely rational considerations, however much the attempt is, and must be, made.[36] As Rahner wrote of *Humanae Vitae*, the rationale which is clear in the encyclical is adherence to the traditional doctrine of Pius XI and Pius XII; but this factor undoubtedly has considerable theological importance, especially since a global "instinct" in particular moral questions can be genuine, even if a pope cannot explain it right up to the final rationale and reflective detail.[37]

*Humanae Vitae* is "prophetic" for a number of reasons. As with Peter himself, Pope Paul was standing "over against" many who were suggesting another teaching. In addition, he acted in such a way as to strengthen and confirm these "others." *Humanae Vitae* is a prophetic insight not only into a spiritual mystery but also into a human meaning. The prophetic nature of this document is also seen in light of the Pope's awareness that he was speaking to a precise situation.[38] As prophetic, then, the Pope is not so much concerned in *Humanae Vitae* with the question of justification of his vision, but rather with an act of observation, of discerning the fact.

In *Humanae Vitae* the Pope enunciated one clear "value emphasis": that of the *bonum prolis*.[39] He was making the prophetic appeal that "procreating" cannot be reduced to "reproducing." In essence, *Humanae Vitae* teaches that although the procreative dimension in human sexuality does not exhaust the intelligibility of sexual intercourse, it is by no means accidental, but is inherently meaningful.[40] The Pope's discernment is singular: to deliberately sever the unitive and life-giving meaning of sexual intercourse is to inherently disrespect the nature of human parenthood. This is an intuition of both faith and reason and thus both of these realities must be present to adequately respond to the encyclical's vision.

### A. Difficulties in Reading Humanae Vitae

There have been three main causes of difficulty in the interpretation of *Humanae Vitae*:

1. The teaching authority of the Church. The 1976 study *Catholic Schools in a Declining Church*[41] put a great deal of emphasis here: That hopes had been raised by the Council for a possible shift in the Church's sexual teaching(s) but these hopes were shattered by the teaching authority of the papal magisterium.[42] In other words, many in the Catholic community were already practicing birth control and hoped for a radical change in the Church's teaching on this subject.

2. The procreative intent of each marital act: As we have seen, a great deal of the theological problem with *Humanae Vitae* lies in questioning the necessity that each and every act of intercourse be open to the transmission of life. The argu-

ments for selective contraceptive acts and practices as
morally permissible are generally these: first, such acts and
practices are well-motivated and efficiently promote
worthwhile goals; second, they need not repudiate the
inherent inter-relationship between the unitive and procreative meanings of marital life as a whole; and third, they
represent the rightful exercise of the dominion over one's
body. This point of view that the procreative goal is a moral
exigency of the entire marital life rather than every sexual
act in the life often points to the Papal Commission on the
Problems of Marriage and the Family.[43] Here one often
finds cited Article 2 of Chapter 2 of the *Theological Report*:
The morality of sexual acts "does not... depend upon direct
fecundity of each and every particular act... (T)he morality
of every marital act depends upon the requirements of
mutual love in all respects." It should be pointed out,
however, that this commission also indicated that contraceptive acts involve "a material privation" and "a negative
element, a physical evil." In brief, however, the majority
report of the commission indicates that each act of sexual
union is, in its external concreteness, an expression of
marital love; but this love culminates in fertility and
therefore finds a basic meaning in fertility. Therefore, each
act gets a moral quality or specification from this fertility,
i.e., choices which either pursue it or exclude it.

3. Natural law. The third problem frequently pointed to has to
   do with *Humanae Vitae*'s use of natural law categories in
   such a way that human realities are identified with biological processes. We have already discussed this particular
   critique. It must be kept in mind that in *Humanae Vitae* the
   formal "rule" enunciated is "In whatever you do, act with
   respect for the person, respect for your own human dignity
   and that of the other." In fact, it is only on the level of the
   singular that a person can effectively respect the universal
   dignity of every other person. It is only in the singularity of
   each person's conduct that universal human dignity is
   authentically respected. A person's body, his or her corpo-
   reality, is not considered simply a part of a person (*pars*

*hominis*), but rather as a human element (*res humana*). Pope Paul VI affirms, then, that the structures and even the biological laws of sexual relationship are not solely *res hominis* but are truly *res humana*.[44]

## B. How to Understand Humanae Vitae

*Humanae Vitae* should be read in such a way as to recall clearly that it is primarily concerned with objective morality: i.e., it is not directly concerned with formal sin, as it is with God's mercy and forgiveness. It is of great importance pastorally to recall that one does not find in *Humanae Vitae* the kind of language one sees in *Casti Connubii*: that "those who indulge in such [acts] are branded with the guilt of a grave sin." It is necessary, moreover, to read *Humanae Vitae* in light of other encyclical letters of Pope Paul VI, especially *Populorum Progressio*; as well as in the light of the Council's document *Gaudium et Spes*. A central assertion of *Humanae Vitae* is in number 12 and its use of the concept *significatio*. This thought cannot simply be translated and understood as "meaning"; but more importantly, that marital intercourse has two *significationes*: of unity and of openness to life. In marital intercourse, then, a couple is simultaneously creating two signs: that they are united and that they are open to life. These signs do not depend on the intention of the spouses, but rather are built into the marital action by God as part of his design and his creation.

Marriage does not, then, really possess two "ends" but rather two *significationes*. In other words, marital intercourse is simultaneously a sign of the union between husband and wife and a sign of their fruitfulness; and what God has joined together, we must not divide.[45] The Pope is affirming that these *significationes* are both worthy of human pursuit.

*Humanae Vitae* thus avoids the distinction between primary and secondary ends of marriage in favor of marital love which intrinsically possesses a connection between unity and fertility.[46] With this vision as foremost, the encyclical represents, with *Populorum Progressio* and *Gaudium et Spes*, a powerful moment for faith in the Church.[47] This "moment for faith" is again discerned in the Pope's prophetic gesture; by recalling the inseparable unity between love and openness to life, the Pope is calling married couples to be open to God. This same holiness was evidenced in the lives of Sarah and Anna and Elizabeth. The sacredness of the unity is achieved by a patient waiting on God, even in sterility and even in old age.

In re-affirming the two *significationes* of marital love, Paul VI is teaching that the most perfect of intersubjective relationships on the human level is one in which there is a free mutual giving and receiving. The two truly become a "we". The beloved is embraced in fidelity in all that he or she is and all that he or she will become; and this is creative fidelity. Such a perfection, however, grows directly out of times of silence for another's address. This "silence" enhances the true possibility of a couple following Natural Family Planning. In other words, there can be no love without distance and no distance without love. *Humanae Vitae* intuits that love is the perfection of relationship and distance is the safeguard. The Pope's counsel of marital chastity is thus a call to wholeness; that silence provides the condition for the possibility of a human conversation. A decision to speak must always be a decision to speak *of* something *to* someone or *with* someone *in* some manner. Concomitantly, if a listener is to genuinely understand what has been said, he or she must in every instance consider what has not been said. In such a relationship, the husband and the wife become a "we"; the subject-object duality is overcome; each coalesces to form a new unity created by neither alone and yet by both together. *Humanae Vitae* is affirming that in marriage human sexuality is a way of expressing the mystery of human incompleteness. It testifies that a man or a woman is fully self only in the "unity" of the couple (the *significationes*).

*Humanae Vitae* refuses to regard sexuality as merely biological. The encyclical's intuition is that human sexuality is never a neutral reality because it is *always* a gesture of communication — for good or for bad. Coitus thus reaches its perfection when it is total, when it accepts the other and all the consequences thereof. When this happens in marriage, there is a tremendous bond that is really more than a mere natural union. This bond is morally good and in itself sanctifies the couple. As *Gaudium et Spes* teaches, marriage is "rooted in the conjugal covenant of irrevocable consent"; it is "a reflection of the loving covenant uniting Christ with the Church" (n 48). In marriage, then, this "tremendous bond" is created because in the power of God the spouses entrust themselves to one another and thus mirror the same relationship which Christ has with the Church. This bond establishes, then, a "community of love" and it is precisely in this love that Christ touches the couple as Perfecter, and Healer, and Bringer of grace and fidelity.

As numbers 49-50 of *Gaudium et Spes* point out, this community-of-love is uniquely perfected through the marital act, where human love is intended to be fruitful, where the couple are co-creators with God (*cooperatores Dei*). Christian marriage is thus the mutually expressed pledge of a man and a woman to begin and carry to conclusion the process of uniting themselves at every level of existence. But because of the finite nature of man and woman, this pledge, if it is to be realistic, must concretely be exclusive and "until death"; and it must embrace the dimension of begetting and forming children, and thus reach out to the transcendent God in Jesus Christ.

*Humanae Vitae*'s vision is that contraception is a counter-gesture which reduces the sexual conversation to utilitarianism; and such a statement will send a marriage in a direction other than that of unity. Thus does the encyclical speak of "one only heart and soul." Its "prophecy" is not that the unity of the *significationes* cannot be separated because the Pope says so; but rather because intrinsically they cannot be separated.

Finally, we must remember that all of us are fashioned by our behavior. To pretend that one's actions have no consequent relation to one's person is an inadequate anthropology. It is important to appreciate here *Humanae Vitae*'s stance against a directly-willed contraceptive act. The encyclical presupposes that the act of marriage is a symbol of self-donation, an act which gestures a gift of one's whole person: and thus any basic reservation in this surrender contradicts the meaning of the act itself. The Pope's intent is not to separate this action from the totality of a person's existence but rather to indicate that the act itself has an objective meaning of its own. This meaning, of course, is not yet finished, because the human conversation of the couple is not yet complete. The sexual act must thus say in the concrete what the person is in essence. The human act, then, must be looked at not simply for what it *does* but also for what it *says*.

A person shapes his or her moral identity by the willingness to choose to act or not to act in certain ways. Contraceptive intercourse is a counter-gesture in the conversation of marital love. It is simply not an isolated act.[48] It demands a "policy decision" regarding openness to life, a choice to adopt a practice; and this mentality can quietly become a dimension of one's existence: one's personal openness to life is pragmatically devalued.[49]

## 3. CONSCIENCE FORMATION AND
## THE MEANING OF DISSENT

We struggle all of our lives to adequately express and develop the meaning that is uniquely ours. As Christians, this struggle takes place within a People and we cannot exist as Christians except in the Church; and we cannot define ourselves except as "of a body." We cannot exist as Christians in isolation. Moral knowledge is thus a shared knowledge; mediated to the individual by the ecclesial community and through the individual's participation in this community. One forms and informs one's conscience, then, by being within the community, by consulting the teachings of the Church. Vatican II's declaration *Dignitatis humanae* thus counsels that "In the formation of their conscience, the Christian faithful ought carefully to attend to the sacred and certain doctrine of the Church."[50] The Christian is the living word of Christ, therefore, only in company with fellow Christians. We find out who we are and what we are to do only in our fellowship with others.

As *Gaudium et Spes* indicates, "The progress of the human person and the advance of society itself hinge on each other... Through his dealing with others, through reciprocal duties, and through fraternal dialogue he develops all his gifts and is able to rise to his destiny."[51] We are living icons of the Lord who are meant to be beings who exist both with and for our fellow men and women.[52] It is this being-for-and-in-existence that forms the bedrock for the meaning of conscience.

It is logical that St. Thomas considered conscience neither a voice nor a feeling, but rather a *process of thinking* based on the total situation. Conscience is *not* simply a matter of personal feeling or motive; it is a process of coming to a moral decision within a community of persons. Conscience is always a "knowing together" that judges various avenues of thought to see what best leads to what is good. Conscience is always prudential: it carefully estimates the entire effect of one's action.[53]

Prudence is a virtue which sustains the inner characteristics of being truthful, wise, docile, alert, unbiased, deliberate, and not given to utilitarianism.[54] Otherwise it is easy to substitute one's illusion for reality. The well-intentioned conscience will never compromise and simply choose the easiest path or the most efficient or simple decision. Conscience is an individual's self-consciousness at any given time, coupled with a sense of what one can and should do.

In light of the question of assent to *Humanae Vitae*, the teaching of the *Dogmatic Constitution on the Church* of Vatican II is of utmost importance:

> In matters of faith and morals, the bishops speak in the name of Christ and the faithful are to accept their teaching and adhere to it with a religious assent of soul. This religious submission of will and of mind must be shown in a special way to the authentic teaching authority of the Roman Pontiff, even when he is not speaking *ex cathedra*. That is, it must be shown in such a way that his supreme magisterium is acknowledged with reverence, the judgments made by him are sincerely adhered to, according to his manifest mind and will. His mind and will in the matter may be known chiefly either from the character of the documents, from his frequent repetition of the same doctrine, or from his manner of speaking.

Both Ladislas Orsy and Francis A. Sullivan[55] have given us important observations regarding the meaning of this conciliar text: "A religious assent of soul" translates *fidei obsequio* which means a "surrender to the truth with an act of faith." They point out that this concept of *obsequium* is a "seminal locution": i.e., the term has not yet fully matured and there is not yet a commonly agreed upon definition; it does convey, however, an insight into a truth, without defining that truth with precision. One can say, however, that *obsequium* means an attitude toward the Church which is rooted in the virtue of religion, the love of God and of the Church. In every concrete case, this attitude will need specification, which could be "respect" or "submission," depending on the progress the Church has made in clarifying its own beliefs. *Obsequium* certainly means:

1. To be one with the Church, in mind and heart, in belief and action.
2. It is ideally perfect when someone is so well united in faith with the Church that he or she believes all that the Church holds firmly, and searches with the Church when some point is in need of clarification.

In this light, the English word "dissent" in terms of magisterial teaching can be very misleading, as the word itself implies a total disregard for and disrespect for the teaching itself, as well as the teaching office. "Dissent" is thus an imperfect term as it starts out on a negative note. It tends to be sweeping, with no boundaries: e.g., it could mean an intellectual stance; a disagreement with the logic of a reasoning; or it can mean a radical opposition to the magisterium, and a readiness to break the bond of unity. Consequently, the counsel of Father Yves Congar is very significant.[56] Congar points out that *la contestation* can never be:

1. Destructive of charity, which wounds the heart.
2. A calling into question of both hierarchical pastoral structures of the Church for which the foundations were laid by the Lord.
3. The denial or the calling in question, in a hasty, thoughtless and irresponsible fashion, of those points of doctrine for which one should rather sacrifice one's life.
4. A rejection of those who think otherwise as bad persons, irretrievably lost.
5. Admitting expressions of *contestation* (or the *opinion differente*) in a liturgical celebration: e.g., in the homily, which creates a climate of tension and agitation.

Orsy and Sullivan conclude that the *corpus* of non-infallible beliefs and opinions may contain much that belongs to the core of our faith and our tradition (the *intuition* of which we have already spoken) but which as yet has not become the object of an infallible "determination." They conclude, then, that it is too simplistic to say that dissent to non-infallibly defined propositions is "legitimate." Joseph A. Komonchak's statement here is helpful:

> Catholics ought to give religious assent to the teaching of the ordinary magisterium. The basis of such assent is the trust that the magisterium is carrying out its divine commission to teach and in so doing is being guided by the Spirit. On this basis, official teaching deserves the presumption of truth. But the manuals also teach that religious assent is conditional, and that the presumption of truth can yield to the truth of evidence. This gives Catholics the freedom to dissent when there are sufficient grounds for doing so. The manuals do not see dissent as undermining the teaching authority of the ordinary magisterium, and at least one manualist, Lercher, recognizes that suspending assent may be a way of protecting the Church from error. However, for the sake of the good of the Church, the manuals are somewhat negative on the possibility of voicing dissent publicly.[57]

This question of dissent needs even further nuance and explanation.

There is one point of view which states that papal teachings which are not set forth as infallible may err.[58] However, in any particular case, the papal teaching is more likely to be correct than is the position of dissent from that teaching. Therefore, in this point of view, dissent from any papal teaching is rarely legitimate. This position allows further scholarly research and discussion on points on which there have been official papal teaching and the presentation of the results of this research and discussion to the hierarchy. In the 1968 statement of the U. S. bishops, *Human Life In Our Day*, the "Norms of a Licit Theological Dissent" seem to presuppose this type of "scholarly discussion": "There exist in the Church a lawful freedom of inquiry and of thought and also general norms of licit dissent. This is particularly true in the area of legitimate theological speculation and research. When conclusions reached by such professional theological work prompt a *scholar* [italics added] to dissent from non-infallible received teaching the norms of licit dissent come into play. They require of him careful respect for the consciences of those who lack his special competence or opportunity for judicious investigation. These norms also require setting forth his dissent with propriety and with regard for the gravity of the matter and the deference due the authority which has pronounced on it."[59]

The 1990 document from the Congregation for the Doctrine of the Faith, *Instruction on the Ecclesial Vocation of the Theologian*[60] also affirms this same attitude toward dissent. In particular, number 30 of the *Instruction* indicates:

> If, despite a loyal effort on the theologian's part, the difficulties persist, the theologian has the duty to make known to the Magisterial authorities the problems raised by the teaching in itself, in the arguments proposed to justify it, or even in the manner in which it is presented. He should do this in an evangelical spirit and with a profound desire to resolve the difficulties. His objections could then contribute to real progress and provide a stimulus to the magisterium to propose the teaching of the Church in greater depths and with a clearer presentation of the arguments.
>
> In cases like these, the theologian should avoid turning to the 'mass media', but have recourse to the responsible authority, for it is not by seeking to exert the pressure of public opinion that one contributes to the clarification of doctrinal issues and renders service to the truth.

Archbishop John R. Quinn of San Francisco has given an important interpretation and explanation of this *Instruction*.[61] In light of our discussion here, it is particularly important to note that Archbishop Quinn indicates that the *Instruction* appears to use the word "dissent" for public and organized manifestations of withheld assent. He comments: "Americans, on the other hand, seem to include in the idea of dissent the more private, personal withholding of assent and do not understand the word only or necessarily as implying public and organized campaigns." The following points of the *Instruction* are thus significant:

1.  "It would be contrary to the truth if, proceeding from some particular cases, one were to conclude that the Church's magisterium can be habitually mistaken in its prudential

judgments, or that it does not enjoy divine assistance in the integral exercise of its mission." (n 24)

2. "In order to serve the people of God as well as possible, in particular by warning them of dangerous opinions which could lead to error, the magisterium can intervene in questions under discussion which involve, in addition to solid principles, certain contingent and conjectural elements. It often only becomes possible with the passage of time to distinguish between what is necessary and what is contingent." (n 240)

3. "What concerns morality can also be the object of the authentic magisterium because the Gospel, being the word of life, inspires and guides the whole sphere of human behavior... By reason of the connection between the orders of creation and redemption, and by reason of the necessity, in view of salvation, of knowing and observing the whole moral law, the competence of the magisterium also extends to that which concerns the natural law." (n 16)

4. "The willingness to submit loyally to the teaching of the magisterium on matters *per se* not irreformable must be the rule. It can happen, however, that a theologian may, according to the case, raise questions regarding the timeliness, the form or even the contents of magisterial interventions." (n 24)

Thesis 8 and Thesis 9 of the 1975 *Theses* of the International Theological Commission are also instructive:

1. Thesis 8: "The specific freedom of theologians... is not an unlimited freedom, for, besides being bound to the truth, it must also recognize that in the exercise of any freedom one must observe the moral principle of personal and social responsibility. At the same time, the theologian's task... is in some sense critical. This criticism, of course, must be of the positive, not the destructive kind."

2. Thesis 9: "The exercise of their functions by the magisterium and by theologians sometimes gives rise to a certain tension. This is not surprising, nor should one

expect that such tension can ever be eliminated here on earth. On the contrary, wherever there is authentic life there will also be some tension. Tension as such is not hostility or real opposition; rather it is a lively stimulus and incentive for both sides to perform their respective tasks in communion with the other, following the method of dialogue."

Theological research and discussion can thus be useful to achieve greater certainty in papal teaching, either by showing that the official position has stood up under critical examination; or by leading to modification of the official teaching. In addition, this understanding of dissent helps us realize that there are different degrees of authority in papal teaching. The *Instruction* thus makes a threefold distinction:

When the magisterium of the Church makes an infallible pronouncement and solemnly declares that a teaching is found in revelation, the assent called for is that of theological faith. This kind of adherence is to be given even to the teaching of the ordinary and universal magisterium when it proposes for belief a teaching of faith as divinely revealed.
When the magisterium proposes "in a definitive way" truths concerning faith and morals, which, even if not divinely revealed, are nevertheless strictly and intimately connected with revelation, these must be firmly accepted and held.
When the magisterium, not intending to act "definitively," teaches a doctrine to aid a better understanding of revelation and makes explicit its contents, or to recall how some teaching is in conformity with the truths of faith, or finally to guard against ideas that are incompatible with these truths, the response called for is that of the religious submission of will and intellect. This kind of response cannot be simply exterior or disciplinary but must be understood within the logic of faith and under the impulse of obedience to the faith.[62]

Consequently, in special circumstances, there is the possibility of limited dissent from papal moral teachings that have not been set forth as infallible. In light of what we have just seen, however, there are certain safeguards which help minimize *illegitimate* dissent:

1. In deciding whether dissent is justified, one must take account of the different degrees of authority attaching to different papal teachings. Dissent against the most authoritative non-infallible papal moral teachings would be justified only rarely and for the strongest reasons. According as the papal teachings are less authoritative, dissent would be justified for less grave reasons. In no case, however, might dissent against a papal teaching be justified for anything less than serious and convincing reasons.

2. Dissent from a papal moral teaching is not justified simply because one is not persuaded by the reasons given in support of the teaching. One should approach any papal teaching with a presumption that it is correct, and with an especially strong presumption that the more authoritative teachings are correct. The *Instruction* calls the theologian, and all of us, to think with the Church (*sentire cum Ecclesia*): in other words, if one values the unity of the Church, one will be disappointed if it appears that an important instrument of that unity has failed in its task.

Anyone who assumes a dissenting posture in the Church to *Humanae Vitae* must first of all make an honest effort to appropriate the prophetic vision of this encyclical, as it affirms the teaching of the Catholic Church as well as all Christian churches up until 1930. As we have seen, dissent comes only at the end of a sincere effort to assimilate the authentic teaching of the Church.[63] This is because the ordinary magisterium holds a privileged place among religious teachers and ought to be given special deference. Its teaching should be approached with an openness to accept and adhere to it.[64]

This openness is marked by being ready to reassess one's own position and the limits of one's own experience and viewpoint. Openness and docility are further marked by a reluctance to conclude that the teaching is erroneous.

## 4. ABSOLUTION

A final word should be said here in this context regarding absolution. If a Catholic couple has prudently come to a decision to engage in individual acts of contraceptive marital intercourse, this should not be reason *in itself* to deny them sacramental absolution. There has been a great deal of confusion in clearly articulating the prophetic vision of *Humanae Vitae*; the evidence from the NORC study points up confusion and malaise more than obstinacy and hardheartedness. Numbers 20 and 21 of the encyclical indicate the difficulty of the teaching and number 25 points to the grave difficulties today involved in married life.

The fact that many couples today tend to judge the importance of an act by its relation to the over-all goals of one's married life might speak more to the conditions of the times than to a doctrine that is no longer relevant. Formal sin might not be involved, then, when a couple do not realize the fullness of the encyclical teaching in each act of marital intercourse. In addition, number 29 of *Humanae Vitae* indicates that "In their difficulties many married couples always find in the words and the heart of a priest the echo of the voice and the love of the Redeemer." And further on, "Let them not be discouraged, but rather have recourse with humble perseverance to the mercy of God." What is essential is that a couple is trying to live responsibly their married life as envisioned by the values stated in *Humanae Vitae*.[65] The words of the U.S. bishops in *Human Life In Our Day* (1968) are important here:

> With pastoral solicitude we urge those who have resorted to artificial contraception never to lose heart but to continue to take full advantage of the strength which comes from the Sacrament of Penance and the grace, healing, and peace in the Eucharist. May we all be mindful of the invitation of Jesus: "The man who comes to me I will never turn away" (John 6:37). Humility, awareness of our pilgrim state, a willingness and determination to grow in the likeness of the Risen Christ will help to restore direction of purpose and spiritual stability.

It would be foolish, however, and pastorally inept, for a confessor to reason that since in a given case there is no formal culpability, there is no problem. It remains the confessor's responsibility to assist the couple to see the validity and value-content of the Pope's teaching.[66]

## 5. CONTRACEPTION AND INFALLIBILITY

In 1978, John C. Ford, Germain Grisez, and Joseph A. Komonchak contributed important articles to *Theological Studies* which addressed the important questions regarding contraception and infallibility.[67] Because of the pastoral importance of this question, it is vital here to discuss the general lines of thinking presented by these authors.

Ford and Grisez point out that Ford and Gerald Kelly indicated in 1963 that the teaching on contraception as intrinsically and gravely immoral is "at least definable doctrine."[68] Ford and Kelly in 1963 judged that the received Catholic teaching on contraception had been infallibly proposed by the ordinary magisterium. This judgment was based on available evidence indicating that a world-wide survey of Catholic bishops would have shown that they all accepted and taught the received teaching.[69] Ford and Kelly pointed out that Pius XI and Pius XII did not propose a new teaching on contraception but repeated a teaching reaching back through the centuries. Even those Anglicans who supported the approval of contraception in 1930 admitted the existence of a long Christian tradition, although they denied the power of this tradition to bind the judgment of Christians today. Ford and Kelly thus wrote:

> For, if the teaching of the Catholic Church on a point so profoundly and intimately connected with the salvation of millions of souls has been the same over such a long period of time, the inevitable conclusion must be that that teaching is true and unchangeable. Otherwise the Church which God has established to interpret the moral law and to guide souls on the way of salvation would be failing substantially in its divine mission.[70]

In the 1978 article by Ford and Grisez, they also argue that the received Catholic teaching on contraception has been proposed

infallibly by the ordinary magisterium. Ford and Grisez argue that
Vatican II's *Lumen Gentium* (*Dogmatic Constitution on the Church*)
teaches that there are four conditions under which the bishops,
disbursed throughout the world, proclaim the doctrine of Christ
infallibly: First, that the bishops remain in communion with one
another and with the Pope; second, that they teach authoritatively on
a matter of faith or morals; third, that they agree in one judgment; and
fourth, that they propose this judgment as one to be held definitively.

Regarding the third point, that the bishops agree in one judgment, Ford and Grisez note that it is the moral unity of the whole body
of bishops in communion with each other and with the Pope that is the
point here, and not the mathematical unanimity of the bishops, which
would be broken by the dissenting voice of any one individual.
Another point about the required universality is, they add, that if this
condition has been met for some period in the past, it is not nullified
by lack of present consensus among Catholic bishops.

Ford and Grisez argue that there is substantial evidence for the
universality of the Catholic Church's teaching on contraception up to
1962. They cite John T. Noonan, Jr.:

> The propositions constituting a condemnation of contraception are,
> it will be seen, recurrent. Since the first clear mention of contracep-
> tion by a Christian theologian, when a harsh third-century moralist
> accused a Pope of encouraging it, the articulated judgment has been
> the same. In the world of the late Empire known to St. Jerome and
> St. Augustine, in the Ostrogothic Arels of Bishop Caesarius and the
> Suevian Varga of Bishop Martin, in the Paris of St. Albert and St.
> Thomas, in the Renaissance Rome of Sixtus the V and the Renais-
> sance Milan of St. Charles Borromeo, in the Naples of St. Alphonsus
> Liguori and the Liege of Charles Billuart, in the Philadelphia of
> Bishop Kenrick, and in the Bombay of Cardinal Gracias, the
> teachers of the Church have taught without hesitation or variation
> that certain acts preventing procreation are gravely sinful. No
> Catholic theologian has ever taught, 'Contraception is a good act.'
> The teaching on contraception is clear and apparently fixed for-
> ever.[71]

Ford and Grisez then conclude "That the historical evidence
shows that Catholic bishops disbursed throughout the world agreed in

one judgment on the morality of contraception, a judgment which remains substantially the same and which was universally proposed at least until 1962."[72] Ford and Grisez then offer a number of substantiating reasons for this conclusion:

1. Not only Jerome and Augustine but also certain Eastern Fathers condemned contraception.
2. Many of those who taught that acts intended to prevent procreation are gravely evil were bishops; many who were not bishops are canonized saints, including several who were Doctors of the Church.
3. The canon law of the universal Church from the 13th century until 1917 included the canon *Si aliquis*: "If anyone for the sake of fulfilling sexual desire or with premeditated hatred does something to a man or to a woman, or gives something to drink, so that he cannot generate, or she cannot conceive, or offspring be born, let it be held as homicide."
4. There is a constant consensus of Catholic theologians in modern times. This consensus is important because any indefiniteness in the tradition regarding methods of contraception, its sinfulness in every single act, and other matters was eliminated either by the explicit statements of the modern theologians or by the general principles which they shared in common. This is especially true of the works in moral theology generally in use in the 19th and 20th centuries. The consensus of modern theologians supports the thesis that the received teaching was universally proposed by Catholic bishops, because the works of the theologians were authorized by the bishops for use in seminaries, and thus the training of confessors who communicated Catholic moral teaching to the faithful in the confessional, in premarital instructions, in the preaching of missions, and so on.
5. Both the Holy See and many individual bishops and groups of bishops in the 19th and 20th centuries insisted upon the received Catholic teaching. This situation is a paradigm case of the ordinary magisterium of the Church, disbursed

throughout the world, agreeing in one judgment and
universally proposing it as if with one voice.

6. When the statements of Pius XI and Pius XII reaffirmed
this existing consensus, there was no significant negative
reaction within the Catholic Church. Not only did the
bishops readily accept the teaching of *Casti Connubii* but
many actively took part in an effort to carry out its program
by encouraging family-life movements, by instructing and
directing their own clergy, and by making public statements
repeating the teaching when such statements seemed called
for. These considerations made clear that the received
Catholic teaching on the morality of contraception was
universally proposed by Catholic bishops in communion
with one another and with the successor of Peter.

Having established the case that the teaching on the morality of
contraception was universally proposed, Ford and Grisez then argue
that the teaching was also proposed authoritatively: i.e., to be held
definitively. The following points are made:

1. There is no evidence that any one handed on the received
teaching as if it were a private opinion, a merely probable
judgment, or a commendable ideal which the faithful might
nevertheless blamelessly choose to leave unrealized. The
teaching always was proposed as a received and certain part
of the obligatory moral teaching of the Church.

2. The teaching is that acts intended to impede procreation are
in species gravely evil — that is, are the matter of mortal
sin. This fact — which was pivotal in the argument for the
binding force of the tradition — makes clear the unqualified
character of the intellectual assent demanded for the
teaching. When the Church proposes a moral teaching as
one which Christians must try to follow if they are to be
saved, she *a fortiori* presents the teaching as one which
must be accepted as certain. The magisterium permitted no
differing opinions about the morality of contraception, and
so probabilism was inapplicable. Thus the conditions under

which the teaching was proposed left no room for doubt in the matter.

3. The insistent repetition of the received teaching in recent times when it was called into question outside the Catholic Church often included and always implied the proposition that this is an obligatory teaching, one which every Catholic must hold even though it is denied by other Christians.

4. The teaching on the morality of contraception often was proposed as a moral norm divinely revealed. Since it was proposed as revealed, *a fortiori* it was proposed as a teaching *to be held definitively* (i.e., the teaching of the encyclical is *constans ecclesiae doctrina*).

Ford and Grisez thus conclude, "We think that the facts show as clearly as any one could reasonably demand that the conditions articulated by Vatican II for infallibility in the exercise of the ordinary magisterium of the bishops disbursed throughout the world have been met in the case of the Catholic Church's teaching on contraception."[73]

Ford and Grisez then cite a statement written by Fr. Ford as a *peritus* for the Pontifical Commission for the Study of Problems of Population, Family, and Birthrate:

The Church cannot change the answer *since this answer is true*. Whatever may be the possibility of a more perfect formulation of the teaching or perhaps of its genuine development, there is no possibility that the teaching itself is other than substantially true. It is true because the Catholic Church, instituted by Christ to show men the sure road to eternal life, could not err so atrociously through all the centuries of its history. The Church cannot substantially err in teaching a very serious doctrine of faith or morals through all the centuries — even through one century — a doctrine constantly and insistently proposed as one necessarily to be followed in order to attain eternal salvation. The Church could not substantially err through so many centuries — even through one century — in imposing very heavy burdens under grave obligation in the name of Jesus Christ as it would have erred if Jesus Christ does not in fact impose these burdens. The Catholic Church could not in the name of Jesus Christ offer to the vast multitude of the faithful, everywhere in the world, for so many centuries an occasion of formal sin and spiritual ruin on account of a false doctrine promulgated in the name of Jesus Christ.

If the Church could err as atrociously as this, the authority of the ordinary magisterium in moral matters would be stultified; and the faithful henceforth could have no confidence in moral teaching handed down by the magisterium, especially in sexual questions.[74]

Ford and Grisez thus conclude that the Church has proposed the moral teaching on contraception as an obligatory norm and a grave one, in the name of Christ, everywhere in the world, through many centuries. Therefore the Church could not err substantially in its teaching on contraception, and so the answer is true. Since the answer is true, the Church cannot change it.

Ford and Grisez then approvingly quote Hans Kung:

We can see now the real reason why the progressive majority of the commission were not able to convince the Pope. To judge from their own progressive report and the progressive official reaction of the commission, they had plainly not grasped sufficiently the full weight of the argument of the conservative group: the moral inadmissibility of contraception has been taught as a matter of course and even emphatically by all bishops everywhere in the world, in moral unity, unanimously, for centuries and then — against opposition — in the present century up to the Council (and the confusion which arose in this connection), as Catholic moral teaching to be observed on pain of eternal damnation: it is therefore to be understood in the light of the ordinary magisterium of Pope and bishops as a factually *infallible truth* of morals, even though it has not been *defined* as such.[75]

Joseph A. Komonchak begins his own assessment of this question regarding infallibility by citing the 1950 encyclical of Pius XII, *Humani generis*:

Nor should it be thought that what is propounded in encyclicals does not of itself demand assent, since the pontiffs do not exercise the supreme power of their magisterium in them. For these things are taught by the ordinary magisterium, to which that word also applies, "He who hears you, hears me"; and quite often what is propounded and inculcated in encyclicals already belongs to Catholic doctrine on other grounds. But if the supreme pontiffs purposely pass judgment on a matter until then under dispute, it is clear to all that the matter, according to the mind and will of the same pontiffs, can no longer be considered a subject of free discussion among theologians.[76]

Komonchak then concludes, as does Ford and Grisez, that from the 3rd to the 20th centuries both the official teachers of the Church and Catholic theologians have consistently and unanimously condemned artificial techniques of contraception. Komonchak then quotes from Vatican I's *Dei Filius*:

> Further, all those things are to be believed with divine and Catholic faith which are contained in the Word of God, written or handed down, and which the Church, either by a solemn judgment or by its ordinary and universal magisterium, proposes to be believed as having been divinely revealed.[77]

At Vatican II, *Lumen Gentium* number 25 spoke of an infallibility of the universal episcopate even outside an ecumenical council:

> Although bishops individually do not enjoy the privilege of infallibility, still when, even though disbursed throughout the world but preserving the bond of communion among themselves and with the successor of Peter, in their authoritative teaching on matters of faith and morals, they agree upon a judgment as having to be held definitively, they infallibly proclaim Christ's teaching.

Komonchak then draws these conclusions:

1. The subject of an infallible exercise of the universal ordinary magisterium is not individual bishops taken singly, but the whole body of bishops who are in communion with one another and with the pope. Individual bishops are not infallible; that degree of authority requires the moral unanimity of the body of bishops. *Lumen Gentium* did require that the bishops be joined by "the bond of communion." This *communio* is one of the most important words in the ecclesiological lexicon of Vatican II, but its meaning is

not always clear. The *Nota explicativa praevia* appended to
the third chapter of *Lumen Gentium* gives a brief indication
of the meaning of "communion" with respect to the episcopal college:

> *Communio* is a notion held in high honor in the ancient
> Church (as also today especially in the East). But it is not to
> be understood as some vague sentiment, but as an organic
> reality which requires a juridical forum and at the same
> time is animated by love.[78]

Komonchak then concludes this point by stating that,

> (T)he requirement in *Lumen Gentium* 25 that the bishops be
> in communion with one another and with the pope refers to
> a *formal* condition necessary for an exercise of their
> authority to be considered infallible. It does not describe the
> actual exercise of their authority. "The bond of commun-
> ion," in other words, describes not the unanimous agree-
> ment of the bishops, but rather a prior condition that must
> be fulfilled for their unanimous agreement to be invested
> with supreme authority.[79]

2.  This object of the universal ordinary magisterium is most
    generally described as *res fidei et morum*. It includes what
    has classically been known as "the primary object of
    infallibility" — revealed doctrine — and what is called "the
    secondary object" — truths not revealed but necessary to
    defend and expound what has been revealed. There has
    been no official determination how far this "secondary
    object" extends; the only principle is that of "necessity" if
    the revelation is to be defended and expounded, and on this
    question, there is a good deal of disagreement among
    theologians.
3.  For an instance of the universal ordinary magisterium to
    constitute an infallible exercise, not simply any presentation
    of the doctrine suffices. In the case of the "primary object,"
    the bishops must present the teaching *tamquam divinitus
    revelata*; in the case of the "secondary object," they must

present it *tamquam definitive tenenda*. The latter phrase is used to avoid the suggestion that the motive for the assent required is the *auctoritas Dei revelantis* to which "divine faith" responds. The phrase does not seem to intend an exercise of episcopal authority inferior to that employed in matters taught as "having been divinely revealed."

Komonchak then indicates that *all three* of the conditions must be fulfilled for a teaching universally proposed by the episcopal body to be considered infallibly proposed: it must concern a matter of faith or morals which, if not divinely revealed, is necessary to defend and explain what has been revealed; it must be proposed by a moral unanimity of the body of bishops in communion with one another and with the pope; and it must be proposed by them as having to be held definitively. If one of these conditions is not met, the teaching does not constitute an infallible exercise of the magisterium. If it cannot be established that any one of them has been met, then the canonical rule applies and the theologian may proceed on the assumption that he is not dealing with an infallibly proposed teaching.

Komonchak concludes that "...there is something like a *consensus theologorum* that the magisterial tradition behind *Humanae Vitae*'s condemnation does not constitute an infallible exercise of the teaching office."[80]


## 6. CONCLUSION

*Humanae Vitae* holds forth a vision of *relational significance*: that when husband and wife respond to the invitation to meet each other in deep fellowship by virtue of their sexual diversity, then they are each other's first "neighbor" and thus establish the *una vita* of the Genesis vision. In conjunction with *Gaudium et Spes*, *Humanae Vitae* is calling married couples to entrust themselves to each other, to give a gift of something decisive; and in this manner they do not so much give something they have, but rather something they are. They thus give a definitive and exclusive gift. And only in respect for the complete significance of the sexual act does one find the total expression of conjugal love as a gift without reservation. This structure must always remain the presumption.[81] A breakdown of action is ultimately a collapse of meaning and a collapse of meaning is inevitably a breakdown of action.

The prophetic vision of *Humanae Vitae* is clear, a vision which can speak to the meaning of married life: human marital sexuality is something essentially profound, a voice from the depths of the human person; it is the utterance of something central and of utmost significance. Procreation is not reproduction.

CHAPTER FOUR

# SEXUALITY, PHYSIOLOGY AND BIRTH CONTROL METHODS

## 1. CONTEXT OF THE QUESTION

In their book *A Sense of Sexuality*[1] Evelyn and James Whitehead demonstrate that the arena of sex is one in which humans differ most from other animals. For most animals, sex is seasonal. For a brief period of time at a biologically determined stage of development males and females are capable of mating. Outside such a mating season most animals display no sexual activity. The attraction and union of women and men, by contrast, does not depend on a mating season. As the Whiteheads indicate, "Sexual activity among humans is less controlled by biological cues."[2]

In most animals, sexual activity is narrowly focused on reproduction. For example, among the primates closest to humans in evolutionary development — the great apes — the female is receptive to the male's sexual approach only during estrus, a recurring but relatively brief period of biological fertility. Among humans, in contrast, sexual interest is not limited to reproductive periods. A woman can experience sexual arousal throughout the menstrual cycle, not just during the limited phase when conception is possible. Both women and men remain interested in and capable of genital behavior long after their biological fertility has come to an end. This would seem to confirm that for the human species sex is about more than reproduction. In humans, therefore, sex is not a neutral ingredient. Sex changes things. Sex generates more than passion; a sexual relationship arouses hopes and enkindles expectations. As sexual

135

sharing continues, promises are made — sometimes explicitly, often in subtler ways. The Whiteheads thus remark, "Recreational sex is bankrupt not because it focuses on pleasure but because it does not keep its promises."[3] For human beings, physical intimacy and psychological intimacy are connected. Sex play reveals more than one's body; it often uncovers hidden hurts and fragile hopes. In other words, in lovemaking, more than pleasure is aroused. We repeat here the Christian conviction made in the previous chapter: An essential connection exists between making love and giving love.[4]

Our sexuality is rooted in a particular consciousness we have about ourselves. This self-understanding comes in part from our own experience, but it is influenced by the messages we receive from our family, our school and church, and from the values and biases of our culture. Our parents' display of their affection for one another teaches us to be comfortable with physical closeness. A school counselor's assistance might well help us accept some of the confusions of the adolescent experience of sex. Problematically, Hollywood's romanticized version of beauty leaves us self-conscious about our physical appearance and envious of others who come closer to the "ideal body." These awarenesses — these understandings of ourself — are the building blocks of our sexuality. The Whiteheads point out that there are three elements of this self-awareness that are crucial:

*First*: A sense of embodiment: What having a body means. We use different images to express the relationship between self and body. Sometimes the experience is one of integration — body and self are one. The Whiteheads remark, "In viewing the film *Chariots of Fire*, even the non-athletes among us could sense this integration as the champion runner declared: 'When I run I feel God's pleasure.' Something similar often occurs in lovemaking, when the barrier of separateness is momentarily transcended and lovers experience a communion that goes beyond the joining of bodies."[5]

Our experiences of embodiment are not always so positive. At times — in illness, perhaps — self and body seem disconnected, linked only in an uneasy truce. We may know periods of even greater antagonism, when an unwilling body cages our spirit or when the unruly demands of the flesh defy the soul. This was the agony that St. Paul experienced: "I see in my members another law at war with the law of my mind and making me captive to the law of sin which dwells in my members. Wretched man that I am! Who will deliver me from this body of death?"[6]

These images of embodiment capture the changing sense of what being a body/self means. Some images may be fleeting: after breaking a leg, we experience our body as a cumbersome burden but the cast is removed and we quickly feel strong and agile again. Other images linger, becoming part of the characteristic way we see ourselves: Our body is clumsy or sickly or fat-and-ugly. These images of our embodiment become a significant part of our sexuality.

*Second*: Gender: What being a woman or a man means. As we have seen, this awareness comes in part from our sex, i.e., from the fact that our reproductive system is male or female. But our sense of self as a man or a woman involves much more than a check of reproductive organs. Gender goes beyond biology to social expectations. If sex is about male and female, gender is about masculine and feminine. Gender says less about how we are equipped than about how we should act. The Whiteheads remark:

> Each culture forms its own roles and rules of gender. By determining what is appropriate for women and for men, the social group establishes its working categories of feminine and masculine. These definitions may differ from culture to culture, but every society develops gender expectations. Our society's expectations about what is masculine and feminine play an important role in our growing sense of what being a woman or a man means.[7]

Our awareness that we are a man or a woman is central to our sexuality. Initially we come to this sense from the messages we receive from others, especially from our parents (what we have previously designated as "gender identity"). From them we learn that "since your are a girl, you shouldn't fight back" or that "our little girl can be anything she wants to be." As we participate in school and church and neighborhood, we learn broader expectations of femininity and masculinity. In our community and in the media, we find role models who show us what being a woman or a man means. We discover both the benefits and the burdens of our gender:

> Being a woman means to locate oneself in the picture of femininity that our culture paints. This is the process of gender identification.

We come to identify ourselves as women, to hold ourselves account-
able to the norms of femininity that prevail in the group that is
important to us. But the match is seldom perfect. As we compare
ourselves to the culture's image of a woman, we find both similari-
ties and differences. Critical to our sexuality is what we do about the
differences.[8]

A cultural image of either masculinity or femininity is always
close to a stereotype, because this image disregards the remarkable
range of individual differences. Every woman, e.g., has feelings and
talents and hopes that do not fit the culture's description of what a
woman is or should be. The parts of themselves that do not fit, that are
not "feminine," often embarrass many women. One may be more
assertive than a "good woman," or too tall or too athletic to be really
"feminine," or "unnaturally" more interested in living out a dream of
personal accomplishment than in having children. Men who confront
the "unmasculine" parts of themselves — tenderness or nurturance or
the desire to be held — experience a similar dichotomy between what
they are and how their culture defines them.

Mature sexuality challenges us to gradually come to greater
confidence and comfort with the way that we are women or men. In
doing this we acknowledge the ways that our experience fits the social
norm, and we accept the parts of ourselves that contradict the culture's
expectations.

In addition, gender differences influence our stance toward
relationships as well as our self-awareness. Both men and women
recognize the benefits of drawing close to others, a sense of belonging, an awareness of inclusion, the possibilities of love. Both women
and men know that close relationships make demands for give-and-
take, for accommodating to the needs of other people, for generosity.
Both men and women recognize the dangers that may accompany
close relationships — domination, control, betrayal. But, as we have
seen, growing evidence reveals fundamental differences between
women and men in their emotional response to close relationships.
The Whiteheads give the following example:

A woman brings to her relationships a sense that "something good
will happen here." Although the situation may be more complex and

conflicted for a woman who has experienced emotional or physical violence from persons close to her, women characteristically approach close relationships with positive expectations.

Men have different internal models. In the imagery of many men, bonds mean bondage. They experience close relationships as emotionally threatening. The net created by close connections feels more like a trap than a safety net. In this image, the links of relationships confine rather than sustain. Characteristically, then, men approach close relationships with caution.[9]

*Third*: The movement of our affections, the feelings that we have toward persons of the same and of the opposite sex. Here again culture is critical, telling us what are appropriate feelings to have toward women and toward men. In this way the culture defines the categories of heterosexual and homosexual experience. Each of us, then, must come to terms with the movements of our affectional life. The Whiteheads remark, "As men, e.g., we learn that our culture permits us to be sexually attracted to women and to show them physical affection. We also learn that the display of physical affection between men is discouraged. Our culture views with suspicion a man who is emotionally drawn toward other men. With this cultural backdrop, each of us has to sort out and accept our own experiences of physical and emotional attraction."[10]

Men and women often find that their own feelings do not fit neatly into the culture's definitions of acceptable heterosexuality. We can be drawn, e.g., to different degrees and with different intensity, toward both women and men. Some find that the strongest emotional orientation is toward persons of the same sex; and some find that the strongest emotional orientation is toward persons of the opposite sex. This level of self-awareness — the ways we are moved emotionally by women and by men, the sense we have of ourselves as primarily heterosexual or homosexual — is part of our sexuality.

Sexuality takes us beyond genital activity and gives us a sense of embodiment, an awareness of gender, and an awareness of the movements of affection. There is an intimate link between sexuality and our emotional life. Emotions are the feelings that move us. Anger stirs us; compassion arouses us; sorrow and guilt cast us down. Our emotions are part of our embodiment. This does not mean that our emotional experiences are genital, but that our ability to respond is an aspect of our sexuality. In other words, our life constricts when we respond to others only in physical arousal and when we express closeness only in genital ways. Attraction and responsiveness remain aspects of sexuality even when they have little to do with genital sex. To be attracted by another's goodness, to be drawn to beauty and nature, to be moved by music and art — these emotional responses often stir us physically and enrich our lives. The Whiteheads instructively comment:

> Evidence from our own lives and from psychological research indicates that these emotional responses are part of the broader experience of sexuality. Hostility toward our body and fear of our emotions is often linked. If we are confused about our masculinity, we may find that reaching out to other people in genuine ways is difficult. If we are afraid of the ways in which our affections are stirred, we may retreat into a stance of no response at all. Soon the experiences of joy and beauty become as alien to us as the unwanted sexual stimulation.[11]

Sex and sexuality are not the same, but they are interrelated. Real connections exist between genetics (a determining factor of sex) and gender (a critical part of sexuality). Our emotional responsiveness and our comfort in being close to other people are linked. In fact, the erotic excitement of romance can lead to the broader commitments of mutual love. The way that we experience these connections is significant, especially to our sexual maturity. Our experience of sex, our awareness of sexuality, our attitude toward close relationships — these all shape our sense of self. As we have noted, sexual maturity is not a state that is achieved once and for all. Rather it is an ongoing process. To mature sexually is to become more confident and more comfortable with the ways that sex, sexuality, and intimacy are a part of our own life. Sexual maturity challenges us to develop a *pattern of life* that is rooted in the wisdom of our own experience and that is responsive to the values and commitments that give our life meaning.[12]

Both Pope Paul VI and Pope John Paul II have spoken to this

question of sexual maturity. In a 1970 address to members of the Equipes Notre-Dame, Paul VI said:

The entire being participates, in the depths of its personal mystery, and of its affective, sensitive, carnal and spiritual constituent parts, thus constituting a more perfect image of God which the married couple has the mission to incarnate day after day, by weaving it with its joys and sorrows, so true is it that love is more than love. There is no conjugal love which, in its exultation, is not an elan towards the infinite, and in this elan, does not wish to be total, faithful, exclusive and creative (See *Humanae Vitae*, 9). The conjugal act, as a means of expression, knowledge and communion, maintains and strengthens love, and its creativity leads the married couple to its full flowering: it becomes a source of life, in the image of God.[13]

John Paul II addressed the members of the Equipes Notre-Dame in 1982 and reaffirmed this same point:

(T)he body is more than the body, it is the sign of the spirit which inhabits it (see General Audience of 28 July 1982); Christian marriage is more than the flesh.... Transfigured by the Spirit, love builds on eternity because "love never ends" (1 Cor 13:8). But at the same time an authentic conjugal love, though filled with tenderness and faithfulness, stops short of fixing an unseemly adoration on the spouse: it moves from the conjugal covenant to the divine Covenant and from the image to its Source.[14]

These three movements of self-awareness of our sexuality give us a good grounding to properly understand the insights of Lisa Sowle Cahill in her important work *Between the Sexes: Foundations for a Christian Ethics of Sexuality*.[15] Cahill points out that the most obvious differences in male and female sexual development and function evidently are controlled by the brain.[16] The brain is influenced by hormones so that it inclines the individual toward certain behavioral characteristics, such as aggressiveness, which appears to differentiate men and women. Hormones influence brain and sex-related behavior normally when they are released in increased levels at puberty. But hormones can also effect abnormal changes in fetal development or in the adult who receives hormones as part of a medical therapy. Cahill reiterates a point we have seen earlier:

> Scientific consensus also supports the conclusion that women generally have better capacities for cognitive activities controlled by the left, or verbal, hemisphere of the brain, while men stand out in those associated with the right, or visual, side. A recent study has provided some evidence that there are not only functional but also structural differences in the human male and female brains, comparable to those already verified in some other species.[17]

What does this suggest? It appears that different physical characteristics, deriving at least in part from their reproductive roles, may create in men and women a tendency toward certain emotional (nurturing, aggressive) or cognitive (verbal, visual) capacities, which may in turn influence the ways they fulfill various social relationships.

With this general framework in mind, we are now better situated to approach the specific question of the physiology of our sexual functions.[18] As we have noted, physical intimacy and psychological intimacy and our sexuality are vitally rooted in a particular consciousness about ourselves. In a book whose primary purpose is to raise the moral and religious issues about human sexuality, it is thus important to also enunciate an understanding of basic physiological sexual functioning.

## 2. THE PHYSIOLOGY OF SEXUAL FUNCTIONS

Physiology is the study of the functions and activities of organs and organisms. An understanding of the physiology of the male and female sex organs helps us to appreciate better what to expect of our bodies during sexual activity.

### A. Sexual Stimulation

Sexual activity begins with erotic stimulation. All healthy humans have the ability to respond to sexual stimulation, and the types of stimuli to which they respond are many: e.g., kisses, caresses, pictures, stories, thoughts. The basic physiological response of the body to sexual stimulation is always the same, but the intensity of sexual arousal that each person experiences during a lifetime can vary from one sexual experience to another. Sometimes sexual excitement reaches a climax in the response known as orgasm. Sometimes it progresses no further than lingering thoughts or vague feelings.

What triggers such responses? It depends on the person. For some, almost anything and everything; for others, very few things. The stimuli may be "sexual" in the ordinary sense of the word, or they may involve factors that have no erotic interest for most people. Katchadourian, Lunde and Trotter point out, e.g., "Young boys, for instance, have been known to have erections in a wide variety of athletic activities (swimming, boxing, riding, skating), emotionally charged events (coming home late, receiving report cards, being chased by police), and even sitting in church or hearing the national anthem. (Unfortunately, no comparable information exists for young girls.)"[19] Nonsexual sources of erotic stimulation generally involve activities and situations that are highly emotional.

As children grow older, sexual or erotic responses tend to become more specific. By the late teens, sexual responses are usually limited to direct stimulation of the genitals or to obviously erotic situations. In later years, sexual stimulation is even more dependent on actual physical stimulation.

Tactile, or touch, stimulation is one of the most important methods of sexual arousal in humans. It is, in fact, the only type of stimulation to which the body can respond reflexively. Because our nerve endings are distributed unevenly, some parts of the body (fingertips) are more sensitive than others (the back). It is the areas of the body with the most nerve endings that have the greatest potential for stimulation.

In addition to the distribution of nerve endings, other differences also play important roles in determining the sensitivity of certain areas of the body. Katchadourian, Lunde and Trotter cite one study where researchers measured breast sensitivity in young men and women and in boys and girls who had not yet reached puberty. Before puberty there were no differences between the sexes with regard to breast sensitivity. After puberty, the tactile sensitivity of the women's breasts was much greater than that of the men's breasts. The researchers also found that the degree of sensitivity of a woman's breast changes, not only at puberty, but during the monthly menstrual cycle and shortly after giving birth.

In addition to the female breasts, there are many areas of the body that are especially susceptible to tactile stimulation. They are called *erogenous zones*. Although it is these areas that are most often involved in sexual arousal, they are by no means the only erogenous zones. The neck (throat and nape), the palms and fingertips, the soles and toes, the abdomen, the groin, the center of the lower back, or any other part of the body may well be erotically sensitive to touch. "Some women have reportedly reached orgasms when their eyelashes were stroked or when pressure was applied to their teeth."[20]

Sight, sound, smell, and taste can be almost as important in sexual stimulation as is touch, with one major difference. Our response to certain types of tactile stimulation, such as genital stimulation, are based on natural reflexive reactions. Our responses to stimulation that comes through the other senses are probably all learned. Almost everyone, e.g., can respond sexually to stimulation of the genitals. Responses to various sights, sounds, smells, and tastes, however, differ far more because of previous learning experiences. And because sexual experiences differ from person to person and from time to time, the sights, sounds, smells, and tastes we learn to associate with sex will vary greatly from person to person and from time to time.

After touch, sight is probably the most important form of sexual stimulation. The sight of genitals, for instance, is a very common source of sexual arousal, even though there appear to be some differences between males and females in this regard.

The effect of sound is less obvious than that of sight but can be a significant sexual stimulant. The tone and softness of voices as well as certain types of music can serve as erotic stimuli. However, responses to such things are learned, so what stimulates one person may only distract or annoy another.

The use of scents in many cultures, as well as interest in body odors, suggests that the sense of smell still has considerable influence. It has been suggested that there may be naturally occurring body odors that are involved in sexual arousal. If there is a naturally occurring, sexually stimulating odor produced by humans, we would expect it to be associated with vaginal secretions or semen, or with the odor of the genital areas. Some researchers claim to have found evidence for the existence of human *pheromones*, chemicals produced by one individual that affect the behavior of another; but the evidence is not conclusive.

Sexual arousal is influenced greatly by emotional states. Even reflexive reactions are usually influenced by the emotions. Stimulation through any or all of the senses will result in sexual arousal if and only if accompanied by appropriate emotional conditions. As we have seen, feelings like affection and trust will enhance; others such as anxiety and fear will inhibit, or hold back, erotic responses in most cases. Our responsiveness, then, is not based solely on the physical situation, but includes the entire store of memory from past experiences as well as thoughts projected into the future. What arouses us sexually is the combination of all these influences: the physical situation, our fantasies, our emotional state, and the context in which these influences act upon us.

Do men and women react differently to sexual stimuli? In a study reported in 1970, for instance, 50 male and 50 female students at Hamburg University were shown sexually explicit pictures under experimental conditions. In general, the men did find the pictures with frankly sexual themes more stimulating, but when the theme had a relational component or affectionate theme (e.g., a couple kissing) women were equally if not more responsive.

Slightly more men than women (40 men and 35 women, out of 50 in each group) reported certain physiological reactions (warmth and pulsations for the women; and an erection for the men). Differences in the sexual aftereffects of the experiment were also slight. About half the subjects in each group reported increased sexual activity during the next twenty-four hours.[21] These studies generally suggest that women today are much more like men with regard to sexual arousal than was previously assumed. However, there are still differences between the sexes. These differences are probably due to a great extent to social and cultural expectations, rather than to biology. Traditionally, in our society, women have been taught that they are not supposed to react as openly as men do to explicit sexual material. This teaching is often enough to inhibit their responses. It seems safe to conclude, then, that the differences between men and

women regarding sexual stimuli are mostly due to cultural expectations rather than biologically built in; even though there may be
biologically based differences as well. Nevertheless, whatever differences do exist between men and women, they are not as great as the
differences that exist among the members of either sex. In other
words, there are many women who will be less responsive to erotic
stimuli than the "average" man. But there are also many women who
will be more responsive than the "average" man. It is likely that there
are a variety of responses that men and women share in varying
degrees, but none of which is exclusive or characteristic of either sex.

Hormones, too, play important roles in sexual arousal, and there
are many behavioral patterns ("body language") as well as quite
obvious and extremely subtle verbal and nonverbal methods of
communicating sexual interest. A great deal of such communication
is so subtle that it is barely recognized consciously, even by the person
manifesting it. In the final analysis, sexual arousal must be understood
in the broad interpersonal and psychosocial context in which it
occurs. It should also be remembered that arousing sexual interest
goes far deeper than mere sexual coquetry or teasing. "It is the first
step in the reproductive effort by which a species maintains itself."[22]

## B. Sexual Response

If sexual stimulation is effective, it leads to sexual arousal. If
sexual stimulation goes on long enough, it can eventually lead to
orgasm. We will here describe the general behavioral characteristics
of sexual response patterns; and the general physiological changes
which accompany these behavioral responses. Of course, there are
many variations on these patterns.

Whenever we are affectively sexually stimulated, a sensation of
heightened arousal develops. Our thoughts and attention turn to the
sexual activity at hand, and we become less and less aware of
whatever else may be going on around us. Katchadourian, Lunde and
Trotter remark:

> Anxiety or strong distractions might shut down sexual arousal in the
> early stages, and it is even possible to suppress excitement or ward
> it off by directing attention to other matters, but if the stimulation,

the time, and the circumstances are favorable, erotic stirrings will be difficult to ignore. As the level of tension rises, external distractions become less effective, and orgasm... becomes more likely.[23]

Sexual excitement can intensify at different rates — rapidly and relentlessly in younger persons, more gradually in older persons. It has also been assumed that men respond more rapidly to sexual stimulation and are capable of reaching orgasm more rapidly than women. There is no known physiological basis for this claimed difference, and females can respond more or less as quickly as males do to affective stimulation. The difference between the sexes in achieving orgasm during intercourse, therefore, does not seem to be related to basic physiological differences between the sexes, but rather to psychological factors and to the effectiveness of stimulation.

When sexual arousal is achieved, reactions may differ greatly from person to person, even though the response to effective sexual stimulation does have some general characteristics. No matter how mild the response, there will always be distinct physiological changes.

*Orgasm* is a very intense and satisfying experience. In physiological terms, it is the explosive discharge of accumulated neuromuscular (relating to both nerves and muscles) tensions. Its subjective counterpart is a state of altered consciousness characterized by intense pleasure, which is experienced with considerable variation from one instance to another. The patterns of response during orgasm vary among individuals and according to age, fatigue, time since last orgasm, and so on; but there is some evidence that each person has a fairly characteristic set of responses.

In adult males the sensations of orgasm are generally linked to ejaculation, but orgasm and ejaculation are two separate processes. Orgasm is the release of neuro-muscular tensions. Ejaculation is the sudden discharge of semen through the urethra. It is experienced only by males past the age of puberty, when the prostate and accessory glands become functional. Although the fluid that lubricates the vagina is produced during arousal, females do not ejaculate, as some people have mistakenly concluded.

Ejaculation occurs in two stages: first, there is a sense that ejaculation is imminent, or "coming," and that one can do nothing to stop it; second, there is a distinct awareness of the rhythmically contracting urethra, followed by fluid moving out under pressure.

In the female, orgasm starts with what some women have described as a feeling of momentary suspension followed by a peak of intense sensation in the clitoris. This sensation then spreads through the pelvis. This stage varies in intensity and may involve sensations of "falling," "opening up," or even emitting fluid. Some women compare this stage of orgasm to mild labor pains. It is followed by a feeling of warmth spreading from the pelvis through the rest of the body. The experience ends with characteristic throbbing sensations in the pelvis. The female orgasm, unlike that of the male, can be interrupted.

Sigmund Freud proposed that females experience two types of orgasm: clitoral and vaginal, although Kinsey and his associates raised doubts about this concept of dual orgasm. The research of Masters and Johnson supports the Kinsey point of view: physiologically there is one and only one type of orgasm, regardless of whether the clitoris, the vagina, or for that matter neither one is directly involved, as when orgasm occurs after breast manipulation only. It may also be that women vary in clitoral and vaginal sensitivity.

The question of dual orgasm has not been resolved to everyone's satisfaction, and researchers are still trying to answer it one way or the other. However, even if there is only one type of orgasm, this does not mean that the experience of orgasm is always the same. The subjective experience of orgasm varies tremendously. But the basis of these differences is primarily psychological and subjective.

The period leading up to orgasm is quite distinct, but the period following it is more ambiguous. In general, the changes gone through after orgasm are the opposite of those leading to orgasm. The rhythmic throbs of the genitals and the convulsions of the body become less intense and less frequent. Neuro-muscular tension gives way to profound relaxation, and the entire musculature of the body relaxes. Immediately following orgasm the person may feel an intense wish to rest, to be at peace. The pounding heart and accelerated breathing return to normal. Congested and swollen tissues of organs resume their usual colors and sizes. As the body rests, the mind reawakens, and the various senses gradually regain their full alertness. For most persons, the predominant feeling is one of peace and satisfaction.

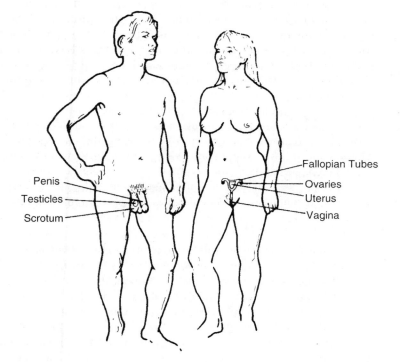

Penis

Testicles

Scrotum

Fallopian Tubes

Ovaries

Uterus

Vagina

A major difference between male and female responses to sexual orgasm involves a *refractory period* in the male cycle. Cells, tissues, and organs do not respond to a second stimulation until a certain period of time has passed since the first stimulus. This period is known as a "refractory period." This refractory period comes immediately after orgasm and extends into the resolution phase. During this period, the male is incapable of physical sexual response, regardless of the type and intensity of sexual stimulation. In other words, he cannot regain full erection nor have another orgasm until after the refractory period, the duration of which varies but has not been precisely determined. It is very brief for some men, especially younger men, and longer for others.

Females do not have refractory periods. In the female, as soon as the orgasm is over, the level of excitement can mount immediately to another climax. Some women can thus have *multiple orgasms*, or orgasms in rapid succession.[24]

The body goes through a great many complex changes during sexual arousal, but most of these changes are the result of two basic processes:

1. *Vasocongestion*: The engorgement, or excessive filling, of the blood vessels and increased flow of blood into body tissues. The erection of the penis and the swelling of the female genitals are the most obvious examples of vasocongestion. When the arteries dilate, the blood rushes in and the tissues become swollen, red, and warm. The cause may be physical, such as when the skin turns red due to heat, or psychological, as during blushing. Sexual arousal is always accompanied by widespread vasocongestion.

2. *Myotonia*: Increased muscle tension. Even when one is relaxed or asleep, one's muscles maintain a certain firmness or "muscle tone." From this base level, muscle firmness increases during voluntary flexing or during certain involuntary contractions, including those of orgasm. Myotonia is present from the start of sexual arousal and becomes widespread, but it tends to lag behind vasocongestion.

*a. Reactions of the Male Sex Organs*

Of all the sex organs, the *penis* undergoes the most dramatic changes during sexual excitement. Erection (*tumescence*) can occur reflexively without erotic feelings, but usually it is positive evidence of sexual arousal. During orgasm rhythmic contractions begin in the prostate, seminal vesicles, and vas, but very soon extend to the penis itself. These orgasmic contractions involve the length of the penile urethra and the muscles around the root of the penis. They begin regularly at intervals of approximately 0.8 seconds, but after the first several strong contractions they become weak, irregular and less frequent.

Ejaculation (*throwing out*) is the forcible ejection of spermatic fluid through the urethra. The fluid, which flows in various amounts, usually about 3 cubic centimeters, is known as semen, seminal fluid, or spermatic fluid. It consists of sperm (only a small part of the total volume) and the products of the prostate mainly, and to a much lesser extent the seminal vesicles.

Ejaculation happens in two stages. During the first phase (emission) the prostate, seminal vesicles, and vas deferens pour their contents into the dilated urethral bulb, and the man feels the inevitability of ejaculation. In the second phase (ejaculation proper) the semen is forced out by strong contractions of the muscles surrounding the root of the penis and by contractions of the various genital ducts. At this point the man feels intense pleasure associated with orgasmic throbs and the sensation of spermatic flow.[25]

In the resolution phase the changes of the first three phases are reversed, and erection is lost, but the penis does not become flaccid all at once. Detumescence occurs in two stages. First, there is the relatively rapid loss of stiffness to a semi-erect state. Then there is a more gradual decongestion as the penis returns to its unstimulated size. Usually, the longer the excitement and plateau phases have been, and the more complete vasocongestion has been, the longer the first state of detumescence will be, which delays the second stage.[26]

During the excitement phase the skin of the *scrotum* contracts, thickens, and loses its baggy appearance. If the excitement phase is prolonged, the scrotum may relax, even though the sexual cycle is not yet completed. The scrotum shows no color changes.

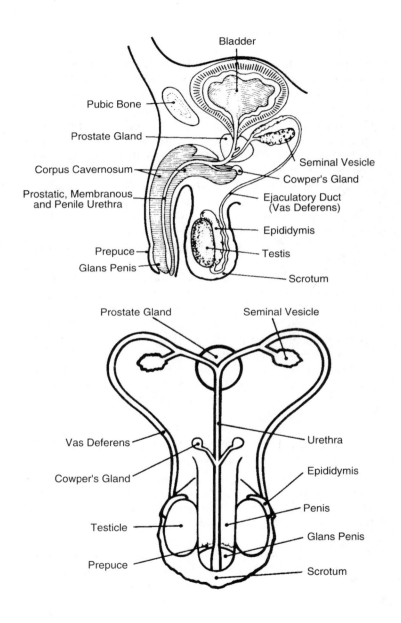

Bladder

Pubic Bone

Prostate Gland

Corpus Cavernosum

Prostatic, Membranous
and Penile Urethra

Prepuce

Glans Penis

Seminal Vesicle

Cowper's Gland

Ejaculatory Duct
(Vas Deferens)

Epididymis

Testis

Scrotum

Prostate Gland

Seminal Vesicle

Vas Deferens

Cowper's Gland

Testicle

Prepuce

Urethra

Epididymis

Penis

Glans Penis

Scrotum

The changes undergone by the *testes* are also distinct. During the excitement phase both testes are lifted up within the scrotum, mainly as a result of the shortening of the spermatic cords and the contraction of the scrotal sac. During the plateau phase this elevation progresses further until the organs are actually pressed against the body wall. Full elevation of the testes is necessary for orgasm and always precedes it. The testes also undergo a marked increase in size, about 50 percent in most cases, because of vasocongestion. There are no further changes during orgasm, and in the resolution phase the size and position of the testes return to normal.

The *Cowper's glands* are almost inactive during sexual arousal. If sexual excitement is sustained, a drop or so of clear fluid, produced by these glands, appears at the tip of the penis. Most men produce only several drops or none at all, but some produce enough to wet the glands or even to dribble freely. This fluid may help neutralize the acidity of the urethra.

Changes in the *prostate and seminal vesicles* take place only during the orgasmic phase. Ejaculation begins as these structures pour their secretions into the expanded urethra. The mixing of sperm from the throbbing vas with the secretions of the seminal vesicles takes place in the ejaculatory duct. Sperm that may have been stored in the seminal vesicles, along with those coming from the vas, are propelled through the duct into the urethra. The prostate and seminal vesicles participate in the rhythmic convulsions of orgasm, and their contractions, along with the filling of the urethra, are responsible for the sensation that orgasm is near.

*b. Reactions of the Female Sex Organs*

Moistness of the *vaginal walls* is the first sign of sexual response in women, and usually occurs within 10 to 30 seconds after erotic stimulation. Just as the penis becomes erect in order to enter the vagina, the vagina becomes moist and lubricates itself in order to more easily receive the penis. The clear, slippery, and mildly scented vaginal fluid not only lubricates the vagina, it also helps neutralize the vaginal canal (which tends to be acidic) in preparation for the semen.

Vaginal fluid oozes directly from the walls of the vagina. The secreting mechanism is not fully understood, but it probably is related to vasocongestion of the walls. The *Bartholin's glands* do produce a fluid, but like that of the Cowper's glands in males, it tends to be scanty, erotic, and probably of little or no lubricating value.

The vagina shows two other changes during the excitement phase: expansion of its inner two-thirds and color change. The ordinarily collapsed interior vaginal walls lengthen, expand, and create a space where semen will be deposited. The ordinarily purple red vaginal walls will take on a darker hue in response to stimulation. This coloring begins in patches, then spreads over the entire vaginal surface, reflecting the progressive vasocongestion of the vagina. During the plateau phase the focus of change shifts from the inner two-thirds to the outer one-third of the vagina. This area may have dilated somewhat during the excitement phase, but in the plateau phase it becomes congested with blood and the vaginal opening becomes at least a third narrower. The congested walls of the outer third of the vagina are called the *orgasmic platform*. It is there that the rhythmic contractions of orgasm are most apparent. During the plateau phase the "tenting effect" of the inner end of the vagina continues, and full vaginal expansion is achieved. Vaginal lubrication tends to decrease at this stage, and if the excitement phase has been long, lubrication may cease altogether in the plateau phase.

Importantly, observations of the vagina during orgasm confirm that it is much more than just a "passive receptacle" for the penis. It is an active participant in coitus, and capable of enveloping and stimulating the penis to a climax.

The *clitoris* is an exclusively sexual organ. It plays no direct part in reproduction. In response to sexual excitement the clitoris becomes tumescent through vasocongestion, but its overhanging prepuce prevents it from standing erect as the penis does.

The clitoris is a highly sensitive organ. Practically all women can feel tactile stimulation in this area, and most women respond erotically to such touches. During the excitement phase the clitoris becomes congested, though in the majority of females the change is so small that a microscope is needed to detect it. Tumescence of the glands of the clitoris coincides with vasocongestive response of the minor lips and comes late in the excitement phase, when the penis has been erect for some time and the vagina is fully lubricated. This response will be more rapid and more obvious if the clitoris and

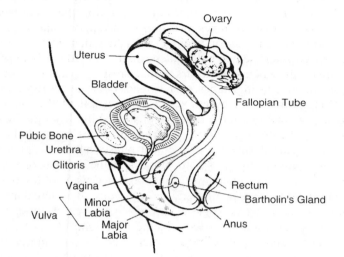

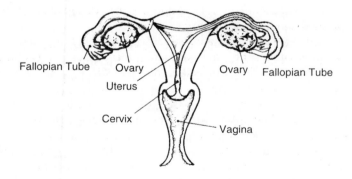

adjoining areas of the *mons* are stimulated directly. Once tumescent, the glands of the clitoris remain so throughout the sexual cycle.

During the plateau phase, the entire clitoris is retracted under the clitoral hood, or prepuce, and almost disappears from view. This reaction is particularly rapid and striking in response to direct stimulation and may result in the clitoris receding to half its unstimulated length. When excitement does let up, the clitoris reemerges from under the hood. And during a long plateau phase there may be several repetitions of this in-out sequence.

Both the *major and minor lips*, or *labia*, undergo changes due to vasocongestion during sexual arousal but there are differences between the changes seen in the labia of women who have not given birth (*nulliparous*) and those who have (*parous*). This is because the pressure of childbirth may cause permanently distended (varicose) veins in the tissues of the labia.

During the excitement phase, nulliparous major lips become flattened, thinned, and more widely separated, "opening" and slightly exposing the external genitals and their congested moist tissues. During the plateau and orgasmic phases, nulliparous lips show no further changes, and at resolution they return to their decongested size and shape and resume midline contact.

The changes in the minor lips during the sexual cycle are quite impressive and remarkably consistent. As excitement progresses to plateau, the minor lips become engorged and double or even triple in size in both parous and nulliparous women. These tumescent lips project between the overlaying major lips and become quite apparent, which may explain the parting of the major lips during excitement.

The vivid coloring of the inner lips at the height of arousal is so closely associated with sexual arousal that these lips have been called the "sex skin" of the sexually excited woman. If erotic stimulation continues beyond this point, orgasm is inevitable; but if stimulation is interrupted, orgasm will not occur. In fact, orgasm will not occur unless congestion of the minor lips reaches this peak. In this sense the "sex skin" is similar to full testicular elevation in men; both are preconditions and good indications that orgasm is near.

*Bartholin's glands* secrete a few drops of clear, slippery fluid rather late in the excitement phase or even in the plateau phase. They appear to be most effectively stimulated by the action of the copulating penis during a long period of time. The contribution of these glands to vaginal lubrication and neutralization is relatively minor.

The *uterus* has long been known to participate actively in the changes of the sexual response cycle. Elevation from its usual position is the first response of the uterus to sexual excitement. This reaction pulls the cervix up and contributes to the tenting effect in the vagina. Full uterine elevation is achieved during the plateau phase and is maintained until resolution. Then it returns to its usual position within 5 to 10 minutes.

In addition vasocongestion causes a distinct increase in the size of the uterus during the early phases. Myotonia is evident in the activity of the muscles of the uterus, resulting in distinct contractions. These contractions start in the *fundus* and spread downward. They occur simultaneously with those of the orgasmic platform but are less distinct and more irregular.

Even though the male breasts do respond to sexual excitement, changes during the response cycle are far more striking in the female *breasts*. Erection of the nipple is the first response. It occurs during the excitement phase as a result of the contractions of "involuntary" muscle fibers rather than of vasocongestion. Engorgement of the blood vessels is responsible for the enlargement of the breasts as a whole, including the areolae. Nipple erection in the male occurs, if at all, in the late excitement and plateau phases.

Sexual activity also results in definite skin reactions, including flushing, temperature change, and perspiration. The flushing response is more common in women. It appears as a color change with the appearance of a rash, in the center of the lower chest as a woman moves into the plateau phase. It then spreads to the breasts, the rest of the chest and the neck. This sexual flush reaches its peak in the late plateau and is an important part of the excited, straining, and uniquely expressive physiology of the person about to experience the release of orgasm.

In addition, the heart races and pounds during sexual excitement. This reaction is not always immediate, and mild erotic thoughts may not change the heart rate. But high levels of sexual arousal and certainly orgasm do not occur without some increase in heart rate. In the plateau phase the heart rate rises from the normal 60 to 80 beats per minute to 100 to 160 beats per minute. Blood pressure also shows a definite increase at this time. These changes are similar to those seen in athletes exerting maximum effort or in persons engaged in heavy labor.

Changes in breathing, or respiratory rate may lag behind those in heart rate but always accompany them. Flaring nostrils, a heaving chest, and a gasping mouth are well-known signs of sexual excitement. Faster and deeper breathing becomes apparent during the plateau phase, and during orgasm the respiratory rate may go as high as 40 a minute (normal is about 15 a minute, with inhalation and exhalation counting as one). Breathing becomes irregular during orgasm.

## 3. CONCEPTION, PREGNANCY, AND BIRTH

Today we know that it is the union of the sperm and egg (ovum) that results in conception, pregnancy, and the birth of a child. Even though there are still aspects of these processes that have yet to be fully explained, the miracle of birth is no longer quite as mysterious as it once was. We will thus study here the major elements in these processes.

### A. Conception

Although we will not deal here with the complex question of ensoulment, it is critical to recall the teaching of the Church on this question. The magisterial teaching on the time of ensoulment is found in the *Declaration on Procured Abortion* (1974) from the Congregation for the Doctrine of the Faith, and was repeated in 1987 in this Congregation's *Instruction on Respect for Human Life in its Origin and on the Dignity of Procreation*:

> This Congregation is aware of the current debates concerning the beginning of human life, concerning the individuality of the human being and concerning the identity of the human person. The Congregation recalls the teachings found in the *Declaration on Procured*

*Abortion*: "From the time that the ovum is fertilized, a new life is begun which is neither that of the father nor of the mother; it is rather the life of a new human being with his own growth. It would never be made human if it were not human already. To this perpetual evidence... modern genetic science brings valuable confirmation. It has demonstrated that, from the first instant, the programme is fixed as to what this living being will be: a man, this individual-man with his characteristic aspects already well determined. Right from fertilization is begun the adventure of a human life, and each of its great capacities requires time... to find its place and to be in a position to act." This teaching remains valid and is further confirmed, if confirmation were needed, by recent findings of human biological science which recognize that in the zygote resulting from fertilization the biological identity of a new human individual is already constituted.

Certainly no experimental datum can be in itself sufficient to bring us to the recognition of a spiritual soul; nevertheless, the conclusions of science regarding the human embryo provide a valuable indication for discerning by the use of reason a personal presence at the moment of this first appearance of a human life; how could a human individual not be a human person? The magisterium has not expressly committed itself to an affirmation of a philosophical nature, but it constantly reaffirms the moral condemnation of any kind of procured abortion. This teaching has not been changed and is unchangeable (Introduction, n 2).

The time when sperm and egg unite is, thus, the time of conception. In order to understand exactly what this means, it is necessary to have some basic knowledge of the cells involved.

(1)  Sperm

Sperm were not discovered until 300 years ago, and even then there was little agreement on what sperm were. The discovery was made in the laboratory of Anton van Leeuwenhoek (1632-1723), a Dutchman who did some of the first scientific investigations of life forms with a microscope. He noted that sperm resembled other microscopic organisms and he named them *spermatozoa* ("seed animals"). It was not until the twentieth

century that it was finally proved that the sperm cell actually
fuses with the egg at the time of conception.

From the union of male and female germ cells, one new cell is
formed. It divides into two cells, then into four cells, then into
eight cells and so on. If all goes according to plan, the result after
approximately nine months is a fully formed human infant. The
process of cell division is called *mitosis*. The information that
guides cells to their division and multiplication is contained in
the *chromosomes*, threadlike bits of material in the nucleus of
each cell.

Human body cells contain 46 chromosomes, 22 pairs and 2 "sex
chromosomes" that determine the sex of an individual. Females
have two XX chromosomes and males have one X and a smaller
Y chromosome. Human germ cells (sperm and egg) are different from other cells. Instead of containing the usual 46 chromosomes, they contain only 23. Thus, when sperm meets egg and
their chromosomes combine, the result is one cell with the usual
46 chromosomes. Germ cells have only half the normal number
of chromosomes because they go through a special type of
reduction division called meiosis.

Sperm are produced in the seminiferous tubules of the testes,
and go through several stages of development beginning with
cells called *spermatogonia* that lie along the internal linings of
the tubules. The spermatogonia divide into *spermatocytes*,
which in turn undergo reduction division, so that the resulting
*spermatides* have only 23 chromosomes. Because this process
begins with normal male cells (having both an X and Y chromosome), half of the spermatides will have an X and half will have
a Y chromosome after meiosis. In females there are two X
chromosomes in each cell. So, when meiosis occurs during the
maturation of eggs, each egg ends up with one X chromosome.
It is the spermatid that eventually becomes a mature sperm. Its
head is pearl-shaped, and it has a cone-shaped *middle piece* and
a tail that enables it to swim. The head of the sperm is about five
microns long, the middle piece another five microns, and the tail
thirty to fifty microns. Enough sperm to repopulate the world
would fit into a space the size of an aspirin tablet. If ejaculation

does not occur within 30 to 60 days, the sperm degenerate and are replaced by the new ones that are being produced all the time.

Billions of sperm are ejaculated by most men during their life times, but few sperm ever unite with an egg. Most sperm die. If ejaculation has occurred during intercourse, the sperm will be deposited in the woman's vagina and will begin to make their way to the uterus. One of the first obstacles they face is the force of gravity. For example, if a woman has arisen immediately after intercourse, the force of gravity will cause the sperm to flow away from the uterus. Even when the woman lies on her back, sperm may be lost through the vaginal opening, especially if this opening has been widened during childbirth. However, the engorgement of the blood vessels around the vaginal opening during sexual arousal creates a temporary orgasmic platform that helps keep seminal fluid in the vagina.

The position and structure of the penis may also affect the journey of the sperm. Continued active intercourse, for instance, tends to disburse the sperm and hinder them on their journey. The semen may also fail to reach the cervix because of incomplete penetration of the vagina by the penis. This may be unavoidable in the case of extreme obesity or because of a condition known as *hypospadias*, in which the opening of the urethra is located under rather than at the tip of the glans.

If the sperm does reach the area of the cervix and remains there, it still faces the obstacle of acidity. The pH of cervical secretions varies, and sperm are extremely sensitive to acidity. If the secretions of the cervix and vagina are strongly acidic, the sperm are destroyed quickly.

Sperm swim at a rate of one to two centimeters an hour (about one inch), but once they are through the cervix and inside the uterus they may be aided in their journey by muscular contractions of the wall of the uterus. Women's orgasms are known to contribute to these contractions, so it may be that if a woman has an orgasm at or near the time of her partner's orgasm there is a greater chance that the sperm will reach the fallopian tubes.

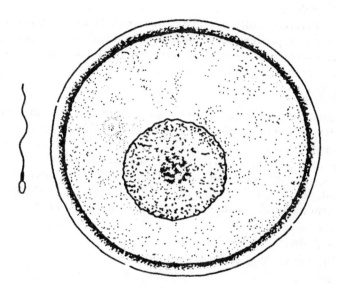

Comparison between the relative sizes of an egg and a sperm.

Once through the uterus and into the fallopian tube, the sperm complete the final two inches or so of their journey by swimming against the current generated by small, wavering, hairlike structures (*cilia*) that line the tube. Even if the woman has ovulated, only about half of the sperm that make it through the uterus end up in the fallopian tube that contains the egg, except on rare occasions when a woman ovulates from both ovaries at the same time.

If one considers all the obstacles that sperm face on their journey it is not surprising that of the several hundred million sperm in the original ejaculation only about two thousand reach the tube that has the egg. And then only one actually unites with the egg.

(2) Ova (eggs)

The discovery of the human ovum, or egg, did not come until 150 years after the discovery of sperm. In 1827 Karl Ernst von Baer (1792-1876), the founder of modern embryology, published a book in which he described his research with pregnant dogs and his discovery of minute specks of matter in the fallopian tubes. The small objects proved to be eggs, the actual germ material essential for reproduction. Later studies of humans confirmed these findings, and the human egg has since been studied in detail.

The human egg is scarcely visible to the naked eye. It is a spherical cell about 130 or 140 microns wide and weighs about 0.0015 milligrams, or approximately 1-20-millionth of an ounce. Although only about 400 eggs are actually discharged from the ovaries during a woman's reproductive lifetime, the ovaries contain about 400,000 immature ova (*primary oocytes*) at birth. It is believed that no new egg cells are produced by the female after birth. It would seem that this vast quantity of eggs would help insure a woman's reproductive ability, but "aging" of the eggs and exposure to radiation or to certain drugs can alter all the germ cells at once and do permanent damage. Possibly related to such "aging" of eggs is the increased incidence of certain defects, particularly Down's syndrome, in children born to older women. A woman in her forties is a hundred times more likely to have a Down's child than is a woman of twenty. For these and other reasons, the age at which it is best for a woman to have a child, biologically speaking, is usually said to be between twenty and thirty-five years.

Eggs begin to mature while still in the ovary, encased in a larger spherical structure known as a *graafian follicle*. The first division of the egg is mitotic and yields a *secondary oocyte* and a much smaller *polar body*, each containing 46 chromosomes. The polar body disintegrates, though it may divide once more before doing so. The secondary oocyte undergoes meiosis, or reduction division, usually after leaving the ovary, and this division produces another polar body, which also disintegrates, and a mature egg with only 23 chromosomes.

In addition to chromosomes, the mature egg contains fat droplets, proteins, and nutrient fluid. It is surrounded by a gelatinous capsule, the *zona pellucida*, the final obstacle to the sperm.

The egg, like the sperm, must travel through the reproductive system to the site of fertilization. This journey begins when the egg is expelled from the ovary at the time of ovulation. Recent research points out too that the fluid from an egg's follicular sac "attracts" sperm: i.e., eggs emit a weak chemical signal that gives out a "message" for a sperm to "come hither."[27] By this time hormonal influences will have caused the graafian follicle to grow to ten or fifteen millimeters in diameter, and it will protrude from the surface of the ovary. The follicle will be filled with fluid, and its wall will have become very thin. The egg flows free in the fluid until the thinnest part of the follicle wall bursts and the egg is carried out with the fluid. This process of ovulation is less like the explosion of a balloon and more like the leakage of water from a punctured sack.

Once out of the ovary, the egg must find its way to the fallopian tube. The process by which it does so is one of the mysteries of conception yet to be solved. The fringed end of the fallopian tube is near the ovary, but there is no direct connection to insure that the egg does not fall into the body cavity. Once the egg has entered the tube (and most do), it begins a slow journey to the uterus, taking about three days to move only three to five inches. Unlike the sperm, the egg does not move on its own. Instead, it is carried along by the movement of the cilia that line the tube. Contractions of the walls of the tube may also contribute to the movement of the egg. If fertilization does not occur during this journey through the fallopian tube, the egg disintegrates.

(3) If sperm and egg successfully complete their journeys, they will meet and unite in the fallopian tube. Each germ cell brings 23 chromosomes to this union, and the combination of these chromosomes results in one fertile cell with 46 chromosomes. Intercourse ordinarily must take place within one or two days before or after ovulation if the sperm and egg are to meet while both are capable of uniting and forming a fertile cell. If intercourse has occurred within 36 hours before ovulation, living sperm may be swimming about in the fallopian tube when the egg arrives on the scene. If fertilization does not occur within 24 to 48 hours of ovulation, conception will be impossible because the egg will no longer have the ability to become a fertile cell. Sperm swim right up to the egg, and many may surround it at the time of fertilization. But only one sperm actually unites with the egg. After a successful union of sperm and egg, a mechanism not fully understood prevents another sperm from entering the egg. This insures that the 23 chromosomes of the sperm and the 23 chromosomes of the egg — and no more — combine to provide the 46 chromosomes necessary for a human being. These chromosomes, half from the mother and half from the father, determine the sex as well as many other characteristics of the child. If the sperm carries an X chromosome, the child will be a girl (XX). If it carries a Y, the child will be a boy (XY).

## Amniocentesis and Prenatal Diagnosis

*Amniocentesis* is a procedure usually not performed until the 14th or 16th week after the last menstrual period. Amniocentesis can be used to find out the sex of a fetus, but it is most often used to test the chromosome makeup of the fetus when some abnormality is suspected.

The procedure of amniocentesis is simple. First, sound waves
are used to make a picture (an ultrasonic scan) of the fetus in the
womb. Once the position of the fetus is known, it is possible to
insert a hollow needle through the abdominal wall into the
pregnant uterus without harming the fetus. Some of the amniotic fluid that surrounds the fetus (and contains cells of the fetus)
is then removed and analyzed. The condition and number of the
chromosomes as well as the presence of either an X or Y
chromosome can be determined with a high degree of accuracy.

Amniocentesis is a relatively safe procedure for both mother
and fetus. Among the serious abnormalities that can be detected
by amniocentesis are Down's Syndrome (mongolism), Sickle-
cell trait, Tay-Sachs disease, Cystic Fibrosis, and Rh incompatibility.

Amniocentesis is most frequently offered to pregnant women
over 35. As women age, as we have seen, they run an increasing
risk of having a child with the wrong number of chromosomes.
Down's Syndrome occurs once in every one thousand live
births, but the risk rises to about one in two hundred for women
over 35 and about one in fifty for women in their 40's.

Scientists can examine the amniotic fluid for other conditions as
well, including nearly one hundred rare genetic diseases. Amniotic fluid can also contain high levels of alpha fetoprotein
(AFP), a chemical signaling that a fetus may be afflicted with
one of two relatively common congenital malformations —
anencephaly and spina bifida, or neural tube defects. These
defects occur very early in pregnancy when, for reasons so far
undiscovered, the primitive nervous system fails to develop
properly.

Amniocentesis is quite expensive, but is reasonably safe. The
technique is not without hazards, however. Among every 200
women who undergo amniocentesis, one or two will spontane-
ously abort afterward. Injuries to the fetus — needle punctures,
e.g. — are somewhat more common. British studies have
revealed additional perils of amniocentesis, such as a small risk

of congenital orthopedic defects like clubfoot, and a risk of premature birth, sometimes with fetal respiratory problems. Physicians do not do amniocentesis until the end of the fourth month of pregnancy, when sufficient fluid is available.

A *sonogram* is a picture taken during an ultrasound scan of the pregnant woman's abdomen. Ultrasound is an increasingly useful medical diagnostic technique and is much more frequently employed than amniocentesis. Ultrasound employs sound waves to form live video images of some parts of the fetus that are invisible to X-rays. It is used to test the fetus for a number of life-threatening conditions and will inform the physician and mother whether a fetus is growing at a normal rate, whether it has one of a large number of genetic disorders or some nonhereditary malformation, whether it is really twins or triplets, and what the sex of the child is. Ultrasound is the most important of the new diagnostic tools used in prenatal diagnosis and it is certainly more versatile and less risky than amniocentesis.

The use of ultrasound has implications beyond diagnosis. The fact that sonograms permit prospective parents to do something they have never been able to do before — observe the fetus — is pushing back parental bonds to before birth. The ultrasound technician often provides a running commentary, interpreting the gray-dappled streaks and blobs so that they are recognizable: Here is the head and spine, there are the tiny arms and legs.[28]

Researchers have also begun to assess the fetus indirectly, without invading the womb. They have found the chemical indicator of neural tube defects (a high level of AFP) in the blood serum of women who were between 16 and 18 weeks pregnant. Because it costs less than other forms of prenatal diagnosis, and because it tests the mother, rather than the fetus, serum AFP screening is the only existing form of prenatal diagnosis besides ultrasound that may eventually be used in all pregnancies.

At the present time, however, the results are ambiguous. For example, some women carrying a fetus with a neural tube defect have normal blood levels of AFP, so the test misses them. Furthermore, out of 100 tests in which the maternal serum AFP is elevated, only one or two fetuses are actually afflicted with anencephaly or spina bifida. Because of this uncertainty about the meaning of high maternal serum AFP, researchers have devised an elaborate series of backup tests to identify the few fetuses that really have neural tube defects.

Newer research includes the prenatal diagnosis called chorion biopsy. In this procedure, the physician inserts a long, slender biopsy instrument through the cervix into the uterus and, guided by an ultrasound scan, takes a sample of tissue from the trophoblast. This tissue is not, strictly speaking, part of the fetus, but it derives from the fertilized egg and is therefore genetically identical to it. The trophoblast gives rise to the placenta and the chorion, which is the outermost fetal structure, surrounding the amniotic envelope that encloses the fetus. In the laboratory, scientists examine the DNA of the tiny threadlike projections or villi, that protrude from the chorion.

From a moral point of view, prenatal diagnosis may never be performed if the intent of the mother (and father) is to abort a child who sustains some abnormality; or is of a sex not desired by the parents.

(4)  Infertility

Most couples are fertile and have no trouble producing children. Others (from 10 to 15% of married couples in the United States) are infertile and can have no children because either the male (in about 40% of the cases), the female or both are sterile.

One of the most common causes of infertility in males is low sperm count. An ejaculation that contains fewer than 35 million sperm per cubic centimeter will almost never result in conception. Frequent ejaculation is one cause of low sperm count. Usually low sperm count has more serious causes: undescended testes; physical damage to the testes; radiation; and infections that affect the testes. Infections of the prostate gland can also affect fertility, as can certain hormone disorders, such as hypothyroidism and diabetes.

The most common cause of infertility in women is failure to ovulate. This may be related to hormonal deficiencies or to other factors, such as vitamin deficiency, anemia, malnutrition, or psychological stress. In addition to failure to ovulate, there are several other problems that can result in infertility. Infections of the vagina, cervix, uterus, tubes or ovaries can cause infertility by preventing passage of the sperm or ova to the site of fertilization. Malformations of the reproductive tract, as well as tumors, particularly cervical or uterine, can also interfere with fertilization. There are also cases in which a woman may be preventing conception without knowing it by using certain commercial douches or vaginal deodorants containing chemicals that interfere with or destroy sperm.

There are numerous tests that can pinpoint fertility problems, and either the man or the woman or both may have treatable disorders.

### B. Pregnancy

The average duration of human pregnancy is 280 days, or approximately 9 months. Pregnancy is often described in terms of 3-month periods called *trimesters*.

### (1) The First Trimester

A missed period is among the first signs of pregnancy, but it does not always indicate pregnancy. Women who are near the beginning or the end of their reproductive years and those who have recently experienced an emotional upset or illness may fail to menstruate. Also, a woman who has recently had a child, particularly if she is still nursing, may not menstruate for 5 or 6 months or more. Missed periods under these circumstances usually do not indicate pregnancy, but contrary to what some people believe, a woman can become pregnant during this time without having had a menstrual cycle since her previous pregnancy. She need only have ovulated.

On the other hand, a woman who is pregnant may continue to have cyclic bleeding, though in smaller quantities and for shorter periods than usual. Such bleeding, which may be confusing to a woman who believes she is pregnant, is called "spotting." It occurs in about 20% of pregnant women, and it is particularly common in those who have already had children. Spotting usually does not indicate a problem, but in some cases it may be an indication of miscarriage.

Another early sign of pregnancy is enlargement and tenderness of the breasts. When hormonal stimulation of the mammary glands begins after conception, a woman usually will become aware of sensations of fullness in her breasts. The nipples in particular become quite sensitive to tactile stimulation early in pregnancy.

Many women also experience so-called morning sickness during the first 6 to 8 weeks of pregnancy. This sickness usually consists of queasy feelings upon awakening, accompanied by an aversion to food or even to odors of certain foods. The nausea may be accompanied by vomiting and great reluctance to be near food. Morning sickness is also experienced by some women in the evenings, but about 25% of women never experience morning sickness, and only about one in two hundred pregnant women in the United States have to be hospitalized because of severe vomiting, which can have serious consequences (including malnutrition) if not treated.[29]

Frequent urination is another common early sign of pregnancy. It is caused by increased pressure on the bladder by the swelling uterus. This symptom usually goes away as the uterus enlarges and rises up into the abdomen, but frequent urination may again become a problem toward the end of the pregnancy when the fetal head descends into the pelvis and puts pressure on the bladder.

Fatigue and need for more sleep, also indications of pregnancy, are often quite obvious during early pregnancy and may be quite puzzling to a woman who is usually very energetic.

A sexually active woman who has missed her period and is experiencing any or all of the above symptoms may have good reasons to believe that she is pregnant. The first time that pregnancy can be detected by physical examination is usually in the sixth week of pregnancy (about four weeks after a missed period). By this time certain changes in the cervix and uterus can be detected during a pelvic examination. One particularly good indicator of pregnancy is *Hegar's sign*, softening of an area between the cervix and the body of the uterus. Various laboratory tests can also be performed to detect pregnancy in its early stages. If performed correctly these tests are 95 to 98% accurate.[30]

Occasionally a woman may become convinced that she is pregnant despite evidence to the contrary. About 0.1% of all women who consult obstetricians fall into this category. Usually they are young women who intensely desire children; but some are women near menopause.

Women suffering *false pregnancy* often experience the symptoms of pregnancy. They often cease to menstruate, and physicians may observe contractions of the abdominal muscles that resemble fetal movements. Even though pregnancy tests are negative, a woman suffering from a severe mental illness like schizophrenia may persist in her delusion for years.

Once pregnancy has been confirmed, the expected delivery date can be calculated by a simple formula: Add one week to the first day of the last menstrual period, subtract three months, then add one year. For example, if the last menstrual period began on 8 January 1980, adding one week (to January 15th), subtracting three months (to October 15th), and adding one year gives an expected delivery date of 15 October 1980. Only about 4% of births occur on dates predicted by this formula; but 60% occur within 5 days of the predicted date.

Once fertilization has taken place, the fertilized cell moves to divide into multiple cells as it moves down the fallopian tube. There is no significant change in size during the first few days, but the original cell becomes a round mass of smaller cells called a *morula*. During the third to fifth day after ovulation, the cells of the morula arrange themselves in a spherical shape, leaving a fluid-filled cavity in the center. This structure called a *blastocyst*, floats about in the uterine cavity. Between the fifth and seventh days after ovulation it attaches itself to the lining of the uterus and burrows in, permitting it to reach the blood vessels and nutrients below. By the tenth to twelfth day after ovulation the blastocyst is firmly implanted in the wall of the uterus, but the woman will still not necessarily know that she is pregnant because her menstrual period is not due for several more days.

The blastocyst, which has embedded itself in the lining of the uterus, will develop from a tiny ball of cells into an easily recognizable human fetus during the first trimester. In the early stages of development a disk-shaped layer of cells forms across the center of the blastocyst. It is from this *embryonic disk* that the fetus grows. The remaining cells develop into the *placenta*, the membranes that will contain the fetus and the *amniotic fluid*, and the *yolk sac*.

Enclosed in the womb, the growing fetus is dependent on its mother for nutrients and for the disposal of waste material. The placenta is the organ through which such materials are exchanged. It grows from both fetal and maternal cells, and during the first trimester it develops into a bluish red, round, flat organ about seven inches in diameter and one inch thick. It weighs about one pound and, along with the fetal membranes, makes up the "afterbirth."

The blood vessels of the placenta are connected to the circulatory system of the mother through the walls of the uterus. The circulatory system of the fetus is connected to that of the placenta by the blood vessels in the umbilical cord, which is attached to the placenta. Oxygen and nutrients reach the fetus through the umbilical vein, and waste products from the fetus reach the maternal system through the umbilical arteries.

The placenta also functions as an endocrine gland, secreting hormones essential to maintaining pregnancy. HCG (*human chorionic gonadotrophin*) stimulates the production of progesterone by the corpus luteum during the first one or two months of pregnancy until gradually the placenta itself begins to produce large amounts of progesterone and estrogen. It appears that the labor process is triggered when the placenta stops producing these hormones just before delivery.

The fetus receives its nourishment through the placenta, but it is very important to realize that other substances — some of them quite harmful to the fetus, particularly during the first trimester — can also reach the fetus through the placenta. Alcohol is, for example, a drug that can cause birth defects. Researchers have found that facial, limb, and heart defects are more common among children of women who drink heavily during pregnancy than among those women who do not drink. Three ounces of alcohol a day or one big binge may be enough to cause damage. Drugs such as heroin and morphine can also pass through the placenta to the fetus and addict the unborn child to the drug. When such an infant is born it must be given further doses of the drug to prevent withdrawal symptoms which can be fatal. Certain viruses can also reach the fetus and have damaging effects on development during the first trimester. One is *rubella* or German measles virus. If a woman has rubella during the first month of pregnancy, there is a 50% chance that her infant will be born with cataracts, heart disease, deafness or mental deficiency.

Another complication is Rh incompatibility, a disorder that can cause serious and even fatal anemia in the fetus. In this disorder, antibodies of the mother travel across the placenta and attack the red blood cells of the fetus. The antibodies occur when the mother's blood is Rh negative and the father is Rh positive. If the mother is Rh negative and the father is Rh positive, Rh incompatibility can develop. This happens in about one of every two hundred pregnancies. In most cases the serious results of this disorder (deafness or brain damage) can be avoided by early detection and treatment.

During the first trimester, there is relatively little change in size of the embryo, but its rather simple structure is transformed into a very complete organism called the *fetus*.[31] By the second week after fertilization, the embryonic disk has become elongated and oval-shaped.

During the third week growth is most obvious at the two ends of the embryo. A prominent "tail" is seen at one end of the embryo, but it will be almost gone by the eighth week.[32]

At the other end the head is beginning to take on a definite shape. By the end of the third week or the beginning of the fourth, eyes and ears become visible. In addition, the brain and other parts of the central nervous system are beginning to form. By the end of the fourth week two bulges appear on the front side of the trunk. The upper bulge represents the developing heart and is called the *cardiac prominence*. The lower one is the *hepatic prominence*, caused by the growing liver.

Between the fourth and eighth weeks the facial features — eyes, ears, nose and mouth — become clearly recognizable. Fingers and toes begin to appear between the sixth and eighth weeks. Bones begin to ossify and the intestines are forming. By the seventh week the gonads are present but still cannot be easily distinguished as male or female. The external genitals cannot be identified as male or female until about the third month.

Between the eighth and twelfth weeks the fetus increases in length from about 1.5 to 4 inches, and in weight from about 2 to 19 grams. Although still very small, the fetus at twelve weeks has a human appearance. From this point on, development consists primarily of enlargement of the structures already present.

One of the most common problems during the first trimester of pregnancy is the unwanted termination of pregnancy — *miscarriage*, or *spontaneous abortion*. Between 10 and 15% of all pregnancies end in miscarriages. About 75% of these miscarriages occur before the sixth week of pregnancy, and most actually occur before the eighth week, long before the fetus or embryo has any chance of survival on its own. The first sign that a woman may miscarry is vaginal bleeding, or spotting. If the symptoms of pregnancy disappear and the woman develops cramps in the pelvic region, the fetus is usually expelled. About 15% of miscarriages are caused by illness, malnutrition, physical trauma (such as a fall), or other factors affecting the pregnant woman. In the remaining 85% the reasons are not apparent, but about 50% of miscarried fetuses are clearly defective in some way.

(2) The Second Trimester

During the second trimester, the nausea and drowsiness of the first few months tend to go away, and worries about miscarriages are generally past. Fetal kicks and movements make the pregnant woman acutely aware of the living fetus she is carrying. A pregnant woman's condition becomes publicly recognizable during the second trimester.

After the twelfth week the fetus is clearly recognizable as a developing human being. It has a proportionately large head with eyes, ears, nose and mouth. The arms and legs, which began as "limb buds" projecting from the trunk, now have hands and feet. The fingers and toes, which began as grooves at the ends of the limb buds gradually appear. At first the fingers and toes appear to be webbed, and in some children this webbing may remain after birth, but this can be easily corrected by surgery.

Very fine hair (called *lanugo*) appears on the scalp and above the eyes in the fifth or sixth month. The skin is quite thin at this time, and small blood vessels beneath the surface may show through. Beginning in the seventh month layers of fat build up beneath the skin, and the fetus takes on its characteristic chubbiness.

The internal organ systems continue to mature during the second trimester, and there is a substantial increase in the size of the fetus. At the end of the third month the fetus weighs about one ounce and is about three or four inches long. At the end of the sixth month it weighs about two pounds and is about fourteen inches long.

During the later stages of pregnancy the fetus alternates between wakefulness and sleep. Its eyes can open, and its arms and legs move, sometimes vigorously. The uterus provides a very sheltered environment for the fetus, but a loud noise near the uterus, a flash of high-intensity light, or a rapid change in the position of the woman can disturb the tranquility of the womb and provoke vigorous movement by the fetus.

## (3) The Third Trimester

A major complication during the third trimester is premature labor and delivery. Since the exact date of conception is not always known, prematurity is defined by weight rather than by age. An infant that weighs less than five pounds, eight ounces at birth is considered premature, and the smaller the infant, the poorer his or her chances of survival. Although an infant born in the seventh month or later can usually survive for a few hours without great difficulty, a premature infant may develop difficulty in breathing and die within 48 hours.

About 7% of all births in the United States are premature. This may be due to various maternal illnesses — such as high blood pressure, heart disease, or syphilis — or to factors such as cigarette smoking or multiple pregnancy. In at least 50% of the cases, however, the cause of prematurity is not known.

One of the most serious complications of pregnancy, if untreated, is a condition called *toxemia*. The cause of toxemia is still unknown, but it seems that a toxin or poison produced by the body causes the symptoms — high blood pressure, protein in the urine, and the retention of fluids by the body. Uncontrolled toxemia is a major cause, along with hemorrhage and infection, of maternal mortality. Six to seven percent of all pregnant women in the United States develop toxemia.

The last three months of pregnancy are a period of growth and development for the fetus. All the essential organ systems have formed, and by the end of the seventh month the fetus is about 16 inches long and weighs about 3 pounds, 12 ounces.

The most common position for delivery and the one that presents the fewest complications, is the *cephalic*, or head-down, *position*. When the fetus is situated in this position, the head appears at the cervix first during delivery. However, during the seventh month about 12% of fetuses are still upright in the womb (the *breech position*), and a few are positioned horizontally (*transverse position*). At full term, only about 3% of babies are still in the breech position.

By the end of the eighth month the fetus is about 18 inches long and weighs about 5 pounds, 4 ounces. During the ninth month the fetus gains more than 2 pounds, and organs like the lungs reach a state of maturity that will allow them to function in the outside world. In addition, less crucial details like hair and fingernails assume a normal appearance. At full term the average infant weighs 7.5 pounds and is 20 inches long. Newborn infants may be as small or smaller than 5 pounds, and weights of 10 or 11 pounds are not uncommon. Ninety-nine percent of full-term infants born alive in the United States survive.

### C. Childbirth

Contractions of the uterus at irregular intervals are among the first signs that pregnancy has come to an end.[32]
Before labor actually begins, several other events occur. Three or four weeks before delivery the fetus drops to a lower position in the abdomen. The next major step in preparation for delivery is the softening and dilation (opening) of the cervix. Just before labor begins there is a small, slightly bloody discharge that represents the plug of mucus that has been blocking the cervix. In a few cases (about 10%) the membranes that surround the fetus burst, and there is a gush of amniotic fluid. Labor usually begins within 24 hours after such a rupture.
*Labor* begins with regular uterine contractions that further dilate the cervix. The mechanism that triggers these contractions is not fully understood, but a number of hormones are known to be involved. The hormones produced by the placenta, for instance, are believed to inhibit uterine contractions, but the placenta stops producing these hormones, just prior to the pregnancy. Other chemicals are known to stimulate the muscles of the uterus and may play a role in initiating labor (i.e., *prostaglandins*). Finally, oxytocin, a hormone produced by the pituitary gland, is released in the late stages of labor, and it causes the more powerful contractions necessary to expel the fetus.
Labor is divided into three stages, the first of which is the longest. It begins with the first contractions and lasts until the cervix is completely dilated (about 4 inches across). This stage lasts about 15 hours in the first pregnancy and about 8 hours in later ones. Uterine

contractions begin at intervals as far apart as 15 or 20 minutes, but they occur more frequently and with greater intensity and regularity as time passes. A woman will usually go to the hospital when the contractions are coming regularly 4 or 5 minutes apart.

The second stage begins when the cervix is completely dilated and ends with the delivery of the baby. This second stage may last from a few minutes to a few hours. If any anesthetic is used, it is usually given before the second stage begins. A spinal anesthetic is currently considered to be preferable to a general anesthetic. Local anesthesia, which blocks the nerves in the vicinity of the vagina, is sufficient for a comfortable delivery for some women who desire a minimum of medical intervention at this stage. Some women prefer no anesthesia during delivery.

In the third stage the placenta separates from the wall of the uterus and is discharged along with the fetal membranes as *afterbirth*. The uterus contracts to a much smaller size during this stage, and there is some bleeding. This third stage of labor lasts about an hour.[33]

If the infant's head is too large or the woman's pelvis too small to permit a regular delivery a *caesarean delivery* may have to be performed. In this operation the infant is removed from the womb through an incision in the walls of the abdomen and uterus. About 10% of deliveries in the United States are performed by caesarean delivery, though the figure is increasing and may be as high as 22% in some hospitals. With modern surgical techniques the rate of complications in this type of delivery is no greater than in a vaginal delivery. The Centers for Disease Control maintain that about one-fifth of all caesarean deliveries may not be medically necessary.

## 4. CONTRACEPTION

Contraception has become a major force in our society and is influencing the history of the human race by its effect on population. In 1975, e.g., almost 80% of the married couples in the United States were using some method of contraception. In this section we will discuss the most-often-used methods of birth control, as well as research trends that will affect the future of contraception. A new study very helpful in this regard is *Preventing Pregnancy, Protecting*

*Health: A New Look at Birth Control Choices in the United States* published by The Alan Guttmacher Institute.[34] We will now review the contraceptive options currently available, and provide a brief description of the methods' basic modes of action. Our purpose here is simply to give an overview of these contraceptive methods, and not at this point to draw any moral implications.

### A. Behavioral Methods

### (1) Periodic Abstinence

The effectiveness of these methods depends both on accurately predicting when ovulation will occur, or detecting when it has happened, and on abstaining from intercourse during the woman's fertile period. There are a variety of ways to determine this fertile period. They include the calendar rhythm method, the basal body temperature (BBT) method, the mucus (Billings or ovulation) method, and the symptothermal method. All of these require users to abstain from intercourse for particular periods in the woman's cycle.

The mucus method of Natural Family Planning is one fully endorsed by the Catholic Church. This method entails watching for changes in the consistency of cervical mucus to determine the timing of ovulation. For couples committed to Natural Family Planning, success rates as high and higher as 92.6% have been reported.

The symptothermal method is a combination of the mucus and the BBT methods, with the additional component of observation of other signs of ovulation to pinpoint the fertile period even more precisely.

Couples can certainly use these methods to predict ovulation or to determine when it has occurred.

A device called the *ovutimer* has been developed by researchers at the Massachusetts Institute of Technology. It can be used to make the periodic abstinence methods more reliable and can also be used by couples who want to know when the fertile days are so that they can try to conceive a child. The ovutimer is a 7-inch long plastic device that, when inserted into the vagina, determines the time of ovulation by measuring the stickiness of cervical mucus, which becomes thin and watery at the time of ovulation.

*(II) Withdrawal*

Withdrawing the penis from the vagina before ejaculation (*coitus interruptus*) obviously requires no drug or device and involves no cost or advanced preparation. Withdrawal is a very ineffective method to use, especially since some active spermatozoa might be present in the mucoid fluid that can emit from the penis during the time before actual intercourse: i.e., pre-ejaculatory fluid may be left in the vagina. Katchadourian, Lunde and Trotter point out that "the decline of the birth rate in Western Europe from the late nineteenth century onward is believed to have been due to the popularity of this method."[35]

When withdrawal is the only contraceptive measure taken, failure rates range from 15 to 30%. This is partly because the male does not always withdraw quickly enough and partly because small amounts of semen may escape before ejaculation. The result: withdrawal is not considered a very effective method of birth control.

**B. Barrier and Spermicide Methods**

*(I) The Condom*

Condoms (also known as "rubbers," "prophylactics," "French letters," and "skins") are thin, flexible sheaths, worn over the erect penis to prevent sperm from entering the vagina. They are the only mechanical birth-control device used by men.

Condoms are cylindrical sheaths with a ring of thick rubber at the open end. The thickness of the sheath is about 0.0025 inches. Each is packaged, rolled, and ready for use. Some condoms also come lubricated. Condoms have been known to burst under the pressure of ejaculation, to leak, or to slip off during intercourse. The failure rates range from 2.5% to 15%. Using condoms with spermicidal cream or foam increases their effectiveness.[36]

Skin condoms are made from lamb cecum, a pouch forming part of the animal's large intestine. They typically cost several times what latex condoms cost. It is important to note that laboratory evidence on whether the AIDS virus can pass through skin condoms is limited to only a few small studies. One study has demonstrated passage; three others have not. Similar studies show that skin condoms do pass the smaller hepatitis-B virus but usually not the herpes virus, which is slightly larger than the AIDS virus.

Consequently, skin condoms work well as contraceptives, but, apparently because of the skins' possible porosity, the Federal Drug Administration (FDA) does not allow their packages to carry the disease-prevention labeling that latex condoms may carry. It remains an open question whether the skins' relative strength outweighs their potential to pass small microbes. In view of this uncertainty, *Consumer Report*'s medical consultants advise latex condoms for disease prevention.

As already mentioned, some condoms now come with a spermicide in their lubricant: nonoxynol-9.[37]

*(II) The Diaphragm*

The diaphragm is a dome-shaped soft rubber cap with a flexible rim that fits in the vagina and covers the cervix. Users are told to place spermicide, in jell or cream form, inside the cup before intercourse. The diaphragm itself blocks sperm from entering the cervix, while the spermicide kills any sperm that may get by the barrier. The diaphragm should remain in place for at least six hours after intercourse. The woman is told to insert more spermicide into the vagina for each additional act of intercourse, while leaving the diaphragm in place.

The diaphragm is available in several sizes, requires a prescription and must be fitted by a physician or other qualified health professional, who then trains the woman in its proper placement and removal. Some women cannot use the diaphragm because they are allergic to rubber or spermicide, or because they cannot be fitted. Because of concern about possible risks of toxic shock syndrome, women are advised not to leave the diaphragm in place for longer than 24 hours. When the diaphragm has been properly inserted, neither partner is aware of its presence during intercourse.

In theory, the diaphragm when used with contraceptive jelly should be highly effective. This is particularly true if the device is unflawed, perfectly fitted, and used correctly during every act of intercourse. In practice, the failure rate for the diaphragm varies between 5 and 20%. Aside from failure to use the diaphragm during intercourse, the reasons for failure include improper insertion, wrong size, and displacement during coitus. Even if the diaphragm is in place before intercourse, it may have slipped by the time of ejaculation.

*(III) The Cervical Cap*

The cervical cap is similar to the diaphragm, but it is smaller and depends on suction to stay in place, fitting closely over the cervix. The cap comes in several sizes and must be fitted by a physician or other qualified health professional. Like the diaphragm, the user places spermicide inside the cap before placement and can insert the spermicide into the vagina if she has repeated intercourse. The cervical cap can be inserted up to 40 hours prior to intercourse, must be left in place for at least 8 hours after intercourse, and should not be left in place for longer than 48 hours. The most popular version in Europe is shaped like a large thimble with a raised rim and is made of either rubber, plastic, or metal. It fits over the cervix in the same way that a thimble fits over the finger. Cervical caps are more difficult to insert than diaphragms and not all women can wear them because of the sizes and shapes of their cervixes. The failure rate for cervical caps is about 8%.

*(IV) The Sponge*

The polyurethane contraceptive sponge comes in only one size, can be purchased without a medical examination or prescription, is disposable and contains enough spermicide to provide protection for 24 hours, regardless of the number of times the woman has intercourse. It must be moistened with water before being placed in the vagina, where it covers the cervix. During intercourse, the sponge releases spermicide and also acts as a barrier by absorbing sperm. The sponge can be inserted several hours before intercourse, but must be left in place for at least 6 hours following intercourse. Because of concerns about toxic shock syndrome, women are advised not to leave the sponge in place for longer than 24 hours.

Some of the potential side effects of the sponge are similar to those found with other spermicidal methods — primarily, a slight burning sensation and an allergic reaction to the spermicide for some women and men. Some men indicate that they can feel the sponge during intercourse.

## (V) Spermicides

Spermicides come in various forms — foams, jells, creams, and suppositories and film that dissolve in the vagina. The active ingredient in all of these preparations is a detergent, usually nonoxynol-9, that immobilizes and kills sperm. Spermicidal protection is expected to last for several hours, but since there is no device to hold the spermicide when it is used alone, it is recommended that it be inserted into the vagina shortly before intercourse to provide maximum effectiveness. Spermicides are probably most effective when used in conjunction with barrier devices (e.g., diaphragm, cap or condom). Some women and men complain of a slight burning sensation with the use of spermicides. Others are allergic to these preparations and cannot use them at all or cannot use certain brands or forms of spermicide.

A plastic applicator is usually supplied for inserting the substance in the vagina. Vaginal foam is a cream packaged in an aerosol can. It is recommended that a full applicator of foam is inserted as soon before intercourse as possible, but no longer than 15 minutes before intercourse.

The failure rates for foams, creams, and jellies is close to 20%, for tablets and suppositories closer to 30%. Statistics indicate that the contraceptive suppository encare oval is very effective when used consistently according to directions.

## (VI) Douching

Douching means washing the sperm out of the vagina immediately after intercourse. Various commercial products are available for douching, and vinegar, lemon juice, soap, or salt are sometimes added as spermicides. These substances, however, add little to the spermicidal properties of tap water and may irritate the vagina. Within one or two minutes or less after ejaculation sperm can be in the cervical canal and out of reach of the douche. The overall failure rate for the douche as a contraceptive method is between 30 and 35%.

*(VII)  Condom for Women*

Ready for marketing is a new condom for women, officially called a *vaginal pouch*. They are made of polyurethane, a thicker latex than male condoms. The pouch is shaped like a tube sock, but instead of putting it over the penis, it is placed inside the vagina like a lining. The sealed end goes inside; the other end, which is open, has a ring that remains outside and keeps the pouch in place. One brand is inserted with an applicator rod, like a tampon; the other is inserted by squeezing a flexible ring at the closed end of the pouch and guiding it in, like the diaphragm. Female condoms can be inserted up to two hours before intercourse and clinical studies have demonstrated thus far that both women and men found sex using a vaginal pouch as pleasurable as sex when not using one. The pouches have effectively blocked the HIV virus in laboratory tests. They sell under the brand names Women's Choice Condomme and Reality Intravaginal Pouch.

### C. Mechanical and Mechanical-Hormonal Methods

The intra-uterine device or IUD is a device which interferes in some way with the implantation of the fertilized egg in the uterus. Properly, then, the IUD is abortifacient.

IUDs come in a variety of shapes, sizes and materials. Two IUDs are currently on the market in the United States: the Copper T 380A (which is sold under the name ParaGard) and the Progestafert. The TCU 380A is a copper-bearing device that became available in 1988. It can be used continuously for up to 6 years, after which the device must be replaced. The Progestafert slowly releases progesterone, a natural hormone; the device must be replaced after one year of use.

The most common problems associated with use of the IUD involve bleeding, pain, partial or complete expulsion of the device, retraction of the string into the uterus so that the woman can no longer feel it, and irritation of her partner by the string. The potential side effects of the different IUDs are similar, except that while the copper IUD tends to increase menstrual bleeding, the Progestafert appears to decrease it. In addition, the IUD carries the risk of more serious complications — pelvic inflammatory disease, ectopic pregnancy, and perforation of the uterus.

### D. Hormonal Methods

#### (1) Oral Contraceptives

Combined oral contraceptives (collectively referred to as the *pill*) are so named because they contain two synthetically produced hormones — estrogen and progestin. The amount of hormone in each pill may be the same throughout the cycle (monophasic pills) or may vary (biphastic and triphasic pills). The doses of estrogen and progestin contained in oral contraceptives today are far less than used in 1960, when the pill first became available in the United States.

Combined oral contraceptives' main mechanism of action is the suppression of ovulation so that no ovum is available to be fertilized by sperm. In the small proportion of cases in which the pill does not prevent ovulation, it prevents pregnancy through other means: it changes the composition of cervical mucus so that sperm have difficulty penetrating it to reach the uterus and fallopian tubes, where fertilization takes place. Oral contraceptives also slow transport of the egg through the fallopian tube and change the uterine lining to inhibit implantation should fertilization occur. In some cases, then, perhaps more than acknowledged, the pill is an abortifacient.

The most frequent side effects reported with oral contraceptive use are spotting and breakthrough bleeding, as well as conditions that are commonly experienced with pregnancy: nausea, weight gain, breast enlargement, headaches and chloasma (blotchy, brown spots that form on the face, often called the "mask of pregnancy"). Such side effects, other than spotting and breakthrough bleeding, are less common with pills used today than they were with the older, higher dose formulations. The lower the dose of estrogen in the pill, the more likely spotting and breakthrough bleeding are to occur.

An alternative form of oral contraceptive contains only progestin. It is often called the *minipill* since it contains a considerably lower dose of hormone than the combined pill. However, the minipill does not suppress ovulation as effectively as the combined pill, and is thus less effective in preventing pregnancy. The minipill also prevents pregnancy by causing a thickening of the cervical mucus, decelerating ovum transport and inhibiting implantation. Irregular bleeding, decreased duration and amount of menstrual flow, amenorrhea, spotting and breakthrough bleeding are commonly associated with the use of the minipill.

Some manufacturers recommend a 21:7 pill program. The pills are the same, but the woman takes 21 pills, then stops for 7 days, then repeats the series again, regardless of when menstruation begins. The advantage of this is that the woman always starts taking pills on the same day of the week. Another way to help a woman remember to take the pill is to have her take one every day — 21 hormone pills followed by 7 placebo (inactive) pills packaged in such a way as to prevent her from taking the wrong pill on any given day.[38]

## (II) Diethylstilbestrol (DES)

The first *morning-after pill* was approved by the FDA in 1975 for use in emergency situations (rape, incest, or where, in the physician's judgment, the women's physical or mental well-being is in danger). The so-called "morning-after pill" contains a potent estrogen, diethylstilbestrol (DES) and is taken in a dosage of 25 milligrams twice a day for 5 days. DES has not been approved for routine use because its safety has not been established. To be effective in preventing pregnancy, treatment must begin within 72 hours of intercourse and preferably within 24 hours.

One of the effects of DES is to prevent ovulation: e.g., in a rape situation if a woman has been assaulted at a point in her cycle when ovulation is imminent and the possibility of conception is high; DES will act as an antiovulatory agent and render fertilization impossible, because the sperm will have died by the time a fertilizable ovum is available. DES also renders the endometrium of the uterus hostile to implantation.

Consequently, the act of administering DES has *two* possible effects: antiovulatory; and abortifacient. In the second edition of their book *Health Care Ethics*,[39] Benedict M. Ashley and Kevin D. O'Rourke conclude: "DES or antiovulant drugs may not be used [in a Catholic Healthcare facility] with the intention of suppressing ovulation unless (a) the physicians responsible have been convinced by reliable research that these drugs have a significant antiovulatory effect and (b) it is doubtful that fertilization has already occurred... Because such treatment is controversial, if the woman herself or the medical staff object on the grounds of a conscientious desire not to risk abortion, their consciences should be respected."

## (III) RU-486

In April of 1991 the Holy See sent a report to all Bishops' Conferences throughout the world on RU-486.[40] The report was developed at the Vatican's request by Gonzalo Herranz, a Spanish bioethicist.[41] We will follow here Professor Herranz's treatment of this subject.

The compound RU-486 is the first "abortion pill." The product was developed in the laboratories of the French firm Roussel Uclaf (from which its name derives). Its scientific name is *mifetriftone*, and in France it is sold under the trade name *Mifegyne*.

RU-486 is a synthetic steroid with very unique anti-hormonal properties (anti-progesterone). It combines naturally at the receptor with the progesterone present in the tissues upon which it acts, including the endometrium, and annuls the action of the progesterone. Since the continued action of this hormone is necessary to continue gestation, especially during the first trimester, administering RU-486 in a sufficient amount can cause early abortion. This is its most well-known action, but not the only one.

RU-486 has other effects. When administered following certain patterns, it can act as a contraceptive. Also, when used in large doses it has an anti-glucocorticoid effect which gives it a certain potential, although it is not fully confirmed, in the treatment of some illnesses.

The principal use that has been made up until now of RU-486 and its effect that has been studied the most is the induction of early abortion. When RU-486 is used alone, the rate of success is too low. It induces incomplete abortions in 15% of women when administered within 5 weeks of amenorrhea (suppression of the menstrual discharge). However, the rate of failure rises to more than 60% when abortion is induced at 9 weeks of amenorrhea.

RU-486 causes an increase in the uterus' sensitivity to other abortion-inducing agents: prostaglandins. When RU-486 and a prostaglandin are used together, the effectiveness grows markedly. A single dose of 600 milligrams of RU-486, followed a day and a half or two days after by an injection of 0.25 milligram of sulprostone or a vaginal suppository of 1 milligram of gemeprost, will produce a complete abortion in most women. This treatment is accompanied by side effects of varying importance: pain that requires analgesia during expulsion of the fetus, hemorrhage which is on the average of 80 milliliters and lasts from one to two weeks. New combinations of RU-486 with prostaglandins are being studied and tested clinically in order to lessen these undesirable effects.

In France (figures from May 1990), induced abortions through the combination of RU-486 and prostaglandin amounted to 45,000. In 1990, nearly 1,000 a week were carried out, which means that this technique is being applied in 1 out of every 3 or 4 abortions. The pregnancy must be of less than 7 weeks. Women are *required* to give their consent to undergo a surgical abortion in the event that the treatment fails or significant hemorrhages are produced.

At this point, some say that only two cases have presented serious complications out of 30,000 abortions induced by RU-486. Others rate serious complications at 5 per 1,000 cases. Significant hemorrhage occurs in 10% of the women treated, out of which 1 in 100 requires a transfusion. Among 5%-20% of cases, the fetus is retained, *and surgical evacuation is required.*

The conclusions reached until now require that early abortion with RU-486 always be done under medical control since frequent complications are to be expected. Until now, these have hindered the free commercialization of RU-486 and thus the possibility of "abortion at home." The complications and the need for a post-abortion ultra-sound control to verify if the abortion was complete are such that RU-486 cannot be used in countries with poor human medical resources, contrary to the desires of some who would see in it the ideal method for abortion in the Third World.

Pre-treatment with RU-486 facilitates abortion in the second trimester induced by the extra-amniotic infusion of prostaglandins in such a way that a marked reduction is obtained both in the interval between inducement and abortion as well as in the total quantity of prostaglandin used.

This method is called by some *pharmacological abortion*. At the moment, the use of RU-486 as a contraceptive remains in the realm of speculation. The necessary clinical requirements have not been carried out yet for verifying and evaluating comparatively its possible capacity as a contraceptive. It seems that the systematic use of RU-486 as a "post-coital contraceptive" or in harmony with the less traumatic designation as a "menstrual inducer" or "monthly contraceptive in a single dose (month-after pill)" must be discarded since it shows *a priori* an insufficient theoretical efficiency, estimated at a 4% failure rate. In reality, the mechanism of RU-486's action which would be taken in the last 4 days of the cycle, in these circumstances would not be contraceptive but anti-implanting or very early abortifacient. In order to act like an efficient monthly contraceptive pill (abortifacient), RU-486 would have to be associated with an anti-hormone freer of gonadotropin or an oral prostaglandin.

For the pro-abortion groups, where surgical abortion is safe, cheap and quick, RU-486 would guarantee a greater ability to choose and, they assure with excessive optimism, the opportunity of having an abortion in private. Those groups postulate that if pharmacological abortion were to arrive at the desired 100% effectiveness and 0% complications, it would be converted into a predominant form of abortion — private, domestic, not medicalized and economical — with obvious effects on population control.

With purely wishful arguments, population controllers state that the "abortion pill" will make abortion more accessible and safer in developing countries and therefore will be very much in demand. It would thus contribute to halting population growth and at the same time avoid a great part of the alleged 100,000 to 200,000 deaths that those countries pay yearly for unsafe or clandestine surgical abortion. However, in the current state of abortion by RU-486, it requires as much or more medical support than surgical abortion, which makes the illusion fade about RU-486 as an easy means of population control.

Many groups see in RU-486 the first step for woman toward making herself truly the absolute mistress of her reproductive capacity. Such groups proclaim the advent of a true reproductive freedom that would arrive when a safe abortion pill were available, freely dispensed, which the pharmacist gives without any medical prescription. This pill would make the guilt feelings disappear that are connected with abortion. Women would no longer have to worry themselves about whether they have conceived or not. Each month they would proceed to clean out their uterus chemically without having to ask any help from the doctor. In this way, women's absolute autonomy would be consecrated with regard to reproductive processes.

Nonetheless, it is doubtful that abortion, including early and deliberately inadvertent abortion, can be seen as free from any psychological traumas. Even though its emotional impact may in some women be less grave than those produced by surgical abortion, with its burden of going to a clinic, undergoing anesthesia and feeling one's body invaded, abortion at home is not free from tension and anxiety. It is the woman herself who, all alone and urgently, takes on the whole psychological and ethical burden of being the sole agent of abortion and who has to wait anxiously for the effect of the treatment. Demedicalized abortion leaves the woman abandoned to herself and in the uncomfortable company of fear, pain and the risk of hemorrhage. The abortion pill favors a woman's privacy and secret, but it condemns her to solitude.

In order to exploit the therapeutic possibilities of RU-486, in some laboratories basic research is proceeding to study new aspects of its interaction with different tissues and functions. Those who are interested in selling RU-486 already know that from the viewpoint of social psychology it would be good to find other clinical uses for the molecule that will redeem it from its "bad reputation" of being an abortifacient and contraceptive. In fact, some clinical uses of RU-486 are already known now.[42] From an ethical point of view, the circumstances in which procured abortion is carried out, whether by a surgical procedure or a chemical agent, do not modify substantially the moral gravity of the action. Consequently, the ethical and moral condemnation of abortion falls, integrally and without any attenuating circumstances, on the abortion produced by RU-486, or on any other chemical compound capable of abortifacient action, with the appearance of a medication that may be used in the future for the purpose of causing an abortion.

Many attempt to annul the sinful nature of abortion by hiding the fact of destroying human life under the veil of new and innocent expressions such as *micro-aspiration, menstrual extraction, voluntary interruption of gestation, menstrual regulation, interception, menstrual pill.* It is considered impolite and in bad taste to speak with regard to abortion about killing, assassinating or destroying human beings, since that terminology indicates that the values have not been grasped of individual autonomy, the right to choose, progressive humanization, population control and ecology.

The introduction and dissemination of chemical abortion in today's society *also requires a terminology of its own.* RU-486's developer Dr. Etienne-Emile Baulieu specifically coined the term *contragestion* in order to designate tactically the abortion induced by RU-486. This new term is required for two reasons: one is the advisability in dealing with RU-486 not to make the slightest reference to abortion; the other is that of pointing out the fact that the abortion pill does not constitute, because it is abortifacient, a novelty in the field of birth control. Baulieu himself has stated, "(T)he use of words with regard to abortion such as *assassination* or *killing* only serve to obscure the real terms of a problem that only has to do with health. For that reason, we have proposed the term *contragestion*, a contraction of *contra-gestation* in order to designate the majority of methods for controlling fertility. It is hoped that the new term will serve to avoid the discussion from degenerating."[43] The intention is obviously to amoralize and thereby place the transmission of human life into an ethically neutral terrain and reduce it to pure biology.

The Vatican report quotes Professor Herranz himself:

> The significance of this type of abortion is extremely important. It will establish as an admitted social fact that the human embryo is a mere product of debris. Not only is the embryo made into a thing, stripping it of all its human value, it is reduced to the negative condition of an excrement. In the same way that a laxative is capable of freeing a sluggish colon of its fecal content, the new pill will enable the gestating uterus to free itself from the embryo growing in it... The transmission of human life, man's supreme capacity to co-create men, that sharing in God's creative power, will be converted into a function of the same physiological, psychological and moral level as micturition or defecation.[44]

## (IV) A Pill for Men

For a number of years, there has been research and testing on using hormones as male contraceptives in order to decrease sperm production. *Vanazol* is a drug that cuts production of male hormone, and thus sperm production. At the same time, it decreases male sexual interest when administered on a daily basis. The mechanism involves suppression of FSH and LH (ICFH) by the pituitary,[45] but when men using this drug are given a monthly shot of destosterone, a healthy sex drive is maintained. The dosage of destosterone, however, must be carefully monitored because too much of it will stimulate sperm production and undo the contraceptive effect of Vanazol. Some researchers, instead of seeking to reduce the number of sperm, are studying ways to keep sperm from moving after they leave the testes. At the present time, no effective male pill has been discovered.

### E. Implants

Contraceptive implants are small capsules that are placed in a woman's upper arm just under the skin. NORPLANT was approved by the FDA in late 1990. These implants slowly release a small amount of progestin and remain effective in preventing pregnancy for up to five years after insertion. Like other progestin-based methods, they act through inhibiting ovulation, promoting thickening of the cervical mucus and deceleration of ovum transport, and inhibiting implantation of a fertilized ovum. Implants' most common side effects are the same as those associated with the progestin-only minipill — irregular bleeding and spotting and amenorrhea.

### F. Injectables

Injectables contain either progestin alone or progestin and estrogen. Medroxyprogesterone acetate (DEPO-Provera, or DMPA) is the most commonly used formulation; norethindrone enanthate (NET) is another. The mode of action and side effects of progestin-alone injectables are similar to those of the minipill and implants. Many long-term users develop amenorrhea. DEPO-Provera has been approved by the FDA for use in the treatment of a number of gynecologic conditions and at menopause, but not as a contraceptive. However, since it is approved for other uses, physicians may prescribe it for contraceptive purposes. Each injection maintains its contraceptive effect for approximately three months, at which time the user must return to a doctor or clinic for another injection.

### G. Surgical Methods

#### (1) Tubal Sterilization or Ligation

Tubal sterilization, also called "tying of the fallopian tubes," involves a surgical procedure in which sections of each fallopian tube are blocked or severed so that the ovum and sperm are not able to meet. It can be performed postpartum or at a time not associated with a delivery. An internal sterilization — one not associated with the postpartum period — can be performed under local anesthesia on an outpatient basis. Sutures, electrocoagulation, clips, bands or rings are used to close or sever the tubes. Tubal ligation or sterilization must be viewed as a permanent method. Although the two ends of the tubes can sometimes be reconnected by microsurgery (depending on the type of technique used, the length of fallopian tube destroyed during the sterilization operation, and the location of the tubal destruction), the surgery can be complicated, expensive and difficult, and success cannot be guaranteed.

In addition to the "traditional methods of tying the tubes," there is also the possibility of the use of chemicals that solidify in the tubes, caps that cover the ends of the tubes, and lasers that heat and destroy a portion of the tubes. Various plastic and ceramic plugs have also been designed for blocking the tubes.

In addition to sterilization by tying the tubes, many women have been sterilized by the surgical procedure known as *hysterectomy*, the surgical removal of the uterus. It is estimated that one-third of all women in the United States have had a hysterectomy by the age of 65. This operation is performed in one of two ways: through an incision in the abdominal wall or through the vagina. The ovaries are left in place, unless there is some medical reason for their removal, so the secretion of female sex hormones remains normal. Hysterectomy is usually not performed solely as a means of sterilization, however, but is done because of some medical problem, such as tumor removal.

Some word needs to be added here regarding the issue of uterine isolation. The specific concern is as follows: Is the isolation of the uterus by tubal ligation morally licit when, because of a number of caesarian sections, the organ itself is weakened to the point of not being further able to bring a pregnancy to term or to be able to do so only with grave danger to the woman?

In the 1940s and before, there had been considerable debate among moral theologians with regard to the situation of a woman whose uterus had been so damaged and weakened by repeated caesarian sections that eventually, on the occasion of another section, the obstetrician would judge that the uterus could no longer be adequately repaired so as to safely support another pregnancy. The moral question was whether or not a hysterectomy, under these conditions, was indeed a contraceptive sterilization; or was it rather the legitimate removal of a dangerously pathological organ?

The leading proponent of the view that such a hysterectomy was indeed a contraceptive sterilization was Father Francis Connell, C.SS.R., Professor of Moral Theology at the Catholic University of America. Father Connell maintained that the damaged uterus did not constitute a danger unless the woman became pregnant and therefore the pregnancy was the cause of the danger.

Father Gerald Kelly, S.J., Professor of Moral Theology at St. Mary's, Kansas, opposed this opinion with the argument that pregnancy was rather the occasion of the danger, the cause of which was the damaged uterus itself. He therefore proposed, as a solidly probable opinion, that the dangerously pathological uterus could legitimately be removed in the same way as any other dangerously pathological organ, even though in this case it was a uterus. He thus maintained that the damage in the uterus itself constituted a legitimate application of the principle of totality, without the consequent sterility being directly intended, but rather being a moral "by-product" and to be viewed legitimately as indirect, under the principle of double effect.

Meanwhile, another moral aspect of the same case of the damaged uterus was being explored. The subsequent question under investigation was whether, in the event that the clinical condition of such a patient contraindicated further surgery (hysterectomy) at the time of the caesarian section — even though hysterectomy was morally indicated because of the damaged and weakened uterus — the surgeon might legitimately isolate the uterus at the tubal adnexa. The rationale of this argument was that there was no moral difference between thus isolating the uterus and removing it. It was pointed out that the hysterectomy part of the surgical technique consists in the clamping and cutting of the fallopian tubes in the process of freeing the uterus. When this has been done, the damaged uterus has already been functionally isolated and at that point one has already passed through the moral issue involved. Whether or not the uterus is now actually removed from the pelvic cavity is without moral significance.

The moral question is precisely this: If the uterus can be removed after repeated caesarian sections because of the danger of rupture, could the procedure be simplified for sound clinical reasons by leaving the uterus *in situ*, and simply isolating the uterus from the fallopian tubes? This could be done by a simple surgical separation procedure whereby the tubes are cut or ligated. The clinical reasons for the simple procedure, as compared to the potentially serious surgical removal of the uterus, could include the fact that the simple cutting or ligating of the tubes would obviate the danger (as in a hysterectomy) of adhesions and the possible need of blood transfusions. In some cases, the woman may be so weakened after a difficult caesarian delivery, that proceeding with the hysterectomy at that time would be contraindicated. An additional reason favoring tubal section or ligation could be a psychological one: the woman may be unduly disturbed and depressed by somehow equating the loss of her uterus with the loss of her womanhood.

It thus seemed reasonable to many authors to conclude that in some particular cases when hysterectomy could be allowed, "uterine isolation" could be chosen as an approved substitute. Father Thomas O'Donnell, S.J., expresses a caution in all of this:

> The legitimate concept of "uterine isolation" applies *only* to the instance in which hysterectomy is indicated because of dangerous pathology within the uterus..., and in which the isolation of the uterus would be an acceptable clinical substitute for a morally and

clinically defensible hysterectomy (in *Medicine and Christian Morality*, p 134).

A key point in this whole argument is obviously the establishment of pathology in the uterus itself: that is, the uterus has been so scarred because of multiple caesarian sections that it cannot reasonably sustain another pregnancy and delivery. From a clinical point of view, organs are by definition essentially functional and not static and thus the terms "pathological" and "non-pathological" have meaning only in relation to whether the organ in question can properly fulfill the function for which it was intended. Many clinicians thus conclude that a uterus which is diseased but which can still fulfill its function is pathological, and a uterus which is so scarred or diseased that it cannot fulfill its intended function at all is by medical definition a *serious* pathology.

The eminent moralist, Father John Connery, S.J., posed the moral question in this way: Does the fact that the organ is pathological prior to the pregnancy make the sterilization indirect even though the danger arises only in connection with pregnancy? He answered the question, "We think that it does." It was Father Connery's position that in such a case, even though the danger comes from pregnancy, since it is associated with the pathology in the uterus, the sterilization is indirect. For Fr. Connery, when the *only* site of the pathology is in the uterus itself *and* when the danger to the woman's well-being or life originates *only* from within the uterus which is now pregnant, and not from some other pathological organ, it is justifiable under the principle of double effect to isolate the uterus rather than perform a hysterectomy. The direct effect of the action and the intention of the surgeon are therapeutic in nature and, therefore, only indirectly contraceptive.

Father Connery and others thus concluded:

(1) That the scarred uterus is pathological in itself, and as such, posed a threat to the health and well-being of the woman;
(2) That tubal ligation was the least invasive way of responding to this threat;
(3) Though a future pregnancy could exacerbate this pre-

existing condition, such a pregnancy was not the cause of the pathology; and
(4) As a result, it would be possible to utilize the principle of double effect in this instance: that is, that the tubal ligation has the direct effect of removing the pathology and only secondarily would it have the *unintended* effect of causing sterility.

Contrary to this argument is the position that the pathology present in the uterus does not constitute an immediate danger to the woman, but rather a more remote danger that becomes present only when pregnancy occurs as the result of sexual intercourse freely entered into by the spouses. In this understanding, such tubal ligation/isolation would be direct sterilization and always illicit. In this way of understanding the moral dilemma, these points are espoused: (1) that the uterus itself does not propose any grave danger to the woman; and (2) that the danger derives solely from the possibility of conception and not from the pathology of the uterus itself: that is, such pathology that does exist is not a grave danger for the woman and is a remote threat that is effectively actuated only by means of an eventual conception which is itself the result of an act of freedom.

In February 1992, Thomas W. Hilgers, M.D. presented a paper at the Eleventh Bishops' Workshop in Dallas, Texas, entitled: "Family Planning Issues: Norplant, Uterine Isolation, and Natural Family Planning." In his treatment of uterine isolation, Hilgers concludes that this practice of uterine isolation is "nothing but direct contraceptive sterilization." Hilgers explains that one of the most important questions that needs to be asked with regard to uterine isolation is, "What are we isolating from?" He replies that it is clear that the uterus is not being isolated from either the sperm or the ovum since they pose no potential of risk. It is equally clear that isolation of the uterus, so proposed, is not isolating the uterus from any known disease condition. The only possible thing that this procedure could be isolating the uterus from is a pregnancy. He concludes, "Thus, it seems equally clear that the primary intent of such a uterine isolation is contraceptive."

I would propose personally that the *fact* of a pregnancy existing in a patient who has previously undergone caesarian delivery does not *in itself* constitute a type of "pathological" condition. A uterus previously operated upon, as in the case of caesarian section, bears a "scar" which it did not previously have. To this degree, the uterus would not be "normal." To the same degree, normality would depart from any organ with a "scar" that was created surgically.

Given this point, it is unreasonable to state that a repeat caesarian section represents *per se* a pathological state that should be treated as such. This "non-normal" condition is complicated by reference to the type of uterine scar: whether it is vertical (midline) or horizontal (transverse) in the lower uterine segment. Most scars are of this latter type. In the midline type, most authorities advocate a repeat caesarian section; whereas in the transverse type the patient is a more ready candidate for vaginal birth after a caesarian (VBAC). Consequently, what was once thought of as a "pathological state" of the uterus is less significant in current thinking on the subject.

In the United States in general, it is rare to have repeat caesarian section constitute a pathological condition, making a future pregnancy truly dangerous. The question of uterine isolation must therefore be answered within *this* context.

Very infrequently, an obstetrician may encounter a uterus so altered by previous surgery that it literally cannot be repaired. More commonly, but still relatively infrequent, an obstetrician may find that the uterus, while technically repairable, is of such a nature, due to past caesarian-induced "scarring" that it would not appear likely to sustain a subsequent gestation, if it were to occur.

Such rare discoveries may necessitate the removal of the uterus, sometimes referred to as a caesarian hysterectomy. In the face of the possibility of such a cataclysmic uterine rupture, of course, this life-threatening situation exists only if there is a subsequent pregnancy.

## *(II) Vasectomy*

Male sterilization involves cutting and sealing the *vas deferens*, a narrow tube through which the sperm travel from the testes, so that sperm will not be present in the ejaculate. A vasectomy is a simple medical procedure that usually takes place in a doctor's office or outpatient clinic under local anesthesia. Complications that may occur are almost always minor and of brief duration — mainly swelling, discolorization and discomfort. It is impossible, however, to estimate the psychological complications sustained by men who have vasectomies. Vasectomy, too, should be considered a permanent method. Reversal is sometimes possible, but the surgery is costly, and success cannot be guaranteed.

The procedure involves a small amount of local anesthetic injected into each side of the scrotum, and a small incision is made on each side in order to reach the *vas deferens*. Each vas is then tied in two places, and a segment between is removed in order to prevent the two cut ends from growing together again. After this operation sperm will no longer be able to travel through the vas from the testes.

No change in sexual functioning occurs as a result of vasectomy. The sex glands continue to function normally, secreting male sex hormones *into the blood*. Ejaculation still occurs because the seminal fluid contributed by the testes through the vas only accounts for about 10% of the total volume. The only difference is that the semen will be free of sperm. Sperm may still be present two or three months after a vasectomy because they are stored in the reproductive system beyond the vas, but these sperm can be flushed out with water or with a sperm-immobilizing agent during the vasectomy. Once these remaining sperm are gone, vasectomy is 100% effective, assuming the procedure is performed correctly.

## 5. NATURAL FAMILY PLANNING

Number 9 of *Humanae Vitae* clearly outlines the characteristic "marks and requirements of conjugal love":

1. This love is first of all fully *human*; that is to say, it is at the same time both physical and spiritual. It is not, therefore, a simple transport of instinct and feeling but also, and principally, an act of the free will, destined to endure and to grow by means of the joys and sorrows of daily life, in such a way that husband and wife become one heart and one soul, and together attain their human perfection.

2. This love is *total*; that is to say, it is a very special form of personal friendship, in which husband and wife generously

share everything, without undue reservations or selfish calculations. Whoever truly loves his spouse, does not love her only for what he receives from her but for herself, happy to be able to enrich her with the gift of himself.

3. This love is also *faithful* and *exclusive* until death. Such in fact do bride and groom conceive it to be on the day when they freely and with full awareness assume the commitment of the marriage bond.

4. This is a love which is *fruitful* and is not exhausted by the communion between husband and wife. Rather is it destined to perpetuate itself by bringing new lives into existence: "Marriage and conjugal love are by their nature ordained to the procreation and rearing of children. Indeed, children are the most precious gift of marriage and contribute immensely to the good of the parents themselves."[46]

In light of these basic "marks," *Humanae Vitae* then indicates in number 16:

(T)he Church is the first to praise and recommend the intervention of intelligence in a work that so closely associates the rational creature with his Creator; but she affirms that this must be done with respect for the order established by God.

If, then, there are serious motives for spacing births, motives deriving from the physical or psychological conditions of husband or wife, or from external circumstances, the Church teaches that it is then permissible to take into account the natural rhythms immanent in the generative functions and to make use of marriage during the infertile times only, and in this way to regulate births without offending the moral principles that we have just recalled.

The Church is consistent when she considers recourse to the infertile times to be permissible, while condemning as always wrong the use of means directly contrary to fertilization, even if such use is inspired by reasons that can appear upright and serious. In reality, there is an essential difference between the two cases. In the first case, the husband and wife legitimately avail themselves of a natural condition; in the second case, they impede the working of natural processes. It is true that in both cases the husband and wife agree and positively will to avoid children for acceptable reasons, seeking to be certain that offspring will not result; but it is likewise true that only in the first case do they prove able to abstain from the use of marriage during the fertile times, when for proper motives procreation is not desirable, then making use of it during the infertile times to manifest affection and to safeguard mutual fidelity. By so doing, they give proof of a love that is truly and fully virtuous.

In light of this teaching, it is critical to help those contemplating marriage and married couples to have a positive appreciation of responsible parenthood through natural family planning (NFP). Pope John Paul II called for such assistance in his 1981 exhortation *Familiaris Consortio.* Number 35 reminds the bishops and faithful alike about the urgent need for a "broader, more decisive and systematic effort to make the natural methods for regulating fertility known, respected and applied." The Pope reiterated this exhortation to "responsibility for love and for life..." in his 14 December 1990 address in Rome on Natural Family Planning.[47] In this address, the Pope indicates in part:

(P)eriodic continence, practiced to regulate procreation in a natural way, requires a profound understanding of the person and of love. In truth that requires mutual listening and dialogue by spouses, attention and sensitivity for the other spouse and constant self-control: All of these are qualities which express real love for the person of the spouse for what he or she is, and not for what one may wish the other to be. The practice of natural methods requires personal growth by the spouses in a joint effort to strengthen their love.

This intrinsic connection between science and moral virtue constitutes the specific and morally qualifying element for recourse to natural methods. It is a part of the complete integral training of teachers and of couples, and, in it, it should be clear that what is of concern here is more than just simple "instruction" divorced from the moral values proper to teaching people about love. In short, it allows people to see that it is not possible to practice natural methods as a "licit" variation on the decision to be closed to life, which would be substantially the same as that which inspires the decision to use contraceptives: Only if there is a basic openness to fatherhood and motherhood, understood as collaboration with the Creator, does the use of natural means become an integrating part of the responsibility for love and life.[48]

It is critically important, from both a moral and pastoral viewpoint, to appreciate the difference between NFP and contraception. In *Familiaris Consortio*, Pope John Paul II teaches: "It [the difference between contraception and the rhythm method] is a difference which is much wider and deeper than is usually thought, one which involves in the final analysis *two irreconcilable concepts of the human person and of human sexuality.*"[49] The Pope goes on to assert that those who use contraception manipulate human sexuality, while those who legitimately regulate births through NFP achieve human love at its deepest level. Why is this so?

What distinguishes an act of contraceptive intercourse from an act of non-contraceptive intercourse is that the former involves the choice to do something before, during, or after the act which destroys the possibility of conception precisely because it is believed that such a choice will indeed negate the possibility of conception.[50] In other words, contraception involves the execution of a choice to exclude conception from an act which by nature involves that possibility: i.e., conception is considered to be an unacceptable possibility here and now. All acts of contraceptive intercourse are anti-generative kinds of acts.

G.E.M. Anscombe argues in *Contraception and Chastity*:[51]

The reason why people are confused about intention, and why they sometimes think there is no difference between contraceptive intercourse and the use of infertile times to avoid conception, is this: They don't notice the difference between "intention" when it means the intentionalness of the thing you're doing — but *you're doing this on purpose* — and when it means a *further* or *accompanying* intention *with* which you do a thing.... Contraceptive intercourse and intercourse using infertile times may be alike in respect of further intention, and these further intentions may be good, justified, excellent... But contraceptive intercourse is faulted, not on account of this further intention, but because of the kind of intentional action you are doing. The action is not left by you as the kind of act by which life is transmitted, but is purposely rendered infertile, and so changed to another sort of act altogether.

The difference, then, between contraceptive intercourse and non-contraceptive intercourse is between their respective present intentions, the intentions inherent in the action that is now being performed apart from any accompanying intentions which may or may not be present. The act of contraception *embodies* the intention of avoiding conception and so makes the coital act a different kind of act (anti-generative) from that which would result if that intention were not operative. Moreover, the intention embodied in the action is a cause or a part-cause of the infertility of the act; the further circumstances which determine the fertility of the act (since not every intrinsically generative kind of act is, in fact, "fertile") include the intention as a cause.[52]

Non-contraceptive intercourse reveals a different structure. It is an intrinsically generative kind of act both physically and intentionally. There may be a further intention to avoid conception (as could be the case in NFP), but the act itself does not embody the present intention to avoid conception as is the case when there is interference by artificial birth control. The further intention to avoid conception does not cause infertility since the act is found to be infertile on its own. The intention to avoid conception is manifested in the determination to avoid intercourse during the woman's fertile period, but this choice does nothing to the sexual intercourse that is chosen during infertile periods to render it anti-generative. Moreover, it should be noted that the choice not to contracept, even when no conception is desired, reveals a fundamentally different attitude toward the procreative aspect of the conjugal act.

Consequently, the essential difference between contraceptive intercourse and non-contraceptive intercourse is located in the intentional structure of the act *as* a human act; the issue is in no way determined by mere biological or physical factors. In *Love and Responsibility*, Pope John Paul II indicates:

> This norm, in its negative aspect, states that the person is the kind of good which does not admit of use and cannot be treated as an object of use and as such the means to an end. In its positive form the

personalistic norm confirms this: The person is a good toward which
the only proper and adequate attitude is love. The positive content
of the personalistic norm is precisely what the commandment to love
teaches.[53]

Within the context of marriage as the lasting union of persons
involving the possibility of procreation, sexual relations must be
evaluated according to this norm as the safeguard against utilitarianism (treating the person as an object). The inseparability of the unitive
and procreative aspects of the marital act is predicated upon this
principle. *Love and Responsibility* thus maintains, "Neither in the
man nor in the woman can affirmation of the value of the person be
divorced from awareness and willingness and willing acceptance that
he may become a father and that she may become a mother."[54] True
personal love demands both the conscious acceptance of the other as
a potential parent and the conscious donation of the self as a potential
parent. If the possibility of parenthood is deliberately excluded from
marital relations by contraception, than the character of the relationship changes radically. The transformation is from a relationship of
authentic personal love toward a utilitarian relationship of mutual
enjoyment which is incompatible with the personalistic norm articulated in *Love and Responsibility*. John Paul II also noted in *Familiaris
Consortio*:

> When couples, by means of recourse to contraception, separate these
> two meanings that God the Creator has inscribed in the being of man
> and woman and in the dynamism of their sexual communion, they
> act as "arbiters" of a divine plan and they "manipulate" and degrade
> human sexuality and with it themselves and their married partner by
> altering its value of "total" self-giving... Thus the innate language
> that expresses the total reciprocal self-giving of husband and wife is
> overlaid, through contraception, by an objectively contradictory
> language, namely, that of not giving oneself totally to the other.[55]

We spoke earlier in this book about sexuality as language. This
concept is reflected in the following remark of Pope John Paul II in
*Reflections on Humanae Vitae*:[56]

It can be said that in the case of an artificial separation of these two aspects, there is carried out in the conjugal act a real bodily union, but it does not correspond to the interior truth and to the dignity of personal communion: communion of persons. This communion demands in fact that the "language of the body" be expressed reciprocally in the integral truth of its meaning. If this truth be lacking, one cannot speak either of the truth of self-mastery, or of the reciprocal gift and of the reciprocal acceptance of self on the part of the other person. Such a violation of the interior order of conjugal union, which is rooted in the very order of the person, constitutes the essential evil of the contraceptive act.

In contrast to the dualist anthropology and separatist understanding of sexuality which undergirds the contraceptive position, the foundations of NFP are personalist and integralist. To regulate births by reading the "language of the body" in truth is a ministration of God's plan which respects the good of the other by respecting the natural dynamism of the marital act toward true self-giving.

NFP is based on the virtue of continence or marital chastity not simply because of the requirement of periodic abstinence, but rather because it is only by mature self-possession of one's psychosomatic subjectivity that the sexual union truly becomes a personal union. The virtue of marital chastity is not a priggish "refraining from," but rather a positive "capacity for." It does not detract from personal love, but rather enhances it. Personal love and chastity are inseparable. John Paul II summarizes this point:

If conjugal chastity (and chastity in general) is manifested at first as the capacity to resist the concupiscence of the flesh, it later gradually reveals itself as a singular capacity to perceive, love and practice those meanings of the "language of the body" which remain altogether unknown to concupiscence itself and which progressively enrich the marital dialogue of the couple, purifying it, deepening it, and at the same time simplifying it. Therefore, that asceticism of continence, of which the encyclical speaks (*Humanae Vitae*, n 21), does not impoverish "effective manifestations," but rather makes them spiritually more intense and therefore enriches them.[57]

A critically important technique of NFP is that of the ovulation method or the Billings method, named after Doctors John and Evelyn Billings, who came to the realization that a women's vaginal mucus serves as a reliable indicator of the hormonal changes which occur at the time of ovulation. Women can easily be taught how to use this method, and an international group, World Organization of the Ovulation Method-Billings (WOOMB), is engaged in the dissemination of this information.[58] Thomas W. Hilgers, M. D., gives the following basic description of the ovulation method for discovering the time of fertility:[59]

1.  The menstrual period at the start of each cycle is considered to be fertile. The reason for viewing the time of menstruation as fertile is that if a woman should have an unusually or unexpectedly short cycle such that the ovulation process were to begin toward the end of menstruation, she would have no warning of this fact since the presence of the menstrual flow would make it difficult for her to examine her vaginal mucus. Thus, as a precaution, women are advised to regard the menstrual period as fertile.

2.  After menstruation, there is a noticeable absence of any vaginal discharge of mucus, and a woman experiences a definite sensation of dryness. During these days of dryness, the woman is infertile.

3.  At the conclusion of this period of dryness, cervical mucus begins to be discharged from the vagina. At first, this mucus is a kind of cloudy, sticky discharge, but it gradually becomes a clear, egg-white, stretchy and lubricative substance. The "peak" or main sign of ovulation is the last day on which this clear and stretchy mucus is present. The women's period of fertility, however, is defined as starting with the first day of the cloudy mucus discharge and continuing up until three days past the peak symptom of ovulation.

4.  From the fourth day after the peak symptom until the start of the next menstrual cycle, a period of infertility occurs.

There are a number of positive considerations in support of NFP:[60]

1. Because couples must be well motivated and mutually cooperative in the use of such methods, the responsibility for family planning clearly comes to rest on both spouses, which is where it belongs.
2. As a result of their increased awareness of, and sensitivity to, their bodies and their natural biological rhythms, many women experience an enhanced sense of personal dignity.
3. The need for periodic abstinence in their lives can encourage spouses to explore and deepen the affective dimension of their sexual lives so that they come to find a true sexual and human fulfillment even when their expressions of love are intentionally directed away from any genital involvement that would encourage or promote orgasm.
4. The presence of periodic abstinence in their lives can help to insure that spouses do not fall victims to a dull sexual routine; the joyful anticipation of renewing their genital relations after a period of abstinence may inspire married couples to more vibrant, exciting and creative acts of love.[61]

## CHAPTER FIVE

# WHAT IS HOMOSEXUALITY?

## 1. SETTING THE SCENE

At his trial Oscar Wilde defined homosexuality as "the love that dares not speak its name."[1] The *Letter to the Bishops of the Catholic Church on the Pastoral Care of Homosexual Persons* of the Congregation for the Doctrine of the Faith[2] begins by stating, "The issue of homosexuality and the moral evaluation of homosexual acts have increasingly become a matter of public debate, even in Catholic circles."[3] Richard A. McCormick, S.J. has indicated that "The inability to deal with homosexuality in an honest, clear way is a symbol of the Church's difficulty to deal in a broader way with sexuality in general."[4] James T. Hanigan recently published a book titled *Homosexuality: The Test Case for Christian Sexual Ethics*.[5] In *Embracing the Exile*, John E. Fortunato writes, "For some gay Christians the pain of their journeys may have been greater; for some it is much less. Their story lines probably go very differently. But my guess is that the major components are common to us all... The denial of our gayness for some period. The questioning of our faith. The seeming irreconcilability of our sexual and spiritual selves. The schizophrenia. The feelings of unworthiness. The guilt. The loneliness. The hiding. The closets. And a sense of being on the fringes, cut off, banished. The story within the story belongs to all of us who are gay."[6] In 1935, in his compassionate "Letter to an American Mother" whose son was homosexual Sigmund Freud wrote:

> Homosexuality is assuredly no advantage, but it is nothing to be ashamed of, no vice, no degradation, it cannot be classified as an

illness... Many highly respected individuals of ancient and modern times have been homosexuals, several of the greatest men among them (Plato, Michelangelo, Leonardo da Vinci, etc.). It is a great injustice to persecute homosexuality as a crime, and cruelty too.[7]

Needless to say, from just this brief overview, homosexuality is an extremely sensitive, delicate and complicated phenomenon. To treat homosexuality differently is to deal with this question with less than an attitude of respect, nuance and analysis that is truly called for.

Although Freud equivocated about whether or not homosexuality was in itself pathological, he did not consider homosexuals as "sick." In a 1903 interview published in the newspaper *Die Zeit* he stated:

> I am... of the firm conviction that homosexuals must not be treated as sick people... Wouldn't that oblige us to characterize as sick many great thinkers and scholars... whom we admire precisely because of their mental health? Homosexual persons are not sick.[8]

Who is a homosexual person? Definitions vary widely and thus it is helpful to view *examples* of the types of "definitions" that one finds:

1. Homosexuals are "those individuals who more or less chronically feel an urgent sexual desire towards, and a sexual responsiveness to, members of their own sex, and who seek gratification of this desire predominantly with members of their own sex..."[9]
2. A homosexual is "one who is motivated, in adult life, by a definite preferential erotic attraction to members of the same sex and who usually (but not necessarily) engages in overt sexual relations with them..."[10]
3. Homosexuality is "a *preference* on the part of *adults*, for *sexual behavior* with members of their own sex."[11]
4. Homosexuals are persons "who feel comfortable and affirmed when intimate with other members of the same sex, while with the other sex, they feel weak, resentful, scared, or simply indifferent, or less comfortable when genital intimacy is possible or occurs..."[12]

Each of these four "definitions" carries a certain bias. For example, the first definition presumes that homosexuality is a *chronic* condition and thus tends to denote a type of sickness. The second and third definitions use the word *preferential*, thus giving the impression that the homosexual person has made a *choice* regarding his or her sexual orientation. The fourth definition represents a homosexual person as being distant from and resentful toward members of the opposite sex. These so-called definitions all misrepresent the homosexual orientation by including these types of biases.

Although no one "definition" completely captures all that needs to be said about the homosexual orientation, the definition given in the *Encyclopedia of Bioethics* seems to represent the orientation most accurately and unbiasedly:

> A homosexual person sustains "a predominant, persistent and exclusive psychosexual attraction toward members of the same sex. A homosexual person is one who feels sexual desire for and a sexual responsiveness to persons of the same sex and who seeks or would like to seek actual sexual fulfillment of this desire by sexual acts with a person of the same sex."[13]

This definition of homosexuality is a useful one because it contains certain commonly employed understandings: that homosexuality is an integral part of one's psychosexual makeup; this psychosexual orientation indicates a fundamental attraction toward persons of the same sex, but does not preclude an interest in, care for and an attraction toward members of the opposite sex; respects the important distinction that the homosexual person has a desire for and a psychosexual responsiveness to persons of the same sex and would like to act upon this sexual fulfillment, but perhaps might not do so, for any number of complicated reasons. Consequently, a person can be homosexual in orientation without having acted upon this psychosexual attraction.[14]

A further nuance in this definition is important. The *homosexual person* is one who sustains all of the components mentioned in the above definition. On the other hand, a *gay person* is one who has identified himself or herself as homosexual and has made this fact known to at least one other individual. In other words, *gay* designates

persons who have accepted their homosexuality as an integral part of
their personalities, and are privately and to a greater or lesser extent
publicly comfortable being known as homosexual. In psychological
terms, these persons are ego-syntonic with their homosexual orientation. The lesbian person is the female homosexual who has, like the
gay person, accepted her homosexuality as an integral part of her
personality.

While some indicate that the word *gay* has its origins in the
usage given to the 17th century troubadours, the actual origin of this
term remains somewhat obscure. On the other hand, most writers
accept the fact that the word *lesbian* derives from the tradition that the
great poetess, Sappho of Lesbos, was homosexual.

In light of this distinction among *homosexual, gay* and *lesbian*,
the insights of James D. Whitehead and Evelyn Eaton Whitehead in
"Three Passages of Maturity" are pastorally instructive.[15] The
Whiteheads employ the metaphor of a *journey* or passage, an image
well known within biblical stories: e.g., Abraham leaving home; the
Exodus event; the Exile; the Diaspora; the itinerant movements of
Jesus (Matthew 11:1). While we all tend to desire permanence ("Let
us build three tents here," Luke 9:33), as Christians our fidelity is
pledged, since Abraham and Moses, to a God whose revelations
require uprooting and repeated departures. Christians thus recognize
their lives as *journeys* with a direction and a purpose.

A journey normally involves the important paradox of *passage*,
a movement which always involves loss and gain: it is a time of peril
and possibility. During a passage we become vulnerable to both loss
and unexpected grace. The Whiteheads give two examples:

> In the death of a parent we lose our beginning and our security. That
> buffer between us and the world, that guarantor of meaning and
> security, which we may have experienced as often in conflict as in
> affection, is taken from us. We are, at last, orphaned. Stripped
> gradually or suddenly of this important person — this part of myself
> — I may well become disoriented, alone on my life journey in a new
> and frightening way.
>
> In the very different experience of a beginning friendship, a
> similar dynamic is at play: amid the excitement and enthusiasm of
> a deepening relationship we may feel a growing threat. If I admit this

person into my heart, I will have to change. This is not because I am selfish or shallow, but simply because my heart will have a new occupant. Most threatened, perhaps, is my sense of independence: to allow you to into my life I will have to let go of some of how I have been until now.[16]

A passage begins, then, in disorientation and the threat of loss. It matures into a second stage as we allow ourselves to fully experience and to name this loss. The terror of a passage appears in this "in-between time." How do I know I can survive without the security and dependability of my parent? How can I be sure that this growing friendship will be better than my well-defended independence? A passage is a narrow, dark subterranean journey; it is something that we "under go." At the same time, however, this time of vulnerability and loss is also a time of grace. We find unexpected strengths; we are startled by our ability to risk and to trust; we emerge not just different, but stronger.

Using this metaphor of journey/passage, the Whiteheads suggest that there are three passages for an individual who is coming to grips with his or her own homosexual orientation. Before looking at this three-fold concept, it is important to note certain reservations about the way which the Whiteheads present this generally good scenario: first, progression from one stage to another is not simply a natural progression, but a careful process of integration and self-assessment; second, the process of movement from stage one to stages two and three should not be interpreted to endorse homosexual activity; and third, only the most weighty reason justifies the movement into the third stage, especially for one who has made public commitments to a celibate life in the Church.

1. *An Interior Passage*: This first passage is more like a revolution and conversion. This is a passage from the closet of ignorance or denial to the light of self-acceptance. This is the passage when one accepts and defends one's own sexual identity. This passage is interior in two senses: it takes place *within* the individual; and it takes place apart from questions of interpersonal expressions of affection and commitment.

Douglas C. Kimmel suggests that a self-identification as homosexual occurs only in one's early twenties.[17] Daniel Levinson's research also endorses the point that many people today require most of the decade of their twenties to come to a sense of their sexual identity.[18]

2. *A Passage of Intimacy*: A second passage appears in the life journey of homosexuals when they experience an invitation or challenge to share themselves with others. In this second passage one is being led to a mode of presence with *others* where one is known for who one is. In this passage there is both a need and a desire to be known and to be loved for who one is. The Whiteheads point out that this second passage merits "special scrutiny." They write, "A common place in both gay and straight experience is the plunge into a second passage of interpersonal intimacy without first traversing the interior passage of self-acceptance."[19] In this passage a person announces him or herself to others in the hope that if he or she is loved, this love will bring about a greater sense of self-acceptance.

In light of the vocabulary mentioned above, the journey from passage one to passage two is the movement from being homosexual to being gay/lesbian.

3. *A Public Passage*: For some gay and lesbian Christians a third passage appears in their life journey. This is the transition into being recognized as homosexual and Christian in the public world. This public passage need not be taken by all gay or lesbian persons. The Whiteheads raise questions here about the possible motives which would incline a person to make this third passage. An obvious motive is an exhibitionist one: a compulsive desire to be seen and recognized. However, at the other end of the motivational continuum is the motive of generativity: i.e., an impulse to care for and contribute to the next generation. In other words, a person's homosexual life becomes a public witness of being both homosexual and Christian. In

this way, one's generativity provides a public observable model of homosexual Christian life.

The Whiteheads wisely counsel, "One cannot enter this passage simply because it is 'the thing to do' or because others have made it. A Christian enters it because he is invited to do so, because he senses himself so called."[20]

This entire approach to homosexuality assumes, of course, that homosexuality is a *condition* or an *orientation*. While many accept the fact of homosexuality as an orientation, many are not able to conceive of homosexuality as a possibility for authentic love: i.e., homosexuality is kept on the level of a physical, sexual urge or drive. It is thus very important here to keep in mind a point made earlier in this book: viz., that one's sexual orientation is integral to one's very self. In other words, one's homosexual orientation does not simply encompass sexual desires, but influences (though it does not determine) the ways one thinks, the ways one decides, the ways one responds, the ways one relates, the ways one creates and structures his or her whole world. All these actions are influenced by one's orientation. While it is possible, then, to make a distinction between a person's orientation and activity, it is also important to understand that it is impossible to quarantine orientation from the rest of one's life.[21] This point is articulated in *Human Sexuality: A Catholic Perspective for Education and Lifelong Learning*:[22]

Sexuality... is a fundamental dimension of every human being. It is reflected physiologically, psychologically, and relationally in a person's gender identity as well as in one's primary sexual orientation and behavior.[23]

Some mention should be made about statistics. Estimates of the number of people in the population whose sexual orientation is exclusively or predominantly toward members of the same sex vary rather widely, often in accord with the sexual orientation of those making the estimates. Complicating the question of numbers still more is the problem of what one means by homosexual orientation. Consequently, using the most restrictive definition and taking the most conservative statistics, about 4 to 5% of the population should be counted as predominantly homosexual in orientation.[24] The 1990 edition of the *Encyclopedia Americana* states that "In Western cultures, 4 to 8% of males and 2 to 4% of females are predominantly or exclusively homosexual in behavior."[25] In the *Official Statements from Religious Bodies and Ecumenical Organizations* of 1991, the point is made that "It is difficult if not impossible to determine the number of homosexuals in the general community. Reasonable estimates suggest that between 4 and 10% of the total population are exclusively homosexual. In terms of absolute numbers this cannot be dismissed as trivial. Many more pass through a homosexual phase in their lives and while such statistics are to be treated with reserve, they do indicate a sizeable proportion of the population."[26]

Finally, we have already noted Hanigan's critique that homosexuality is a "test case" for Christian sexual ethics. Several of the aspects which create this phenomenon are worth mentioning.[27]

There is the extensive cultural mythology about and resulting social antipathy toward homosexual individuals which create for them an inevitably distorted social situation. As John E. Fortunato points out in *Embracing the Exile*, many homosexual persons have been forced to live in a situation of hiding and of relating to others under false pretenses. Often, their sexual orientation is the source of jokes or at best something of an odd curiosity.

This type of phenomenon creates the problem of *homophobia*.

Combined with a distorted social situation, and closely related to it, is the incomprehension of the majority heterosexual community: i.e., for numerous heterosexual persons to comprehend the outlook and the problems of a homosexual individual. The "unnaturalness" of homosexual attraction and desire and the consequent immorality of homosexual activity seems almost self-evident to many heterosexual individuals. Repulsion and fear of homosexual persons create in many people an almost pathological fear of homosexuality and homosexual people, a fear which we have come to call homophobia. As Hanigan remarks, "Parents have been known to disown children, friend to reject friend, when homosexual attraction reared its head. It is, then, little wonder that most homosexual persons are not initially eager to admit to others or even to acknowledge to themselves the true state of their sexual feelings and inclinations."[28]

We have already noted that an individual's sexual orientation *de facto* influences all of one's life: i.e., the ways one thinks, decides, responds, relates, and structures one's world. Hanigan thus importantly remarks:

> We sometimes gloss over this difference in experience for heterosexual and homosexual people too readily which is surely a mistake... Heterosexual individuals enter into personal relationships or engage in daily social interaction without any need either to hide or to proclaim their sexual orientation. They simply take it for granted... Such personal relating or social interaction takes place and flows naturally, as it were, from this taken for granted, unreflexive preconsciousness.
>
> Though we rarely pay attention to the fact, heterosexual women relate differently to men and heterosexual men relate differently to women than they do to members of their own sex. I do not refer here to the subjects they talk about, or to the language they use, or to the social and cultural roles they play, or even to the social chauvinistic or sexist attitudes and biases they bring to their relationships. I refer rather to the emotional tone and unspoken feeling quality of the relationship, the physical and emotional comfortableness or disease one feels in the presence of the other. When one stops to think about it, one attends differently to members of the opposite sex than one attends to members of the same sex. I find, for one instance, that in classes or lectures before a sexually diverse audience, I usually become aware that there are physically attractive women in the audience, and some not so attractive. But I do not have a clue as to whether there are physically attractive men present. From the depths of preconscious awareness springs the unreflective knowledge of and consequent relatedness to members of the opposite sex as potentially desirable or undesirable sexual partners or sexual aggressors which generates a range of feeling and emotional tone toward them which is simply different than what is felt toward members of the same sex.[29]

The person with a homosexual orientation finds himself or herself in a "different world." It is not members of the opposite sex but of the same sex who become the dominant focus of one's sexual curiosity, desiring and energy. There is thus an interesting parallel between the importance sexuality takes on for homosexuals and the importance race takes on for African American people in racially discriminatory societies. The social world, if it discriminates against people on the basis of sex or race, makes these factors of a person's existence matters of primary importance to individuals. One's color, or race, or sexual orientation, is something that one must come to grips with as a central feature of one's own identity and place in the world.[30] Hanigan's further remarks are useful:

> Given this difference in the heterosexual and homosexual experi-
> ence, and the problems resulting from the difference for the homo-
> sexual person, it should not be surprising that an alternate lifestyle
> develops around the homosexual orientation, just as a lifestyle
> different than married life develops around the life of consecrated
> celibacy and around the still uncommitted life of the single hetero-
> sexual person in the world. But it is only in the case of the
> homosexual person that one's sexual orientation is the explicit,
> conscious focus of that lifestyle and so of one's personal identity, as
> well as being the focus of social hostility and personal attack... The
> homosexual individual very frequently does have the need to in-
> clude his or her sexual orientation in every affirmation of self
> identity, and understandably so. But in that case, sexuality and
> sexual relationships tend to become excessively important in one's
> understanding of what it is to be human.[31]

## 2. HISTORICAL OBSERVATIONS

In *Sexuality and Homosexuality*[32] Arno Karlen gives a good and helpful overview and perspective on major historical aspects regarding homosexuality. Karlen points out that historical and biographical data give sufficient evidence to conclude that homosexuality has existed in all places and times and has even flourished in periods of great artistic and cultural vitality: e.g., in da Vinci, Michelangelo, Wilde. In centuries and even millennia before the Greeks, many people from the Easter Mediterranean to Sumeria worshiped a god-dess whose rites included both heterosexual and homosexual inter-course. The worshiper of the "Great Mother" probably united himself with the deity by joining his body to that of the priest. Karlen thus mentions, "Homosexuality... [was]... widespread among these cult-ists."[33] He further demonstrates that the Jewish people had a long-standing and strict prohibition against both male and female homo-sexuality, which they came to associate with worshipers of the Great Mother: e.g., in Deuteronomy 22:23; 1 Kings 14, 15, 22; 2 Kings 23; Hosea 4.

In analyzing the long period of time before the Greeks, as well as the Greek influence itself on the question of homosexuality, Karlen comes to these conclusions:

1. Mistrust and hostility mark the relationship between the sexes because of the downgrading of women and this fact marked a clear backdrop for homosexuality.

2. Classical Greece rewrote Mycenean myth to fit its own sensibilities: i.e., a romantic revision. Many gods were two-sexed in order to demonstrate their double power and infinite generation and immortality. By the end of the fourth century B.C., however, these gods became more "between the sexes," an object of erotic aesthetics rather than serious worship. In art after this time, e.g., the aesthetic ideal was the rounded youth and a small-breasted, waistless goddess.

3. Most Greek homosexuality was between men and adoles-cents, and not between adult males. Karlen writes, "Typical praise was of 'a beardless, tender and beautiful youth' with 'sweet and lustrous' thighs, 'flashing eyes and blushing cheeks,' and long hair. The hair on the head was sometimes left very long; this, along with depilation of the body, must have produced an appearance somewhere between the sexes. Most of the comparisons and metaphors used by homosexual lovers evoke a picture either of a slender sapling or a boy-girl creature, coquettish yet naive, or a fuzzy little blooming peach."[34] Homosexuality was associ-ated in the Greek mind with the separation of the sexes, the military ethos, male nudity, physical culture and the gymnasia. Only a wealthy few could have had the time to spend their days in the gymnasium. Therefore, the question remains: Did any but the most well-born in Sparta and Crete have homosexual mentors?

There were many male/boy prostitutes but "...there is no
evidence that homosexuality met with any general social
approval..."[35] Karlen thus concludes, "One gets an over-all
impression of shallow adolescence, romanticism in grown
men, and often of mercenary affairs and callous bed-
hopping by a psychosexually disturbed leisure class."[36]

   In Greece, the exclusive homosexual was generally
considered laughable and despicable. The corruption of
boys by homosexual tutors was a constant theme in literature; and once the "boy" reached twenty-one he was
expected to take the dominant male role. Many a homosexual man married to put up a heterosexual front and thus
escape scorn.

4.  The Stoics condemned homosexuality as unnatural. For
    example, Lucian made a female character say, "I do not
    care for a man who himself wants one."[37] Therefore, Karlen
    concludes, "In ancient Greece homosexuality was consid-
    ered a deviation; it was given positive value only by a
    minority of homosexuals, bisexuals and apologists... The
    fact that homosexuality was a factor in the lives of many
    great men only speaks for its prevalence among the lei-
    sured, literate elite from which artists and statesman
    came."[38]

   Karlen indicates that in the Rome of the first and second
centuries there was a great amount of sadism and indiscriminate
bisexuality. He gives evidence that homosexuals wore revealing and
semi-transparent clothes and often wore yellow (*galbus* in Latin);
thus did *galbinus* become synonymous with homosexuality. Since
masculinity was equated with aggressiveness and dominance, it was
permitted that an older man could use a younger male as a passive
sexual object without loss of maleness. Karlen also indicates the
emphasis of Christianity on heterosexuality, especially with its emphasis on the complementarity of the sexes; and the importance of
reason; and of procreation.

   The *Code of Justinian* in Novella 77 (538 A.D.) claimed that
famine, earthquakes, plagues and even total destruction awaited cities
harboring homosexuals. During the Middle Ages one finds a good

deal of radical antisocial behavior; and during the time of the
Renaissance we find the emergence of a new literature of "Platonic
love," which sprang up from the troubadours. However, claims
Karlen, homosexuality remained a capital crime and an object of
contempt.[39]

During the Reformation period, Martin Luther viewed sex as a
base, raging beast. He agreed that the desire for sexual pleasure was
"awful" to God and to marry for passion was a sin. Luther claimed that
the power of lust was so great, its paint so deep, that no human could
resist it. Even marital sex was unclean but, said Luther, "God winks
at it."[40] John Calvin taught in the *Institutes* that "The licentiousness of
the flesh, which unless it be rightly restrained, transgresses every
bound."[41] Calvin maintained that few men were capable of celibacy
and he was probably thinking about homosexuality when he said that
men should not take vows they cannot live up to, for God would then
send them "secret flames of lust" and "horrible acts of filthiness."[42]

The greatest spokesman during the Puritan era was John Milton
who wrote that the goal of man and woman was "a human society;
where that cannot be had there is no true marriage." During this
period, then, no one would have claimed that homosexual love was
just as sincere, profound or worthy as heterosexual love. Milton thus
stressed that married love was the happiest fate that could happen to
a person; and this was "true Puritanism."[43]

In France, Louis XIV despised homosexuals and would have
scourged them from the earth were it not for his own brother who was
homosexual. His homosexuality was called "the Italian vice."[44] Louis
XIV's son was also involved in a homosexual scandal when he was
a young boy and the King ignored his existence from that time on (the
boy died at age 16). Tradition also has it that the King discovered that
some of the nation's highest nobility had formed a secret society
sworn to avoid women except to produce one heir.

A great source on the sexual life of the time is Pierre de
Bantome's *Lives of Galant Ladies* (1665). The author writes that
lesbianism was common in France, a love called *donna con donna*.
Interestingly, lesbians were not considered as "odious" as male
homosexuals probably due to the fact that wives were kept ignorant
of the refined pleasures of sex, for such would lead to adultery and the
breakdown of social and moral restraints. Pierre de Brantome indi-

cated that some husbands would urge their wives to have lesbian affairs in order to avoid adultery. Karlen points out importantly that it must be kept in mind that one is reading here a *de facto* projection of male homosexuality: i.e., the assumption that women would not fall in love with other women, would not form deep emotional attachments and find real sexual fulfillment.

The eighteenth century was a time of libertinage. The record of sexual deviation is more copious, detailed and extravagant. Upper classes often married for wealth and position and then continued their old rounds of seduction and whoring. Children were raised by servants, instructed by tutors, shipped off to boarding schools and convents: "They knew their caretakers better than their parents."[45]

Women were widely viewed in the most debased manner (Swift wrote, "A species hardly a degree above a monkey"[46]). What flourished then, was delinquency: assault, rape, drunkenness and whoring. There was a furious desire to outrage every moral convention. Private clubs arose devoted to sexual indulgence, blasphemy and satanic ritual. One of these clubs was the *Mollies*. Members met in women's clothes and thus this word was generally used for homosexuals. There were "molly houses" that provided quarters for homosexual prostitution.

Industrialization was growing and so were the cities as a consequence. In the literature of this time, there is a growing mention of a middle and lower class of homosexuals. There were many police drives against them in the 1780s and there was the discovery of homosexual rings in London and Exeter. Outlets existed for every special sexual interest and commodity, and pornography at this time became a rather large industry (especially with increased literacy). It was during this time that the pornographic work, *Fanny Hill*, was written. Most of society, however, still viewed these "special sexual interests" as "deviations": e.g., the penalty for homosexual relations remained death, and even attempted homosexual acts were punished. During the 1720s police were at work in trapping homosexuals.

In France at this time a great deal of erotic literature was produced which gave homosexuality more and more emphasis. Lesbianism was more widely documented. The 1755 earthquake in Lisbon was believe to be a punishment by God for homosexuality. Homosexual prostitution was widespread in Paris and in 1702 an organized system was discovered which catered to a very high-class clientele.

In Sweden at this time the punishment for homosexuality was worse than for murder, sorcery and treason. In Holland, the names of convicted homosexuals were published and their wives were free to remarry or resume their maiden names.

In 18th century Europe, sin, insanity, rage, unreason and lust were all usually equated. Overt homosexuals were locked up with psychotics and imbeciles. Even for the better minds of the 18th century, the trinity of madness, vice and unreason defined extreme deviants much as witchcraft, blasphemy and sodomy had in the Middle Ages. One of the greatest revolutionaries of the time was the *Marquis de Sade* (born in 1740). In his writings he poured out a world of compulsive anger, sex and argument and his basic moral was that vice always triumphed; and should. Sex was divorced from all emotions, except anger. He claimed that the timid invented love, virtue and morality.

The French revolutionaries highlighted the importance of individual rights and old laws concerning marriage, divorce and sexual behavior were secularized. The Civil Code enacted by Napoleon made homosexual acts illegal *only* if they involved force or public display. However, "Homosexuality was no longer a sin, nor even a crime, but it was still antisocial and subject to informal sanctions."[47] In 1845 when some 50 homosexuals were arrested in the *"Rue Basse des Ramparts"* scandal, the French blamed the increase of homosexuality on the Arabs!

Capital punishment was abolished in England in 1837, except for such crimes as murder, rape and sodomy. But in the 1840s there were still many homosexual brothels in England. At this time Victorianism was at its height with its expressed fear of sex and its anger at all impulse. In general, Victorianism was a smug denial of sex which arose in a wave of prudery, guilt and religious reformism in the second half of the 18th century (and thus did "Victorian" predate the rise of Queen Victoria to the throne in 1837, and lost its hold especially in the upper classes long before her death in 1901). In this era, however, there was a rigid fear of all sensual and impulsive expressions.

The *scientific study of sex* began after the middle of the 19th century. Sex became a "problem" and could no longer be treated the way that we have just seen. It was a time for investigation, reform and a new idealism. There was, e.g., a voluminous literature on masturbation. In 1717 the *Urtext* on masturbation claimed that sex, and especially masturbation, soiled body, mind and soul and produced diseases, vapors, epilepsy, madness, lying, swearing, and perhaps murder.[48] By the middle of the 19th century it was almost universal medical doctrine that sexual excess, especially masturbation, led to "masturbatory insanity" and that masturbation caused homosexuality. Doctors at this time thus recommended cages, bandages, mittens and straitjackets to restrain the weak-willed. Karlen remarks, "Science had replaced religion as a justification of traditional mores."[49]

In 1835 the English psychologist Pritchard introduced the concept of "moral insanity," a "morbid perversion" of the feelings and impulses without delusion or loss of intellect. For almost a century scientists would classify homosexuality as a form of moral insanity. Doctors assumed that convulsive disorders were connected with sex and treated them with castration in men and cauterization of the clitoris and ovariectomy in women.

The most advanced views about homosexuality after mid-century were put forth by medico-legal experts of Germany and France, Doctors Casper and Tardieu. In 1852 and 1863 Casper made the distinction between "innate" and "acquired" homosexuality. The majority of homosexuals, he said, were congenital; there was no "depraved fancy" at work in them, but in some "the taste for this vice had been acquired in life, and is the result of over satiety with natural pleasures..."[50]

In 1856 Tardieu portrayed homosexuals as degraded monsters, morally and physically different from other people. The first serious work exclusively about homosexuals was written by Karl Heinrich Ulrichs, himself a homosexual. He wrote that the homosexual was neither criminal nor insane, but the product of abnormal embryonic development: at an early stage of development of the human embryo the genital tissue is differentiated; and in the male homosexual the genitals became male but the same differentiation failed to take place in the part of the brain that determines the sex drive. The result is an animal *muliebris virile corpore inclusa*, a female soul in a male body. This is inborn and unchangeable, but not any more pathological than color blindness. (He further added that most homosexuals whistle poorly or not at all!) Ulrichs created the classification of "active" and "passive" homosexual, as well as "sexual preference" in the homosexual. He further taught that all sex is basically repugnant and this accounts for anti-homosexual prejudice. He thus actively supported full legal rights for homosexuals, including their right to legally marry one another.

In 1869 a Hungarian doctor, Benkert, wrote under the pseudonym Kertbeny. He coined the word *homosexual* from the Greek *homos* (same). In the same year in Berlin, Dr. Karl Westphal in the journal *Archiv fur Psychiatrie* dubbed "contrary sexual feeling" for homosexuality and said that it was a kind of moral insanity due to "congenital reversal of sexual feeling."[51]

The next crucial writing on this subject was "Inversion of the Genital Sense" by Charcot and Magnan in 1882. They maintained that the cause of psychosexual problems was constitutional nervousness, weakness due to hereditary degeneration. Magnan taught that the male homosexual had a woman's brain and a man's body; and others then adopted their terms "invert," "inversion" and "stigmata of degeneration." In other words, the damage to genes came from nervous disorders, and also perhaps from alcoholism.

The famous Russian sexologist, Benjamin Tarnowski, decided that in some cases homosexuality was acquired: e.g., these people read dirty books, kept bad company, lived luxuriously, and were so jaded by sexual excess that they took up homosexuality and other bizarre practices. He further taught that born homosexuals could not help themselves since their condition came from damage to their parents' genes resulting from hysteria, epilepsy, alcoholism, anemia, typhus, debauchery, soil, climate and altitude. Scientists everywhere agreed, attributing homosexuality to a failure to pass beyond a primitive, ancestral condition of bisexuality.

The Italian psychiatrist and criminologist Cesare Lombroso taught that acts called criminal in civilized society are natural among animals and common among primitives. In the civilized world, then, the homosexual is an *atavism*, a case of moral insanity. He "proved" this by measuring skulls, bodies and features of criminals, prostitutes, idiots, arsonists, the poor, and homosexuals. In *Criminal Man* (1876) he showed how he found in them such primitive characteristics as jutting jaws, malformed craniums and close-set eyes. Once discovered, he said, these people should be separated from the rest of the community and kept from reproducing.

In Germany, Hirschfeld and Fliess studied left-handedness in homosexuals. They taught that it was an important sign of "inverted sexual characteristics."[52] Studies were also made of homosexuals' facial hair and body hair. The Italian doctor Mantegazza created a scandal in the 1870s and 1880s in his work *Sexual Relations of Mankind* where he called homosexuality "one of the most terrifying facts to be met in human psychology."[53] He said that there are three possible causes: genital nerves were distributed around the rectum; psychic origin "specific to intellectual man, cultivated and frequently neurotic"; and *larghezza desolante*, a desolating largeness of the human vagina, which made some men turn to the cozy tightness of the male rectum.

The pinnacle of this era's sexology was Richard von Krafft-Ebing's *Psychopathia Sexualis: A Medico-Forensic Study* (1887). He believed that sex was meant for reproduction and that "man puts himself on a level with the beasts if he seeks to gratify lust."[54] He also taught that the male homosexual's brain had been feminized and argued that even acquired homosexuality could exist only if there was some hereditary weakness of the nervous system. He called for the repeal of the harsh anti-homosexual Article 175 of the German Criminal Code because one should not punish a sickness, especially one for which there was so little hope for cure. He taught that *predisposition* was critical in homosexuality: "Psychological forces are insufficient to explain manifestations of so thoroughly degenerated a character."[55]

By the turn of the 20th century, a major scientific view had emerged that homosexuality was *congenital*, caused by hereditary damage that appeared as neuropathy and was exacerbated by masturbation. Fere even added that trying to "cure" a homosexual of his innate drive was an attempt to pervert his true instincts. Fere concluded that the homosexual should make chastity his ideal. (Karlen emphasizes the importance of remembering that throughout this same period of time there was a "nightmare vision of sex" which frequently appeared in Western literature: e.g., woman was turned into a harpy and a destroyer and a lesbian. This view was especially common in French art and literature.)

At the turn of the 20th century, a Berlin doctor, Magnus Hirschfeld, was becoming the world's leading expert on homosexuality. He coined the popular phrase "the third sex" and insisted that homosexuality was congenital and non-pathological, probably due to the interplay of hormones and the nervous system. Today his theories are mostly discredited, but he was a pioneer in research methods and reform. He also said that homosexuals have special virtues: their world has less regard for caste and status than the heterosexual's world, and thus they were more democratic.

Havelock Ellis was born in 1859. In his *Studies in the Psychology of Sex* he taught that homosexuality was an inborn abnormality, quite non-pathological, even though there were a fair number of neurotics among homosexuals. He claimed that homosexuality was like color blindness or perhaps more like synesthesia, such as color-hearing, which makes some people equate visual and aural impression and say that a sound is "red." Thus heterosexuals and homosexuals differ no more than red and yellow roses. All sexual acts are alike before God, claimed Ellis, and should be alike before the human community.

Most of the early accounts of non-Western homosexuality are sweeping and brief. In these later centuries, both boys and men who played women's parts in the all-male Chinese theater were notoriously homosexual and were also known for homosexual prostitution. There were many male brothels in Peking; and many also in Canton in the south. There is some evidence in Japan of homosexuality, especially between religious masters and their disciples. In India, Hinduism puts a heavy emphasis on abstinence and self-control. There was a class of boys called *hinjras* who were said to prepare themselves to be male prostitutes but "...they were held in deep contempt by other Hindus."[56]

On the other hand, the Indian Muslims were constantly accused by English and French writers of homosexuality, both male and female. However, there were also accounts of scorn and avoidance of homosexuality in Muslim India: "The Muslims... officially condemned homosexuality but enforced the ban inconsistently — sometimes harshly and sometimes hardly at all."[57]

Arab homosexuality is said to be the result of the separation of the sexes called for by the Koran. This system is called *purdah* and requires a harem, a forbidden place. It is usually accompanied by a low status for women and even contempt for them. It was a noted long-time practice in parts of the Arab world that mass sodomitic rape was used as a punishment and as a humiliation: "This was almost surely done to Lawrence of Arabia by his Turkish captors..."[58] There is no doubt that eunuchs, boy prostitutes and homosexuals of both sexes existed through much of the Arab world and Muslim Asia, probably more than in much of Europe.

The laws of the Aztecs of Central Mexico and the Mayas of Yucatan and Central America both condemned homosexuals to death by stoning.

The Finnish writer Edward Westermarch wrote *The Origin and Development of Moral Ideas* which appeared between 1906 and 1908. Regarding homosexuality, his thinking was very close to that of Ellis, whom he freely quoted. He kept emphasizing cultural influence and said that homosexuality was sometimes a matter of instinctive preference and sometimes due to circumstances inhibiting normal intercourse. Widespread homosexuality in both sexes, he said, went hand in hand with isolation of women and a premium on chastity. He suggested that free relations between men and women would reduce its frequency. He dismissed the idea that homosexuality was practiced as a form of birth control and he felt that the real reason for the hostility toward homosexuality in the West was its traditional connection with heresy and unbelief.

Not long before his death, Oscar Wilde said, "I never came across anyone in whom the moral sense was dominant who was not heartless, cruel, vindictive, log-stupid and entirely lacking in the smallest sense of humanity. Moral people, as they are termed, are simple beasts. I would sooner have 50 unnatural vices than one unnatural virtue."[59] This led the editor W.P. Stead to write, "If all persons guilty of Oscar Wilde's offenses were to be clapped into gaol, there would be a very surprising exodus from Eton and Harow, Rugby and Winchester, to Pentonville and Halloway."[60]

Homosexual-hunting then became a common fact of life. And a new revolution was being prepared and a new ideology was being shaped by Sigmund Freud.

### Analysis

This long history gives us a good opportunity to see why certain *myths* are still quite prevalent regarding homosexual people, myths which foment homophobia:

1. Homosexuality is caused by sinfulness. A contemporary example may be found in *The H Persuasion*,[61] a product of the aesthetic realist movement which sees homosexuality as "contrariness." In addition, contemporary fundamentalists view homosexuality as sinful, with the obvious consequence that to be homosexual is an arrogant and sinful act of volition.
2. Homosexuality is caused by mental illness. In this point of view, the "depravity" of homosexuality involves genes or twisted parenting. Homosexuality is clearly a pathological problem and persons with this "illness" need medical and/or psychological treatment. There is the additional belief here that homosexuality comes from being confused about one's gender, desiring to be a member of the opposite sex.[62]
3. Homosexuality is a form of sexual addiction, analogous to bestiality, and thus inhuman and vulgar, certainly at the hinterland of sexual abnormality.

The 1981 study *Sexual Preference: Its Development in Men and Women* did surface some extraordinary conclusions:

1. Nearly 1 in every 4 lesbians and 1 in every 5 gay men surveyed had attempted to kill themselves at least once during their life. Among heterosexuals, the numbers were about 1 in 10 and 1 in 30, respectively.
2. Roughly one-quarter of gay Whites who attempted suicide were driven to their first attempt by the time they were 17 years old. The proportion was even higher for gay African Americans.
3. Well over half of those attempting suicide for the first time did so for reasons of unhappiness concerning their homosexuality; and the problems of trying to fit into a hostile world.

Craig O'Neill and Kathleen Ritter demonstrate in *Coming Out Within* (1992) that homosexual persons face serious *losses* in their lives which often lead to feelings of isolation, depression and self-loathing. What are these losses?

*1. Family*

a) Homosexual persons are usually accepted within their *families of origin* as long as they maintain a heterosexual image. This situation changes drastically for many homosexuals when they disclose their orientation. Many parents thus give to their children two choices: either "please yourself and lose me" or "lose yourself and please me."

b) Many homosexual persons lose the *family of dreams*: i.e., the normative heterosexual marriage with children which most people try to match with an almost unconscious blueprint or model.

*2. Work*

a) Some homosexuals become so broken that they are no longer able to imagine that anything they plan will materialize.

b) Many homosexuals fail to realize their potential due to prejudicial treatment in their work environment.

c) Some homosexuals fear exposure and thus remain underemployed relative to their talents and skills.

d) Some homosexuals sustain an inability to focus on vocational plans because so much energy is given to issues related to their sexual orientation.

e) Some homosexuals achieve work-satisfaction and accomplishment but at the price of pretense. Lifelong disillusionment thus sets in.

*3. Health and Safety*

a) Violent assaults on gay men and lesbians have been increasing.

b) HIV infection and AIDS has claimed the lives of thousands of homosexual people.

## 4. Religion

a) A large number of homosexual persons do not feel that their basic human goodness is affirmed by their religion; they feel thrust into a struggle between a personal sense of "rightness" and a perceived sense of "sinfulness."
b) A number of homosexual people feel alienated from religion and thus from a sense of belonging to a religious community.

## 5. Community

a) Many homosexuals feel a pervasive sense of not belonging, something akin to James Baldwin's comment, "It is a great shock at the age of five or six to find that in a world of Gary Coopers you are the Indian."
b) Joseph Campbell has pointed out that shaping stories or myths help us to understand our passage from birth to death, to find out who we are, to touch the transcendent, and to discover "the rapture of being alive." In many cases, the messages conveyed to homosexual persons make them feel left-handed in a right-handed world and give them no life-images to take into account. This leads to the inability to reconcile one's inner world with the outside world.

Such "extraordinary conclusions" as these can help us see well the possible consequences of homophobia (or as some now say homo-hatred) where certain *myths* about homosexual people have forced them into what Fortunato calls an "exile." Homophobes sometimes justify their prejudice against homosexuals by alleging that homo-sexuality is contagious — that young homosexuals become that way because of older homosexuals and that homosexuality is a social corruption (homosociality). Such beliefs form the core of the organized anti-homosexual movement. Homophobia is surely a form of bigotry that needs to be clearly condemned.[63]

## 3. THE CAUSES OF HOMOSEXUALITY

We saw in Chapter Two that each of us experiences our sexual lives within certain limitations, mainly rooted in our gender self-assessment, a self-evaluation which moves along three separate dimensions: gender identity; sexual orientation; and sexual intention. We noted that these three dimensions, separately or together, are basically parts of a subjective, psychological, intrapsychic phenomenon. Our sexual identity is only *one part* of our many-faceted self, and exists alongside many other "identities," such as political, ethnic, religious, generational, vocational.

In discussing sexual orientation, we saw that adult subjective orientation refers to the intrapsychic images of people that attract and provoke sexual arousal. Adults can be considered homoerotic who think about, are attracted to, or aroused by images of persons of the same sex. Consequently, any attempt to search out the causes of one's homosexuality is by necessity going to be as complex and as limited as would be the search for the origins and roots of one's heterosexuality or bisexuality. It should be noted as well that there are a number of writers who argue that all research into the "causes" of homosexuality is intrinsically hostile to homosexual persons.[64] These writers suggest that such research is motivated by the premise that homosexuality is pathological and is most often grounded in rigid assumptions about what constitutes true "maleness and femaleness." In addition, as we have seen, the debate about the major causes for a homosexual orientation very much depends on one's "definition" of homosexuality. We have already taken the position (which some label the *essentialist* point of view) that one's homosexuality refers to an individual's inner, authentic self: that one's sexual orientation is intimately intertwined with one's identity as a human being. (Most defenders of homosexual rights then argue that expression of that identity is essential to human wholeness.)

On the other hand, there are those (sometimes referred to as the constructivists) who argue that homosexuality is a behavior and perhaps a preference for certain behaviors, the meaning of which is ambiguous for the understanding or labeling of a person. In this view, homosexuality should not be considered an identity as such, especially because homosexual behavior takes varied forms from culture to culture.[65] The landmark work in this so-called constructivist approach is Greenberg's *The Construction of Homosexuality*.[66]

Recognizing, then, the necessary care that must be had in approaching this subject, we can indicate that the major causes for a homosexual orientation that have been proposed include genetic, prenatal/hormonal, adult (postnatal)/hormonal, and psychological factors.[67]

### A. Genetic Factors

Early research[68] into the causes of homosexuality suggested a strong genetic component, but these results have not withstood further tests. It is generally concluded today that studies of frequency of homosexuality in identical and fraternal twins, and in near-relatives of homosexuals, suggest that there is some degree of genetic influence in the development of the homosexual orientation operative in some persons.[69]

Recently, some scientific data is converging on the conclusion that sexual orientation is innate. For example, a recent study by Simon LeDay, a neurobiologist at the Salk Institute, reported a difference in the hypothalamus, a part of the brain that develops at a young age, between homosexual and heterosexual men. In addition, the scientific research of Michael Bailey of Northwestern University and Richard Pillard of the Boston University School of Medicine has likewise demonstrated that male sexual orientation is substantially genetic.

John Money believes, however, that "According to currently available evidence, the sex chromosomes do not directly determine or program psychosexual status as heterosexual, bisexual, or homosexual."[70] In other words, he argued that even though there is genetic influence for some, there is no "sexual orientation gene." Sexual orientation is probably indirectly influenced by other factors that are controlled by a person's genes and these factors may predispose some people to homosexuality.

### B. Prenatal/Hormonal Factors

Several studies have administered abnormal sex hormone levels to animal fetuses in their mother's wombs to study the effects this has on sexual differentiation and development of sexual behavior patterns in adult animals. It has been shown that the right dose of sex hormones given to an animal fetus at a critical time can result in that animal showing sexually "inverted behavior" when mature, including homosexual behaviors exhibited in conjunction with mating. These effects are complex and multifaceted, and have been taken by some as evidence suggesting that similar hormone variations must be causal factors in human homosexuality.[71]

While experiments directly manipulating hormones in the womb cannot be performed with human fetuses, a number of naturally and accidentally occurring medical conditions have served almost as "quasi-experiments." These studies have shown that some human fetuses exposed to abnormal hormone levels during development can show radically altered physical development, brain functioning, gender orientation, and sexual behavior of the person.

Does this research suggest that prenatal hormonal factors cause homosexuality? There are theorists who propose that the animal experiments and their human "quasi-experimental" parallels strongly suggest that homosexuality is biologically determined.[72] These theorists specifically propose that human sexual orientation is largely determined between the second and fifth month of pregnancy by fetal exposure to the principal sex hormones. Because of the problems regarding the applicability of the animal research to humans and the fact that few of the human "quasi-experiments" deal with homosexuality in isolation, it is critical to examine the three major types of direct evidence of this hypothesis.

The first group of evidences are the reports suggesting that the brains and/or entire neurohormonal systems of male homosexuals (no significant research in this area has been conducted with lesbians) are different from their heterosexual peers, being significantly "feminized." For instance, some research suggests that homosexuals are less right-handed than heterosexuals,[73] that they have different mental abilities than heterosexuals based on different brain structures,[74] and that their hormonal response to an injection of estrogen is more like a woman's than a heterosexual man's (or at least is intermediate between those extremes). At the present time, there is significant reason to doubt the persuasiveness of the evidence on each of these points.

The second type of evidence for prenatal causation suggests that the most powerful predicator of adult male homosexuality is striking gender non-conformity or inappropriateness early in childhood. In other words, boys who are strikingly effeminate as young children appear to be much more likely to become homosexual men than their more typically masculine peers.[75] Some effeminate children do not grow up homosexual, however, and many homosexuals do not report gender-inappropriate behavior as children. There is no conclusive evidence for why early gender behavior distortion occurs. While some regard it as evidence for the prenatal hormone hypothesis, there is some evidence that the causes could be psychological.[76]

Finally, research has been cited which lends indirect support to the prenatal cause hypothesis. The most frequently cited are those showing that an unusual number of homosexuals were born to German women who were pregnant during World War II.[77] These researchers argue that the stress of war produced hormone disturbances which produced homosexuality in the children.

While there is an impressive amount of research cited in favor of the parental causation hypothesis, the direct research in support of this hypothesis is far from conclusive. It seems most reasonable to conclude that prenatal/hormonal influences may be a facilitating contributing cause of homosexual orientation in some individuals. These influences cannot be considered operative in all homosexuals, and there is no evidence that such factors can by themselves "cause" homosexuality.[78]

### C. Adult Postnatal/Hormonal Factors

There are still anecdotes reported suggesting that male and female homosexuals have too much or too little of certain sex hormones compared to others, or that they have too much of the hormones of persons of the other gender. The research in this area is quite clear, however, that there are no substantial hormonal differences between homosexuals and their comparable heterosexual peers. Research which was once thought to show such differences has been shown to be plagued by inaccurate methods of measuring hormones and inaccurate ways of categorizing the sexual orientations of subjects in the studies.[79]

## D. Psychological Factors

Psychoanalytic theory is the "standard" psychological theory of causation and almost all of the psychoanalytic research has been directed at male homosexuality. In this view, homosexuality is due primarily to a profound disturbance in parent-child relationships.[80] If a boy has a father who is distant, unavailable, or rejecting; and a mother who is overly warm, smothering, and controlling, the boy's desire to identify with the father may be frustrated. An ambivalent feeling of fear of and yet longing for closeness with another male may result. There is some evidence that similar dynamics are present for lesbians as well, where the major disturbance seems to be in the relationship with the mother. Lesbians report greater than expected frequencies of rejecting and negative relationships with their mothers.[81] A smothering relationship with the mother can make sexual relationships with women threatening. This in turn can lead to avoidance of normal heterosexual activities both because of fear of the aggressiveness of other males with whom the boy is competing and fear of the sexuality of women. At the same time, the boy is attracted to other men because of his longing for closeness to a male.

The evidence of this basic theory is substantial, yet inconclusive. Much of the research is based upon the clinical impressions of practicing psychoanalysts, and some see the evidence as contaminated by the biases of the therapists. The bulk of empirical research[82] on the families of homosexuals documents patterns that would be predicted by the psychoanalytic theory, even though it cannot be argued that those results support only that theory.[83]

Several studies have produced evidence that would seem to contradict the psychoanalytic hypothesis.[84] It seems that there is not enough evidence to prove the psychoanalytic hypothesis, but there is too much evidence to dismiss it at this time.

The other major type of psychological theory is learning theory. These hypotheses suggest that early sexual and other learning experiences shape sexual orientation. For instance, the first sexual experiences of a boy shape sexual orientation: a boy with troubled family relationships and a preexisting tendency toward effeminate behavior may be more likely to be homosexual. Such early experiences could shape the child's perception of himself, his sexual fantasies, and his choices of subsequent sexual experiences, with the eventual result of adult homosexual orientation. The evidence in support of the learning approach is much less substantial and more indirect than that of the psychoanalytic hypothesis.[85]

### Conclusion

There is a general consensus today that no one theory of homosexuality can explain such a diverse phenomenon. There is certainly no single genetic, hormonal or psychological cause of homosexual orientation. There appears to be a variety of factors which can provide a "push" in the direction of homosexuality for some persons, but there is no evidence that this push renders human choice irrelevant. The complex of factors which result in the orientation toward homosexuality probably differs from person to person. While we do not know what causes the orientation, we undoubtedly know that the forces that go into the creation of a homosexual person are more complex and mysterious than most had earlier appreciated. There is, then, substantial reason to approach the scientific topic of homosexuality with caution and respect, as the overwhelming complexity of the issue merits.[86] A final word should be added about the possibility of changing one's homosexuality to heterosexuality. A number of studies have been conducted on this conversion and these studies claim a certain success rate. The psychological methods used have ranged from psychoanalysis[87] to directive behavioral sex therapy.[88] There has been at least one empirical research report of change via religious means through a church lay counseling and healing ministry.[89] Reported success rates have never been outstanding or suggestive of an easy path to change for the homosexual person. These "success" rates have ranged from 33% and 50-60%. In *Homosexuality In Perspective* (1979), e.g., Masters and Johnson reported a 50-60% cure or improvement rate for highly motivated clients using sex therapy methods and behavior therapy methods. This report was later questioned, however, on the grounds of whether or not those studied were *de facto* truly homosexual or heterosexual.

One author has said, pointing to the somewhat common continued experience of homosexual feelings even when the "converted" person is functioning heterosexually, "...the finding that one can with great effort graft apparently heterosexual behavior over an earlier homosexual orientation" is hardly a ringing endorsement of the change process.[90] Even the most optimistic advocates for change by psychological means conclude that change is most likely when motivation is strong, when there is a history of successful heterosexual functioning, when gender identity issues are not present, and when involvement in actual homosexual practice has been minimal.

It is critical to return here to a point made earlier regarding our understanding of what it means to be homosexual. If one begins from the point of view that homosexual orientation is part of the core identity of an individual, then the evidence regarding change would cause one to question the utility of attempts at change. Another way of expressing this is to draw parallels to radically different conditions: Is homosexuality more like left-handedness (once thought of as an abnormality and deficiency, but now understood as a normal variation which we would not want to waste effort changing), or like a psychological personality disorder (where treatment efforts persist because of the professional consensus that the pattern is a problem)?

Today there are many Christian ministries which attempt to provide opportunities for growth and healing for the homosexual.[91] Many of these groups are represented by the umbrella *Exodus International* organization. These groups offer a variety of approaches, but generally agree that change from homosexuality is a difficult and painful process of renouncing sinful practices and attitudes and reaching out to grasp the promise of God's help. These groups suggest that struggling with homosexual attraction is a life-long task, but that the person who takes on that struggle can expect gradual change, especially with God's grace. Some aim for conversion to heterosexuality; others aim at freedom from overpowering homosexual impulses and increasing capacity to experience one's sexuality as fully as would be desired for any Christian single person.

## 4. HOMOSEXUALITY AND SELF-ASSESSMENT

It is certainly clear that the assessment of one's gender identity is no easy matter and an individual comes to an authentic sense of his or her own sexual orientation only slowly. In assessing one's sexual

orientation, in this case one's homosexuality, three levels of evalua-
tion/assessment are important:

(1)  *The Level of Attraction*: Here a person assesses with
     honesty and integrity both one's dreams and fantasies, as
     well as one's conscious attractions: e.g., When I walk down
     a street, when I walk along a beach, who is the first type of
     person I tend to notice? Or, when I enter a room, do I tend
     as a general rule to notice the men or the women?
(2)  *The Level of Arousal*: Here one faces an important question:
     What type of persons do I find sexually erotic and arousing?
(3)  *The Level of Experience*: Here one carefully evaluates
     actual sexual and, if present, genital experiences if they
     have taken place. For example, it is possible that an indi-
     vidual is a pseudo-homosexual[92] and experiencing an
     experimental stage in one's sexual life-experience; or one
     may find that a homosexual genital experience was not
     satisfying, comforting or erotically stimulating. Such
     experiences must be carefully assessed and weighed in
     order to evaluate precisely one's level of experience.[93]

Numerous authors have pointed out that sexuality is not an "all
or nothing" behavior, any more than intelligence or athletic ability.[94]
Sexuality forms a continuum with homosexuality on one end and
heterosexuality on the other. Thus, men who define themselves as
heterosexual may well have males in their lives whom they deeply
love; and women who define themselves as homosexual may have
men in their lives whom they deeply love. Consequently, it is more
realistic to think in terms of being "more" (predominantly) heterosexual than homosexual or "more" (predominantly) homosexual than
heterosexual.[95] In addition, at different points in one's life, a person
may gravitate more toward one end of the scale than the other (e.g.,
through experimental or variational homosexual experiences).

In addition, it is very important to realize that sexuality can be
either psychological or physical or both: e.g., a person could be both
psychologically and physically homosexual; a person could be both
psychologically and physically heterosexual; a person could be
psychologically homosexual but not physically, i.e., have a homo-

sexual orientation but not actualize it physically; a person could be psychologically heterosexual but not physically, i.e., have a hetero- sexual orientation but not actualize it physically; a person could have a homosexual psychological orientation but engage in heterosexual physical behavior; a person could have a heterosexual psychological orientation and engage in homosexual behavior.

The view that sexual orientation is dichotomous, i.e., hetero- sexual or homosexual, was dismissed over forty years ago by Kinsey, Pomeroy and Martin:[96]

> The world is not divided into sheep and goats. Not all are black nor all things white. It is a fundamental of taxonomy that nature rarely deals with discreet categories and tries to force facts into separated pigeon holes. The living world is a continuum in each and every one of its aspects. The sooner we learn this concerning human sexual behavior the sooner we shall reach a sounder understanding of the realities of sex.

Out of their findings, Alfred C. Kinsey and his associates developed a 7-point scale in which 0 represented exclusive hetero- sexuality and 6 represented exclusive homosexuality. Three (3) on the scale indicated equal homosexual and heterosexual responsive- ness. Individuals were rated on this continuum based upon their sexual behavior and psychic reactions: i.e., physical attraction to desired partners.[97]

Although this continuum notion better represents the realities of the world, the Kinsey Scale has many limitations for accurately describing an individual's sexual orientation. First, the scale assumes that sexual behavior and erotic responsiveness are the same within individuals. As we have seen, this is not always the case. Some authors thus suggest the conceptualization of sexual orientations embracing physical, interpersonal, and intrapsychic factors.[98] The physical and intrapsychic factors describe the components of sexual behavior (physical) and erotic fantasy (intrapsychic factors). Inter- personal affection refers to associations involving love or affection that may or may not include genital contact. Here too there may be great discrepancies between these three scales within a given indi- vidual. In several important articles, some researchers have thus suggested a 7-point Scale for the various dimensions of one's sexual orientations:[99] sexual attraction; sexual behavior; sexual fantasy; emotional preference; social preference; self-identification; and hetero/gay/lesbian lifestyle. In this Scale, one is asked to assess these 7 points in terms of one's Past, Present, and Ideal. A respondent's past and present are defined by the preceding year, and the "ideal" refers to an individual's ideal choice. We must not forget also that there are a number of social and demographic variables which may be of equal or greater importance in this analysis of one's sexual orientation: e.g., class, race, income and religion. Bell and Weinberg thus conclude:

> Before one can say very much about a person on the basis of his or her sexual orientation, one must make a comprehensive appraisal of the relationship among a host of features pertaining to the person's life and decide very little about him or her until a more complete and highly developed picture appears.[100]

A final word should be added here regarding the 1973 decision of the American Psychiatric Association (APA). In the *Diagnostic and Statistical Manual of Mental Disorders*, 3rd edition, the category of Homosexuality is replaced by Ego-dystonic Homosexuality, described in this fashion: "The essential features are a desire to acquire or increase heterosexual arousal, so that heterosexual relationships can be initiated or maintained, and a sustained pattern of overt homosexual arousal that the individual explicitly states has been unwanted and a persistent source of distress."[101] The *Manual* goes on to describe Ego-syntonic Homosexuality as no longer "classified as a mental disorder."[102] In this form (ego-syntonic) an individual is not upset by his or her orientation.

In 1974, a significant minority of the members of the APA did not accept the *Manual's* revision of the category of homosexuality. Representative of the minority, Dr. Irving Bieber objected to the revised classification on the score that it is a developmental abnormality, although not a disease or mental illness. It might be called heterosexual dysfunction or inadequacy.[103]

## 5. MAGISTERIAL TEACHING

We noted in Chapter Three that *Gaudium et Spes* gave clear confirmation about the interrelationship between the unitive and procreative meanings of human sexuality. This document reaffirms this double purpose of sexual relations, even though these two purposes are not ordered hierarchically.[104] This document also explicitly recognizes the integral goodness of sexual acts in marriage even when procreation is neither possible nor desired: "Therefore, marriage persists as a whole manner and communion of life, and maintains its value and indissolubility, even when offspring are lacking — despite, rather often, the very intense desire of the couple" (n 50). Hanigan thus concludes, "Sex finds its deepest and lasting meaning as an expression, celebration and deepening of the two-in-one flesh unity of the couple."[105] In addition, as we have seen, *Humanae Vitae* likewise affirms an indissoluble link between the procreative and unitive meanings of human sexuality, a link established by God and revealed by nature.

Early in 1974 the American bishops, through their Committee on Pastoral Research and Practice, issued a set of guidelines specifically designed to assist priests in their dealings with homosexuals: *Principles to Guide Confessors in Questions of Homosexuality.*[106] This document recognizes the fact that homosexuality is a "complex question" and encourages confessors to "avoid both harshness and permissiveness"; and homosexuals are to be encouraged to form stable friendships. While respecting the probability of reduced culpability on the part of a homosexual who performs homosexual acts, the document reiterates traditional Catholic teaching that "Homosexual acts are a grave transgression of the goals of human sexuality and of human personality, and are consequently contrary to the will of God." The document also insists that "Genital sexual expression... should take place in marriage" and that there is a two-fold meaning for sexual intercourse, unitive and procreative, neither of which may ever be deliberately excluded.

On 29 December 1975 the Congregation for the Doctrine of the Faith issued its *Declaration on Certain Questions Concerning Sexual Ethics (Persona Humana).*[107] This document affirms traditional Catholic moral principles: There is an inner law within all persons that must be obeyed, a law that can be grasped by reason. This law is not dependent on cultural variance and the Church is the authentic interpreter of this law. As authentic interpreter, the Church teaches that homosexual acts are unnatural, even for the incurable homosexual (where there is a pathological condition); these acts lack an essential and indispensable finality and thus are seriously disordered, even though one may not be personally responsible for the activity. The *Declaration* thus draws the distinction between homosexual acts and a homosexual orientation and condemns the former as seriously wrong and disordered.

On 11 November 1976, the American bishops published a document on the moral life titled *To Live in Christ Jesus*.[108] This document teaches that morality is not imposed on us from without but is ingrained in our being; it is the way we accept our humanity as restored to us in Christ. The document again insists that the love-giving and life-giving meanings of genital intercourse are inseparable. One might not always act to realize both of these values but one must never deliberately suppress either of them. In this context, the document argues that sexual intercourse is a moral and human good only within marriage, for only within marriage are such relations symbolic of God's image of unconditional love.

*To Live in Christ Jesus* importantly teaches that homosexuals should not suffer from prejudice and should take an active role in the Christian community:

> Some persons find themselves through no fault of their own to have a homosexual orientation. Homosexuals, like every one else, should not suffer from prejudice against their basic human rights. They have a right to respect, friendship and justice. They should have an active role in the Christian community. Homosexual activity, however, as distinguished from homosexual orientation, is morally wrong. Like heterosexual persons, homosexuals are called to give witness to chastity, avoiding, with God's grace, behavior which is wrong for them, just as non-marital sexual relations are wrong for heterosexuals. Nonetheless, because heterosexuals can usually look forward to marriage, and homosexuals, while their orientation continues, might not, the Christian community should provide them a special degree of pastoral understanding and care.[109]

In summary, these three documents restate the Catholic Church's traditional teaching on homosexuality: (a) Homosexual activity is a sin *contra naturam* since it excludes all possibility of the transmission of life; (b) Homosexual activity represents an inordinate use of the sexual faculty, which possesses as one object the procreation of children; and (c) Homosexual activity is evaluated under the traditional rubric of material and formal sin: objectively (materially) homosexual acts are disordered and thus sinful, although subjectively (formally) one may not be responsible for the performance of such acts.

What does this distinction mean? The traditional authors of moral theology taught that formal sin is *realized* sin since it is the act of freely and knowingly violating the law of God. A formal sin always entails knowledge of the wrongness of the action that is being performed and freedom to do or to omit that action. Formal sin never occurs unless one acts knowingly and freely. Edwin F. Healy in *Moral Guidance*[110] teaches that "Formal sin entails only the sinfulness that is apprehended in the act itself or in the cause, for there is no sin without knowledge." On the other hand, material sin is the act of unknowingly violating a law. Classic authors taught that material sin "is not really a sin in the ordinary sense at all, for there is no moral guilt involved in this type of action. Hence it should not be mentioned in confession."[111]

In this regard it would be helpful to return to a matter we discussed in the first chapter regarding parvity of matter and acts which are *intrincese malum*. The Church teaches that homosexual activity is an intrinsically evil act for two reasons: (a) The physical structure of the homosexual act violates the complimentary structure of male and female anatomy and (b) Such an act is closed by its very nature to the procreative good. Consequently, such acts can never be fit objects for deliberate moral choice and no intention of the moral agent can make them fit objects. Or, in more precise language, an act of homosexual sex can never be an act of Christian love which proceeds from faith, no matter what the intentions of the actors may be. When such acts are deliberately chosen, therefore, they constitute mortal sin.[112] A homosexual act is, then, always objectively wrong, even though the wrongness neither of the act nor of the intention is necessarily and consciously apparent to the agent. Hanigan provides a useful explanation to help us understand this teaching: "To intend a moral evil, even for an ultimately good purpose, is to intend evil, no matter what other rationalizations may be offered in defense of that choice. Such an intention cannot be an act of love, not because of a defect in the agent, but because of the nature of the object intended. And no mere intention of the agent can change the nature of reality."[113]

In 1986 the Congregation for the Doctrine of the Faith issued the *Letter to the Bishops of the Catholic Church on the Pastoral Care of Homosexual Persons.*[114] This *Letter* refers in n 3 to the 1975 document *Persona Humana*, a document which noted the distinction between "the homosexual condition or tendency and individual homosexual acts." These acts were described as deprived of their essential and indispensable finality, as being "intrinsically disordered," and able in no case to be approved of. The *Letter* goes on to state that subsequent to 1975 discussion regarding this distinction gave "an overly benign interpretation... to the homosexual condition itself, some going so far as to call it neutral, or even good." In light of such benign interpretations, this *Letter* then teaches:

> Although the particular inclination of the homosexual person is not a sin, it is a more or less strong tendency ordered toward an intrinsic moral evil; and thus the inclination itself must be seen as an objective disorder.

For reasons we have already seen, the Church teaches that homosexual acts cannot be fit objects for deliberate moral choice because they are always disordered. The *Letter* is emphasizing this point, especially when one notes that the above quotation is in the same paragraph which teaches, "The particular inclination of the homosexual person is not a sin...." In "Toward an Understanding of the Letter 'On the Pastoral Care of Homosexual Persons,'"[115] Archbishop John R. Quinn explains this "objective disorder":

> This is philosophical language. The inclination is a disorder because it is directed to an object that is disordered. The inclination and the object are in the same order philosophically... In trying to understand this affirmation, we should advert to two things. First, every person has disordered inclinations. For instance, the inclination to rash

judgment is disordered, the inclination to cowardice, the inclination to hypocrisy — these are all disordered inclinations. Consequently, homosexual persons are not the only ones who have disordered inclinations. Second, the letter does not say that the homosexual person is disordered. The inclination, not the person, is described as disordered. Speaking of the homosexual person, the letter states that the Church "refuses to consider the person as a 'heterosexual' or a 'homosexual' and insists that every person has a fundamental identity: a creature of God and, by grace, His child and heir to eternal life" (no. 16). Consequently, the document affirms the spiritual and human dignity of the homosexual *person* while placing a negative moral judgment on homosexual *acts* and a negative philosophical judgment on the homosexual *inclination* or orientation, which it clearly states is not a sin or moral evil.[116]

N. 4 of the *Letter* indicates that some claim "that Scripture has nothing to say on the subject of homosexuality..." The *Letter* affirms the fact that the Scriptures have a good deal to say about this question, and it is to this subject that we now turn.

## 6. HOMOSEXUALITY AND SCRIPTURE

The *Letter* situates its scriptural discussion of homosexuality within the theology of creation found in Genesis. It teaches:

> Human beings... are nothing less than the work of God himself; and in the complementarity of the sexes, they are called to reflect the inner unity of the Creator. They do this in a striking way in their cooperation with him in the transmission of life by a mutual donation of the self to the other... To choose someone of the same sex for one's sexual activity is to annul the rich symbolism and meaning, not to mention the goals, of the Creator's sexual design. Homosexual activity is not a complementary union, able to transmit life; and so it thwarts the call to a life of that form of self-giving which the Gospel says is the essence of Christian living.[117]

Keeping this perspective in mind, we need to also recall that the concepts "homosexual" and "homosexuality" were unknown during the time of the Bible's composition. While Scripture does speak about homosexuality, it does not recognize homosexuality as a sexual orientation since the biblical writers took it for granted that all people were created with a natural attraction to members of the opposite sex and their genital activity would and should reflect this fact. Consequently, any homosexual behavior was likely to be judged negatively. It is helpful to look at the basic texts in the Bible which speak to this question:

## A. *Genesis 19:1-11* [118]

> The two angels came to Sodom in the evening, and Lot was sitting in the gate of Sodom. When Lot saw them, he rose to meet them, and bowed himself with his face to the earth, and said, "My Lords, turn aside, I pray you, to your servant's house and spend the night, and wash your feet; then you may rise up early and go on your way." They said, "No; we will spend the night in the street." But he urged them strongly; so they turned aside to him and entered his house; and he made them a feast, and baked unleavened bread, and they ate. But before they lay down, the men of the city, the men of Sodom, both young and old, all the people to the last man, surrounded the house; when they called to Lot, "Where are the men who came to you tonight? Bring them out to us, that we may know them." Lot went out of the door to the men, shut the door after him, and said, "I beg you, my brothers, do not act so wickedly. Behold, I have two daughters who have not known man; let me bring them out to you, and do to them as you please; only do nothing to these men, for they have come under the shelter of my roof." But they said, "Stand back!" And they said, "This fellow came to sojourn, and he would play the judge! Now we will deal worse with you than with them." Then they pressed hard against the man Lot, and drew near to break the door. But the men put forth their hands and brought Lot into the house to them, and shut the door. And they struck with blindness the men who were at the door of the house, both small and great, so that they wearied themselves groping for the door.

Victor Paul Furnish in *The Moral Teaching of Paul*[119] writes that "later biblical writers were not themselves preoccupied with [the] homosexual dimension" of this story.[120] For example, Jeremiah writes

that Sodom's sins were adultery, persistent lying and an unwilling-
ness to repent (23:14). Ezekiel claims that the crimes of Sodom's
people were "pride, gluttony, arrogance [and] complacency"; moreover, the inhabitants of Sodom "never helped the poor and needy; they
were proud and engaged in filthy practices..." (16:49-50). The Wisdom of Solomon identifies the evils of Sodom as folly, insolence and
inhospitality (19:13-14). Sirach indicates simply that God "did not
spare the people with whom Lot lived, whom he abhorred for their
pride" (16:8).

Jesus makes reference to Sodom in Luke 10:10-12 and Matthew
10:14-15. Here, Jesus himself seems to associate Sodom with the evil
of inhospitality. There are two late New Testament texts (2 Peter 2:4-
10 and Jude 6-7) which do give a predominantly sexual interpretation
to the Sodom story.

It seems clear, then, that the citizens of Sodom were involved in
numerous offenses. In this regard, it must be remembered that God's
decision to destroy Sodom and the surrounding cities was made *prior*
to the angelic visit. That is what Abraham's great debate with God was
about in the preceding chapter. The messengers were sent from God
to warn Lot and his family to flee, regardless of the reception the
messengers themselves received.

Homosexual activity, therefore, was one among many sins for
which Scripture condemns Sodom. The word "know" in the story is
paralleled in Judges 19:22-30 where the word is quite literally
translated as "to have intercourse with," which was also the way this
word was used in Genesis 4, and commonly in the Old Testament. The
point is inescapable: whereas sexual intercourse was legitimate in
Genesis 4, because Adam and Eve had been given to each other in
marriage, it was an abomination and an act of wickedness in Genesis
19 and in Judges 19, because the relationship is not marital but is one
of contemplated homosexual rape.

In *Women and Sexuality,* Lisa Sowle Cahill adds yet another
dimension-of-interpretation to this story:

> The historical setting renders the act an outrage not only as an
> instance of sexual violence, but also because it would have amounted
> to a vile betrayal of the duty of hospitality, without which travelers
> could not even have survived in the deserts of the ancient Near East.

Lot's proposed resolution of the affront is a frightening revelation of the dark side of a male piety only too ready to identify women's social and religious status in terms of the worth of their sexuality to fathers and husbands... Lot was willing to sacrifice his two daughters as an offering to the assailants, and proferred them with the encouragement that they were virgins. To have raped them would apparently have fallen significantly short of the "wickedness" about to be perpetrated on the pair of male visitors. (20-21)

### B. *Leviticus 18:21b-23 and 20:13*

I am the Lord. You shall not lie with a male as with a woman; it is an abomination. And you shall not lie with any beast and defile yourself with it, neither shall any woman give herself to a beast to lie with it; it is perversion...

If a man lies with a male as with a woman, both of them have committed an abomination; they shall be put to death, their blood is upon them.

The earliest specific law against homosexuality in Israel occurs in Leviticus 20:13. The same law is present in Leviticus 18, but without reference to the death penalty. The Holiness Code in which this law stands (Leviticus 17-26) had its origin in the 6th century B.C. The purpose of this legislation, made plain early on in the Code, was to establish the "holiness" of the Israelites over against their neighbors:

You shall not do as they do in the land of Egypt, where you dwelt, and you shall not do as they do in the land of Canaan, to which I am bringing you. You shall not walk in their statutes. You shall do my ordinances and keep my statutes and walk in them. I am the Lord your God (18:3-4).

In this Holiness Code the people of Israel were required to maintain their identity and integrity as the people of the one true God. The prohibition of males lying with males, like many of the other laws in this Code, sought to identify and condemn practices that had been, and ought always to remain, essentially foreign to Israel's life.[121]

Some have argued that what is really being proscribed here is either a kind of homosexual temple prostitution or the imposition of sex by one man on another, by one woman on another or by a human being on an animal.[122] In other words, homosexual rape is forbidden, as is bestiality.

On the contrary, the words "as with a woman" clearly suggest that what is permissible for a man to do with a woman is not permissible for him to do with another man. If one reads cultic prostitution into the passage, one makes it say that homosexual sacred prostitution is forbidden, but presumably heterosexual prostitution is permissible. If one reads rape into the passage, one makes it say that homosexual rape is forbidden, but presumably heterosexual rape is not. Clearly, Scripture speaks decisively against both cultic prostitution and rape. Consequently, these passages indicate that what is permitted between the sexes in marriage is not permitted between members of the same sex.

## C. *1 Corinthians 6:9-11 and 1 Timothy 1:8-11*

Do you not know that the unrighteous will not inherit the kingdom of God? Do not be deceived; neither the immoral, nor idolaters, nor adulterers, nor homosexuals, nor thieves, nor the greedy, nor drunkards, nor revilers, nor robbers will inherit the kingdom of God. And such were some of you. But you were washed, you were sanctified, you were justified in the name of the Lord Jesus Christ and in the Spirit of our God (1 Corinthians 6).

Now we know that the law is good, if any one uses it lawfully, understanding this, that the law is not laid down for the just but for the lawless and disobedient, for the ungodly and sinners, for the unholy and profane, for murderers of fathers and murderers of mothers, for manslayers, immoral persons, sodomites, kidnappers, liars, perjurers, and whatever else is contrary to sound doctrine, in accordance with the glorious gospel of the blessed God with which I have been entrusted (1 Timothy 1).

Furnish suggests three important points that should be kept in mind when studying the Pauline/deutero-Pauline texts:

1. The concepts "homosexual" and "homosexuality" as a sexual orientation were unknown in Paul's day. These terms presume an understanding of human sexuality that was possible only with the advent of modern psychological and sociological analysis.[123] Ancient writers did not know, e.g., of our concept of "sexual orientation." Dio Chrysostom, for instance, presumed that the same lusts that drove men to engage female prostitutes could drive them eventually to seduce other men.[124] Similarly, Philo wrote of the Sodomites' sexual intercourse with men as if it were one form of their "mad lust for women." Moreover, these writers and their contemporaries presumed that one could by force of will *control* these appetites and conform oneself to the sexual behavior dictated by reason or by "the law of nature."[125]

2. Homosexual behavior was invariably associated with insatiable lust and avarice. Seneca, for instance, portrayed it as a rich man's sport.[126]

3. Writers of this period were convinced that homosexual behavior necessarily involved one person's exploitation of another. For example, the influence of stoicism was widespread, and is detectable not only in several of the writers of the period but also in the teaching of St. Paul.

In the 1 Timothy 1 text, "sodomites" is *arsenokoitai*, which literally means "[men] who have intercourse with [other] males." In *The New Testament and Homosexuality*,[127] Robin Scroggs argues for this translation of 1 Timothy 1:

(U)nderstanding this, that the law is not laid down for the just but for the lawless, rebellious, impious, sinner, unholy, profane, patricide, matricide, murderer, *pornoi, arsenokoitai, andrapodistai,* liar, and perjurer, and whatever else is contrary to sound doctrine..."

Scroggs demonstrates that *pornos* means "male prostitute": the one who sells himself, or the slave in the brothel house (in normal Greek usage); in the New Testament usage, it normally means sexual crimes in general. Since *pornos* is here in juxtaposition to *arsenokoites*, it may have the same meaning vis-a-vis *arsenokoites* as does *malakos* in 1 Corinthians 6, the first term denoting the passive homosexual role and the second term the active. Scroggs then concludes that the phrase could be translated, "Male prostitutes, males who lie [with them], and slave dealers [who procure them] (*andrapodistai*)."

Scroggs' point becomes more evident when analyzing the 1 Corinthians 6 text. The two Greek words in question here are *malakoi* and *arsenokoitai*. The root meaning of the first term is "soft" or "weak," and by extension, "effeminate" (as in fact some translations render this text). It is significant that this is the very term that a number of writers at the time used to describe "call-boys," those who offered their bodies for pay to older males. However, the term can denote men as well as boys.[128] That Paul is using it in a sexual sense here seems likely, because it stands in a list where several other terms referring to sexual immorality also appear, e.g., "fornicators" and "adulterers."

Although 1 Corinthians 6:9 is the first documented use of the word *arsenokoitai*, it is difficult to avoid the conclusion that it refers to males who engage in sexual activity with other males. The juxtaposed term *malakoi* supports this interpretation. Scroggs argues that the word is simply a literal rendering in Greek of the Hebrew phrase *mishkav zakur*, "lying with a male," the usual way of referring to male homosexual intercourse in early rabbinic literature. Both *arsenokoites* and *mishkav zakur* appear to be terms coined from the prohibition of homosexual acts in Leviticus 18:22-23 and 20:13. Since *malakoi* would refer to the "effeminate" or passive partner in such a relationship, *arsenokoitai* doubtlessly refers to the male who assumes the more active role. Furnish thus translates the phrase in 1 Corinthians 6:9-11 as, "Don't deceive yourselves: Neither the sexually immoral, nor idolaters, nor adulterers, nor effeminate males, nor men who have sex with them, nor thieves, nor money-grabbers, nor drunkards, nor slanderers, nor swindlers will get into God's kingdom."[129]

What, then, did Paul have in mind as he recites a list of vices which includes references to "effeminate males" and "men who have sex with them"? Given what we have learned about the forms of homosexual activity with which Paul's world was most familiar, it would appear that these references are, respectively, to youthful call-boys and their customers. According to various ancient writers who condemn this practice, the one partner has violated the male role that by nature is his; and, by taking advantage of this, the other partner has also violated his proper role. Such conduct Paul regards as one of the forms of unrighteousness by which "unbelievers" are distinguished from "saints."

### D. Romans 1:22-27

> Claiming to be wise, they became fools, and exchanged the glory of the immortal God for images resembling mortal man or birds or animals or reptiles. Therefore, God gave them up in the lusts of their hearts to impurity, to the dishonoring of their bodies among themselves, because they exchanged the truth about God for a lie and worshipped and served the creature rather than the Creator, who is blessed forever! Amen. For this reason God gave them up to dishonorable passions. Their women exchanged natural relations for unnatural, and the men likewise gave up natural relationships with women and were consumed with passion for one another, men committing shameless acts with men and receiving in their own persons the due penalty for their error.

Richard B. Hays has given us an important context with which to interpret this text.[130] Hays indicates that a *keynote* for understanding this text is to appreciate Paul's basic theological view that the believer was to proclaim God's righteousness (God's faithfulness and justice). God's wrath is thus displayed against those who do not acknowledge and honor him. In Paul's theology, all depravities *follow from* the human person's *unrighteousness*; and this is the meaning of the "exchange" rhetoric: because some persons fell into idolatry and "exchanged" worship of the true God for false gods, God "exchanged" in them the natural for the unnatural. In this light, it is important to note that this is the first and only time in the whole Bible that one encounters the condemnation of female homosexual activity.

In this text, Paul, like his non-Christian contemporaries, supposes that homosexual behavior is something *freely chosen* by an individual; in Greek as in English the verbs "exchanged" and "gave up" imply a conscious decision to act in one way rather than another. Paul associates this choice with *insatiable lust*; the men, he writes were "consumed with passion for one another." Paul regards such activity as *a violation of the created order*: "natural" heterosexual relations were abandoned in favor of those which were "against nature." It is not surprising, then, to find Paul including sexual immoralities among those vices to which the pagans had been led by their own idolatry: lustful impurity and the degradation of their bodies (1:24), and "dishonorable passions" as evidenced by homosexual intercourse (1:26-27). In this connection he too can speak of the Gentiles having received "the due penalty for their error" (1:27). The "due penalty," then, indicates the very "exchange" itself, rather than some form of venereal disease or even (incredibly) AIDS, as some have recently suggested.

### Conclusion

Robin Scroggs and many contemporary writers seek to answer the question, "What specifically was it that the New Testament was reacting to when it speaks of what we might term 'homosexuality'?" As we have seen, Scroggs makes a good case for the position that the New Testament (especially Paul) was reacting against pederasty. Scroggs and others then imply that since this is the case, it is not correct to draw further conclusions about the New Testament position on homosexuality. In other words, one can say nothing based on the New Testament about whether it condemns any other form of homosexual behavior. This argument is flawed.

To discern what particular form/manifestation of a phenomenon an author is reacting to is not the same thing as to say why he is reacting against it. In other words, the specific manifestation is not the cause. Scroggs and others have to a certain extent confused these two things. For example, let us say that a series of particularly heinous murders has taken place in San Francisco over recent months, murders of a ritual nature which in some way mock the Church. Under such circumstances, if Church spokesmen were interviewed by the news media they might well express their indignation and utter disapproval of this particular form of murder. They might even dwell on the fact that the form in question is especially despicable. But would it be correct to conclude that they are not really opposed to murder as such but only to *this particular form of murder*? Of course not. The same thing is true of the New Testament's view of homo-sexuality. In other words, Scroggs and others have made a very good and convincing case for the position that pederasty was most probably the particular form of homosexuality to which the New Testament is by-and-large reacting. But this does not mean that the New Testament opposes only pederasty, but would find other types of homosexual behavior permissible. Consequently, the question comes down to this: did/would Paul see a homosexual relationship by mutual consent as against God's will or not?

In Romans 1:26-27 when Paul speaks of "natural" sexual relations versus "unnatural," Scroggs and others deny that this has anything to do with "any theories of natural law."[131] Even though once again some notion of pederasty might be the example of such behavior Paul might have had in mind, it seems a strain on credibility to think that he does not mean "unnatural" in somewhat the same sense we would now use the term in reference to deviant sexual activity. What Paul writes in these verses seems to bear this out. Note also that he uses the language of "males with males" (rather than men with men), not "men with boys," as one might expect if the reference were only to pederasty. Given the reference to the "unnatural" quality of this behavior, and the generic terms "male(s)" and "female(s)," and the unique reference to female homosexuality, it is difficult not to conclude that Paul is referring to something more than pederasty.

As we noted earlier, while it may be possible to demonstrate certain specific manifestations of homosexual behavior that New Testament authors probably had in mind in their anti-homosexual statements (e.g., pederasty), this does not prove that these remarks were limited to this one manifestation of such behavior. However widespread pederasty may have been in the Mediterranean world of the first century, surely no one could claim that sexual activity between adult males was unknown then, even though it may be less well documented. Pauline and deutero-Pauline texts provide some evidence to support the contention that the condemnation was in fact broader.

First, evidence comes from what New Testament authors *do not say*. Nowhere *in the New Testament* can one find reference to any sexual vice specifically referring to "boys." The extra-biblical *Didache*, on the other hand, contains a list of moral prohibitions based on the decalogue in which *ou paidophthoreseis* ("thou shalt not corrupt boys") occurs between "thou shalt not commit adultery" and "thou shalt not commit fornication" (*Didache* 2:2) — thus it is connected to the sixth commandment. Furthermore, *arsenokoitai* cannot be restricted to minors nor, as mentioned earlier, can *malakoi*.

Second, we should look again at what the New Testament authors *do* say. The term they use in contexts condemning homosexual behavior is *arsenokoitai* (1 Corinthians 6:9; 1 Timothy 1:10). Like rabbinic *mishkav zakur*, this is undoubtedly a coinage based on Leviticus 18:22 and 20:13, the Old Testament passages that provide the clearest and strongest condemnation of homosexual activity. There is no evidence to suggest that the Leviticus texts refer to acts committed with boys rather than men, and this holds true for the rabbinic expression as well. Because of the widespread phenomenon of pederasty in New Testament times, it is quite possible that pederasty was the *specific form* of homosexual behavior that New Testament writers would have come into contact with most often. But this does not mean it was the only form they had in mind. The fact that Paul and the author of 1 Timothy made use of a term based on the legal texts in Leviticus, passages rejecting homosexual acts *in general*, supports the view that what they were condemning was broader than pederasty. These facts make it impossible to endorse Scroggs' conclusion: "Biblical judgments about homosexuality are not relevant to today's debate."[132]

In addition, the New Testament's clear pro-marriage statements (heterosexual) are of vital importance in expressing its view about homosexuality. This is a point of major significance and should not be overlooked.

In conclusion, although it cannot be proven absolutely from scriptural evidence alone, there appears to be sufficient basis from which to assert that both the Old and New Testament writers express disapproval of homosexual behavior *per se*. The reasons are not always clearly stated, which certainly makes the biblical, moral and pastoral task more difficult.[133]

## 7. OUTING

In the Congregation for the Doctrine of the Faith's *Declaration on Certain Questions Concerning Sexual Ethics* (1975) and the *Letter to the Bishops on the Pastoral Care of Homosexual Persons* (1986), the affirmation is clear that no person should be discriminated against because of his or her sexual orientation.

The moral principles of equality and justice have been attacked in the political arena and sustain potential for attack in the religious realm. In 1987, e.g., Representative Barney Frank of Massachusetts announced that he was homosexual. Subsequently, he stood accused of a long-running affair with a male prostitute who claimed that Frank ran a bisexual prostitution ring in his Capitol Hill apartment. In a 1989 interview with *Newsweek*, Frank claimed, "I threatened to name the names of gay-bashers... They're entitled to privacy, but they're not entitled to hypocrisy. You can't vote for the 55-mile-per-hour speed limit and drive 80 mph." The same question emerged in the case of Terry Dolan, a founder of the National Conservation Political Action Committee. Dolan's stance of publicly voting against gay issues while being a "closeted homosexual" has led to the phenomenon called the "Terry Dolan problem."

In August of 1991 the national gay news magazine *Advocate* carried a story that a high-level Defense Department official is gay and the *Advocate*'s Editor-in-Chief defended the story by stating, "We commit ourselves to this singular instance of outing in the name of the 12,966 lesbian and gay soldiers who have been ousted by the military since 1982." The Editor maintained that it is "hypocritical" for this official "to front for the Pentagon..."

A spokesman for the Defense Investigative Service, which conducts background checks on civilians for the military, said that homosexuality is considered "like adultery, alcoholism or criminal activity" — as something that could present a security risk if it is a secret because it might render an employee vulnerable to blackmail. He noted, "An open gay, that's not a problem as a general rule."

Since the Church clearly upholds a position of non-discrimination and equality for all citizens, is forcing certain closeted homosexuals out of their private lives a form of public "political cannibalism"? Is this political tactic simply a bloodthirsty willingness to "do somebody in?"

These questions pointedly moved from the political to the religious sphere during the August-September 1989 convention in San Francisco of Dignity. During that convention, some participants felt it was time to move beyond anger at the Church and to cease unnecessary Church-bashing. A document issued at that meeting asserted that "...being gay or lesbian is God's blessing and gift" and that "...our sexuality and its expression is the holy gift of God."

Equally as vocal, however, has been the AIDS Coalition to Unleash Power (ACT-UP) which specifically proposes a tactic of revealing the names of homosexual clergy and religious who hide their sexual orientation and habits but who attack homosexuals who do not. ACT-UP has coined the term "outing" for the tactic of revealing the closeted homosexuality of politicians and religious people who oppose gay interests. The specific aim of "outing" is to select those politicians and clergy who abuse their moral authority by injecting themselves forcefully into civil and religious issues of gay rights. One delegate to the San Francisco Dignity Convention who holds such a view draws this analogy: "(I)f a child were abused by a neighbor, I would feel morally obliged at some point to report that neighbor's abuses, even though I liked that person, and even though that would constitute an invasion of their privacy and no doubt cause them some serious pain." The aim of "outing" is, then, to expose closeted homosexuals to force them to help the gay/lesbian movement; or at least to nullify them as opponents.

Advocates of "outing" are concerned about three critical religious areas:

1. Members of the hierarchy who refuse to acknowledge the numbers of homosexuals within the clergy.
2. Official Church documents which undermine the possibility of homosexual people realizing the "giftedness" of their homosexuality. Often-cited examples here include the reluctance of the Archdiocese of New York to comply with the terms of a New York City anti-discrimination ordinance in the hiring of homosexuals; and the 1986 document of the

CDF, *Letter to the Bishops...*, which calls the homosexual "tendency" "an objective disorder" (n 3).
3. Homosexual priests who evidence "In their private lives, clandestine [homosexual] behavior..."

This tactic needs a clear moral analysis.

First, do we have a right to know about the private lives of those persons who hold authoritative positions, be it in politics or the Church? A well-publicized case was that of Gary Hart and Donna Rice. Their private relationship caused many to conclude that the public has a right to know about the character and personality of its leaders in order to assess carefully their over-all ability to lead and to inspire confidence. Similarly a 1982 Gallup Poll indicated that support for homosexuals has grown in recent years; but it is equally clear that the discovery or the announcement of an individual's homosexuality does create a negative difference in public opinion regarding that person's capacity to hold authoritative positions. Consequently, it is not possible to totally divorce one's private life from one's public capacity to inspire confidence and trust.

Second, the tactic of "outing" represents violence to a person's right to privacy. Human dignity is truly not sustained by destroying another's individual dignity. Forcing a person into the "passage" of public disclosure is an act of violence against one's right of personal recognition and acceptance and a violence against human dignity.

Third, the legal ramifications regarding "outing" should not be overlooked. As one example, the 1970 case *Henrickson v. California Newspapers, Inc.* (48 Cal. App. 3d 59) demonstrates that a suit for invasion of privacy which is based on the public disclosure of private facts includes these elements: public disclosure; the facts disclosed are personal facts; and the matter made public is one which would be offensive and objectionable to a reasonable person of ordinary sensibilities.

Is not the public disclosure of another's sexual orientation an invasion of privacy? This disclosure becomes especially problematic when it is aimed at a person in retaliation. Such an announcement would doubtlessly be offensive and objectionable to most reasonable people. The tactic of "outing" is morally and legally outrageous; and demonstrates a complete disregard for intrusion into the private lives of individuals and the impact that this labeling would have on their relationships to various publics. From a legal point of view, then, the tactic of "outing" is subject to causes of action for slander, invasion of privacy, and possible intentional infliction of emotional distress.

Every person must be assisted to understand and accept his or her own sexual orientation. For persons who have made a celibate commitment, integrity of lifestyle is essential and expected; and politicians need to assess their own lifestyles in order to bring their public advocacy of individual rights into harmony with their own personal ways of living and acting.

Confrontational tactics as proposed in "outing" are a violence against human dignity and a threat against the need to continue to uphold nondiscrimination toward persons in light of their sexual orientation. The problem with "outing" is that it claims an unjustifiable right to sacrifice the lives of others.[134]

## 8. DISCRIMINATION, HOMOSEXUALITY AND
## PUBLIC POLICY

The *Encyclopedia of Homosexuality* states that "The campaign for anti-discrimination ordinances parallel to those protecting other minorities will be a major part of gay movement activity in the decades ahead, as removing the negative sanctions in the law is only the first, though necessary step." This article concludes by indicating that in the future homosexuals will be seeking "positive guarantees of... fundamental liberties" in order to become "full-fledged members of modern society."[135]

This assertion offers an interpretive backdrop for the concerns expressed in "Some Considerations Concerning the Response to Legislative Proposals on the Non-Discrimination of Homosexual Persons," a document sent to all U.S. bishops on 25 June 1992 from the Congregation for the Doctrine of the Faith. On 23 July 1992, the Vatican's press office offered an explanation of this document: "For some time, the Congregation for the Doctrine of the Faith has been concerned with the question of legislative proposals advanced in various parts of the world to deal with the issue of the non-discrimination of homosexual persons. A study of this question culminated in the preparation of a set of observations which could be of assistance to those concerned with formulating the Catholic response to such legislative proposals."

This clarification goes on to say that the observations " were not intended to be an official public instruction on the matter from the Congregation but a background resource offering discreet assistance to those who may be confronted with the task of evaluating draft legislation regarding non-discrimination on the basis of sexual orientation." It notes further that since the observations had become public, a "slight revision of the text was undertaken and a second version prepared."

The document's Foreword gives precise focus to the Congregation's concern: "Recently, legislation has been proposed in various places which would make discrimination on the basis of sexual orientation illegal."[136] It is critical to note that the *fundamental* caution raised in these observations is that "Such initiatives... may in fact have a negative impact on the family and society."[137] This concern is repeated several times: the nature and rights of the family are placed "in jeopardy" when homosexual activity is seen to be equivalent to or as acceptable as "the sexual expression of conjugal love;"[138] bishops should keep as their "utmost concern" the defense and promotion of the family;[139] and provisions of proposed measures must be evaluated carefully: "How would they affect adoption or foster care? Would they protect homosexual acts, public or private? Do they confer equivalent family status on homosexual unions, for example, in respect to public housing or by entitling the homosexual partner to the privileges of employment which might include such things as 'family' participation in the health benefits given to employees."[140]

This emphasis comes to its conclusion in the final paragraph of the document: "The Church has the responsibility to promote family life and the public morality of the entire civil society on the basis of fundamental moral values, not simply to protect herself from the application of harmful laws."[141]

On 22 June 1992, Archbishop Daniel E. Pilarczyk, President of the N.C.C.B., issued a letter which also endorses this primary focus: "The Congregation's concern is that proposals to safeguard the legitimate rights of homosexual persons not have the effect of creating a new class of legally protected *behavior*, that is, homosexual behavior, which, in time, could occupy the same position as non-discrimination against *people*, because of their race, religion, gender, or ethnic background. The document rightly warns against legislation designed more to legitimate homosexual behavior than to secure basic civil rights and against proposals which tend to promote an equivalence between legal marriage and homosexual lifestyles." The document's interest seems primarily aimed at protecting and upholding the centrality of family life.[142] Discrimination and homosexuality are thus evaluated *in relationship to* the family in society.

Since the document is not intended to be an official instruction from the Congregation, certain standard features in Roman curial documents are lacking: (a) the document bears no Letterhead of the Congregation, nor does it bear a date; (b) it does not *per se* indicate what type of document it is: e.g., a decree, an instruction, a letter; (c) it does not bear the signature of the Prefect of the Congregation, nor of the Secretary; and (d) it does not indicate papal approbation. Archbishop Pilarczyk's comment is thus helpful as to how these observations are to be used: "Bishops will continue to evaluate local legislation with these considerations clearly in mind. However, as the considerations note, 'It would be impossible to foresee and respond to every eventuality in respect to legislative proposals in this area...'" The counsel given in the Congregation's 1986 *Letter* also explains: "...(T)hey [bishops] should decide for their own dioceses the extent to which an intervention on their part is indicated. In addition, should they consider it helpful, further coordinated action at the level of their National Bishops' Conference may be envisioned... In a particular way, we would ask the bishops to support, with the means at their disposal, the development of appropriate forms of pastoral care for homosexual persons."[143]

### Discrimination

In its personal and social dimension, discrimination refers to treatment that disadvantages others by virtue of their perceived membership in a group.[144] Historically, discrimination against homosexual people has created a pattern of ostracism and homophobia which has driven many homosexual persons into concealment and deception in order to avoid moral, economic and social penalties which a discriminatory environment causes and encourages. Discrimination creates people and groups considered to be stigmatized, criminals and outcasts.

While the Civil Rights Act of 1964 made it illegal to discriminate against persons on grounds of racial or ethnic origin, discrimination based upon a person's sexual orientation has been generally upheld by the courts and attempts to include homosexuals within the protections afforded cultural, religious, and racial minorities have met uniformly with failure.

Only gradually have groups concerned with civil liberties come to believe that discrimination against homosexuals violated their civil rights. The struggle to include "sexual orientation" in the protected list of anti-discrimination laws began in the 1970s and has led to the passage of some 50 municipal ordinances with such guarantees.

Since the late 1940s, the United States federal government has maintained that homosexual conduct is immoral and that homosexuality in itself establishes unfitness for employment. While more recent court decisions have somewhat limited the Civil Service Commission in this area, they leave open the possibility that homosexual conduct might justify dismissal where interference with efficiency could be proved. The military establishment has been almost uniformly successful in defeating suits brought against it by homosexual and lesbian members of the armed forces threatened with discharge and often loss of benefits as well.

Homosexual teachers and counselors often face dismissal on the basis of substantive rules that disqualify such an employee for "moral turpitude" or "immoral or unprofessional conduct." Because popular belief wrongly identifies the homosexual with the child molester, public school teachers have faced a particularly invidious type of discrimination.

Recently, a few courts have held that an employee's private life should not be of concern to an employer unless it could be shown to affect the employee's ability to perform his or her duties. In practice, the criterion has often been the employee's visibility: if the person's sexual activity is covert and unknown to the community, the school official can overlook it; but if it becomes publicly known, they feel obliged to "protect the reputation of the institution." Such is also the logic of court decisions that uphold the right of an employer to dismiss a gay activist whose political overtness has made him or her publicly identified.

Discrimination in housing is another barrier that homosexuals face. Single homosexuals who "pass" are not likely to encounter difficulty. When two prospective tenants of the same sex apply for housing, they may be denied at the whim of the owner — or as the result of company policy. The argument is voiced that their presence will have a "morally corrupting influence" on the children of families living in the same building or in the general area.

### Church Teachings

This brief overview gives focus to two important points in Church teachings:

### A. Human Sexuality

The Congregation for the Doctrine of the Faith's document *Declaration on Sexual Ethics (Persona Humana)* affirms:

> ...(T)he human person is so profoundly affected by sexuality that it must be considered as one of the factors which give to each individual's life the principal traits that distinguish it. In fact, it is from sex that the human person receives the characteristics which, on the biological, psychological and spiritual levels make the person a man or woman, and thereby largely condition his or her progress towards maturity and insertion into society.[145]

In 1977 the National Conference of Catholic Bishops published *Sharing the Light of Faith: National Catechetical Directory for Catholics in the United States.* Here we read:

> Sexuality is an important element of human personality, an integral part of one's overall consciousness. It is both a central aspect of one's self-understanding (i.e., as male or female) and a crucial factor in one's relationship with others. (n 191)

In 1983 we read in the Congregation for Catholic Education's *Educational Guidance in Human Love*:

> Sexuality is a fundamental component of personality, one of its modes of being, of manifestation, of communicating with others, of feeling, of expressing and of living human love. Therefore it is an integral part of the development of the personality and of its educative process. (n 4)

Finally, in *Human Sexuality: A Catholic Perspective for Education and Lifelong Learning* (1990), the United States Catholic Conference teaches:

> Sexuality... is a fundamental dimension of every human being. It is reflected physiologically, psychologically, and relationally in a person's gender identity as well as in one's primary sexual orientation and behavior. For some young men and women, this means a discovery that one is homosexual, that is, that one's 'sexual inclinations are oriented predominantly toward persons of the same sex.' (p 54)

The Church's teachings about human sexuality are thus quite clear and pointed: human sexuality must be considered one of our principal traits, an integral part of our personality, and a fundamental dimension of every human being. Human sexuality is "... a voice from the depths, the utterance of something central and of utmost significance."[146]

## B. Prejudice and Discrimination

On 11 November 1976, the American bishops published a document on the moral life, *To Live in Christ Jesus*. This document maintains that homosexuals should not suffer from prejudice and should take an active role in the Christian community:

> Some persons find themselves through no fault of their own to have a homosexual orientation. Homosexuals, like everyone else, should not suffer from prejudice against their basic human rights. They

have a right to respect, friendship and justice. They should have an active role in the Christian community. (n 4)

In *Human Sexuality*, the U.S.C.C. "reaffirms" this teaching and "strongly" echoes the 1986 *Letter* from the Congregation for the Doctrine of the Faith: "It is deplorable that homosexual persons have been and are the object of violent malice in speech or in action. Such treatment deserves condemnation from the Church's pastors wherever it occurs."[147] *Human Sexuality* continues:

> We call on all Christians and citizens of good will to confront their own fears about homosexuality and to curb the humor and discrimination that offend homosexual persons. We understand that having a homosexual orientation brings with it enough anxiety, pain and issues related to self-acceptance without society adding additional prejudicial treatment... (W)e affirm that homosexual men and women "must certainly be treated with understanding" and sustained in Christian hope.[148]

Clearly, Church teaching affirms that homosexuals should not suffer prejudice against their basic human rights.

This point can also be found in these Considerations, affirming of the 1986 *Letter*:

> The Church... does not limit but rather defends personal freedom and dignity realistically and authentically understood. (n 3)
>     What is essential is that the fundamental liberty which characterizes the human person and gives him his dignity be recognized as belonging to the homosexual person as well. (n 8)

### Some Points of Interpretation

1. The Considerations stress the Congregation's teaching in the 1986 *Letter* [149] that the homosexual orientation is an objective disorder. The Considerations add that " 'Sexual orientation' does not constitute a quality comparable to race, ethnic background, etc. in respect to non-discrimination." (n 10) N 13 adds that "... there is no right to homosexuality" and states in n 14:

An individual's sexual orientation is generally not known to others unless he publicly identifies himself as having this orientation or unless some overt behavior manifests it. As a rule, the majority of homosexually oriented persons who seek to lead chaste lives do not publicize their sexual orientation. Hence the problem of discrimination in terms of employment, housing, etc. does not usually arise.[150]

It is important to note here that while the Considerations state that "there is no right to homosexuality" and refer to n 10 of the *Letter*, there is a critical difference between the documents: the *Letter* states that it is "homosexual activity" that is the "behavior to which no one has any conceivable right..." and not homosexuality *per se*. Archbishop Pilarczyk's commentary is thus helpful and correctly interpretive of the *Letter*: the legitimate rights of homosexual persons need to be safeguarded, while not creating a "new class of legally protected *behavior...*"

This focus finds emphasis in the teaching of *To Live in Christ Jesus*, "Some persons find themselves through no fault of their own to have a homosexual orientation," as well as the CDF's *Letter* that "the particular inclination of the homosexual person is not a sin..." (n 3) and *Persona Humana* that "...sexuality... must be considered as one of the factors which give to each individual's life the principal traits that distinguish it." The U.S.C.C.'s *Human Sexuality* thus counsels that "...parents and other educators must remain open to the possibility that a particular person, whether adolescent or adult, may be struggling to accept his or her own homosexual orientation."[151]

2. The Considerations uphold the possibility of discrimination in certain specified areas: consignment of children to adoption or foster care; employment of teachers or coaches; and military recruitment.[152] In addition, discrimination is "obligatory" in the case of "objectively disordered external conduct" or of "culpable behavior."[153] Number 12 concludes with a critically important phrase that helps exegete possible discrimination: "in order to protect the common good." In other words, the document suggests that discrimination is "sometimes" (the document's word) licit when external conduct is harmful to the common good. Since the Foreword states that it is "impossible to anticipate every eventuality" and that this document is thus concerned with identifying "principles and distinctions

of a general nature," it is clear that Church authorities are being asked to exercise discrimination only in those cases where the common good is being harmed.

3. The Considerations raise concern about legislation which confers "...equivalent family status on homosexual unions, for example, in respect to public housing or by entitling the homosexual partner to the privileges of employment which could include such things as 'family' participation in the health benefits given to employees." (n 15)

Across the U.S., major efforts have been underway to change laws regarding "close and committed personal relationships involving shared responsibilities." Statistics indicate that of the nation's 91 million households, 2.6 million are inhabited by unmarried adults of the opposite sex, and some 1.6 million households involve unmarried adults of the same sex. These latter households lie at the center of a growing national debate over whether gay couples should be allowed to declare themselves "domestic partners." We will deal with this question again in more detail in the next chapter on Nonmarital Sexuality.

It is enough to say here that domestic partnership is damaging to society and objectionable to the Church because it further weakens the institution of marriage and encourages heterosexual couples to forego the marital commitment.

4. N 13 of the Considerations raises concern about the homosexual orientation "as a positive source of human rights, for example, in respect to so-called affirmative action, the filling of quotas in hiring practices." From the late 1960s onward,[154] laws and guidelines have been enacted in the U.S. that call for "affirmative action" to increase the numbers of women and ethnic minorities in fields from which they have traditionally been excluded or limited to low-level menial positions. These have even included actual quotas that an employer needs to meet to comply with the law. However, none of these programs has contained any measure to increase the number of homosexuals in any firm or industry, although there have been consent decrees which various government agencies have agreed to which include affirmative action policies for gay and lesbian persons.

The Considerations endorse this posture by claiming that while such qualities as race, ethnic background (n 10), sex and age (n 14) do not constitute a reason for discrimination, homosexuals should not be designated as a special group for affirmative action. Anti-discrimination laws indicate that it is wrong to discriminate in employment and housing against an individual on the grounds of sexual orientation. Affirmative action laws, on the other hand, create a special and privileged group, often with specific time-tables and targets to meet quotas in employment and housing. It is this latter category which the Considerations do not support: "Including 'homosexual orientation' among the considerations on the basis of which it is illegal to discriminate can easily lead to regarding homosexuality as a positive source of human rights, for example, in respect to so-called affirmative action or preferential treatment in hiring practices." (n 13)

### Conclusion

Archbishop Pilarczyk's final words of comment are a fitting conclusion to these remarks: "I believe that the bishops of the various local Churches in the United States will continue to look for ways in which those people who have a homosexual orientation will not suffer unjust discrimination in law or reality because of their orientation. In our teaching, pastoral care, and public advocacy, bishops will, of course, continue to strive to be faithful to Church teaching on homosexuality, to uphold the values of marriage and family life, to defend the basic human dignity and human rights of all and to condemn violence, hatred and bigotry directed against any person."

CHAPTER SIX

# NONMARITAL SEXUALITY

## 1. CONTEXT OF THE QUESTION

A number of changes have taken place in our society that deeply affect attitudes toward nonmarital sexuality:

(1) *Availability of Contraceptives*: Today there exists a more "safe" attitude toward engaging in sex because of the availability of effective contraceptives. In addition, abortion is considered by many in our society as a simple "follow-up method" if normal contraceptives fail. Katchadourian, Lunde and Trotter remark, e.g., "Abortion has been used as a form of birth control for thousands of years in numerous cultures, whether or not the procedure was considered legal... As a back-up procedure when contraception fails... abortion is becoming increasingly popular, and although it remains a highly controversial issue on ethical and moral grounds, it is widely practiced in the Soviet Union, parts of Eastern and Central Europe, and Japan."[1] With this almost casual attitude toward contraceptives, many people are led to sex at a premature age.

(2) *Cultural Aspects*: Many today live in an anonymous social setting and have *de facto* adopted an attitude that says, "*My* sexual conduct is none of your business."

(3) *The Emancipation of Women*: The so-called "double-standard" in American sexual mores no longer exists, and there is a growing sense and acceptance of the equality of

271

the sexes. The "standard" about virginity regarding women
and men has radically changed.

(4) *Stress on Self-Determination*: Today freedom of behavior
and autonomy are greatly stressed with the result that many
persons automatically shun any type of excessive personal
and/or social intrusion into their lifestyle and sexual
decisions.

(5) *Longer Time between Puberty and Marriage*: The "premarital period" is a rather recent phenomenon in history and
creates an atmosphere that produces an "acceptable" and
conducive environment for sexual expression, especially
when many people are getting married at a later age.

For these and many other reasons, sexual intercourse before
marriage is oftentimes simply taken for granted; and even encouraged. In this context, the *Declaration on Sexual Ethics* teaches:

> Today there are many who vindicate the right to sexual union before
> marriage, at least in those cases where firm intention to marry and an
> affection which is in some way conjugal in the psychology of the
> subject require this completion, which they judge to be connatural.
> This is especially the case when the celebration of the marriage is
> impeded by circumstances or when this intimate relationship seems
> necessary in order for love to be preserved.[2]

The *Declaration* goes on to say that such an opinion is "contrary
to Christian doctrine," and reaches this conclusion for several reasons:

(1) Every genital act must be within the framework of marriage: *Gaudium et Spes* teaches that "the sexual nature of
man and the human faculty of procreation" find their moral
goodness only within the conjugal life, where sexual acts
are ordered properly to true human dignity.[3] The Church
holds this principle from revelation and from her authentic
interpretation of the natural law which states that the use of
the sexual function has its authentic meaning and moral
rectitude only in true marriage.

(2) Nonmarital sexuality does not get its moral goodness from the intention of those who practice such premature sexual relations, no matter how firm or convincing such intentions may be. The fact remains that these relations cannot insure sincerity, fidelity, and the interpersonal relationship between a man and a woman; nor can they protect this relationship from whims and caprices.

(3) Jesus willed a stable union and restored its original requirement, beginning with the sexual difference: "Have you not heard that the Creator from the beginning made them male and female and that he said: This is why a man must leave father and mother, and cling to his wife, and the two become one body? They are no longer two, therefore, but one body. So then, what God has united, man must not divide."[4] St. Paul is more explicit when he teaches that if unmarried people or widows cannot live chastely they have no other alternative than the stable union of marriage: "It is better to marry than to be aflame with passion."[5]

(4) In marriage, the love of married people is taken up into that love which Christ irrevocably has for the Church,[6] while dissolute sexual union defiles the temple of the Holy Spirit which the Christian has become.[7] Sexual union is, therefore, only legitimate if a definitive community of life has been established between the man and the woman.

The *Declaration* concludes these reasons by stating that this is "what the Church has always understood and taught."[8] The *Declaration* then notes:

Experience teaches us that love must find its safeguard in the stability of marriage, if sexual intercourse is truly to respond to the requirements of its own finality and to those of human dignity. These requirements call for a conjugal contract sanctioned and guaranteed by society — a contract which establishes a state of life of capital importance both for the exclusive union of the man and the woman and for the good of their family and of the human community. Most often, in fact, premarital relations exclude the possibility of children. What is represented to be conjugal love is not able, as it absolutely should be, to develop into paternal and maternal love. Or, if it does happen to do so, this will be to the detriment of the children, who will be deprived of the stable environment in which they ought to develop in order to find in it the way and the means of their insertion into society as a whole.[9]

This perspective is reiterated in the U.S.C.C. document *Human Sexuality*.[10] This document reaffirms the Church's clear teaching that sexual union is legitimate (i.e., has its true meaning and moral rectitude) only in the context of marriage.[11] Outside of this "definitive community of life" called marriage, however personally gratifying or well-intended, genital sexual intimacy is objectively morally wrong. Relational misunderstandings and break-ups, the sense of being used or betrayed, the trauma of unexpected pregnancies, sometimes followed by abortion, constitute some of the real personal harm that can result from sexual intimacy expressed apart from the bonds and fidelity of marriage.

This document recognizes the fact that it is common in our American culture for couples engaged to be married or couples contemplating formal engagement or even couples who feel close affection and friendship, even if marriage is not likely, to engage in intimate sexual expressions, including sexual intercourse: "The romanticism of theatrical, film, or television dramas; the lure of media advertisements building on 'love story' themes; the peer pressure to be sexually intimate fairly early in a budding relationship; and the strong personal need or drive for swift and immediate closeness all coalesce to foster what we believe is a premature and misguided focus on sex and genital expressions."[12]

*Human Sexuality* recognizes that all too often, particularly among teenagers and those inexperienced in human relationships, sexual exploitation preempts any attempt at true love and commitment. Too often casual sexual intercourse is carried out primarily for one's own selfish pleasure and this has caused real psychological, social and spiritual damage.

As we have seen, and this document endorses, many social scientists suggest that our current American society is marked by tendencies toward excessive individualism and a preoccupation with self-gratification. So also, the consumerism of our age, with the correlative practice of built-in obsolescence and disposable goods, tends to make permanence, commitments and fidelities seem "old-fashioned" or even unattainable.[13] The young and inexperienced are particularly vulnerable to manipulation through false pledges of love and fidelity. Their fragile egos and adolescent sense of self make them easy prey to sexual demands couched in the language of romantic love.

The document goes on to say that this potential harm is not limited to psychological and spiritual damage alone. The procreative potential of sex means that a third party, a new member of the human family, can get affected, at least potentially, by every act of intercourse. For example, recent statistics indicate that more than half of America's teens have experienced sexual intercourse by the time they are seventeen. More than one million teenage girls in this country become pregnant each year. That has resulted in a 200% increase in the birth of children to unwed teenage mothers in recent decades. Even with this dramatically increased birthrate, still more than 400,000 teenage girls now have abortions each year.[14] In addition, each person engaging in nonmarital sex runs the risk of being infected or infecting others with sexually transmitted diseases (STD). Obviously, these can cause serious mental and physical harm, frequently including infertility and sometimes even death.[15]

A word should be added here about the phenomenon of *cohabitation* between the sexes. Nonmarital sexual intercourse and living together without marriage are not identical issues or questions. *Faithful to Each Other Forever* thus remarks, "Couples may engage in sexual intercourse without living together; other couples, particularly those sharing homes for financial reasons, might live together without having sexual intercourse."[16] While cohabitation, by definition, does not necessarily involve genital sexual intimacy, it does establish a context in which avoidance of nonmarital sex becomes exceptionally difficult, particularly for those couples bound by affection or even contemplating marriage. When two people move in together without exchanging formal wedding vows and live "externally as husband and wife," they can create more difficulties for themselves and can cause a potential scandal for others by weakening the sanctity and respect society has for marriage itself. In addition, empirical data raises doubts about cohabitation as a healthy or helpful preparation for married life.[17]

We have just seen that *cohabitation* and *nonmarital sexual intercourse* are *de facto* not identical issues or questions. It is helpful, though, to make further distinctions:

### A. Premarital Sex

At one extreme, the term "premarital sex" is used to describe the practice of "sleeping around," or engaging in a protracted series of one-night stands. Such behavior is often a sign of profound problems with identity and self-acceptance, particularly when it is pursued as a form of rebellion. In such cases, the behavior is only incidentally sexual.[18] As we have now often stated, to make of sexual expression anything other than an act of serious personal commitment is to trivialize sex; and this is the same as trivializing ourselves. Reputable studies have demonstrated, for instance, that promiscuous sexual activity during adolescence makes it virtually impossible for a person in later life to achieve sexual love.[19]

Sigmund Freud wrote about the importance of "attachment," which later came to be called by some "imprinting."[20] The Attachment Theory has important repercussions for the development of affection and love, for it is within the bond of affection formed between mother and child, and later father and child, that the essential human interaction of growth and development will take place. It means that significant interaction, which is worthy of the name "human," always occurs in the context where affective feelings are present. This differentiates the personal dimension of human relationships from the impersonal, where roles are exchanged such as are necessary for work and the transaction of social life. Since sex is such a fundamentally human experience, it loses its vitality when it occurs in the absence of an affectionate personal interaction.

In this light, the adolescent who has sex is often led to believe that he or she "has arrived." Young men and women are often pressured to have intercourse as a sign of adulthood, for they can boast afterward that they have had sex, thus hoping to gain respect and recognition. This is a great temptation, but one that fails the test of human integrity, for sex is much more than a social marker. What is often not realized by those who advocate coitus as a sign of adulthood is that psychologically coitus carries with it an intense degree of exclusivity. It is felt as a most powerful personal sign of "this man" or "this woman" making love to "me". It is therefore quite inappropriate that it should become an occasion for social achievement. We must not forget, then, that sexual activity always has some personal result.

We spoke earlier of the virtue of chastity and we return now to that conversation. Abstinence is neither as easy as some have advocated nor as impossible as society currently accepts. There are psychological and physiological forces, which vary from person to person, driving toward orgasmic release. In our society these internal pressures are widely aided and abetted by social sexual titillation. Sexual abstinence is never easy but becomes easier after thought (and prayer) and when an effort is made to achieve it. It is facilitated too when the personal and loving dimension becomes the primary reason.

The prevailing view of premarital sex is, at its worst, one of hedonistic pursuit and, at its best, that each sexual occasion is one of instant and temporary bonding with no lasting or enduring meaning. Such a view permits and encourages casual sex, but discourages the rich potential of sexual intercourse. In its human dimension, the sexual instinct is integrated within the whole personality and is a symbol of a loving commitment of exclusiveness, faithfulness and permanency. Through exclusiveness, a couple are promising to love one another to the exclusion of others. Through faithfulness, they are offering to love one another without fear of rejection and loss of this love to a third party. Through permanency, they are offering one another what all human beings long for and have been conditioned to in childhood, namely continuity, reliability and predictability.

The uniqueness of the genital union consists in the marital promise, "I take you, for better, for worse, until death." This is the love-pledge one does not make even to one's children. Sexual intercourse is, therefore, an act which testifies to a couple's mutual and full self-giving that does not hesitate to assume an unconditional responsibility for each other. True love is thus distinct from physical sex. Sex is not the ultimate proof of love; the greatest proof of love is caring for others even to the point of self-sacrifice.[21]

The creation accounts of Genesis 1:27-28 and Genesis 2:24

reflect that both the *procreative* and the *unitive* expressions of
sexuality are an imitation of God's promise of fidelity to his people.
A committed love-relationship has traditionally been regarded as a
required setting for genital sexual expression: this can be appreciated
only when one understands that the qualities of God's love for
humanity are both creative and eternally faithful and are reflected in
the full richness of human sexual love through the characteristics of
procreativity and permanent fidelity.

Before engaging in premarital expressions of genital intercourse, then, every person should raise certain questions about his or
her prospective sexual partner: e.g., "Can I honestly say that if I ever
have a child it will be with you?" or, "Are you the one I want to be the
mother or father of my child?" or, "Are you the one I want to be with,
to care for, and to be cared for, for the rest of my life?" In human
persons, sexuality cannot be reduced to mere biological or physical
realities. All sexual activity, in other words, has a moral content.
Persons who are contemplating premarital intercourse should always
truthfully remember that circumstances change, engagements are
broken, and promises are not vows. Words of love do need the
strengthening that comes from the willing support of the community
of faith and the sacramental grace of marriage.

To say that marriage is a sacrament is to say that it is a "special
point of contact" between God and his people. It always says that in
loving each other, two people intend to enter into and share the quality
of love that exists between Christ and his people. On their wedding
day, then, a man and a woman *become sacraments* or living and
effective signs of God's love. This is much better than to say simply
that "they receive the sacrament of matrimony." The essence of
marriage lies in the exchange of vows and the mutual consent of the
couple. But in order for the full richness of marriage as a sacrament
or a sign of God's creative and faithful love to be exposed and
appreciated, it is necessary for a man and a woman to proclaim their
love in a social context so that the sign may be seen and heard. If
marriage is really a sacrament or a sign, then it is necessarily social.
It requires witnesses.

As we have seen, chastity is a matter of honesty in sex.
Therefore, no physical expressions of love should go beyond the
degree of interpersonal commitment that is found in a relationship.

Since sexual intercourse is best and morally expressed only in a marital relationship where two people have pledged themselves to mutual unconditional responsibility for each other in marriage, it is unwise and frustrating to engage in heavy premarital expressions of affection (e.g., petting; deep kissing; etc.). Sex cannot and does not create a relationship. Sex is a very small part of love, a part which cannot be allowed to dominate a relationship. Once a relationship becomes dominated by sex, the relationship has probably gone too far.

## B. Pre-Ceremonial Sex

Pre-ceremonial sex refers to the case of two people who are engaged, formally or informally, but have not yet taken part in a marriage ceremony. Such cases vary considerably, but at least at times, the two appear to be fully committed to each other and intend that commitment to be lifelong. In such cases, some authors refer to sexual activity between the couple as "pre-ceremonial" because the elements of true marital consent and intent are present in this commitment.

As we have seen, the essence of marriage lies in the exchange of vows and the mutual consent of the couple. In order for the full richness of marriage as a sacrament or sign of God's creative and faithful love to be exposed and appreciated, it is necessary for a man and a woman to proclaim their love in a social context so that the sign may be seen and heard, and so that through this new promise of love, people may be reminded of the greatness of God and of his love.[22]

Paul Ramsey thus noted that if an engaged couple, by means of genital relations, intend "to express the fact that their lives are united and that they now are willing to accept all that is entailed in sexual intercourse as their unity in one-flesh and possibly into the one flesh of the child, then it is simply impossible for them to engage in premarital sexual relations."[23] In Ramsey's eyes, this couple is in some sense already married and therefore their genital involvement is only pre-ceremonial, not premarital.

Along with Genovesi and others, I would object to this view because of its implications; and in addition to the implications, this approach to pre-ceremonial sex is against the teaching of the Church.

If marriage is really a sacrament or sign, then it is necessarily social. Thus an engaged couple who privately profess their love in a genital way cannot be considered married, whatever else might be said about the good faith of their mutual commitment. Genovesi raises important points:

> (W)e must insist that other considerations do enter into the discussion: our actions have unavoidable repercussions upon ourselves and others, and we must not avoid asking whether or not we and others are prepared to face these repercussions; we must also contend with the difficulty of knowing our true motives and intentions in our protestations of love. Is the commitment as strong and real as we think, or are we really not thinking, but merely feeling? Will our "commitment" survive the passing of such feeling?[24]

We cannot undercut the importance of the social dimension of the wedding ceremony, of love, commitment, unity, of having a child and raising the child. We all need more than a personal encounter, for in every one of us there is an essential social dimension. The decision to relate permanently to another human being in love and raise a family is as much a social as a personal statement and needs the involvement and the support of society. A wedding ceremony, with witnesses from the community, acts as a guarantee of the personal love between spouses. In Christian terms the marriage is a sacrament, and perspectives on sexuality in both Testaments require the institutionalization of sexuality in heterosexual, monogamous, permanent, and procreative marriage that furthers the cohesiveness and continuity of family, church, and body politic, and that respects and nurtures the affective commitments in which spouses give sexual expression.[25]

## C. Nonmarital Sex

Cases exist that do not precisely fall into the categories of premarital or pre-ceremonial: i.e., a man and a woman drawn to one another who enjoy each other's company, feel real affection for each other, and in some sense even love each other. For various reasons, though, they are not even thinking of making a permanent commitment to each other. Sexual intercourse may seem to them to be a good and understandable expression of their affection and their love. In such cases it is again important to recall the significance of human sexuality in terms of the two aspects that are at the heart of the traditional norm of marriage: *committed partnership* and *procreation*. *Humanae Vitae* speaks of these two meanings as constituting "true mutual love."[26] *Gaudium et Spes* also mentions "mutual self-giving and human procreation in the context of true love."[27] Building on and interpreting these meanings of sexuality, then, the essential criteria of Christian sexual responsibility can be formulated as: (1) An intentionally permanent commitment of partnership and love; and (2) The willingness of the couple to welcome and nurture as a couple any children that result from their union.[28]

The friendship and commitment of a man and a woman to one another is a truly splendid phenomenon. It is a commitment *to be there* for this other person. As a decision, it is an achievement of the human mind and spirit. However, because we are not pure spirits, this decision is often symbolized and realized in bodily expression. Very often, sexual intercourse expresses realities different from the two-fold norm presented above: e.g., affection, concern, caring, pleasure. As we have noted, the desire to find an outlet for sexual energy is powerful, and its roots are deep.

We must always remember, however, that the desire to find another person to whom we can give ourselves without reserve has roots which are deeper than sexual expression, and sexual expression can oftentimes hinder this search. Unless our sexual energy is an expression of this type of transcendence, sought and found, we will never find joy and abiding peace. Neely's comments are helpful:

> Our real sexual gambits are intended to lead to something more than the pent-up release of the moment. However therapeutic that may appear to be, the wisdom of the ages is that man and woman are reaching out to each other for something more... Notwithstanding all modern sexual license, we all crave someone beyond ourselves to live for and to die for. Those who claim that they are free-swinging spirits are merely at a way station where tentativeness is god. What they really seek is farther along the way, where the risk is surely greater, but the rewards become permanent.[29]

## D. Extramarital Sex

If premarital and nonmarital sex are a violation of sexual integrity, extramarital sex (adultery) is even more so. All of these forms of sex are violations of personal integrity, against the unitive dimension of sexuality seen as a source of life: a life of attachment and personal love, and the means of new life. Marriage carries an exclusive commitment which is betrayed in extramarital affairs, and the personal dimension loses its meaning when it is diverted from the spouse.

The physical act of adultery which serves to betray one's spouse is preceded usually by a lack of caring and concern: complacency, neglect and lack of communication between spouses are warning signs to be heeded that the relationship needs attention if it is to survive and thrive.

Adultery was proscribed in the Ten Commandments.[30] In a patriarchal society such as existed at the beginning of God's revelation, there was emphasis on the rights of the husband, and a focus on external deeds.[31] But the decalogue was concerned with more than the external act: it explicitly noted the wrongness of coveting one's neighbor's wife.[32]

Adultery was frequently mentioned in the Old Testament. Adultery was seen to attack the heart of the marriage covenant itself, and strike at every person guarded by that covenant. Commenting on the significance of the story of human origins in Genesis, Pope John Paul II summed up the teaching of the Old Testament, "Adultery... means a breach of the unity by means of which man and woman only as husband and wife can unite so closely as to be 'one flesh.'"[33]

As we have already seen, Jesus clearly taught that not only the external deed of adultery is sinful but the desire for it as well.[34] Although Jesus forgave the woman caught in adultery, he cautioned her not to sin again.[35] Jesus made it clear that adultery violates the rights of both husband and wife, and it desecrates the covenant of marriage.[36]

St. Paul saw a sexual union between man and woman in marriage as a communion-in-being, a "one flesh" unity, symbolizing the intensely personal union between Christ and the Church.[37] Paul taught that a Christian becomes one body with Christ in baptism.[38] He stressed that the body of the Christian is a temple of the Holy Spirit, a "vessel" to be held in honor as a God-given and sacred reality.[39] Consequently, precisely because sexual activity and the body are so meaningful and precious, Paul taught that any act of sexual immorality was an act of desecration, for in such an act the person who had already become one body with Christ was taking something holy, his or her own person now living in Christ, and defiling it.[40]

This brief summary makes it evident that the New Testament considered adultery to be wrong and incompatible with one's life as a Christian. As Hebrews teaches, "Let marriage be held in honor among all, and let the marriage bed be undefiled; for God will judge the immoral and adulterous."[41]

The friendship of marriage is of a special character and differs from other types of friendship in a number of ways. It is rooted in the covenant of irrevocable personal consent, a consent that establishes the man and the woman as irreplaceable and nonsubstitutable spouses, as husband and wife.[42] It is therefore a friendship that is exclusive of others in the sense that husband and wife pledge to be with and for each other until death, and aspire to a unity of personal intimacy, to a communion in being.[43] Marital friendship is essentially related to the most basic and intimate of human communities, the family. This friendship, unique among all kinds of human friendships, is the ground of the family and is nourished and expressed in the life of the family. The intimacy of this friendship, so fittingly expressed in the conjugal act, the unity of the spouses in a common life, and the open-ended demands of procreating and raising children require that marital friendship be the permanent and exclusive relationship that Christian teaching holds marriage to be.

Adultery obviously inflicts great harm on spouses and on their children. The deep personal hurt and betrayal experienced by the victims of infidelity, the breaking of the bonds of trust and love, the painful effects of divorce — all these evils and many more are the commonly known effects of adultery. These evils do not exist in each and every case of adultery; but evils of this type are the natural consequences of the harm to marital friendship that is necessarily involved in every act of adultery.

## 2. DOMESTIC PARTNERSHIPS

Across the country, major efforts are underway to change laws regarding "close and committed personal relationships involving shared responsibilities." In Los Angeles, e.g., a task force has been investigating *discrimination against domestic partners* by insurance companies, health clubs, credit companies, and airline frequent-flyer programs. In Seattle, the city's Human Rights Department ruled in June of 1990 that the AAA automobile club of Washington had illegally discriminated on the basis of marital status by refusing to grant associate membership to a gay man's domestic partner. In Washington State, a domestic-partnership benefits commission has been established to explore extending benefits to the partners of municipal employees.

Statistics indicate that of the nation's 91 million households, 2.6 million are inhabited by unmarried adults of the opposite sex. Some 1.6 million households involve unmarried adults of the same sex. These figures include a disparate array of personal arrangements: young male-female couples living together before getting married, elderly friends who decide to share a house, platonic roommates, and romantic gay or straight lovers. There is a growing national debate over whether gay couples should be allowed to declare themselves "domestic partners."

Homosexual groups maintain that this issue is particularly pressing for them for two specific reasons: heterosexual couples have the option to marry if they wish to be eligible for family benefits; and the spread of HIV/AIDS raises the importance of medical coverage, bereavement-leave policies, pension rules, hospital visitation rights, and laws giving family members the authority to make medical decisions and funeral arrangements.

In the last census, a category was included for adults living together as "unmarried partners." According to the Census Bureau, it was hoped that this new category will "get at the true unmarried-couple situation where there is intimacy between partners."

How does one assess this domestic partner question?[44]

Since its inception, our society has provided to married couples and families certain benefits that are not available to nonmarried individuals (e.g., tax incentives, health care rights, pension and survivor benefits). At the root of this traditional societal and governmental concern for marriage and the family has been the belief that marriage constitutes the most beneficial environment for raising the next generation of citizens. Society has thus perceived itself to have a vested interest in supporting strong, stable, committed marital relationships so that children will have a stable and nurturing environment in which to be raised.

It is particularly important to recognize this point: the benefits accorded to families by government and society are not primarily benefits rendered to individuals who are married (though they do extend to married couples without children and to couples whose children are grown). Even so, benefits are rendered to establish a nurturing environment for children. Any discussion of domestic partnership that misses this point will become mired in confusion, for it is impossible to justify special benefits to married couples if these benefits are seen first and foremost as benefits to the spouses themselves.

The domestic partnership idea rests upon a sociological fact and a value judgment. The sociological fact is that there is a great diversity of living arrangements in our society today. The value judgment is that individuals in all or at least some of these living arrangements have an equal right to the benefits that government and society presently give to married couples.

As the above statistics clearly show, substantial numbers of Americans live in nontraditional households. Those who favor domestic partnerships say that government should recognize this diversity and distribute benefits without regard to whether it is a traditional marriage, a committed partnership without benefit of marriage, or merely a temporary arrangement of convenience.

While it is true that domestic partnership proponents frequently speak of giving benefits only to truly committed couples, the *majority* of legislative proposals advanced would have the legal effect of providing such benefits without any requirements for a long-term committed relationship.

Extending equal benefits to couples who are living together without benefit of marriage would have two deleterious moral effects in our society. First, the government would be *punishing couples for being married*. Married couples *de facto* undertake certain substantive legal responsibilities: the obligation to support their spouse in times of illness or unemployment; community property obligations; and joint responsibility for debts incurred by a spouse. Under every proposed domestic partnership ordinance, domestic partners would receive all of the legal benefits extended to marriage, but assume none of the legal responsibilities. Thus the government is put in the position of actually punishing people for getting married (as it already deters some of the elderly from getting married through financial disincentives).

Second, the government would be sending a strong message to couples that it does not matter whether they are married or not. After all, in the United States, civil law is often taken to be a reflection of moral law; people believe that what is legal is also moral. Thus the content of civil law has a strong pedagogical role in our society. By extending to domestic partners all of the legal benefits extended to married couples, the government is teaching that nonmarried relationships are equal to married relationships, or at the very least are equally worthy of protection, and that it really does not matter whether one is married or not.

We should not overlook the fact that some changes are needed in civil law to address inequities created by the increasing diversity of American family life: e.g., it is unjust for people who are living together not to have the right to visit their partner in the hospital as would "family," or to receive bereavement leave from work upon the death of their partner. However, domestic partnership is damaging to society and objectionable to the Church because it further weakens the institution of marriage and encourages heterosexual couples to forego the marital commitment.

## 3. STATISTICAL DATA[45]

Statistical data from the late 1980's reveal that 68% of never-married girls and 78% of never-married boys report having sexual intercourse by the age of nineteen. This demonstrates a sharp contrast to the Kinsey studies (1948 and 1953) that reported 20% and 45%. Surveys throughout the 1970's reveal pronounced increases, primarily in the rates of young women.

The proportion of adolescents with sexual experience rises sharply with age: for girls — 18% at age 15, 29% at 16, 40% at 17, 54% at 18, and 69% at 19. Data on adolescent boys show that 29% have become sexually active by age 16, 48% by 17, 64% by 18, and 78% by 19. However, the figures represent incidence of sexual intercourse, not frequency, which is often occasional and limited to few partners. Comparison of 1980 and 1988 reports indicates virtually no change, suggesting that the upward trend of increased activity has leveled off. There is some indication, however, that girls under the age of 15 are engaging in intercourse at earlier ages and in increasing proportions.

Contributing factors to adolescent sexual activity are early and frequent dating, peer pressure, experimental sexual activity, incidents of sexual abuse and incest, lack of parental support, unfulfilled emotional needs, minimal religious instruction, depression, low educational achievement, lack of personal long-term goals, drug abuse and poverty.[46]

Each year of the approximately 11 million adolescent girls who are sexually active, about one million become pregnant. Of these pregnancies, approximately 40% are aborted, 10% end in miscarriage or stillbirth, and 50% result in live births (roughly one-fifth of all births annually). Approximately 93% of unmarried adolescent mothers who give birth choose to keep their babies. Adolescent pregnancy rates in the United States are highest among the Western nations and are, in fact, twice as high as England and five times as high as Sweden and the Netherlands. This is in spite of the fact that rates of adolescent sexual activity are similar among all four countries, and Sweden's rates of sexual activity are actually higher.[47]

Statistics on adolescent pregnancy represent a great deal of human suffering. Young women are less likely to receive prenatal care, and if they do, are more likely to initiate it later in pregnancy. Pregnant teens have higher rates of pregnancy complications, are more likely to die during pregnancy, and have higher rates of infant mortality than women in their twenties. Pregnancy is the number one cause of school dropouts by adolescent girls (some studies indicate 80% leave school and do not return) and 9% of teenage mothers attempt suicide (a rate seven times the average for adolescent girls without children).

Studies of adolescent sexual activity and pregnancy also reflect a pervasive cycle of poverty in American society. One-third of families run by persons under 25 years of age are single-parent households, and 75% of families maintained by a woman under 25 are living in poverty. Fifty percent of all Aid to Dependant Children expenditures went to families in which mothers were adolescents when their first child was born. Government expenses for these families totaled $16.6 billion in 1985.[48]

A recent study of sisters in poor families found no difference between women who gave births as teenagers and their sisters who gave birth later or did not give birth at all.[49] Such evidence suggests that, for many young women, poverty continues to be a reality in their lives, whether they give birth or not. Having little access to education and employment, many will continue to be poor, regardless of their sexual decisions.

Issues of poverty and teenage pregnancy are particularly critical for young women of color. Approximately one-third of family households run by persons under 25 years of age of single-parent households are "usually headed by mothers who are predominantly black or Hispanic. In 1985, 75 percent of families maintained by a woman under 25 years of age were living in poverty."[50] For low-income adolescents, lack of educational opportunities, vocational options, and health benefits perpetuate cycles of poverty that foster and reinforce patterns of early childbearing. All these difficulties are compounded by the dynamics of racism.

Unintended pregnancy is not the only consequence of adolescent sexual activity. Health professionals express concern that young people are particularly at risk in contracting sexually transmitted diseases, including HIV/AIDS. Behaviors, such as child prostitution, drug and alcohol abuse that impairs judgment, and needle sharing among intravenous drug users, put adolescents in jeopardy of becoming infected. Of particular concern are studies indicating that most adolescents do not feel they are personally at risk and are not inclined to change their sexual practices or reduce their level of sexual activity.[51]

Since many of today's adolescents experience sexuality as violent and coercive, particular attention must be given to *nonstranger abuse among peers*. Statistics on date and acquaintance rape indicate that some teens almost expect coercion to be a part of sexual relations. In one survey, 54% of a group of teenage boys said that forcing a girl to have sex is acceptable under certain circumstances, and 42% of a similar group of girls agreed. According to this study, force is justified if the girl says "yes" and then changes her mind, if she had "led him on," or if "she gets him sexually excited." Under those circumstances, the teenagers said, the girl is responsible for what happens. Force may be acceptable if the couple has had sex before, if he is "turned on," or if she has slept with other boys, or if she agrees to go to a party where she knows there will be drinking and drugs.[52]

Our culture bombards young people with images of what it means to be a "real man" and a "real woman." For young men, claiming one's sexuality can mean adopting a brand of masculinity that requires making sexual advances and seeing them to their resolution in genital sexual acts. In women, on the other hand, it is learning passivity to their own sexual feelings, expecting to be "swept away" by the overpowering conquest of man and romance. One author has written, "The social construction of heterosexual sexuality in this culture has been largely based on patterns of dominance and submission in which men are expected to be dominant and women are expected to be submissive."[53]

Studies show that adolescents engage in unwanted sexual activity for many reasons, including threats to end the relationship, the desire to be popular, peer pressure, questioning one's sexuality, being under the influence of alcohol or drugs, and feeling obligated because of time or money expended by the other person. In addition, relationships between women and men of all ages typically develop through patterns of sexual "game-playing" — patterns that rely on both verbal and nonverbal clues and signals. Since erotic messages are encoded with mystery and suggestiveness, they are vulnerable to many levels of misinterpretation.

Young men (as well as older men), e.g., may interpret a young woman's desire for cuddling and kissing as a desire for intercourse, and young women learn to send ambiguous messages when they feel the need to offer token resistance to having sexual relations in order not to appear "easy." In a study on attitudes toward coercive sex, teens said they thought that boys wore open shirts, tight jeans, and brief swimsuits to reflect their clothing choices, but they thought girls wore tight jeans, no bra, and short shorts as a "come on" for sexual activity. This report concludes, "In cases where the boy misreads the girl's cue, the stage seems set for nonstranger rape."[54] Until patterns of erotic communication between men and women are infused with a fundamental honesty and mutual respect, such miscommunication will contribute toward patterns of violent and coercive sexual relations.


## 4. ADOLESCENT SEXUALITY

The U.S.C.C. document *Human Sexuality* comments:

> Many young people today consider genital sexual activity, including intercourse, to be acceptable behavior, a "right" of sorts, even outside the context of marriage. However, the Catholic tradition affirms that genital sexual intimacy, particularly intercourse, is a right and privilege reserved to those who have committed themselves for life in marriage. It is only in the context of the marital covenant that genital sex finds its full meaning as an embodied expression of the intimacy and fidelity of the couple. We urge parents and teachers to insist on sexual abstinence and preparation for marital responsibility for adolescents. We believe this to be inscribed in our human nature as well as in the Christian call from God. Adults who guide adolescents in their moral development need to be forthright and clear in this regard, acknowledging and supporting the courage it may require from young people.[55]

In "Adolescent Affection: Toward a Sound Sexuality," Richard A. McCormick has presented an extremely fine and balanced approach to this question of adolescent sexuality.[56] By "adolescent affection" McCormick is referring to heterosexual fascinations such as kissing, embracing and fondling, which classical moralists referred to as *actus impudici* ("sexually stimulating acts").

McCormick comments that immorality has come to be largely identified in a great deal of American thought with that which causes harm to another and almost inevitably such an anemic morality tends to identify harm with *physical tangible harm*, hence to devour unwittingly the very spiritual goods it would protect. "It is thus that the controlling principle in such modern premarital sexual ethics has reduced itself to the avoidance of pregnancy."[57] The unspoken conclusion is that physical intimacy of all kinds is "tolerable," barring the outcome of pregnancy. McCormick then wisely counsels that a sound pastoral approach in this area will certainly recognize sin but also *go beyond* the identification of sinfulness in human behavior and courageously explain why certain conduct is sinful, thus highlighting the missing goodness. Pope Pius XII insisted on this same point:

> Many men have learned too well in their youth to avoid evil rather than to do good, to fear punishment much more than to give themselves up to love of their Father. They have been told of death and the dangers of life but too little of the joy of life. The precipices, where each step was risky, have been signalized, but nothing was said of the summits which beckoned them...[58]

McCormick then outlines some basic principles regarding premarital chastity. He recognizes the fact that during adolescence a young person is struggling toward maturity in general; and one aspect of this general development is the growth toward sexual maturity: the virtue of chastity, i.e., purposeful, control of the sex instinct according to one's state of life. The concept *purposeful control* is very important here. At no time is chastity simply a static continence, a pointless plateau of control which one reaches without aim or understanding. In fact, a non-integrated control runs its own risks and is no less prejudicial to sexual maturity than uninhibited incontinence. If it is purposeful control, what is the purpose? The purpose is to bring order into the area of sexual instinct, and this in either of two ways: by regulating the instinct according to the ends of married love; or, in the case of celibacy by assuring the Spirit total dominance over this instinct. Chastity thus produces real liberation by freeing one's self from the tyrannical excesses of sex when this has become purposeless. In other words, authentic chastity renders a person capable of true love, of self-donation.

Authentic chastity, then, controls without destroying the urges of instinct and should be *de facto* an integral part of one's personality. The adolescent needs to be *taught* to have a genuine desire for chastity. As Dietrich von Hildebrand wrote:

Reverence is the presupposition for every response to value, every abandonment to something important, and it is, at the same time, an essential element of such response to value... This can be verified by examining moral attitudes on the different levels of life... Reverence for the mystery of the marital union, for the depth and tenderness and the decisive and lasting validity of this most intimate abandonment of self, are the presuppositions for purity.[59]

McCormick likewise points out that an attitude of normalcy toward adolescent affection is very important: these sexual fascinations are quite normal and a part of normal psychosexual development. McCormick quotes Fr. Sterckx:

There is no cause for scandal in the amorous groping of the adolescent, in this reciprocal fascination of the young man for the young woman and the young woman for the young man... He is a poor educator indeed who is shocked at this, or has but derision for it, or worst of all, simple incomprehension and an intransigent attitude toward the manifestations of instinct...[60]

In furthering this discussion, McCormick points out the importance of recognizing that the physical expressions of affection which satisfy desire at one stage will not for long be thrilling. The individual will soon find himself or herself requiring further stimulation to experience the same degree of satisfaction received earlier. The thrill of pleasure that came several weeks ago just from holding hands is now impossible without kissing, and the satisfaction once derived from kissing is soon lacking unless there is caressing of the body. Thus the couple moves, though not inevitably or necessarily, from one rung of the ladder to the next. Ultimately, of course, no mutual caress short of intercourse will be satisfying. Such progression clearly does not make control any easier. To the adolescent it must continually be pointed out that to express sex is not to free oneself from it, but to encourage a stronger grip. This is the psychological law derived from the mechanics of arousal.

Consequently, many forms of sexual affection (e.g., deep kissing, petting) must be evaluated in light of this almost inevitable sexual progression, especially for younger people. We noted much earlier in this book that the body "has a memory." In other words, the body has many "go-ahead" signals, and few "stop" signs. Hence physical intimacy is not simple and uncomplicated; it is more like an appetizer. Because certain types of kissing, e.g., evoke not only an exchange of pleasant thoughts but also an exchange of physical feelings, and because these feelings are quite naturally concerned with genital areas of the body, prolongation tends to focus on these areas, hence to suggest not "I like you," but "I like your body." As pleasure increases, attention narrows and tends to exclude other considerations and draw increasing attention to itself.

It is in such a situation that expression of affection can easily pass over into exploitation, the use of another as an instrument for personal pleasure, the more so with an adolescent whose notion of affection is likely to be *purely* instinctual. It means that I forget for the moment that this other is a *person*.

In light of the point made earlier that sexuality is a language, McCormick's final counsel is important:

> In still other words, a kiss can say many things: "I love you and want to devote myself completely to you, and protect you"; "Thanks for a nice evening, stranger"; "I'm hungry and need you for gratification." If one uses it repeatedly in the less noble senses, it gradually may become identified with them and when the person wants them to say "I love you" he realizes with horror that they no longer speak such language.[61]

### Conclusions

From a Catholic perspective, marriage is the reference point in evaluating all nonmarital sexuality. Marriage sustains the elements of decisiveness, stability and social recognition, components which are deficient in one way or another in all nonmarital sexuality. As we have seen, young people must necessarily learn in their own way, and step by step, to speak the heterosexual language. They should not force themselves, nor be forced by others, into adult situations. Unfortunately, communication between people before marriage has greatly come to be identified with one specific act, coitus. It is very important before marriage that a couple ascertain that the dimensions for authentic love be truly present in their relationship and realize that sex can be an obstacle to this: i.e., sex can make it impossible to distinguish the presence of human love from its mere expression. St. Augustine's point is well taken that one may be infatuated to the point of blindness (*amabam amare*, "I loved to love"). Sex should never be separated from human love. It is interesting to note that Sigmund Freud understood the psychological essence of perversion as precisely this: the segmenting of the act of intercourse from its intrinsic relation to the total self, which he stressed as degenerative self. Whether the act actually leads to generation is beside the point; in the structure of the act, Freud taught, generativity must be present *implicitly*.

Authentic human sexuality must, then, entail emotional and spiritual components, intellectually perceived ideals and interiorized values. When these are taken from one's sex life, one is reduced to the impersonal, arrested world of prostitution sex. *Human* sexuality must be penetrated and modified and elevated by human emotionality and human rationality, by the sum of all human qualities, physical and non-physical. Love itself is profound communication, whether one refers to such communication as "decentralization of the self" (Mounier); "availability" (Marcel); "disarmament of the self" (Nouwen); or "mutuality" (Erikson). Communication is a primordial fact and requirement of human development in all its dimensions.

To prevent a sexual relationship from losing this outward, self-giving direction, the permanent commitment to love in marriage must be invoked. It is the marriage commitment that makes the difference. Among many other things, this commitment holds in check the downward slide into self-love and makes the sexual act affirm symbolically the self-giving that exists in all the areas of one's life. In marriage, the sex act can truly say what it is designed to communicate, namely: "I love you not only now, not only for your body, not only for a part of you. I love you, for yourself, for always. I love you because of your continuing self-giving to the family, and I affirm my fidelity without limit to you."

Without the marriage commitment, sexual intercourse tends to lose its communicative character by disengaging itself from the persons of the lovers, and degenerating into mere genital contact and surface sensation. Sexual escalation outside marriage terminates by its own natural downward spiral into a body-centered and not person-centered erotic juxtaposition. This is not communication.

Sexual intercourse is a sign of total surrender, and a perpetual socialized fidelity (marriage). When intercourse takes place outside this context, the act then is being made to say something which its intrinsic symbolism denies. There is a type of pernicious problem here and somehow, although it may not at first be recognized, its effect will be felt in the human psyche. Trust and communication go hand in hand. From infancy through adulthood, when basic patterns of trust are present, they will hold in check the fear of abandonment, physical or emotional, and so create a stable condition in which a person is willing to share his or her inner feelings and thoughts.

Premature genital sex thus risks forming a relationship in which the couple engages in physical sex at a superficial and impersonal level where masculinity and femininity cannot appropriately develop.[62] Edward Malloy has thus wisely remarked:

> Those of us who are Christian can draw upon a legacy of reflection about sexuality, both in general and in the pre-marital context. This tradition contradicts many of the claims of contemporary spokesmen who want to argue that sexual intercourse before marriage is natural or its repression is psychologically harmful or that it contributes to marital adjustment or that somehow marriage is an outdated institution. This Christian wisdom suggests that Scripture and tradition as well as insightful understandings of the functions of sexual intercourse can be persuasive arguments against certain of these contemporary tendencies. No one wishes to be hung-up or outdated or written off as irrelevant to contemporary discussion. That is why the most effective argumentation about the matter of pre-marital sexuality is given by Christian couples who have attempted to live by this Christian ethic with as much integrity as they can muster.[63]

In responding well and reasonably to questions of nonmarital sexuality, it is helpful to recall again some basic and critical characteristics of human sexuality:[64]

*First*: Human sexuality is a totalizing experience. Sexuality is not something that has to do with sexual organs alone. Sexual experience is totalizing not just because erotic emotion invades every part of a person's physical and mental being. Sex is also a total experience because we instinctively put our whole self into it. Of course, a person can plan tomorrow's schedule while having sex, but it is going to be a rather low-grade sexual experience, and insulting and dehumanizing for the partner. The prostitute can, e.g., deliberately disassociate sexual activity from her or his real self, but she or he cannot do so repeatedly without psychological damage. To segregate sexuality, to isolate it in a nether region of the self, is personally disastrous.

*Second*: Human sexuality has a certain surplus value: i.e., the meaning of sexuality is not exhausted by its procreative power. Sexual relations serve many other purposes, some good, some less so. Sexuality can be a means of affirming the value of the other, or of self-affirmation. It can be used as a sign of casual caring or of total commitment. It can be a way of manipulating, or hurting, or exploiting, or shaming. Or it can be a way of celebrating togetherness, a rejoicing in life, or in comforting the despondent, lonely and discouraged spouse. Sexual experience as a human event surely has many meanings beside the purely biological ones.

*Third*: Human sexuality is plastic: not in the sense of artificial, but in the sense of moldable. In most lower animals and insects, sexual behavior is genetically programmed. How spiders, bees, fish, birds and most animals mate is not a matter of personal taste but a procedure dictated by instinct. How sexuality fits into a given human life, however, is something determined by a person's *choices*. How physical affection is displayed varies with cultural backgrounds and personal tastes. What meaning various types of sexual behavior have in a certain person's life is a result of how sex is in fact used. As in so many other human areas, sexual mastery is a lifelong project. People only gradually mold their sexual selves through a long process of experiment and restraint, of physical evolution and emotional integration. That is why sexual consciousness is so much a part of one's unique selfhood.

*Fourth*: Human sexuality is other-directed. Autoeroticism is a human possibility, and thus other-directedness is not automatic, even though it is built into the natural scheme of human growth. In human beings there is something deliberate about the orientation of sexuality beyond the self to the other. Furthermore, animal sexual activity does not ordinarily affirm the partner as a unique self. Almost always, egoistic sex is immediately perceived as dehumanizing, brutalizing and subhuman. There may be an inevitable, immature, self-centered stage in the development of sexual expression; but this is a stage to grow beyond. To regard others as instruments of one's own pleasure, to see them as sex objects, is to reduce them to something less than human and even to diminish an aspect of what it is to be human in one's self. Where a person is unable to go out of himself or herself to others, or where his or her sexual self does not radiate in the world, or where genital sexual behavior is not fixed on another unique self, there a human personality is not fully implemented, and there sexuality is not truly humanized.

*Fifth*: Human sexuality is self-giving: i.e., it is always in some basic way procreative. Human sexuality is life-giving in a number of ways beyond the merely biological: the gift of self in sexual love is one of the most dramatic ways we have of saying to someone that they are truly loved and worthwhile. When the unique beloved tells you that you too are that special other for him or her, whether in word or gift or sexual gesture, the effect is far deeper than casual compliments from others. Such sex is then life-giving. It makes it possible to grow and unfold as a person. In addition, just as autoeroticism is an immature stage of sexuality that needs to become other-directed, so romantic love that absorbs the couple alone is an immature stage of love. It might be necessary for lovers to pass through a period of being lost in each other, but we recognize that this is an immature stage of love's development. Mature love instinctively goes outward. Marital partners who surrender their unique self to the unique other in sexual embrace are also strengthened to go out in loving concern for the whole world. Since they feel secure, fulfilled, realized in their mutual sexual relationship, the larger world is neither threatening nor enticing. In fact, no further sexual partners are necessary or even really possible. It is only when there is no real interpersonal exchange of sexual behavior that others become more or less interchangeable, more or less desirable alternative sexual objects. For mature lovers the world beyond the beloved is opportunity for service and concern, for expression of love in a less specific and genitally sexual sense.

*Sixth*: Human sexuality is a language. One has to first acquire a certain maturity for both communicable language and authentic sex. Thus, if sexual expression comes to mean for a certain person casual affection, or impersonal fun, or manipulation, it cannot very easily come to mean a sign of final commitment. Like language too, sexuality is both a unique personal possession and a fully social reality. Everyone has his or her own personal way of using language. In much the same way each person's sexual style is unique. How erotic feelings and sexual behavior are integrated into each person's life and into relationships with others is something he or she builds up over a long period of time. On the other hand, sexuality is also a social possession as well. No one learns to talk all alone. Language is something we develop in interchanges with everyone around us, as it is something we can exercise only in a social context. Similarly we develop our personal sexual style through interaction with others, and particularly with others of the opposite sex. People isolated from others or who do not relate much at all with others do not develop a balanced sexual personality. Human sexual expression is in large measure a natural sign, but the actual sign value it has, its meaning in a given person's life, is something acquired.

It is important here to repeat that a person can use sexuality to mean all sorts of things. Genital sex can be an insignificant fun episode; it can be a way to get something else like power or status. But once that sort of thing becomes established as one's personal meaning for genital sex, this natural sign is no longer available as a sign of final commitment. Just as it is wrong to poison the meaning of interpersonal verbal communication by prevarication and deception, so it is at least equally wrong to muddy the possibilities of sexual communication.

We noted in Chapter One that our deepest fulfillment is only to be found within our union with God, and human sexual expression can only mirror this totality of personal union. Jesus is the model who gives meaning to our living of a moral life. It is through our human nature that God's love becomes manifest in the world. In sexual expression, as in other manifestations of love, we dedicate our bodily selves to the service of building the Kingdom of God.

Human sexual activity should imitate Jesus' own self-giving: its effectiveness as an instrument of love derived from the paschal mystery itself. Authentic moral formation must seek to bring an individual to the level of personal spiritual maturity that accepts responsibility for cooperating in Christ's work on earth.

Sexuality is a *dual* gift: it affirms our biological need to be touched; and our psychological/emotional need to be intimate. When we attempt to get in touch with our needs, we should always ask, "Do I need intimacy? or Do I need to be touched? or Both?" We should not forget how often "touch" is recorded in the Scriptures and how it is intimately associated with healing and unction. A good part of our contemporary society responds to the dual gift of sexuality by insisting on a simple answer: all human needs and feelings are addressed by sexual intercourse. We have seen here, however, that physical "touch" never *in itself* satisfies the human need for intimacy and love. A well-developed sense of one's own identity and worth is a necessary prelude to the real work of life, of genuine loving.

## CHAPTER SEVEN

# MASTURBATION: MORAL EVALUATIONS

## 1. OVERVIEW OF THE QUESTION

The 1975 *Declaration on Certain Questions Concerning Sexual Ethics* of the Congregation for the Doctrine of the Faith teaches:

(B)oth the Magisterium of the Church — in the course of a constant tradition — and the moral sense of the faithful have declared without hesitation that masturbation is an intrinsically and seriously disordered act. The main reason is that, whatever the motive for acting in this way, the deliberate use of the sexual faculty outside normal conjugal relations essentially contradicts the finality of the faculty. For it lacks the sexual relationship called for by the moral order, namely the relationship which realizes "The full sense of mutual self-giving and human procreation in the context of true love." All deliberate exercise of sexuality must be reserved to this regular relationship.[1]

This text reflects clearly the consistent Catholic tradition which has held that autoerotic or solitary genital sexual behavior is immoral and, in the objective sphere, can never be ethically justified. As we noted in Chapter Six, the Church teaches that human sexual expression ought to be linked to marital intercourse, which, by definition, serves both love-making and life-giving purposes. It follows that masturbation is not procreative; nor is it unitive in any interpersonal sense. As the U.S.C.C. document *Human Sexuality* points out, "This is not intended to deny the psychological or sociological data, which indicate that such behavior is common, especially among the young. Modern behavioral sciences provide us with much valid and useful information for formulating better contextual judgments and more sensitive pastoral responses."[2] However, the 1975 *Declaration* also teaches:

> Psychology helps one to see how the immaturity of adolescence (which can sometimes persist after that age), psychological imbalance or habit can influence behavior, diminishing the deliberate character of the act and bringing about a situation whereby subjectively there may not always be serious fault. But in general, the absence of serious responsibility must not be presumed.[3]

Respecting, then, the psychological and sociological data that is available, it is necessary as well to always keep our focus on the development of the whole person, understanding masturbatory actions in context, seeking their underlying causes more than seeking to repress the actions *in isolation.*[4] *Human Sexuality* thus encourages parents, teachers and counselors to "undramatize masturbation" and not to reduce a person's esteem and benevolence in dealing with this subject:

> We encourage all educators and counselors to help those who masturbate to move toward better social integration, to be more open and interested in others, in order eventually to be free from this form of behavior. Thus, they will advance toward the kind of interpersonal love proper to mature affectively. At the same time, we encourage people who struggle with masturbation "to have recourse to the recommended means of Christian asceticism, such as prayer and the sacraments, and to be involved in works of justice and charity."[5]

The teachings found in these documents lead to certain important conclusions:

(1)  The Church teaches that masturbation is a seriously disordered act. It divorces sexual activity from its proper conju-

gal context and consequently cannot be either self-giving or life-giving.

(2) Masturbation is a sign of a difficulty which all people have in attaining psychological sexual maturity; consequently, anxiety and destructive guilt are not in themselves helpful ways to confront this reality.

(3) Masturbation should be seen as a troubling sign of just how unintegrated our sexuality often is and how difficult the achievement of sexual maturity can be.

(4) Avoidance of masturbation involves a good deal of self-control and asceticism (prayer) in order to bring about mature sexual love, which must be the norm and criterion according to which certain practices can be judged as unworthy of our free choice.

## 2. AUTOEROTICISM[6]

Anthropological records indicate that masturbation is practiced by various species of animals, including monkeys and apes; and it is probably practiced in all cultures. In the widest sense *masturbation* is self-stimulation for erotic pleasure. This includes manipulation of one's own genitals, but it can also include a wide variety of autoerotic activities. In a narrower sense masturbation includes only deliberate acts of self-arousal that result in orgasm. Traditional moralists referred to such acts as *perfect orgasm*: i.e., masturbatory acts which lead to orgasm. Most often this behavior occurs in private, but two or more people may masturbate together (mutual masturbation). Many authors do not consider such activity as "mutual masturbation," but rather as petting, homosexual or heterosexual play, or foreplay. Consequently, masturbation involves a variety of sexual behaviors that overlap with other forms of sexual expression.

### A. Techniques

Predictably, the highly sensitive external sex organs are the primary targets of stimulation. The physiological reactions of such stimulation are vasocongestion and muscular tension. The first is usually beyond voluntary control, but the second can be deliberately used to heighten sexual tension.

Masturbation has certain common characteristics in both sexes. Physical differences between the sexes, however, as well as many social, cultural and life-history differences among people lead to a great variety of techniques of masturbation. *The Hite Report*,[7] e.g., lists a number of basic types of female masturbation and describes variations within these types.[8] Manual techniques of masturbation are commonly used by both sexes.

In male masturbation, there are two major physiological stages:

First, about six organ contractions take place at which time the internal sphincter of the urinary bladder closes. These contractions are accompanied by a sensation of inevitability where the male no longer feels in control. Secondly, there is the relaxation of the external sphincter of the bladder to allow fluids to flow into the penile urethra, with accompanying contractions and pressure. During this stage the male feels a sense of subjective contractions.

Female masturbation sustains both a physiological (a brief episode of physical relief) and a psychological (a subjective perception of a peak of physical reaction to sexual stimuli) phase. In female masturbation there are certain physiologic factors: i.e., a total body response. The male's sense of ejaculatory inevitability may have its counterpart in the female's subjective identification of orgasmic onset.

In female masturbation there are also a number of psychologic factors: a sensation of suspension, followed by an isolated thrust of intense sensual awareness; there is then a suffusion of warmth, followed by a feeling of involuntary contraction.[9]

It should be mentioned here that many men assume that orgasm occurs simultaneously with ejaculation, a two-phase response consisting of emission and actual ejaculation. However, some men can have orgasms without ejaculating. This phenomenon is exceptional, but important because it illustrates the dichotomy between the physiological response of ejaculation and the psychological perception of orgasm. Paraplegics, e.g., with severed cords can become aroused and have orgasms. Depending on the location of the injury on the spinal cord, a paraplegic might also have erections or ejaculations or both, but he would not be able to feel them. These experiences of orgasm indicate that sexual responses can depend more on impulses in the brain than from the genitals.

### B. Fantasy

Fantasy is very often an important part of masturbation. The intensity and level of mental imagery varies considerably from person to person. Some may concentrate on the physiological sensations they are experiencing and have no erotic thoughts; but most people do fantasize while masturbating. Masturbatory fantasies often involve memories of past experiences, but erotic photographs or literature are sometimes used as sources of stimulation. A number of surveys have indicated that the most commonly mentioned type of fantasy during masturbation involves sexual intercourse with a loved person (reported by three-quarters of all men and four-fifths of all women). But in the case of nearly half the males and more than a fifth of the females, masturbatory fantasies involve various acquaintances and individuals in a variety of sexual encounters. Among the other fantasies mentioned in the Kinsey Studies, e.g., were intercourse with strangers (47% of males and 21% of females), sex with several persons of the opposite sex simultaneously (33% of males and 18% of females), being forced to have sex (10% of males and 19% of females), forcing someone to have sex (13% of males and 3% of females), and homosexual contacts (7% of males and 11% of females).[10]

Masturbatory fantasies often provide "safe" expression of a wide variety of sexual interests that the fantasizer might find impossible or unacceptable in real life. We spoke earlier about the importance of assessment of one's levels of attraction and arousal. To this point, Katchadourian, Lunde and Trotter add this point:

> Among the many purposes served, masturbatory fantasies are also used to test one's inclinations. For example, a 17-year-old woman who had fears about hidden Lesbian, or homosexual, tendencies was reassured of her heterosexuality by the fact that she could not reach orgasm while visualizing naked females.[11]

To fantasize sexually can be, then, extremely informative for the knowledge of oneself as a sexed being, although it needs to be added that such fantasy need not necessarily be connected with masturbatory stimulation.

### C. Prevalence and Frequency

Numerous statistics indicate that masturbation is a widely-used sexual outlet. It is prevalent among males and much more common among females than was generally believed in the past. Prevalence figures from different studies differ somewhat, but all have been high. In the Kinsey sample,[12] 92% of males and 58% of females were found to have masturbated to orgasm at some time in their lives. The Kinsey sample indicates that only a small proportion of males had masturbated to orgasm by age 10 (even though the majority had attempted self-stimulation, stopping short of orgasm). Between the ages of 10 and 15 years the incidence curve climbed dramatically and then leveled off as it approached age 20. Practically every man who was ever going to masturbate had already done so by this age. The Kinsey survey also indicated that up to the age of 45 years, more and more women were still discovering this outlet by experiencing orgasm through masturbation for the first time.

What was the frequency of masturbation among men? As with total sexual outlet, age and marital status made a great deal of difference. In boys from puberty to 15 years of age, among whom masturbation reached a peak, the mean, or average, frequency was about twice a week. If we exclude those who never masturbated, the weekly figure increases to 2.4 times. Beyond age 15 the figures dropped steadily with age: in the total unmarried population the 46-to-50-year-old group averaged fewer than one orgasm every two weeks. Frequencies for married men were small, no more than once every two or three weeks.

These figures, of course, represent group averages, and as with most forms of sexual behavior there was a wide range of variation. There were apparently healthy men who never masturbated or did so only once or twice in their lives. Others may had averaged 20 or more such orgasms a week over many years. The average (mean and median) frequencies for the active female sample were quite uniform at various age levels (up to the mid-fifties) and did not show the steady decline with age that was characteristic of males. The average unmarried woman, if she masturbated at all, did so about once every two or three weeks. For married women it was about once a month.

The range of variation in frequency in female masturbation was very wide. In addition to many who never masturbated, some masturbated yearly, monthly, weekly, or daily; and some reported reaching staggering numbers of orgasms in a single hour. These few individuals inflated the female means to two or three times the corresponding medians.

Surveys conducted since these original Kinsey studies indicate changes in attitudes which are reflected in masturbatory behavior, particularly among women. Attitudes, though still ambivalent, have become more liberalized, and the prevalence of masturbation has increased. One of the most distinct changes is that both boys and girls appear to start masturbating at earlier ages. The increase in prevalence rates of masturbation since the Kinsey study is not restricted to adolescents. The rates for single young males have gone up moderately, and those for young females even more so. Currently, 60% of women between the ages of 18 and 24 report some masturbatory experience, as opposed to a 25 to 35% rate for young women in the Kinsey study. More than 80% of the women in *The Hite Report* (see above) reported masturbating. Frequency rates have also increased. For young males the frequency has gone from 49 to 52 times a year; for young females from 21 to 37 times a year.

Biological, social, and situational factors affect masturbation as they do other types of sexual behavior. Among Kinsey subjects, for instance, males who reach puberty at a younger age were more likely to masturbate and to do so more frequently than boys who reached puberty later. (The same did not hold true for females.) Social factors, as measured by educational and occupational status also affect masturbation. The better-educated person (especially if female) is more likely to masturbate, but class-related differences appear to be less significant than in previous years.

Current data also indicates an increase in the prevalence of masturbation among young married men and women. In the Kinsey study about 40% of the husbands in their late 20's and early 30's masturbated (about 6 times a year); now about 70% do so (about 24 times a year). For wives of corresponding ages the percentages have gone up from 30 to 70%, but the median rate has not changed (about 10 times a year).

Why would married people masturbate at all? The most recent data do not suggest that increased masturbation is in compensation for frustrations in marital coitus. Instead, modern married persons, especially those who are younger, appear relatively freer to rely on masturbation as an additional outlet for sexual pleasure and related needs.

The most common reason for masturbation by married men and women is the temporary unavailability of the spouse — through absence, illness, pregnancy, disinclination. Of all the alternatives to marital coitus, masturbation is seen by many to be the "least threatening" to the marital relationship.

### D. Masturbation and Health

As we noted in the history of homosexuality, masturbation has been erroneously suggested at one time or another to be associated with insanity; epilepsy; various forms of headaches; numerous eye diseases; intermittent deafness; redness of the nose and nosebleeds; hypertrophy and tenderness of the breasts; pains of various kinds (e.g., heart murmurs named by some as the "masturbator's heart"); and skin ailments ranging from acne to wounds, pale and discolored skin, and "an undesirable odor of the skin in women."

There is absolutely no evidence to support claims that these or any other type of physical harm result from masturbation. Yet for more than 200 years and until recently these dire effects have held an unshakable place in the beliefs of many of the medical elite in the Western world.

The most frequently mentioned motive for masturbation is the release of sexual tension. The need for such release is often to compensate for the lack of a sexual partner or the temporary unavailability of one. Masturbation is often relied on as an additional source of gratification, by single as well as by happily married persons. Other motivations are non-sexual: e.g., to combat feelings of loneliness. People also rely on masturbation to release tensions caused by occupational or personal problems or simply to relax in order to get to sleep. In light of these points, a proper *psychological* evaluation of masturbatory behavior can be made only in the context of the individual's overall life. Clearly, masturbation can become a true liability if it is relied upon compulsively at the expense of interpersonal encounters. In other words, masturbation can be a convenient shortcut that can have the potential of shortchanging an individual's maturation process. The problem in such cases is not primarily masturbation but rather of other, more fundamental psychological difficulties.

In "Putting Sex in Perspective,"[13] Dr. Michael Cavanagh insightfully remarks that every individual sustains the three basic needs of love, esteem and security. In one way or another, these three needs are fulfilled by interfacing with "things," "others" and a "significant other(s)." Cavanagh maintains that if love, esteem and security are not being met especially by a significant other, a type of "pressure cooker" phenomenon begins to occur in an individual's life which inevitably will result in some type of "explosion": e.g., drug abuse; alcohol abuse; over-eating; masturbation. In such cases, then, masturbation itself might not be the problem but rather the symptom of a much more profound and deep difficulty: a lack of love, esteem and/or security. The wise parent and counselor will always look, then, "behind" the masturbatory activity to see what type of difficulty might be present which is causing the masturbation.

A general social acceptance of masturbation seems clearly on the rise as can be judged by the explicit discussions of it in popular and literary works, and by the endorsement of the practice in popular sex manuals. Sex researchers, such as Masters and Johnson, encourage women who have never reached orgasms with partners to seek orgasm first through masturbation.[14] A very popular book of some years ago on human sexuality thus stated:

> (T)he pleasurable sensations resulting from self-stimulation may not be interpreted as having sexual content. Deliberate self-stimulation or masturbation can be pleasurable without proceeding to orgasm in the female or to ejaculation in the male. But, since most of the erotic areas that one can reach, other than the head and neck, are those which society and most families would prefer to be covered, this self-stimulation requires privacy. And, even thumbsucking, and pacifiers are frowned on in some families, even

among those who recognize the pleasurable sensations of this kind of activity. So, nailbiting and thumbsucking in the slightly older child are carefully regulated to the privacy of the bedroom. This kind of activity in any individual, like other kinds of self-stimulation, only becomes a problem when it is compulsive, guilt-ridden, and a substitute for something missing in other areas of one's life.[15]

## Conclusions

1. Autoerotic activities seemingly constitute a large degree of many people's sexual behavior. The most common forms of autoeroticism are sexual fantasies, erotic dreams and masturbation. Social science studies indicate that autoeroticism has come to be accepted by many people as a "legitimate" way of enjoying sex.
2. Erotic fantasies take many forms — from fleeting erotic thoughts and images to intricately woven fantasies. Erotic fantasies are a significant form of autoeroticism throughout life for most people.
3. While the person doing the fantasizing is usually the main character in erotic fantasies, the other characters and the content of the fantasies are limited only by the dreamer's imagination. The degree of arousal that accompanies these fantasies varies from no arousal in some cases to intense feelings of excitement in others. Some individuals are reportedly able to reach orgasm through fantasy alone.
4. Erotic fantasies are a source of unpleasant feelings for some people: i.e., the source of profound guilt and embarrassment. In general, erotic fantasies in themselves are not considered to be harmful unless they are particularly disturbing or lead to the acting out of antisocial thoughts.
5. Clinical studies show that many people come to accept their own gender identity through erotic fantasies. Fantasies are often a substitute for sexual experiences that are otherwise unavailable or unattainable.
6. Neurophysiological studies indicate that everyone has regular periods of dreaming every night. These dream

periods are accompanied by rapid eye movements (REM) and intense physiological activity, including erections in males in many instances. Sexual arousal during sleep is not always accompanied by erotic dreams, but most people have erotic dreams from time to time.

7. Nocturnal orgasms — often accompanied by erotic dreams — do not make up a large percentage of total sexual outlets, but many females and most males experience them. It is important to note that nocturnal orgasms are *involuntary acts* and as such are a "natural" outlet for accumulated sexual tensions. Nocturnal orgasms in themselves should not be, then, a source for anxiety and guilt. They occur more often in males than females and thus are often referred to as "nocturnal emissions," or "wet dreams."[16]

8. The techniques of masturbation are numerous and usually involve manipulation of the genitals with the hands. One author thus defines masturbation as:

Masturbation or pollution is complete sexual satisfaction (orgasm) either obtained by some form of self-stimulation or procured by immodest actions with the other sex, exclusive of sexual intercourse. Mostly, however, the term masturbation designates sexual gratification by self-stimulation, which is also the more frequent form. It is also called self-abuse, the solitary sin, ipsation. Orgasm is usually brought about by manipulation or friction of the genitals (therefore the term "masturbation"); but it can also be procured by sexual fantasies, desires and touches of another person. The term onanism, which is likewise sometimes used, refers rather to unlawful avoidance of conception in the sexual union of married people.[17]

9. Masturbation is said to be a very common sexual outlet. According to the Kinsey survey, more than 90% of males and at least 60% of females engage in it at some time or other. Statistics indicate that young males masturbate on an average of 2 to 3 times per week, with this figure tending to decrease with increasing age. Female averages are lower, but recent surveys suggest that both males and females are beginning to masturbate at an earlier age and are doing it more often than in previous generations.[18]

## 3. MAGISTERIAL TEACHING

While the general teaching of the Bible clearly upholds purity and holiness of life, exampled especially in St. Paul (for instance in 1 Corinthians 6), there is no specific or explicit condemnation of masturbation in either the Old or New Testaments.[19] The Old Testament does make reference to seminal discharges (Leviticus 15:16) and nocturnal emissions (Deuteronomy 23:9-11), and indicates that such discharges/emissions make a person temporarily unclean and ritually impure. In the New Testament, we are told to use our bodies in a way "that is holy and honorable, not giving way to selfish lust..."[20] and "people of immoral lives" are warned that they will not inherit the Kingdom of God.[21] Scripture scholars agree, however, that there is no convincing proof that any passages cited in the Scriptures pertain to the morality of masturbation as such.

There exists, however, a long line of magisterial pronouncements against masturbation. In 1054, e.g., Pope Leo IX taught that "Masturbators should not be admitted to sacred orders." In 1904 the Sacred Penitentiary indicated that complete masturbatory acts of a woman during the absence of her husband are gravely illicit and that any confessor who approves this practice should be denounced to the Holy See. In 1929 the Holy Office said that direct masturbation is not permitted for the purpose of obtaining semen. The Congregation for Religious in 1961 wrote, "Any candidate who has the habit of solitary sins and who has not given well-founded hope that he can break this habit... is not to be admitted to the novitiate... A much stricter policy must be followed in admission to perpetual profession and advancement to Sacred Orders... unless he has acquired a firm habit of continency and has given... consistent proof of habitual chastity."

In 1971 *The Ethical and Religious Directives for Catholic Health Facilities* (of the United States Bishops) repeated the teaching of the 1929 statement of the Holy Office: "The use of the sex faculty outside the legitimate use by married partners is never permitted even for medical or other laudable purposes, e.g., masturbation as a means of obtaining seminal specimens" (n 21). In 1974 the Congregation for Catholic Education issued *A Guide to Formation and Priestly Celibacy* and gives the following advice: "One of the causes of masturbation is sexual imbalance. The other causes are generally of an occasional and secondary nature, albeit contributing to its appearance and continuation. In education, efforts should be directed rather towards the causes than to attacking the problem directly... Fear, threats, physical or spiritual intimidation are best avoided. These could encourage the formation of obsessions and compromise the possibility of a balanced sexual attitude... Success as always will depend on the degree of awareness of the real causes of the problem... Self-abuse upsets the kind of life which is the educator's aim. He cannot remain indifferent to the close-up attitude which results from it. Nevertheless, he should not over dramatize the fact of masturbation nor lessen his esteem and goodwill for the individual afflicted... In trying to meet each difficulty, it is better not to offer a readymade take-it-or-leave-it solution. Rather, using the occasion for real interior growth, help and encourage the sufferer in such a way that he finds his own remedy" (n 63).

Brockman offers this summary:

> Masturbation is objectively a serious sin ... and the average person who gives in to masturbation, either as a teenager or as an adult, commits sin. Through confession and the sacraments, a person of good will can obtain the grace to overcome this habit, if he or she is willing to mortify the self and to avoid occasions of sin.[22]

## 4. THEOLOGICAL RESPONSES

Theological stances vary regarding the moral approach to this question of masturbation. As one example, Lawler, Boyle and May teach in *Catholic Sexual Ethics*[23] that the Church is "certain" that of its very nature masturbation is gravely wrong and this certainty is first of all rooted in divine revelation. These authors cite these texts: Genesis 38:8-10 (Onan); 1 Corinthians 6:9 (where Paul lists those excluded from the kingdom and specifically mentions the *malakoi*); and Romans 1:24 (where Paul indicates that those who reject God dishonor their own bodies). These authors recognize the fact that contemporary scholarship points out that these texts "do not unambiguously refer specifically to masturbation."[24] However, these authors conclude that "In condemning irresponsible uses of sex generally, Scripture certainly does include a condemnation of masturbation."[25] This conclusion is *logical* in light of the statement in the 1975 *Declaration on Certain Questions Concerning Sexual Ethics*: "Even if it cannot be proved that Scripture condemns this sin by name [masturbation], the tradition of the Church has rightly understood it to be condemned in the New Testament when the latter speaks of 'impurity,' 'unchasteness,' and other vices contrary to chastity and continence."[26] *Catholic Sexual Ethics* then concludes, "A teaching so seriously proposed over so many centuries is certainly authoritative for believers. In fact, it would not be implausible to count her teaching on masturbation as part of the infallible exercise of the ordinary magisterium of the Church."[27]

In "Contemporary Attitudes on the Morality of Masturbation,"[28] Brockman identifies other moral stances regarding masturbation. One may be called "the diminished freedom view":

> Masturbation is far from being a simple sexual sin, but is part of the complex process of maturation. While it is always objectively sinful, habitual masturbation usually involves a significant diminishing of freedom, so that in many cases it is unwise to consider the person who has this problem as being morally responsible, at least in regard to serious sin.

Another view is the one involving a person's "fundamental option":

> While masturbation is a moral question, for the average person it is not necessarily to be regarded as seriously sinful. A particular individual action has meaning insofar as it makes incarnate and intensifies the fundamental moral choice that man must make between God and creatures, which ultimately means self. It is difficult to imagine that an act of masturbation could be regarded as such a fundamental choice.

Finally, Brockman presents "the neutral attitude" toward the morality of masturbation:

> Masturbation is such a normal part of growing up that the only serious evil that can be attached to it arises from the unfortunate guilt

feelings that come from early training and negative attitudes toward sexuality. Masturbation represents the phase through which a person grows toward interpersonal relationships.

Some comment should be made here regarding the historically important article "Masturbation and Objectively Grave Matter" by Fr. Charles E. Curran (1968).[29] Curran begins his presentation by citing the traditional authors on the question of masturbation; for instance, Zalba taught, "Direct and perfectly voluntary pollution is always and intrinsically a grave sin."[30] To the contrary, however, Curran concludes that masturbation is not always a grave matter, an action which is *ex toto genere suo grave.*

Curran gives three major reasons for coming to this conclusion: psychological studies indicate that masturbatory actions are generally symptomatic;[31] the majority of adolescents go through a more or less prolonged period of masturbatory activity; and confessional practice indicates that most often the masturbator has not broken his or her relationship to God.

After outlining the meaning of sin in a fundamental option perspective, Curran revisits the classic tradition which teaches that a sin is mortal *ex toto genere suo* if it is against the love of God (e.g., blasphemy) or against love of neighbor (e.g., adultery).[32] In addition, an injury is also done to God when the order of nature is broken since God is the author of nature: i.e., when there is a substantial inversion of an order of very great importance.[33] Curran then asks: Does the single act of masturbation constitute a substantial inversion of a very important order of nature? His answer is "No," for several reasons:

1. A total human consideration must embrace much more than the mere biological emission of semen.
2. Masturbation might indicate a narcissistic behavior pattern, a period of temporary stress, or a developing stage of adolescent sexuality; it thus involves a multitude of relationships and must not be considered solely in terms of procreation.
3. Traditional arguments against masturbation stressed teleology of the semen; but this does not explain the reality of female masturbation.

4. Traditional theologians have illegitimately transferred to the individual act the importance that belongs to the sexual faculty.

5. There has been an over-emphasis on sexual sins because of the influence of Gnosticism and Jansenism.

Curran then concludes that there is no conclusive proof that the Scriptures mention the malice or gravity of the matter of masturbation; the Fathers of the Church are practically silent on the simple question of masturbation; and masturbation is not a matter which is always and everywhere and necessarily grave.[34]

### Conclusion

The teaching of the magisterium on masturbation must remain normative in all moral and pastoral perspectives on this question: i.e., masturbation is an objectively serious sin since its very nature contradicts the self-giving and life-giving meanings of the sexual faculty. It is also important to recognize the fact that the Church herself acknowledges that on occasion a person may possibly experience a curtailment of freedom in his or her behavior, so that while the act of masturbation remains objectively a serious sin, an individual may not be subjectively responsible for this sin. At the same time, this does not imply that a person is not in need of such assistance as counselling and spiritual direction. The 1975 *Declaration on Certain Questions Concerning Sexual Ethics* thus states:

> On the subject of masturbation modern psychology provides much valid and useful information for formulating a more equitable judgment on moral responsibility and for orienting pastoral action. Psychology helps one to see how the immaturity of adolescence (which can sometimes persist after that age), psychological imbalance or habit can influence behavior, diminishing the deliberate character of the act and bringing about a situation whereby subjectively there may not always be serious fault. But in general, the absence of serious responsibility must not be presumed; this would be to misunderstand people's moral capacity.[35]

It is always necessary, then, to take seriously the act of masturbation and to realize that it is doubtlessly symptomatic of some phenomenon in an individual's life. The value judgment of the magisterium is thus significant: that masturbatory activity precludes life-giving and love-giving meanings. Consequently, masturbation must be evaluated in terms of its incompatibility with the meaning and purposes of human sexuality. Genovesi thus rightly remarks:

> If, in the full richness of its physical dimension, human sexuality is meant to be understood and valued as being not only love-giving, unitive and interpersonal, but also life-giving, procreative and heterosexual, then masturbation must necessarily be lacking in the ability to express faithfully sexuality's full meaning and purpose. In this inability, this failure, to reflect the richness of human sexuality, lies the moral problem with masturbation; "to stunt one's growth intersubjectively and heterosexually... is a serious matter."[36]

## 5. PASTORAL SUGGESTIONS

Sexuality is a powerful presence in all of us and while recognizing its importance we must also resist its urge for immediate gratification. Our sexuality is God's way of calling us into communion with others and thus we must be on our guard against self-centeredness and self-preoccupation. In this context, the moral danger of masturbation is obvious: it can entrap a person in such a way that he or she becomes so fixed on bodily gratification and sensual pleasure that the capacity for authentic love in a relationship ceases to be functional.[37]

While recognizing this potential threat to authentic sexual maturation, we must also recall that *some acts* of masturbation may be purely hedonistic: i.e., done simply for the sake of the pleasure involved, without any direct relationship toward isolation and self-centeredness.[38] There may be times in the ordinary course of events that certain masturbatory acts do not give birth to selfishness or a curtailment of other-directedness. Recognizing always that the meaning of human sexuality lies in its potential to confer love and life, recourse to masturbatory activity can be at times solely a means of pleasure. This point is made not to justify such activity, but to recognize that an over-interpretation of masturbatory activity can be as harmful as no interpretation or a neutral interpretation. In assisting ourselves and others, then, in a moral evaluation of specific acts of masturbation, it is always important to appreciate the context of a person's life and thus situate that act within a more comprehensive awareness of an individual's personality. Genovesi is again helpful:

> It can happen that masturbation may have little or nothing to do with sexuality and may simply serve as a response to various kinds of psychological or emotional pressures arising from school, work or inter-personal relationships; sometimes masturbation may be an expression of sexual curiosity, or function as an attempt to deal with sexual feelings and desires that have not yet been perfectly inte-grated.[39]

We have seen that both psychologists and theologians have come to emphasize the fact that fantasies which accompany autoeroticism can be important and useful indicators of what mastur-bation means, humanly and pastorally. Genovesi remarks:

> That fantasies in general ought to be taken very seriously when attempting to determine the human and moral significance of mas-turbation seems to be confirmed by a fact which has been verified by both clinical psychologists and priests engaged in pastoral counsel-ing, namely, that the guilt "which arises as a result of masturbatory activity does not so much arise from the act itself as from the fantasies which accompany it."[40]

The fantasy-life involved in autoeroticism is very important for assisting individuals to truly see their level of *gender identity* (as mentioned earlier): e.g., they might see themselves as exploitive or manipulative of others; as a person yearning for a closeness with another individual; a person in need of controlling a relationship; a person who experiences profound vulnerability; a person who wishes himself or herself to be someone other than the person one is.[41]

If masturbation occurs, it should be brought *in a regular fashion* to the Sacrament of Reconciliation. Regular confession can truly assist an individual not to accept masturbation into his or her life as an integral life-expression. In fact, alternation in a person's life between periods of masturbation and abstinence seems to indicate an action unwillingly accepted and an expression of weakness, a sign of tested, tried and failed virtue; rather than a sign of non-commitment to God and to others:

> A person's very lack of complacency, the unwillingness to grant masturbation a permanent and undisputed place in one's life, argues strongly that in such circumstances masturbation may more inspire a person to humility than be an expression of basic and serious sinfulness.[42]

In view of the power of sin both in the world and in ourselves, we also should not hesitate to think of masturbation and the anxieties which it causes many people as Satan's way of making good persons feel bad about themselves.

Bernard Haering wisely comments in this regard that anyone experiencing difficulty with masturbation should not be discouraged "If, at the same time, he has developed the capacity to love others generously and commit himself to worthwhile causes for the common good."[43] The *Declaration on Certain Questions Concerning Sexual Ethics* makes this same point:

> It is true that in sins of the sexual order, in view of their kind and their causes, it more easily happens that free consent is not fully given; this is a fact which calls for caution in all judgment as to the subject's responsibility. In this matter it is particularly opportune to recall the following words of Scripture: "Man looks at appearances but God looks at the heart" [1 Sam. 16:7]. However, although prudence is recommended in judging the subjective seriousness of a particular sinful act, it in no way follows that one can hold the view that in the sexual field mortal sins are not committed.[44]

Mortal sins are possible in the area of sexual expression and in the area of masturbation but we must be extremely cautious in assessing these matters so as not to assume that every masturbatory activity occurs with "free consent," and thus lessening or eliminating one's subjective culpability (formal sin).

A number of years ago, John R. Connery and Richard A. McCormick wrote articles extremely helpful in dealing with the question of masturbation, especially adolescent masturbation.[45] They wisely suggest that there are certain pessimistic attitudes which must be avoided in dealing with this question:

(1) There is really no hope of overcoming this activity in adolescence.

(2) Creating an alarmist mentality: e.g., being juridical (don't do that); being interpretative (you'll neglect your studies); being a policeman (how many times a day do you do that?); being hysterical (you'll go blind); giving foolish recipes (keep clean, tie your hands, flee sex, take a daily shower); being too casual or commonplace (it's like brushing your teeth).

Connery and McCormick also caution against optimistic attitudes:

(1) Daily communion is an automatic solution. They comment that this is a very poor pastoral practice because it can lead many to become extremely discouraged when daily communion doesn't "solve" the problem and thus they might unwittingly lose an important faith-perspective in the importance of the Eucharist. In addition, some might not be able to receive communion daily, with the result of further discouragement.

(2) This activity is merely a matter of "growing up" and needs no ethical or moral comment. Such an approach can suddenly lead to sustaining a person at an autoerotic level.[46]

Genovesi points out that in trying to limit sexual temptation and the sense of frustration that often accompanies it, we will be greatly helped if we are prudent in choosing our reading materials and our forms and places of entertainment: "Basically, we have to keep in mind what kind of person we want to be; then we must truthfully analyze what are our 'occasions of sin,' i.e., where, when and with whom are we most likely to betray our ideals and settle for being less than we are called to be and really want to be. Once we identify our proven 'troubled spots,' we put ourselves on the line to see how sincere we are trying to avoid them in the future."[47] We must not forget that the urge and need for sex are not a part of us in just the same way as the urge and need for food and drink are. Rather, our sexual tendencies depend for their arousal upon external stimuli to a far greater degree than is true of hunger and thirst. It is thus important to monitor our mental "in-take" if we wish to avoid unnecessary turmoil in the struggle for sexual integrity.

## 6. CELIBACY AND MASTURBATION

In 1990 the Congregation for Institutes of Consecrated Life and Societies of Apostolic Life issued *Directives on Formation in Religious Institutes*.[48] These *Directives* counsel that:

> Chastity frees the human heart in a remarkable manner (1 Cor. 7:32-35), so that it burns with a love for God and for all people. One of the greatest contributions which religious can bring to humanity today is certainly that of revealing, by their life more than by their words, the possibility of a true dedication to and openness toward others, in sharing their joys, in being faithful and constant in love without a thought of domination or exclusiveness. The pedagogy of consecrated chastity will consequently aim at: Helping in matters of self-control on the sexual and affective level... (n 13).

The Code of Canon Law also reflects this point. Canon 599 states: "The evangelical counsel of chastity assumed for the sake of the kingdom of heaven, as a sign of the future world and as a source of more abundant fruitfulness in an undivided heart, entails the obligation of perfect continence in celibacy." And canon 277 states: "Clerics are obliged to observe perfect and perpetual continence for the sake of the kingdom of heaven and therefore are obliged to observe celibacy, which is a special gift of God, by which sacred ministers can adhere more easily to Christ with an undivided heart and can more freely dedicate themselves to the service of God and humankind. Clerics are to conduct themselves with due prudence in associating with persons whose company could endanger their obligation to observe continence or could cause scandal for the faithful."

In their commentary on canon 277, Coriden, Green and

Heintschel[49] comment, "This canon represents an important commitment of the Western Church upheld by the Second Vatican Council.
The law of celibacy was reaffirmed... in Article 16 of *Presbyterorum
Ordinis*: 'Perfect and perpetual continence for the sake of the kingdom of heaven was recommended by Christ the Lord' (Mt. 19:12)."

The celibate's commitment to chastity is thus a commitment to
a life where the autoerotic activity of masturbation is eliminated. In
"The Sexual Celibate and Masturbation,"[50] Bernard J. Tyrrell indicates that a masturbation-free existence truly calls for an authentic
faith perspective, one rooted in the awareness that an unreflected
celibate life is impossible to live: i.e., one needs to give a *raison d'etre*
for one's celibacy. A celibate is not an a-sexual being but must learn
to express his or her sexuality in appropriate ways. Tyrrell comments
that it is necessary to avoid a pessimistic view that a masturbation-free
celibate existence is impossible. With the help of grace, freedom in
this area is possible and self-fulfilling destructive prophecies must be
avoided. In this regard, William F. Kraft gives sound advice:[51]

> Workaholic religious, who are compulsively project oriented and
> who are so busy that they seldom take time out simply to be, are also
> candidates for masturbation. An attractive feature of masturbation is
> that by using this means, one does not take time to slow down, rest,
> and relax. Obviously, a key therapeutic challenge is to look behind
> the mask of masturbation in order to restructure one's life in ways
> that foster more embodied and integrated living.
>
> To help oneself and others, it is important to look behind the
> mask of masturbation and see what is hidden and neglected. We have
> noted that masturbation is often a sign of more basic issues like
> disembodiment, functionalism, affectivisim, and aborted spiritual-
> ity. Usually one part of our lives (activity, thinking, feeling) is
> maximized, sexuality is not integrated, or feelings (loneliness,
> boredom, frustration) are avoided. Masturbatory acts say something
> about our whole lives. Their main message is that our sexuality
> (embodiment) and spirituality are not well integrated.
>
> To view masturbation as a challenge for spiritual growth, we
> must listen to and learn from the uncomfortable feelings that often
> underlie and motivate masturbation. Feelings of disembodiment,
> fatigue, loneliness, boredom, and depression are telling us some-
> thing about our lives. Instead of silencing their message, we should

listen to their invitations to grow holy as well as wholly. We should strive to see the spirit that is hidden behind the mask of masturbation. Rather than remaining only with ourselves, we should listen to the call of the spirit of sex to go beyond ourselves.[52]

## *Excursus*

A final note should be added here regarding certain presuppositions about celibacy:[53]

(1) Celibacy is a mode of Christian existence. Celibacy is not a series of practices, though it implies practices. Rather, it is a way of existing in which the person is able to love others without centering on a single partner as in marriage. For the Christian celibate, it is the personal love of Christ first which is most important in relationships. In addition, the love of one's sisters and brothers serves to form that love of Christ in an ever more expanding circle of love.

(2) Celibacy involves a capacity to love both men and women affectively and effectively. Ideally, a celibate should be able to do this in an integrated manner. This means that one is drawn toward others in Christ in one's whole being in a manner that reflects one's relationship to them. Thus, despite one's sexual orientation, one's physical, emotional, intellectual and volitional attraction to others befits their sex and one's relationship to them. A celibate will love men and women in an integrated way as teacher to student, as pastor to parishioner, as counselor to client, as friend to friend. The love manifested will depend upon the kind of relationship, its stage of development, and the depth of commitment of the persons to one another.

Celibate love implies in a broad way a warmth in being present to one's brothers and sisters, a sensitivity to their needs, a respect for their individuality and privacy, a concern for their welfare and growth, an ability to expose to them one's own vulnerability, an acceptance of their ministering to oneself, and an expression of one's love in a fitting manner. To the contrary, it is a defect for a celibate to lack the ability to be affective or effective in love for both men and women; it is a defect to be drawn only toward one sex; it is a defect when one is drawn toward others in a purely physical way; it is also as much a defect for a celibate to be affectively distant.

It is a mistake to think of celibacy as the mere absence of genital contact. Rather, since celibacy is fundamentally the presence of a consuming love for Christ, it is also an integrated love of all persons and thus eliminates the need to focus on a centered relationship to one as in marriage. Since genital activity is, in the Christian tradition, the expression of the deeply committed centered relationship of marriage, celibates renounce that kind of an exclusively centered relationship. The presence of such genital activity manifests either that one is not called to celibacy or that one has not yet matured as a celibate.

3. *Both heterosexually and homosexually oriented persons can be celibate.* A celibate is one in whom the attraction toward Christ living in all overtakes the orientation of the individual, whether heterosexual or homosexual. What must progressively predominate in a celibate is one's movement of integrated love for all in Christ.

For both heterosexual and homosexual persons, the perfection of celibacy is not an immediate attainment. At the same time, the call to celibacy includes the call to chastity; seminarians and those in novitiate experiences must thus refrain from sexual relationships from the beginning of their preparation for ordination or religious vows. Indeed, some time frame of about three to five years of chaste living should be a prerequisite for entrance into seminary or religious formation programs. In the stages of the development of their vocations (in the seminary or novitiate), all celibates are more or less fragile. They need to mature in circumstances where they are challenged to grow; at the same time, they should not be confronted by obstacles too difficult for their present capacities.[54]

## CHAPTER EIGHT

# RESPECT FOR HUMAN LIFE

The human person is made in the *image* and *likeness* of God. From such a perspective, life has its boundaries. It is not a possession to be grasped. Life is not my individual personal property to do with as I will. Neither is life an absolute good which must be preserved at all costs. The good steward sees earthly existence and all creation as provisional. The good steward is neither a vitalist nor a pessimist; but is a person of hope.[1] Consequently, there is no obsolete human being to whom we do not owe what Paul Ramsey calls "canons of loyalty."[2]

Since the human being is the image of God, an authentic spirituality is one which must include an ethical world view that leads to actions which are always peace-building. We are called to be stewards of creation: to care for, and to share, the goods we hold in trust.[3] In "Practical, Utopian, and Poor — Just Stewards," Weber offers a provocative point:

> In his book *Situation Ethics*, Joseph Fletcher presents a hypothetical situation to make a point about the nature of Christian morality. Suppose, he says, that you are in a burning building and could save only one of two persons from the fire. The two persons are your own father and a medical genius who has just discovered a cure for a common fatal disease. What would you do? Fletcher's own position is that you should save the medical genius. He argues that Christian morality is consequentialist in nature and that whatever course of action provides the greatest good for the greatest number is the loving and right thing to do. The medical genius would be of greater benefit to more persons than your father.

Those who disagree with Fletcher's analysis of this case need not disagree with the emphasis on consequences. Some would argue that social consequences are very important in determining what should be done, but one does not need to calculate social consequences in the same way that Fletcher does. One can argue, rather, that concern for social consequences should lead us to save the father, for society is better served by fostering sound attitudes and values (like familial loyalty and gratitude) than by improving the physical health of people. *The most important consequences are not always the most tangible ones.*[4]

We approach the question of human life from this perspective: We are all made in the image of God and the most important consequences are not always the most tangible ones.

## 1. INSTRUCTION ON RESPECT FOR HUMAN LIFE IN ITS ORIGIN AND ON THE DIGNITY OF PROCREATION

This *Instruction* was issued by the Congregation for the Doctrine of the Faith on 22 February 1987. This *Instruction* presents certain important presuppositions in properly approaching and evaluating the nature of human life.

The Introduction stresses that it is always incumbent upon us to safeguard the human person. The *Instruction* stresses that technology serves the person and not vice-versa. Commenting on this perspective, Thomas A. Shannon and Lisa Sowle Cahill note:

Because of the holistic nature of the person — his or her psychosomatic unity — there is no such thing as a merely technical intervention. Insofar as the interventions are purposeful and performed on the human, they have an inescapable moral dimension. Thus the concept of respect for persons, both physically and spiritually, stands as the touchstone of the moral analysis of the reproductive technologies.[5]

A person is a "unified whole," a single body-soul entity, and this must be the fundamental perspective from which the criterion for all decision-making regarding the human person is made. What is technically possible is, then, not by that very fact morally admissible. Chapter One of the *Instruction* deals with the embryo. The document states that the human being must be respected from the first instance of its existence: i.e., from the "moment of conception," when the zygote has formed.[6] The *Instruction* then includes this "doctrinal reminder," which provides the fundamental criterion for the solution of the various problems posed by the development of the biomedical sciences in this field:

> (S)ince the embryo must be treated as a person, it must also be defended in its integrity, tended and cared for, to the extent possible, in the same way as any other human being as far as medical assistance is concerned.[7]

Prenatal diagnosis is, then, possible if it safeguards the integrity of the embryo and the mother and provides no disproportionate risk to either. In addition, the *Instruction* teaches, prenatal diagnosis may never be done for the purpose of inducing an abortion (e.g., to ascertain evidence of malformation or hereditary illness). Such a purpose equals "a gravely illicit act."[8] The *Instruction* then condemns any civil or health programs which "favor a link" between prenatal diagnosis and abortion. Therefore, procedures on embryos are licit only if they are directed toward healing or survival and the consent of the parents is given.

Clearly the *Instruction* teaches that embryos must be respected as human beings:

> To use human embryos or fetuses as the object or instrument of experimentation constitutes a crime against their dignity as human beings having a right to the same respect that is due to the child already born and to every human person.[9]

It is clearly against the teaching of the *Instruction* to use fetal tissue as a source of experimentation or research. The document indicates that embryos are not to be kept alive *in vivo* or *in vitro* for experimental or commercial purposes.[10] Embryos that are obtained *in vitro* are human beings and it is immoral to produce such embryos to be exploited as "biological material." The *Instruction* thus "condemns" the destruction of embryos obtained *in vitro* for research purposes as this equals "kill(ing) [of] defenseless human beings."[11]

The *Instruction* warns that *in vitro* techniques can lead to other illicit attempts at fertilization: e.g., human and animal gametes; gestation of human embryos in the uterus of animals; constructing artificial uteruses for the human embryo. The *Instruction* concludes that such techniques are contrary to human dignity: i.e., "The right of every person to be conceived and to be born within marriage and from marriage."[12]

Chapter Two of the *Instruction* deals specifically with *interventions*. The document indicates that *in vitro* procedures usually do not transfer all ova into the genital tracts of the woman (and thus some embryos are "spared" or "frozen" or "sacrificed"). Such techniques are "contrary to the doctrine on procured abortion."[13]

The *Instruction* then points out that responsible procreation must be the fruit of marriage: there is the "reciprocal respect of their right to become a father and a mother only through each other":[14]

> The child has the right to be conceived, carried in the womb, brought into the world and brought up within marriage: it is through the secure and recognized relationship to his own parents that the child can discover his own identity and achieve his own proper human development.

The *Instruction* condemns heterologous artificial fertilization because it is *contrary to the unity* of marriage and to the dignity of the spouses and to "the child's right to be conceived and brought into the world in marriage and from marriage."[15] Consequently, any recourse to a third person for sperm or ovum equals a violation of "the reciprocal commitment of the spouses" since an "essential property of marriage... is its unity":

> Heterologous artificial fertilization is contrary to the unity of marriage, to the dignity of the spouses, to the vocation proper to parents, and to the child's right to be conceived and brought into the world in marriage and from marriage.[16]

Logically, then, the document condemns surrogate motherhood for it is contrary to the unity of marriage and the dignity of procreation: it equals a division of the physical, psychological and moral elements of the family.

The *Instruction* then deals with *homologous artificial fertilization*. The document insists that there is an inseparable connection between the unitive and the procreative meanings of the conjugal act and thus homologous artificial fertilization is "not the fruit of a specific act of conjugal union" and thus *separates* the two meanings:

> (P)rocreation is deprived of its proper perfection when it is not desired as the fruit of the conjugal act, that is to say of the specific act of the spouse's union.[17]

The *Instruction* recognizes that sterility is a source of suffering but "an openness to the transmission of life" is not sufficient for making a positive moral evaluation of *in vitro* fertilization between spouses. *In vitro* fertilization and embryo transfer "cannot borrow its definitive moral quality from the totality of conjugal life of which it becomes part nor from the conjugal acts which may precede or follow it:

> Homologous IVF and ET is brought about outside the bodies of the couple through actions of third parties whose competence and technical activity determine the success of the procedure. Such fertilization entrusts the life and identity of the embryo into the power of doctors and biologists and establishes the domination of technology over the origin and destiny of the human person.[18]

The so-called "simple case" (homologous IVF and ET procedure that is free of any compromise with the aborted practice of destroying embryos and with masturbation) remains a technique which is "morally illicit because it deprives human procreation of the dignity which is proper and connatural to it."[19] The *Instruction* does recognize, however, that "homologous IVF and ET fertilization is not marked by all that ethical negativity found in extra-conjugal procreation":

Although the manner in which human conception is achieved with IVF and ET cannot be approved, every child which comes into the world must in any case be accepted as a living gift of the divine Goodness and must be brought up with love.[20]

The *Instruction* teaches that "Marriage does not confer upon the spouses the right to have a child, but only the right to perform those natural acts which are *per se* ordered to procreation":

> The child is not an object to which one has a right, nor can he be considered as an object of ownership: rather, a child is a gift, "the supreme gift" and most gratuitous gift of marriage, and is a living testimony of the mutual giving of his parents.[21]

The document recognizes the "sad situation" which sterile couples face but encourages them to see in this sterility "an opportunity for sharing in a particular way in the Lord's Cross":

> Sterile couples must not forget that "even when procreation is not possible, conjugal life does not for this reason lose its value. Physical sterility in fact can be for spouses the occasion for other important services to the life of the human person, for example, adoption, various forms of educational work, and assistance to other families and to poor or handicapped children."[22]

Chapter Three of the *Instruction* speaks to the *moral and civil law*. The document maintains that the State must place its power at the service of the rights of each citizen, especially the more vulnerable. The law must provide appropriate penal sanctions "for every deliberate violation of the child's rights." In addition, the document maintains, legislation must prohibit embryo banks, *post mortem* insemination and surrogate motherhood.

The *Instruction* comes to its *conclusion* by stating that its intent is not meant to halt further reflection but "rather to give it a renewed impulse in unrenounceable fidelity to the teaching of the Church."

## 2. SCIENCE AND THE UNBORN

Two works are important for helping us appreciate better the meaning and ramification of the teachings in the *Instruction: Religion and Artificial Reproduction* by Thomas A. Shannon and Lisa Sowle Cahill[23] and *Science and the Unborn* by Clifford Grobstein.[24]

Shannon and Cahill review the history of artificial reproduction. They point out that in the 1950s "The Pill" guaranteed a separation of sexuality and reproduction; and in the 1990s scientific advances have made possible intercourse without reproducing, and reproducing without intercourse: e.g., artificial insemination; in vitro fertilization — which also makes the embryo available for other procedures; and the surrogate uterus/mother.

These birth technologies present certain *general risks* for the woman: e.g., loss of privacy/intimacy of one's sexual life; endometrial biopsy, which requires a scraping of the uterus with a sharp instrument; the uterus and oviducts may be filled with dye; hormonal treatments; the possibility of general anesthesia during laparoscopy; anxiety-producing risks and strain on the spouse's relationship; the life-threatening risk of ectopic pregnancy. At the same time, these birth technologies have several benefits: e.g., the possibility of having a child; the possibility of learning the cause of one's infertility. With these birth technologies, the pregnancy rate varies with the number of ova implanted: 21% in the transfer of a single fertilized egg, to 30% with two, and 40+% with three mature eggs. The critical statistic is still the number of children actually born, and that number appears to be quite low.[25]

Costs vary for these birth technologies: e.g., the cost for screening to enter a program is almost $2,465.00; and the cost for the actual procedure is about $5,590.00 (these are 1983 figures). Thus the initial attempt costs a little over $8,000.00 and each additional attempt costs another $5,000.00. Something in the order of $38,000.00 would be required to insure roughly a 50% chance of a live birth for a particular patient.[26]

Shannon and Cahill then review the Church's tradition regarding sexuality, marriage and parenthood. As we have seen, in Catholic teaching the meaning of sex is tied to the interpersonal communion/ love of the partners, thus giving to human sexuality an intrinsically positive meaning. For St. Thomas, sex was primarily for procreation, the procreation which occurs within a relationship characterized by a strong and appropriate affective bond and commitment.

In the 1917 Code of Canon Law, the possibility that marriage is first and foremost an interpersonal love relationship was virtually ignored. And as recently as 1930, Pope Pius XI in *Casti Connubii* defends procreation as the primary purpose of marriage and upholds the proper submission of wife to husband. In a strikingly different tone, *Gaudium et Spes* speaks of conjugal love which involves "the good of the whole person" and is expressed appropriately in "the marital act" that is "noble and worthy" and which signifies and promotes "the mutual self-giving" of spouses.[27] It is important to note that *Humanae Vitae* also indicates that procreation is not the primary purpose of marriage or of sex. The "two great realities of married life" are "conjugal love" on the one hand and, on the other, not procreation as such but "responsible parenthood."[28] Pope John Paul II's *Familiaris Consortio* (1980) stresses that the "unitive" and "procreative" meanings of the "conjugal act" are "inseparable."[29] In other words, morality is based on both the unitive and procreative meanings of the conjugal act and not simply on the physical structure of the reproductive processes.

In his classic work *Contraception*, John T. Noonan suggests that the teaching of the Church in this regard protects five core values:

1. Procreation is good.
2. Procreation of offspring reaches its completion only in their education.
3. Innocent life is sacred.
4. The personal dignity of a spouse is to be respected.
5. Marital love is holy.[30]

In Chapter Three of their book, Shannon and Cahill then give an overview of the *Instruction*. They stress that the document emphasizes that the meaning of science and technology must be drawn from the nature of the person and his or her moral values. Science and technology cannot of themselves show the meaning of existence and of human progress. Thus, there is an inherent check on science and technology: *the nature of the person.*

Because the person is a psychosomatic unity, there is no such thing as a merely technical intervention. Every intervention has an inescapable moral dimension. Consequently, the concept of respect for persons, both physically and spiritually, stands as the touchstone of the moral analysis of the reproductive technologies. Interventions are possible, then, only if they respect the life of the embryo and the mother and do not subject them to disproportionate risks.

Shannon and Cahill focus on the two critical rights enunciated in the *Instruction*:

1. The right of the child to be conceived, carried in the womb, and brought into the world and brought up within marriage (II:1).
2. The right that a child must never be considered an object of ownership (II:8): in other words, marriage does not confer on the spouses the right to have a child.

The fidelity of the spouses involves "reciprocal respect for their right to become a father and a mother only through each other" (II:1) and thus are these three dimensions inseparable:

1. The right to become a father and a mother only through one another.
2. Fidelity makes possible the procreation of the child.
3. Fidelity of the spouses reflects the unitive and procreative dimensions of the conjugal act.

Chapters Four, Five and Six contain several conclusions:

1. Conception is the definitive beginning point of personal existence and from that time forward the pre-embryo must be accorded full human rights (we will look further at this point in a moment).
2. Reproductive technologies separate sex not only from love, but also from procreation, since they enable conception to occur without a sexual act.[31]
3. Homologous fertilization is not marked by all the ethical negativity found in extra-conjugal procreation.[32]

4. Family and marriage constitute the setting for the birth and upbringing of children.
5. A child cannot be conceived as the product of an intervention of medical/biological techniques; but, should this occur, the child must be the object of his or her parents' love.
6. Conception may be assisted but never dominated by technical assistance for domination constitutes a violation of human sex and conception precisely as human events.
7. The values of love and procreation are inseparably linked to "each and every act" of sexual intercourse.

The *Instruction* makes numerous references to such terms as conception, zygote, fertilization, pre-embryo, fetus. Although not written in conversation with the *Instruction*, Clifford Grobstein's book is extremely useful in assisting us to understand the meaning of these and other terms found in the document. Consequently, we will here review the main components of Grobstein's book. This discussion will also benefit by the important insights of Shannon and Wolter in "Reflections on the Moral Status of the Pre-Embryo."[33]

In Chapter One, Grobstein maintains that the question regarding the personally human status of the pre-embryo cannot be answered on scientific grounds alone, for a human person has his or her definition not only in terms stemming from a scientific definition, but also from moral and religious contexts.

He explains that implantation is the physiological beginning of actual maternal pregnancy, as well as of the offspring's significant dependency on the mother. Until this time, the developing entity is *within the mother* but *not interactive with the mother*. Grobstein indicates that there are several reasons for this conclusion:

1. The woman within whom the egg is fertilized is normally unaware of when fertilization occurs.
2. It is not until implantation that hormonal changes announce the beginning of the pregnant state.
3. The independence of the pre-implantation phase is dramatically demonstrated in the few IVF cases in which an externally developing offspring has been transferred to the

uterus of a woman who is not its genetic mother. Development continues in such a substitution gestational mother.
*Thus, genetic and gestational motherhood can be sepa-
rated.*

Grobstein wisely indicates that the *status* of the single zygote is
of extreme importance since this "entity" can physically be separated
from its mother. Consequently, there is a need to preserve the special
quality and dignity of human life, especially in light of the increasingly powerful and precise ability of science and medicine to intervene in human reproduction and either inadvertently or deliberately
diminish the meaning of what it means to be human.

In Chapter Two, Grobstein indicates that to be an individual is
to be a single and particular entity, recognizable as both *unitary* and
*unique*. Unity refers to singleness and unique refers to being particular, in the sense of having an identity distinguishable from others.
These two properties (unitary and unique) do not arise simultaneously
in the process of becoming. There are six separable aspects of
individuality:

1. Genetic (hereditary uniqueness).
2. Developmental (the achievement of singleness).
3. Functional (the diverse activities essential to survival).
4. Behavioral (integrated activities of the whole in relation to
   environments).
5. Psychic (inner experiences accompanying behaviors).
6. Social (self-aware interaction).

The critical question here is when does a *particular individual
life* begin? This question is the crux of this entire issue.[34]

Fertilization has two major consequences: it activates what has
been a dormant state of the egg in the ovary, so that it completes its
maturation and continues development; and it combines hereditary
contributions from both parents into a new and unique hereditary
constitution (genotype or genome).[35] Fertilization substantially alters
the properties of the egg, not only by activating it but also by
providing it with a new joint genome derived from both genetic
parents (it takes an expert observer to detect that fertilization has

occurred during the first few hours after sperm penetration). At this point, the fertilized egg/"zygote" has acquired a very important *first aspect of individuality* in its unique genome, which combines contributions from both parents but does not duplicate either of them. Therefore, the new genome is a fundamental first step in establishing a new total individuality.

Uniqueness in the genetic sense has been realized but, e.g., unity or singleness has not. The zygote may give rise to either natural or induced twinning or to two or more individuals with identical heredity. Consequently, the new genetic message established at fertilization is unique, but it is still far from realization in a *particular human individual*. Genetic particularity or uniqueness is established at fertilization, then, and singleness arises independently and at a significantly later time.

When does human *developmental* singleness first appear? About 10 to 14 days after fertilization and by a process still only dimly understood, human *developmental* singleness first appears. It is this transitional stage, referred to as the *blastocyst*, that arrives in the uterus and begins the process of implantation into the uterine lining. The blastocyst is no longer merely a bundle of cells: it is a multicellular entity. Within the blastocyst there are now two distinguishable cell populations, those of its external layer and those of a smaller, cellular mass extending into the inner cavity. Only this inner cell mass is the precursor of the embryo. The external cells and their descendants become the placenta and extra-embryonic membranes, which are discarded at birth. Each can contribute to any part of the embryo, and separation of the mass into two parts can still yield two or more embryos. It is only when the later-stage blastocyst has penetrated and implanted in the uterine wall that properties of the inner cell mass change and it becomes committed to the production of a single individual.

This stage of commitment to developmental individuality is referred to as *primary embryonic organization*: the beginning of formation of the embryo proper. The first sign that primary organization is underway is the appearance of what is called the *primitive streak*. Before these primary organizing events occur, there is no recognizable embryo but only a two-layered disc of cells that is

## Fertilization of the Egg

A large number of sperm encounter the mature egg. All attempt to penetrate the envelope of the egg and occasionally more than one will succeed in doing so at the same time. Only the one, however, which first reaches the nucleus is able to fertilize the egg.

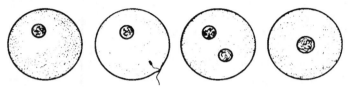

The miniscule head of the sperm absorbs the liquid of the egg till it becomes one with the nucleus itself. When the two are fused, the development and the cellular division of the fertilized egg begins. The first division is into two cells, then four, then eight, then sixteen, etc.

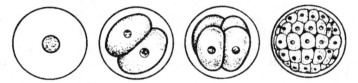

Meanwhile the packet of cells (also referred to as the *morula*) enters the uterus and, shedding its noncellular envelope, attaches itself to the uterine wall, blocking menstruation. Then, in the first, second and third months of pregnancy the human embryo forms (note below the approximate sizes).

precursor to it. From the time of the appearance of the streak, singleness of future development of an organism is being established.

The major activity of the embryonic period is the process of diversification into parts as organs, known as *organogenesis*. This organogenesis continues until about the end of the eighth week, though organogenesis continues well beyond eight weeks in particular organs and parts: e.g., in the formation of teeth. As more mature functional activities are realized, the offspring's potential for existence independent of the mother is increasing. This living potential is manifested as increasing *functional individuality*. The end of the eighth week (organogenesis) is known as the transition from the stage of the embryo to that of the fetus.

Spontaneous movement appears to occur in the absence of known stimulation and raises the question of whether there is inner volition and even possible sentience. Grobstein maintains that movement should be cited only as representing the onset of behavioral individuality. Psychic individuality refers to inner, subjective experience, variously designated as sentience, self-awareness, consciousness, or psychic individuality. It is very difficult to identify this inner experience in a being that cannot communicate through some form of behavior. However, the absence of behavioral signals from the fetus cannot prove that it has no inner experience or psychic individuality. This leaves a considerable zone of uncertainty as to the precise time or onset of psychic individuality during the developmental course.

Social individuality is conferred by recognition of others. Therefore, it is not an intrinsic property but a conferred one. Thus, when the developing offspring becomes recognizably human either in appearance or behavior, *recognizability* may itself become a significant factor in social reactions and decisions about its status.

Grobstein comes to these conclusions:

1. The six aspects of individuality represent a progression in levels of complexity: e.g., independent behavior detectable by ultrasonic imaging as early as six or seven weeks raises the question of independent volition and possible sentience, properties associated with psychic individuality. Thus, human development is a translevel phenomenon.
2. The six aspects of individuality arise separately, gradually,

with significant overlap in time, but roughly in the order presented.
3. A case can be made for considering the set of six to be more significant than their simple sum, perhaps because of the overlap and interaction among them. In this sense, the character of the entity itself, in all its aspects at a given stage, might be the indicator for status assignment. Consequently, the concept of continuing emergence of individuality cannot be ignored in considering status for the unborn. Individuality in its several aspects comes successively into existence.

In Chapter Three, Grobstein deals with the neural substrate of individuality. Roughly twenty weeks to birth, neural maturation has progressed far enough to raise serious question as to whether psychic individuality may have appeared in the form of minimal sentience. The nervous system is the structural and functional substrate for the behavioral, psychic, and social individuality that become the substance of status. In other words, neuronal transmission is the essential substrate that enables large and complex multicellular organisms to function.

Grobstein maintains that neither behavior nor its simplest neural substrate exist in the unborn prior to at least six weeks of development and thus there is no objective basis for assuming even the most minimal inner experience, including pain, during the first half of the first trimester. However, the same cannot be said with equal certainty in the second half of the initial trimester, when new and more localized movements occur and the neural substrate is also increasing markedly in its maturation below the level of the brain. He concludes that based on the limited information available, it can be said that brain-dependent inner experience such as pain is unlikely even up to twenty weeks.

In Chapter Four, Grobstein embarks on the important discussion of the pre-embryo. The scientific concept of an embryo is one of an individual multicellular organism in the process of forming major parts and organs from rudimentary beginnings. Until implantation is achieved, there is not yet a rudimentary individual or embryo. During the preceding stages, there is only an unorganized aggregate of precursor cells that lie within a cellular peripheral layer. This peripheral layer is busy with preparation for and then actual engagement in implantation.

Prior to implantation, then, the developing entity is *internal to the mother* and floats freely in the fluids of her oviduct or uterus *without* direct contact or interaction with either.[36]

The early stages of human development primarily involve the establishment of non-embryonic trophoblast. This process is a necessary prelude to formation of the placenta but provides the continuing essential exchange of substances between the embryo and the mother. During these early stages, the developing entity is not designated and understood as an embryo, but rather as a pre-embryonic phase necessitated by the ancient mammalian commitment to internal gestation.

There is ambiguity in the way scientists use the term "embryo." It is critical, however, to make the distinction between pre-embryo and embryo for purposes of clarity. In Catholic teaching, to prevent implantation is to preclude development to birth and, hence, effectively to terminate the life of the potential offspring. In *Roe vs. Wade* (1973) the Supreme Court denied the pre-embryo any competing status to the unborn as a person with external "viability."

It must be stated clearly, then, that the pre-embryo is unquestionably human in biological terms: e.g., it sustains fundamental biological characteristics as the number, size, and shapes of its chromosomes; the sequence of the components (nucleotides) in its hereditary DNA; and the sequence of analogous components (amino acids) in its proteins. Pre-embryos awaiting transfer to the maternal uterus in an IVF laboratory dish are, therefore, unquestionably *alive* by scientific criteria. They are not only human but "in being."[37] Although not all of equal weight, Grobstein then reaches these conclusions about the pre-embryo:

1. The pre-embryo is not a *person.*
2. Pre-embryos should be respected for their biologically human quality.
3. Pre-embryos must have a status that embodies awareness of, and a special concern about, their potential to become persons.[38]

4. Pre-embryos are members of the human community with specifically recognized kinship and important community roles within it.[39]

In Chapter Five, Grobstein deals with the status of the *embryo*. He points out that during the period of embryonic organogenesis, the embryo is totally dependent on the uterine environment supplied by its mother, often with little awareness on her part. During this time, the embryo can be characterized as totally passive and behaviorless. At this time, however, the embryo is an entity in the process of extraordinarily rapid, fundamental and complex change.

As early as six or seven weeks after fertilization, there are occasional tentative movements, harbingers of behavior: these are in the form of weak, almost flickering twitches of the head and neck that appear to be random and uncoordinated, but certainly represent the onset of premonitory behavior. This can be taken to be the marker for *transition from embryo to fetus*. During this time, one must be very careful about agents that can induce structural and functional defects. Exposure to alcohol, to other drugs, or to workplace toxins can exert such effects, sometimes even before a woman knows she is pregnant.

Consequently, once pregnancy is established, the intimacy of the association between fetus and mother is such that the interest of neither party can be served without significant consequence to the other. Two recent technological advances have provided new means of diagnostic access to the human embryo:

1. Imaging: using ultrasound which allows visualization of the embryo and fetus without surgical intrusion. Ultrasound can detect a number of anatomical abnormalities, as well as the nature and pattern of movements.
2. Amniocentesis: this process samples the cells and the fluids surrounding the fetus.[40]

In the second to eighth weeks of pregnancy, as organogenesis is at its height, there are transient periods of heightened sensitivity, known as critical periods, in the various parts of the embryo. A number of common exposures — to radiation, alcohol, certain drugs, cigarette smoke — clearly can contribute to abnormality arising during the embryonic period.[41]

*Donum vitae* (*Instruction on Respect for Human Life...*) declares, as we have seen, that "All research, even when limited to the simple observation of the embryo, would become illicit were it to invoke risk to the embryo's physical integrity or life..." The only exception is "experimental forms of therapy used for the benefit of the embryo itself in a final attempt to save its life." In magisterial teaching, then, destruction of human embryos for research purposes "usurps the place of God" because the researcher "arbitrarily chooses whom he will allow to live and whom he will send to death."[42]

Grobstein argues that the integrity and future welfare of the embryo should be strictly protected in order to safeguard its movement toward complete individuality.[43]

Chapter Six of Grobstein's book turns to the status of the *fetus*. The human fetus begins about the end of the eighth post-fertilization week when the embryo passes without sharp boundary into the fetal stage. The fetal stage then normally ends at birth. Fetal "viability" refers to the capability to survive disconnection from the placenta. It does not imply complete independence. Under current legal interpretation, viability confers new status on the yet-unborn fetus when it is known to be capable of survival externally with appropriate care.[44]

By thirteen weeks, which marks the traditional end of the first trimester, a "basic motor repertoire" has been established. Such movements, more noticeable as the fetus enlarges, are felt by the mother as "quickening" before the midterm of pregnancy, and their continuance gives assurance that the fetus is alive and well.

In light of all of this data, Grobstein argues that there are five recognizable periods that possibly warrant different status:

1. Pre-embryo (0 to 2 weeks)
2. The embryo (3 to about 8 weeks)
3. The early fetus (9 to 20 weeks)
4. The middle fetus (20-1 to 30 weeks)
5. The late fetus (30-1 weeks to birth)

Grobstein then reaches these conclusions:
1.  A new generation comes into existence at fertilization with

the establishment of a *unique genetic individuality* in a *single living and human cell.* This step is fundamental because in achieving multicellularity (which comes about following a number of subsequent cleavage divisions) all additional levels of human complexity become possible.

    Accordingly, the status of this early multicellular stage, or pre-embryo, deserves human respect.

2. The embryo is alive, genetically individual, with potential to become a person in the fullest sense of that term. Its structure and function are rapidly changing and emerging into new levels of individuality and this characteristic is the hallmark of the embryo.

3. At about eight weeks, the embryo emerges into the fetus, a phase of rapid growth and maturation that is especially characterized by the onset of movement as overt behavior. Movement is critical because it signals behavior, in terms significant to social status. Also, movement is dependent on, and therefore diagnostic of, the level of neuronal maturation in the central nervous system.

4. During the entire unborn period, the developing offspring is biologically *human* and therefore deserving of respect and protection against denigration of its human character.

    The work of Shannon and Wolter provides additional insights into this complicated question of moral status.[45] They point out that a critical discovery in the past two decades is that of *capacitation*, the process by which sperm become capable of fertilizing eggs.[46] As we have seen, human sperm need to be in the female reproductive tract for about seven hours before they are ready to fertilize the egg. This process removes or deactivates "a so-called decapacitating factor that binds to sperm as they pass through the male reproductive tract."[47] Fertilization is not just a simple penetration of the surface of the egg. Rather, it is a complex biochemical process in which a sperm gradually penetrates various layers of the egg. Only after this single sperm has fully penetrated the egg and the haploid female nucleus, one having only one chromosome pair, has developed, do the cytoplasm of the egg and the nuclear contents of the sperm finally merge to give the new identity its diploid set of chromosomes. This process

is called *syngamy*: it takes about 24 hours to complete and the resulting entity is called the zygote.[48]
Fertilization accomplishes four major events:

1. Giving the entity the complete set of 46 chromosomes.
2. Determination of chromosomal sex.
3. The establishment of genetic variability.
4. The initiation of cleavage (the cell division of the entity).

After the various cell-divisions,[49] when the embryo approaches the entrance to the uterus, it is in the 12-16 cell stage, the morula. This occurs on the fourth day. On around the sixth or seventh day the organism, now called the blastocyst, reaches the uterine wall and begins the process of its implantation there so that it can continue to develop. This process of implantation is completed by the end of the second week, at which time there is primitive uteroplacental circulation.[50] The next major stage of development is that of the embryo. This is the beginning of the third week of pregnancy. This phase begins with the full implantation of the pre-embryo into the uterine wall and the development of a variety of connective tissues between it and the uterine wall. After Shannon and Wolter detail embryonic development up to the eighth week they conclude that this development shows a dramatic process from the initiation of fertilization to the formation of an integrated organism around mid-gestation.

They also point out that a critical finding of modern biology is that conception biologically speaking is a *process* beginning with the penetration of the outer layer of the egg by a sperm and concluding with the formation of a diploid set of chromosomes. This is a process that takes at least a day. They suggest that the term "moment of conception" frequently used in Church documents thus be understood as referring to this process as a whole:

> (I)t seems that the theologians who framed these carefully crafted documents wished to convey the idea that at the moment of conception (whatever stage of development of human life obtains) everything is present that is required essentially for this human organism to be a person in the philosophical/theological, if not psychological, sense of the term: a rational or immortal soul has been created and

infused into the organic body. At the same time, while they wished to set forth guidelines, they declared it was still a theoretically open question and hence they did not want to specify, or define, the moment when such passive conception (as it was called by Catholic theologians for many centuries) took place.[51]

Clearly and without any doubt, then, once biological conception is completed we have a living entity and one which has the genotype of the human species. Similar to Grobstein, Shannon and Wolter point out that "Because of the possibility of twinning, recombination, and the potency of any cell up to gastrulation to become a complete entity, this particular zygote cannot necessarily be said to be the beginning of a specific, genetically unique individual human being. While the zygote is the beginning of genetically distinct life, it is neither an ontological individual nor necessarily the immediate precursor of one."[52]

Shannon and Wolter conclude that "there is no reasonable way in which the fertilized egg can be considered a physical individual minimally until after implantation. Maximally, one could argue that full individuality is not achieved until the restriction process is completed when cells have lost their totipotency. Thus the range of time for the achievement of physical individuality is between one and three weeks. One simply cannot speak, therefore, of an individual's being present from the moment of fertilization."[53] It is important to note, however, that the recognition of this biological fact (individuality is not present from the moment of conception) *does not preclude the recognition of the pre-embryo as human and thus deserving of respect and care*, for all of the reasons mentioned by Grobstein.

## 3. THE ABORTION QUESTION

The history and status of the abortion question are very complicated and detailed and I do not intend here to discuss all of the complexities of this question. We will deal with certain specified questions *within* the abortion debate.[54]

## A. Resolution on Abortion

In 1989 the American bishops issued a *Resolution on Abortion* at their annual November meeting.[55] In this *Resolution*, the bishops expressed their "reaffirmation" and "conviction" that "all human life is sacred whether born or unborn." In light of the materials we just reviewed regarding science and the unborn, it is critical to see here again that the magisterial position clearly upholds the sacredness of *all human life* from the "moment of conception." Thus, even though the status of individuality does not come until after fertilization, conception establishes a new human *genome*, which is sacred and deserves utmost affirmation and respect.

Consequently, the bishops state in the *Resolution* that "No Catholic can responsibly take a 'pro-choice' stand when the 'choice' in question involves the taking of innocent human life." They conclude, "We urge public officials, especially Catholics, to advance these goals in recognition of their moral responsibility to protect the weak and defenseless among us."

## B. A Consistent Ethic of Life

In order to set the Church's teaching on abortion in a holistic moral framework, Cardinal Joseph Bernardin urged in 1983 that the question be placed within a consistent ethic of life.[56] This Consistent Ethic of Life (or seamless-garment approach) argues that there should always be a *presumption against taking human life*. In a limited, sinful world, however, there are some *narrowly defined exceptions*: e.g., the just war ethic in Catholic theology.

In the last thirty years or so, the presumption against taking human life has been strengthened and the exceptions have become *more* restrictive: e.g., Pope Pius XII *reduced* the traditional three-fold justification for going to war (defense, recovery of property, and punishment) to the single reason of defending the innocent and protecting those values required for decent human existence. In the case of capital punishment, the action of Catholic bishops, and Pope Paul VI and Pope John Paul II, has been directed against the exercise of that right by the State.

Cardinal Bernardin and others have argued that there is a need for a "consistent ethic" which cuts across the issues of genetics, abortion, capital punishment, modern warfare, and the care of the terminally ill. Opposition, e.g., to abortion and nuclear war must be seen as *specific applications* of this broader attitude. Consequently, a consistent ethic or "seamless-garment" approach pushes the moral, legal and political debate beyond an *ad hoc* or "single-issue" focus. The Church sustains, then, an enduring commitment to the sacredness of human life, based at least on these three principles:

1. Human life is a basic gift and good, the foundation for the enjoyment of all other human goods. Precisely because human life is sacred from the point of conception to the point of natural death, the taking of even one life is a momentous event.
2. There is a strong presumption against any taking of human life, but in a world marked by the effects of sin, there are some narrowly defined exceptions where life can be taken (e.g., in the just war theory).
3. A dedication to the sacredness of human life involves not only the commitment to minimize the taking of human life, but also a commitment to enhance the quality of life at all stages through policies on nutrition, health care, income assistance, and family life.

Why should abortion and all other life issues be placed within a "consistent ethic of life" context? First, technology today poses a series of related threats to life at its various stages of existence. The Church's resistance to these threats is linked by a foundational dedication to the sacredness of human life and to the principles which undergird it: e.g., the Church's traditional principle that the direct taking of innocent human life is always immoral. Second, a sensitivity to any particular threat to the sacredness of human life would be enhanced by a deepened sensitivity to all the threats that are posed to life. And third, the credibility of the Church's stand on any particular life issue will be strengthened by its consistent commitment to life issues.

What are the problems which are often raised with this "consistent ethic of life"? The first criticism one often hears is that the Church makes several exceptions to its general defense of the sacredness of human life: e.g., the killing of combatants in a just war. The question then arises: How consistent is this? Secondly, while the Church may voice its consistent defense on all of the life issues (abortion, nuclear war, capital punishment, euthanasia, medical care), it devotes far more resources to the struggle against abortion than to any of the other issues; thus there is no consistency of energy in the Church's stand on the life issues. In the third place, since most anti-abortion politicians tend to oppose the Church's position on the other life issues, and most politicians who support the Church's stands on nuclear war, capital punishment, and welfare policies tend to reject the Church's position on abortion, how can a citizen translate the "consistent ethic of life" into voting behavior? It seems almost impossible to find a politician to vote for who is consistent on the life issues. Therefore, how is the Catholic in good conscience to prioritize these issues?

These are certain shortcomings of the "consistent ethic of life." But in spite of these shortcomings, the "consistent ethic" framework remains the best tool for bringing to the consciences of Catholics and non-Catholics alike the respect for the sacredness of life in all of its dimensions.[57]

## C. The Bishops' Position on Abortion and Civil Law

The Church teaches that there is a difference between morality and civil law. Morality represents the ethical obligations of individuals and social groups. Civil law touches upon only those ethical obligations which are necessary to promote domestic tranquility, insure public welfare, and provide for the healthy functioning of the civil order. Law cannot deal with all that is morally desirable or attempt to remove every moral taint from society. Even in acknowledging that not all ethical obligations should be the subject of civil law, the Church teaches that it is certainly part of the obligation of civil law to decide where the right to life begins and ends. It is the very essence of government to defend its citizens against threats to their life, and thus civil law must of its very nature touch upon the issue of abortion.

While acknowledging that women face great suffering in being forced to continue unwanted pregnancies, particularly in cases of rape and incest, the Church teaches that this suffering does not justify the taking of innocent human life, and government should not let its unborn citizens be killed by refusing to outlaw abortion. Mario M. Cuomo, the Catholic Governor of New York, has articulated a response to this magisterial position on abortion and public policy.[58] Governor Cuomo asks three questions: (1) Is abortion morally wrong? (2) Do I have a responsibility to try to eliminate abortion in our society? and (3)Is the outlawing of abortion the best way to do this?

Cuomo considers the first two questions to be religious/moral questions and he answers "Yes" to each. He considers the third question to be an essentially political one. He argues that a law against abortion would not be obeyed because there is no public consensus against abortion in the United States: "Our public morality... depends upon a consensus view of right and wrong. The values derived from religious belief will not — and should not — be accepted as part of the public morality unless they are shared by the pluralistic community at large by consensus." Consequently, Cuomo (and others) has argued that while he believes abortion is wrong and has a responsibility to try to eradicate it in our society, he has no obligation to support anti-abortion laws *because there is no existing consensus supporting them.*

The fallacy inherent in Cuomo's approach can be seen when one applies his methodology to other questions of great moral consequence in history. If a Senator before the Civil War were to ask Cuomo's three questions about eradicating slavery (Is it moral: yes; Do I have a responsibility to end it: yes; Is there a public consensus supporting it: no), then the Senator would have concluded that the moral decision would have been to oppose anti-slavery legislation. The same would be true if one applied Cuomo's logic to the anti-apartheid legislation in South Africa or anti-discrimination legislation in Nazi Germany. The problem with Cuomo's logic is that it fails to recognize that there are certain moral questions which are of such import that there is a moral obligation to support legislation even in the absence of a clear moral consensus supporting that legislation. Abortion is such an issue.[59]

In "Catholic Abortion Rates and the Abortion Controversy,"[60] James R. Kelly reports that The Guttmacher Institute found that Catholic women were as likely as the general population to have

abortions, while Protestant and Jewish rates of abortion were proportionately less than the national average. The two scholarly articles
which constitute this report from The Guttmacher Institute stated
several statistical conclusions:

1.  Only 1% of their sample gave rape or incest as a reason for
    abortion; and only 7% reported a health problem.
2.  Women interviewed gave several reasons for having
    abortions: about one-half of them said they did not want to
    be single parents, or they had relationship problems.
3.  Women skilled in contraceptive use often became know-
    ingly pregnant to test the commitments of their partners
    and, when the male refused the obligations of family life,
    resorted to abortion.
4.  The level of unintended pregnancy is in part a reflection of
    poor contraceptive practices among American women.
5.  There is a high rate of abortion for Afro-Americans and
    Hispanics, both groups with higher than average objections
    to abortion on opinion polls. This fact suggests some lack
    of meaningful choice in abortion. The Institute's study
    reports that 77% of women under or just over the official
    poverty line said they were having an abortion because they
    could not afford to have a child. The report concludes in
    this regard that women reporting a family income of less
    than $11,000.00 were twice as likely as other women to
    have abortions.

### D. The Eucharist and A Pro-Choice Position

St. Paul instructs the Christian community that the table of the
Lord must always be a place of unity. In 1 Corinthians 10:16-17, he
writes: "The cup of blessing which we bless, is it not a participation
in the blood of Christ? The bread which we break, is it not a
participation in the body of Christ? Because there is one bread, we
who are many are one body, for we all partake of the one bread." In
light of this unity which the communion of the Lord both signifies and
establishes, Paul goes on in chapter 11 of 1 Corinthians to abhor that
disunity caused by certain Christians around the Eucharist. He writes,

"I do not commend you, because when you come together it is not for the better but for the worst. For, in the first place, when you assemble as a church, I hear that there are divisions among you... When you meet together, it is not the Lord's supper that you eat.... What shall I say to you? Shall I commend you in this? No, I will not" (vv 17-22).

It is not surprising, then, that Paul concludes chapter 11 by a strong counsel: "Whoever, therefore, eats the bread or drinks the cup of the Lord in an unworthy manner will be guilty of profaning the body and blood of the Lord. Let a man examine himself, and so eat of the bread and drink of the cup. For anyone who eats and drinks without discerning the body eats and drinks judgment upon himself" (vv 27-29).

Clearly, St. Paul gives to the Christian community a central focus for the celebration and the reception of the Eucharist. The Eucharist is a sign of unity in the Church; it is a moment to celebrate charity; and all persons need examination to approach the table worthily, to receive the Eucharist in a spirit of unity and not disunity.

The Church's law reflects this scriptural tradition when it understands the Eucharist as "the most august sacrament" in which Christ is contained, offered and received, and by which the Church constantly lives and grows (canon 897). This canon goes on to state importantly that the Eucharist is "the summit and the source of all Christian worship and life; it signifies and effects the unity of the people of God and achieves the building up of the body of Christ. The other sacraments and all the ecclesiastical works of the apostolate are closely related to the Holy Eucharist and are directed to it." Vatican Council II also teaches that "the Eucharist shows itself to be the source and the apex of the whole work of preaching the Gospel."[61] Clearly, then, the Eucharist is the sacrament which both signifies and brings about the unity of the Christian people. Conversely, the table of the Lord must never be the place for public displays or proclamations of disunity or disharmony.

It is for this reason that the law of the Church asserts the right of the faithful to receive the sacraments of the Church (canons 213 and 843) and teaches that a presumption must always favor a person's appropriate disposition to receive the Eucharist worthily.

It is by way of exception that the Church prohibits giving the Eucharist to the faithful and teaches that this prohibition applies only to one "who obstinately perseveres in manifest, serious sin."[62] The official commentary on this canon thus states, "Any prudent doubt about either the gravity or the public nature of the sin should be resolved by the minister in favor of the person who approaches the sacrament."[63]

We see here clearly that the Church's law both follows and endorses St. Paul's injunction that the Eucharist must always be a place of unity and harmony. The Church's law gives every presumption of the doubt to the Christian faithful. It seems only right and just, therefore, that the faithful must approach the Eucharist with the same disposition and point of view: participation in the Eucharist is communion in "the most august sacrament," and the table of the Lord should never be a place for a public display of disagreement, opposition and disharmony within the body of Christ. The 1987 *Instruction, Eucharisticum Mysterium* teaches that "All the faithful show this holy sacrament the veneration and adoration which is due to God himself" (n 3) and "The Rites of the Catholic Church" likewise instructs that "Those who intend to receive the body of the Lord must approach it with a pure conscience and proper dispositions of soul..." (I:23).

In a letter to the world's bishops on 19 May 1991, Pope John Paul II reaffirmed the conviction about the sacredness of all human life. The Pope decries the veritable "slaughter of the innocents" which is taking place through abortion on a world wide scale.[64] The Holy Father expresses particular concern about "The fact that people's moral conscience appears strikingly confused and they find it increasingly difficult to perceive the clear and definite distinction between good and evil in matters concerning the fundamental value of human life." In order to address this confusion, and to break the "vicious circle" of the moral insensitivity of people's consciences, the Pope indicates that "It seems more urgent than ever that we should forcefully reaffirm our common teaching, based on sacred Scripture and tradition, with regard to the inviolability of innocent human life."

Addressing the bishops, the Pope concludes that "All of us, as pastors of the Lord's flock, have a grave responsibility to promote respect for human life in our dioceses." He encourages the bishops to make "public declarations at every opportunity" about this "slaughter of the innocents" and thus "contribute, through the civilization of truth and love, to another fuller and more radical establishment of that 'culture of life' which constitutes the essential prerequisite for the humanization of our society."

The magisterium of the Church makes certain *teaching pronouncements* which present and explain the values of the Catholic tradition: e.g., the recent teachings of the American bishops in *The Challenge of Peace: God's Promise and Our Response* (1983); and in *Economic Justice For All* (1986). Catholics are obliged, as a key aspect of their Catholic identity, to accept the public moral values these teaching pronouncements contain and to work to promote them in their private and public lives. Catholics should also show deference and respect for the ethics of the magisterium when they urge passage of measures fostering such values.

Catholics are thus disloyal to the Catholic tradition if they advocate something the Catholic tradition positively sees as opposing moral values of the public order. In this connection a clarification again of the overall Catholic view on abortion is in order:[65]

1. In the Catholic tradition to take life in the womb is to destroy the value of human life itself. The Catholic tradition believes that the legal sanctioning of abortion on demand opposes the values of human life and the common good.

2. The Catholic value system sees abortion as a matter belonging to the public order and not simply as a matter of personal decision. Every person does have a right to privacy. That right is grounded in the fact that each individual has a uniqueness which of its very nature demands a sphere of privacy. The law does not confer this right; it merely recognizes it, and rightly so. However, the right to privacy is not an absolute right. This right is conditioned in its exercise by the rights of others. Abortion is *not only* a personal decision of the mother, but is also a matter belonging to the public order because it involves the taking of human life in the womb. And because the life of another is of such great importance for the common good, the Church believes that the State does have a proportionate reason for invading the privacy of the mother (and of the father). Accordingly, for Catholics to declare that the abortion

decision is a purely private matter is to disagree with a significant value teaching of the Church.

3. The Catholic moral system of values sees as a *grave public disorder* a condition in which a society believes it is a good that every woman be accorded the legal right to abortion for any reason whatsoever simply because the fetus is within her and is totally dependent upon her. According to Catholic teaching, total dependence does not confer total rights to dispose of the other; rather it demands responsibility for the welfare of the other. To legitimate by law a mentality which extols the freedom to dispose of another because the other is physically dependent on oneself is to begin to erode the public virtue upon which a free society rests. Thus, the Catholic tradition does not see the abortion itself as the only public moral evil. It sees the free choice mentality, the mentality that favors abortion on demand, as also harmful to the public good.

Accordingly, no one who accepts the Catholic value system may advocate the free choice mentality on abortion as a good in itself.

Some Catholics choose to demonstrate their opposition and dissent to this Catholic teaching by wearing T-Shirts to communion that read, e.g.: "CATHOLICS FOR FREE CHOICE." This manner of dissent not only demonstrates a disloyalty to the Church's teaching, but it also misuses the Eucharist by making communion a platform for disagreement and opposition. In view of St. Paul's counsel and the Church's law and teaching on this subject, it is certainly inappropriate and misguided to use the table of the Lord as a forum for expressing one's disagreement with or dissent from Church teaching. All Catholic faithful should thus refrain from such demonstrations of disunity and disharmony in the very sacrament which expresses unity and *communio.*[66]

## 4. REPRODUCTIVE TECHNOLOGIES

We have seen that *Donum Vitae* stresses the "special nature" of the transmission of life in marriage.[67] This "special nature" is understood in magisterial documents as *conjugal intercourse* which canon 1061 specifies as intercourse of the couple "performed between themselves in a human manner."

Many argue that *in vitro* processes do not respect human life but rather treat it as "raw material" used to manufacture a baby. This reasoning argues that the child is thus treated as an object, a thing manufactured out of an egg and sperm, subject to quality control and domination by others. As one theologian comments, "A human life, the life of a being that is the bearer of inviolable and inalienable rights, is not to be considered as a product inferior in nature and subordinate in value to its producers."[68] *Donum Vitae* teaches that a human person is to be begotten, not made: i.e., only if conception is the fruit of human love and not of deterministic technique, will the human being enter history supported by love and free from biotechnological influence.

In *Religion and Artificial Reproduction*,[69] Shannon and Cahill argue these points in terms of *Donum Vitae*:

1.  A key ingredient in the contemporary Western moral understanding of sex and marriage is an enhanced appreciation of the fact that it is the interpersonal relationship of the couple which is at the heart of marriage.

2.  In *Gaudium et Spes* and *Humanae Vitae* the relationship of the spouses moves to center stage. Another example of this general shift is in the 1983 Code of Canon Law which includes the fact that spouses give consent to the *consortium*, the partnership of the whole of life. This language contrasts sharply with the 1917 Code's understanding of consent as directed toward the "right over another's body" for the acts ordained to procreation (cc 1055:1 and 1057:2).

    Stated succinctly, the general contemporary Catholic view is that marriage is a partnership which should be characterized above all by mutual love, which is expressed sexually, and which is conducive to children.

3.  This "paradigm shift" in Roman Catholic teaching reflects certain important factors:
    (1) The partnership of the couple is the basic category; the partnership opens out onto family and society.

(2)  The biological structure of the sexual act is secondary
      to (not absent from) its moral meaning.
Once this shift is recognized, then acts must be evaluated in the context of marital relationship. For instance, acts
of procreation which rely on a procreative partner outside
the marriage are morally illicit because they seem to make
the desire to procreate more important than the fundamental
marital relationship and bring a third party (via shared
parenthood) into the nexus of basic human relationships
which marriage is supposed to support and protect. In
addition, third-party methods violate the promise of exclusivity, which is a fundamental quality of Christian marriage.

Cahill and Shannon reach these conclusions:

1.  It is always important in this discussion to appreciate the
    "inseparability" of sex, love and procreation.[70]
2.  Third-party methods of obtaining ova and sperm intrude a
    third *person* into the marriage, even if he or she is suppos-
    edly affectively uninvolved and is recognized only as a
    biological contributor.
3.  To create deliberately a reproductive situation in which any
    *prima facie* connection between genetic and social parent-
    hood is from the outset denied and suppressed is again to
    treat dualistically a fundamental and powerful relationship
    of the human *person*. In third-party methods, the parties act
    as though there were no morally important relation of
    genetic reproduction either to a marital or a parental
    personal relation.
4.  The love commitment of the spouses sets reasonable,
    humane and Christian parameters in which to undertake
    parenthood. The partnership of spouses is the humanly
    appropriate context for childbearing.

### A.  Current Technology For IVF-ET

IVF-ET is the retrieval of the preovulatory ovum from a
woman's ovary followed by fertilization in a culture dish and devel-

opment of the conceptus to the 2 to 8 cell stage. It is then transferred into the woman's uterine cavity. This procedure began in 1944 when John Rock and Miriam Menkin reported the first *in vitro* fertilization of a human ovum. They described two ova which developed to the two cell stage and one which progressed to the three cell stage. Thirty-four years later, Louise Brown was born, a result of the first clinically successful IVF-ET pregnancy reported by Drs. Steptow and Edwards in England. In the years since 1978, IVF-ET programs have become available worldwide with over 100 IVF centers in the United States alone reporting on now over 3,000 births resulting from IVF-ET.

IVF (*In Vitro Fertilization*) and ET (*Embryo Transfer*) was used initially only to treat women with surgical loss of both fallopian tubes or irreparable tubal damage. The indications for IVF-ET have now been expanded to include all causes of infertility (except azoospermia or total lack of sperm) after traditional medical and/or surgical therapy has failed. The indications for an IVF-ET process include:

1. A generally healthy husband and wife.
2. Accessible ovaries.
3. Normally functioning uterus.
4. Normal or correctable menstrual function.
5. Maternal age under 40.
6. One of the following uncorrected problems:
   (1) Tubal factor
   (2) Male factor [except azoospermia]
   (3) Endometriosis
   (4) Unexplained infertility
   (5) DES exposure
   (6) Cervical factor
   (7) Immunologic factor or anovulation

There are four major steps of IVF-ET:

1. Controlled Ovarian Hyperstimulation

   a. The first IVF-ET cycles used the woman's natural cycle but the success rates were poor. This was partially due to the production of only one oocyte per cycle making it possible to implant only one embryo, since later experience showed that

transfer of more than one embryo improved pregnancy rates.
The natural cycle also proved to be inconvenient since
oocyte retrieval had to be timed to the woman's LH surge
necessitating surgical and laboratory teams to be available at all
hours.

The concept of controlled ovarian hyperstimulation was
thus developed in which multiple preovulatory oocytes were
produced and the timing of oocyte retrieval could be manipulated to occur during normal surgery hours.

b. The most common protocols utilize clomiphene citrate
(CC), human menopausal gonadotropin (HMG), or follicle
stimulating hormone (FSH) alone or in combination to override
the normal mechanism by which only one dominant follicle is
selected for ovulation each cycle. Human chorionic gonadotropin (HCG) is then used as substitute for the luteinizing
hormone (LH) surge which ordinarily causes follicular rupture.

c. Follicular growth is tracked in most protocols by daily
ultrasound examinations starting about day six to nine of the
cycle and serum estradiol levels measured daily beginning
somewhere between day three and nine of the cycle. Some
protocols also call for daily monitoring of vaginal and cervical
changes, the so-called "biological shift."

d. The objective in the hyperstimulation protocols is the
development of two or more follicles to a preovulatory size
(approx. 1.8 cn.) with adequately rising estrogen levels. When
adequate hyperstimulation is thus attained, the HMG is discon-
tinued and ten thousand units of HCG is given 48 hours later.
Follicular development is adequate in about 65-75% of stimulated cycles. If the estradiol levels and/or follicular growths are
not adequate, that stimulated cycle can be cancelled (prior to
laparoscopy) and a different regimen of controlled ovarian
hyperstimulation used for the next cycle.

2. Oocyte Retrieval:

a. If adequate follicular stimulation does occur, the woman
then enters oocyte retrieval. This is done via laparoscopy which
is scheduled 34-36 hours after the HCG trigger is given.

b. At laparoscopy, the ovary is stabilized with a grasping

forceps and a long stainless steel beveled needle is introduced through a third small incision for the operating laparoscope itself.

c. The follicles are punctured and the follicular fluid along with the ovum and cumulus mass is aspirated into a trap.

d. The fluid is immediately examined in the laboratory for the presence of a preovulatory oocyte. Oocytes are retrieved over 95% of the time. Most Centers aspirate all possible follicles, particularly if they have the availability for oocyte or embryo cryopreservation (freezing).

e. If excess oocytes cannot be frozen for later use, some authors have advised stopping when six oocytes are obtained.

While most oocyte retrievals are accomplished via laparoscopy, some programs have now initiated the use of ultrasound-directed oocyte retrieval through the abdominal wall, bladder or vagina. Ultrasonic methods of oocyte retrieval avoid surgery and anesthesia, and are applicable even when the ovaries are inaccessible by laparoscopy.

. Insemination and Cleavage:

a. This is the fertilization process. After the maturity of the oocytes is evaluated, they are incubated in Hams F-10 media + 7.5% fetal cord serum in 5% CO for 3-8 hours.

However, immature oocytes may be incubated longer, up to 24 hours. The degree of maturation is important because fertilization rates have been shown to be higher with more mature oocytes.

The embryologist is looking for a well dispersed *corona radiata* and the presence of the first polar body (evidence that the first meiotic division of the oocyte has occurred and the oocyte is at the proper stage for insemination).

b. During the incubation period, the husband produces usually by masturbation a semen specimen which is washed, centrifuged, and allowed to "swim up". This process removes sperm antibodies, decapacitation factors, bacteria and abnormal sperm, concentrating the progressively motile, normal sperm in the supernatant.

Capacitation, a biochemical change in the sperm necessary before it is able to fertilize the oocyte, is thought to occur during this preparation time.

c. The concentration of sperm is then adjusted and a total of 50,000 to 100,000 sperm are added to the oocytes and allowed to incubate for 12-18 hours. When the sperm enters the oocyte, the second polar body is intruded and two pronuclei are formed.

If it appears that fertilization has occurred, the pronuclear oocyte is transferred to another culture dish and allowed to incubate another 24 hours at which point a two cell embryo should be noted if development is progressing normally.

4. Embryo Transfer:

a. Embryo transfer is accomplished 48-72 hours after fertilization.

b. The woman is placed in the supine or knee-chest position. After the embryos are loaded into a transfer catheter, the tip is inserted into the uterus within 1-2 cns. of the fundus and the embryos are injected. After the catheter is reexamined to insure that the embryos are still not in it, the woman remains at rest for the next six hours. She is then discharged and told to stay in bed as much as possible over the next 2 to 3 days.

c. It is at the transfer stage where most IVF-ET cycles fail. The percentage of embryos implanting is reported to be 8 to 12 per cent. Many reasons have been given to explain the inefficiency of embryo transfer, one being the inability to assess the quality or viability of the embryo.

Many embryos which appear to be normal do not implant while some thought to be abnormal result in normal infants.

The timing of transfer may also contribute. In IVF-ET, the embryo arrives in the uterine cavity several days before it would arrive in a natural cycle and so the synchrony between embryo and uterine lining may not be optimal.

In stimulated cycles, the higher estrogen levels may also contribute to an abnormal development of the uterine lining.

And, finally, the transfer procedure itself may be traumatic or stimulate uterine activity which would expel the embryo.

One study using embryo-like microspheres showed that only 45% remained in the uterus at one hour.

## B. Pregnancy Rates and Outcomes

About 20-30% of the clinically recognizable IVF pregnancies will end in spontaneous miscarriage. Multiple pregnancies are reported in about 10-20% of cases and are related to the number of embryos transferred, especially when that number is greater than four. Congenital abnormalities in IVF pregnancies are, in general, lower than in spontaneous pregnancies with the U.S. Centers reporting 1.7% and the Australians reporting 2.6% at the Fourth World Congress. Obstetrically, these pregnancies have a higher rate of prematurity and low birthrate which are related to the increased incidents of multiple pregnancies.

The following analysis of data from February 1983 to April 1986 is instructive regarding controlled ovarian hyperstimulation:[71]

| | |
|---|---|
| Number of Patients | 296 |
| Number of Laparoscopies | 443 |
| Number of Oocytes Recovered | 1595 (3.6/patient) |
| Number of Oocytes Fertilized | 1356 (85%) |
| Number of Embryo Transfers | 409 |
| Number of Embryos Transferred | 1372 (3.2/patient) |
| Clinical Pregnancies | 151 (11%) |
| Multiple Pregnancies | 17 Twins |
| | 2 Triplets |
| Total | 19 |
| | |
| Miscarriages | 32 (21.2%) |
| Ectopic Pregnancies | 1 (0.7%) |
| Congenital Anomalies | 1 (0.7%) |
| Total Live Births To Date | 81 |
| Live Births: Embryo Transfers Ratio | 19.8% |
| Live Births: Embryos Transferred Ratio | 5.9% |
| Embryo Loss Ratio | 9.1% [72] |

## C. GIFT (Gamete Intra-Fallopian Transfer) and ZIFT (Zygote-Intra-Fallopian Transfer)

The GIFT procedure and its variations are the most recently developed of the new reproductive technologies. GIFT is the "direct transfer of preovulatory oocytes and washed sperm into the fallopian tube in an attempt to mimic the early physiologic processes that lead to gestation in the human." The major difference between GIFT and IVF is that in GIFT both sperm and ovum are placed in the normal site of fertilization in the woman and fertilization is allowed to occur *in vivo* or within the women's fallopian tube rather than an *in vitro* culture dish. Because the fertilization process does not occur extracorporeally, some authors have commented that GIFT might be considered morally licit within the context of *Donum Vitae*. This positive critique runs into a certain clear difficulty when one considers the point strongly made in Chapter Five of the Introduction of *Donum Vitae*: i.e., human procreation must be achieved and actualized in marriage through specific and exclusive acts of husband and wife.

GIFT is thought to be effective by virtue of being able to bypass deficiency in transport of the oocyte or sperm to the site of fertilization. It has been utilized in patients with unexplained infertility and endometriosis where it is thought that deficient oocyte pickup and/or oocyte entrapment (the "luteinized and ruptured follicle syndrome") are preventing pregnancy, as well as in male factor, cervical factor and immunologic factor infertility where deficient number of sperm at the site of fertilization are implicated.

A GIFT treatment cycle begins with one of the ovarian hyperstimulation protocols as in IVF-ET. Superovulation is necessary, because, as with IVF, pregnancy rates are improved if more than one oocyte is transferred up to a maximum of 3-4. Daily hormone assessment and ultrasonic tracking of follicle growth are also carried out as in an IVF-ET cycle. Finally, oocyte retrieval is accomplished 36 hours after the LH surge or HCG.

The oocytes obtained are then taken to the embryology laboratory and their maturity is evaluated according to a grading system. The embryologist is looking for a second polar body and a well expanded corona radiata. Two hours prior to the oocyte retrieval, semen is obtained usually by masturbation. The sample is washed, resuspended, allowed to "swim up" and then adjusted to a concentration of approximately 100,000 motile sperm 25 microliters.

Some comment should be made here again about the question of masturbation for such purposes as IVF. Authentic Catholic teaching in this regard maintains that "deliberately induced masturbation" is an intrinsically immoral act and does not become acceptable for any motive or under any circumstance. This teaching can be found in the *Declaration on Certain Questions Concerning Sexual Ethics* (1975) of the Congregation for the Doctrine of the Faith; as well as in the *Ethical and Religious Directives for Catholic Health Care Facilities* (1971) of the National Conference of Catholic Bishops (Directive 21). Other methods for obtaining sperm have been proposed and evaluated by Catholic moral theologians.[73] Some procedures are designed to obtain sperm directly from the male patient in ways that do not involve masturbation (e.g., Electroejaculation).[74] Other methods involve the recovery of sperm subsequent to a "substantially integral marital act between husband and wife," either by aspiration of some of the husband's ejaculate from his wife's vagina or by retaining some of his ejaculate in a punctured condom worn during their marital intercourse. O'Donnell comments, "In these latter methods, the limited but not essential, modification of the marital act is morally acceptable because of the importance of knowing how to treat the infertility of the male partner to the marriage."[75] Even though such procedures are approved for obtaining a specimen of spermatozoa for analysis in cases of male sterility, it would be questionable whether such authors would approve the use of a punctured condom, e.g., for purposes of IVF, since this procedure itself is unacceptable to the teaching of the Church.

After the sperm sample in the GIFT procedure is washed, resuspended, and allowed to "swim up," instead of inseminating the oocytes in a culture dish, the most mature ova and 25-50 microliters of the prepared sperm are loaded into a 50-cm.-16 gauge Teflon catheter (it is at this point that the procedure differs from IVF-ET). The catheter is prepared under sterile conditions and brought to the surgeon who lifts the tube atraumatically and after advancing the catheter 1.5-4 cms. into the fimbrial end of the tube, the gametes are injected. To further improve the success rates, some researchers fertilize the egg in a laboratory dish and then place the pre-embryo, or zygote, directly into the fallopian tube — a procedure known as ZIFT (zygote intra-fallopian transfer). The Teflon catheter is taken back to the laboratory to assure that the oocytes and sperm have indeed been expelled. The process is usually repeated with the other fallopian tube as well, transferring up to 4 ova at a time. Once the woman recovers from the anesthetic, she is discharged from the hospital. Following the transfer procedure, progesterone supplementation is usually used to support the luteal phase of the cycle and a pregnancy test is done 11-16 days later.

The factors which have made GIFT a rapidly expanding technology are several. Most important, pregnancy rates seem to be higher than in IVF-ET in the range of 30% per transfer. This is thought to result from a decreased manipulation of the gamete; and the undefined beneficial effect of the tubal environment on the conceptus; and a better synchrony between the endometrium and the arrival of the embryo in the uterus.

GIFT is also seen as a technically simpler procedure which requires less of both the laboratory and the embryologist's time. Because it is simpler and does not require embryo transfer, GIFT cycles are about 25% less expensive than the estimated $6,000 per cycle cost of IVF-ET. However, this difference would be minimal if ultrasound, rather than laparoscopy, were used for oocyte retrieval in IVF-ET cycles.

Outcomes of GIFT pregnancies reveal a 20-25% spontaneous abortion rate as in IVF. Ectopic pregnancies account for 4.4% to 7.5% of fetal wastage, most cases occurring in patients with mild tubal adhesions. A large cooperative study of 800 GIFT procedures reported an ectopic rate of 2.9%, a figure not significantly higher than that for IVF-ET. So whether GIFT will supercede IVF-ET based on improved pregnancy rates and similar complication rates remains to be seen.

### D. Low Tubal Ovum Transfer (LTOT)

In LTOT, insemination and fertilization are the result of normal coitus. The process involves ovarian hyperstimulation, laparoscopic oocyte retrieval, and transfer of the oocytes to the proximal portion of the fallopian tubes. At present, continuing research on LTOT is not being done, due to the low percentage of actual pregnancies.

## E. Artificial Insemination

We have already dealt with a moral analysis of artificial insemination in the over-view of *Donum Vitae*. We will look here, then, at the biological factors involved. Generally speaking, AI refers to any procedure in which semen or a sperm preparation from the husband (AIH) or a donor (AID) is introduced into the women's vagina, cervix, or uterus. Thus, one may have intravaginal, intracervical or intrauterine inseminations.

Artificial insemination requires timing ovulation in the woman either by Basal Body Temperature (BBT), cervical mucus (LH surge, estradiol levels) or ultrasound. Inseminations are carried out at a variable number of times (from 1-9) around the time of ovulation. This timing is obviously important.[76] Consequently, insemination is defined as the insertion of sperm directly into the uterus of the wife by normal marital intercourse or by an assisted technique of catheterization of the cervix with insertion of the sperm previously collected by various techniques.

Insemination may also be defined as the application of sperm from the husband directly onto the eggs harvested from the wife by surgical techniques and collected in a Petri dish before these eggs are inserted back into the uterus.[77] By shortening the distance of the sperm to travel within the female genital tract — which is accomplished by the application of sperm directly into the cavity of the uterus — the chance for a successful natural fertilization of eggs arises. As we have seen, *Donum Vitae* strictly forbids this type of assisting fertilization, even when the sperm is produced by the husband. There are two objections: masturbation, even serving for diagnosis and therapy, is reprehensible and evil;[78] and the generative and unitive aspects of the sexual act must be in one inseparable physical union.[79]

We have noted that sperm can be obtained which are produced during marital intercourse and thus without recourse to masturbation by the husband. Thus, the possibility of a natural fertilization would not be excluded if after intercourse the physician obtains a sample of sperm from the vagina and then prepares it for insemination directly into the body of the uterus by catheter technique. This method is very attractive from a medical point of view, as the quality (number and motility) of sperm obtained after intercourse is much better when analyzed than the quality of sperm obtained after masturbation.

## 5. DIRECT STERILIZATION

The 1980 *Statement on Tubal Ligation* (STL)[80] indicates that the traditional teaching of the Church "clearly declared the objective immorality of contraceptive (direct) sterilization even if done for medical reasons."[81] In 1968 *Humanae Vitae* also taught, "Equally to be excluded... is direct sterilization of a man or a woman, whether this be temporary or permanent."[82] The 1971 *Ethical and Religious Directives for Catholic Health Care Facilities* of the United States Catholic Conference affirms this teaching and makes the further clarification: "Procedures that induce sterility, whether permanent or temporary, are permitted when: (a) They are immediately directed to the cure, diminution, or prevention of a serious pathological condition and are not directly contraceptive (i.e., contraception is not the purpose); and (b) A simpler treatment is not reasonably available."[83]

The *Pastoral Guidelines for the Catholic Hospital and Catholic Health Care Personnel* of the Ad Hoc Committee on Pro-Life Activities of the N.C.C.B. (1973) also affirms that "A Catholic hospital should make it clear... sterilizations are forbidden... Sterilization... may not be used as a means of contraception."

In March of 1975, the Congregation for the Doctrine of the Faith issued its *Reply on Sterilization in Catholic Hospitals*. This *Reply* states: "Any sterilization which of itself, i.e., of its own nature and condition, has the sole immediate effect of rendering the generative faculty incapable of procreation, is to be considered direct sterilization... Therefore, notwithstanding any subjectively right intention of those whose actions are promoted by the care or prevention of physical or mental illness which is foreseen or feared as a result of pregnancy, such sterilization remains absolutely forbidden according to the doctrine of the Church... (S)terility intended in itself... damages the ethical good of the person..., since it deliberately deprives foreseen and freely chosen sexual activity of an essential element."

In 1977 the N.C.C.B. issued a *Commentary* on this *Reply*. This

*Commentary* proposed to make several comments on the *Reply* in light of the American context. Several points are significant:

1. Sterilization may not be used as a means of contraception nor may it be used as a means for the care or prevention of physical or mental illness which is foreseen or feared as a result of pregnancy.
2. Procedures that induce sterility are not always forbidden; they are permitted when they are immediately directed to the cure, diminution, or prevention of a serious pathological condition and are not directly contraceptive; and a simpler treatment is not reasonably available.
3. A Catholic hospital can in no way approve the performance of any sterilization procedure that is directly contraceptive. Such contraceptive procedures include sterilizations performed as a means of preventing future pregnancy that one fears might aggravate a serious cardiac, renal, circulatory or other disorder.[84]

These basic teachings are repeated in the 1980 *Statement on Tubal Ligation*. Specifically, this *Statement* indicates that "Formal cooperation in the grave evil of contraceptive sterilization... is forbidden and totally alien to the mission entrusted by the Church to Catholic health care facilities."

The 1975 *Reply* of the Congregation for the Doctrine of the Faith, while declaring that it is unbecoming for the Catholic hospital to cooperate in direct sterilization "for any reason," does affirm the Church's traditional teaching regarding material cooperation. Specifically, the *Reply* teaches:

1. The traditional doctrine regarding material cooperation, with the proper distinctions between necessary and free, proximate and remote, remains valid, to be applied with the utmost prudence, if the case warrants.

   These distinctions are meant to be a calculus to help judge whether or not there are adequate grounds for material cooperation. The category of *necessary* means that there must be grave duress where serious harm will occur if cooperation does not happen; and the category of *free* indicates that personal or corporate freedom is not truly lost: i.e., one could choose to do otherwise. The categories of *proximate* and *remote* refer to the degree of involvement present.

These categories refer to important points on a calculus which must be weighed and discerned in each particular situation and set of circumstances.

2.  In the application of the principle of material cooperation, if the case warrants, great care must be taken against scandal.

The 1977 *Commentary* of the N.C.C.B. further interprets and applies this principle of material cooperation. Specifically, the *Commentary* declares:

1.  Material cooperation will be justified only in situations where a hospital because of some kind of duress or pressure cannot reasonably exercise the autonomy it has: i.e., when it will do more harm than good.

2.  Because of the extraordinary nature of the decision concerning material cooperation, the Bishop of the diocese or his representative must be involved in the decision.

3.  If the cooperation is to remain material, the reason for the cooperation must be something over and above the reason for the sterilization itself. This same point is made in n 4 of the 1980 *Statement on Tubal Ligation*.

4.  Material cooperation should not occur with any frequency and each case must be decided on its own merits.[85]

## CHAPTER NINE

# HIV/AIDS AND THE CHURCH

The bishops of the United States have addressed the question of HIV/AIDS on two separate occasions. In 1987 the Administrative Board of the U. S. Catholic Conference issued *The Many Faces of AIDS: A Gospel Response*[1] and in 1989 the full body of bishops issued *Called to Compassion and Responsibility: A Response to the HIV/ AIDS Crisis.*[2]

*Called to Compassion* roots itself in *The Many Faces of AIDS* and recalls the commitment of the conference of bishops to issue a further document on this subject.[3]

In *Called to Compassion* the bishops recognize that many factors have emerged since the 1987 statement: e.g., public discussion concerning HIV had intensified; new facts, fears and initiatives had emerged regarding HIV/AIDS; the crisis itself had worsened; the need for compassion had grown more urgent; the 1988 Report of the Presidential Commission on the Human Immunodeficiency Virus Epidemic had been issued,[4] which calls upon religious groups to be of "special assistance," especially by emphasizing "the worth and dignity of every human being."

*The Many Faces of AIDS* made several important points:

1. AIDS is an illness to which all must respond in a manner consistent with the best medical and scientific information available.
2. As members of the Church and society, we must reach out with compassion to those exposed to or experiencing this

disease, and must stand in solidarity with them and their
families.

3. As bishops, we must offer a clear presentation of Catholic
   moral teaching concerning human intimacy and sexuality.
4. Discrimination and violence against persons with AIDS and
   with HIV infection are unjust and immoral.
5. Social realities like poverty and oppression, and psychological factors like loneliness and alienation, can strongly
   influence people's decisions to behave in ways which
   expose them to the AIDS virus.
6. Along with other groups in society, the Church must work
   to eliminate the harsh realities of poverty and despair.
7. The expression of human sexuality should resemble God's
   love in being loving, faithful and committed. Human
   sexuality in marriage is intrinsically oriented to permanent
   commitment, love and openness to new life.
8. The spread of AIDS will not be halted unless people live in
   accord with authentic human values pertaining to
   personhood and sexuality.
9. Since AIDS can be transmitted through intravenous drug
   use, there is need for drug treatment programs, a halt to
   traffic in illicit drugs and efforts to eliminate the causes of
   addiction.
10. Considering the widespread ignorance and misunderstand-
    ing about HIV infection and its modes of transmission,
    educational programs about the medical aspects of the
    disease and legitimate ways of preventing it are also
    needed.

In his lecture "AIDS and the Church: A Stimulus to Our
Theologizing,"[5] Jon D. Fuller wisely remarks:

> I would... suggest that the experience of the HIV/AIDS epidemic
> challenges our understanding of certain aspects of human sexuality,
> of sexual development, and of our role in developing public policy.
> Just as the Church has always had to develop its tradition in the face
> of new challenges, so do we need to evaluate the experience in the
> light of our tradition as we develop our response to a new and
> apparently permanent part of the human landscape.[6]

We will deal here in this chapter with some fundamental points of our Catholic tradition that inform a proper response to the HIV/AIDS epidemic.

## 1. OVERVIEW

It is important to recognize that the AIDS epidemic (what many now name a *pandemic*) has reached frightening levels at the present time. We are looking not just at an epidemic, but at a new *endemic* disease that we will have to learn to live with for the foreseeable future. And unlike most of the plagues of the past, HIV infection is preventable by education and behavior change.[7]

America's AIDS epidemic has entered what scientists call the "mature" phase, an agonizing long-term presence with a slowly shifting profile. The virus is no longer spreading explosively among gay men and drug users as it did in the late 1970s and early 1980s, infecting huge numbers before most realized what was happening. Largely because of that early sweep, Federal experts believe, perhaps one million living Americans carry HIV, an awesome personal and social tragedy that will play itself out over two decades or more. So far, 200,000 people have developed outright AIDS, according to the current definition of the disease, and more than 125,000 of them have died.

Now, perhaps 50,000 more people become infected with the virus each year, according to very rough estimates by the Centers for Disease Control. To describe who these people are is to describe the prevention challenge. Compared with the population as a whole, the newly infected are much more likely to be people of color, much more likely to be residents of inner cities, much more likely to be economically disadvantaged.

They include teen-age boys discovering their homosexuality, not believing that even a single unprotected encounter may hold deadly risk. They include new recruits to the underworld of intravenous drug addicts, too desperate or self-destructive to faithfully use sterile needles. They include female crack addicts who trade their bodies for drugs. Increasingly they include homeless men and women, who may shoot drugs, prostitute themselves or both.

# Who has AIDS

Racial breakdown of those who have been diagnosed as having AIDS in the United States through September 1991.

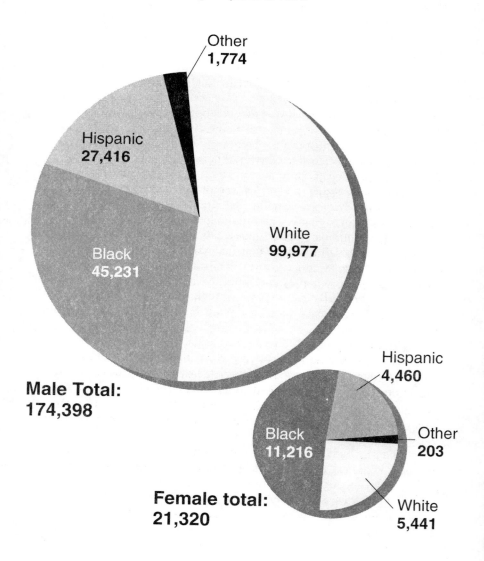

Other
1,774

Hispanic
27,416

Black
45,231

White
99,977

Male Total:
174,398

Hispanic
4,460

Black
11,216

Other
203

Female total:
21,320

White
5,441

Source: Centers for Disease Control

To a very minor degree they include men who receive the virus from one of a multitude of heterosexual partners. Far more they include women, black or Hispanic, who are infected by a husband, boyfriend or casual sex partner; women, who, even when they suspect the danger, are often powerless to persuade their men to use condoms. And they include babies: some 1,500 to 2,000 born with the virus each year. And, last of all, there are a very restricted number who caught the AIDS virus through a blood transfusion before the blood supply was being carefully monitored.

Fighting heterosexual spread, even knowing how to talk about it credibly has posed special problems. Early on, some experts dismissed the risk as negligible. As more women came down with AIDS who were sex partners of drug addicts but insisted that they had never used needles themselves, and as evidence poured in from Africa, the threat began to seem less remote. On the other side, some who were out to gain attention and funds exaggerated the risk, evoking the improbable specter of a runaway national plague.

Actually, the Federal scientists who chart the epidemic have been quite consistent in their statements. AIDS is a sexually transmitted disease, they have long said, and heterosexual intercourse with an infected partner carries some risk, however small. The change of transmission is vastly lower in vaginal than anal intercourse, studies have shown, and the virus passes much more easily from man to woman than the other way. Transmission is eased by the presence of venereal diseases such as syphilis.

Voluntary testing for HIV is a cornerstone of prevention strategies. The theory is that the sooner people learn of their infection, the sooner they can obtain helpful medical care. They also, experts believe, will be less likely to pass the virus to others. Even for the lucky ones who test negative, the agony of waiting for results may teach a chilling lesson.

But it is one thing to be tested if you have access to care, another if, like so many prospective AIDS patients, you are poor and uninsured.

For many who are likely to spread HIV in the years ahead, society cannot keep its end of the bargain. All too often, poor people who test positive get a session of counseling and a list of phone numbers of overburdened public clinics. Many never get the expensive immune tests and drugs that can prolong their lives. In New York

City clinics, there can be a one-to-four-month waiting list just for an initial appointment. Then it takes all day at the clinic, so if you have a job you have to take the day off.

Many poor people with HIV infections do not qualify for Medicaid, the Federal-state insurance program, until — in a horrible catch-22 — they are declared "disabled" because they develop outright AIDS. Hence they may miss the irretrievable chance to stave off the disease as long as possible.

The epidemic was first recognized in the United States in 1981. By 1988, at a time when women accounted for just 9% of all U.S. cases, AIDS had become the nation's eighth leading cause of death among women aged 25-44, and in New Jersey it was the leading cause of death in this age group, exceeding causes two and three combined (unintentional injuries and heart disease).[8] By 1990 AIDS had become the leading cause of death among young Black women in New York State, and in 1991, with women representing at least 11% of all cases, AIDS became the fifth leading cause of death among all young women in this country. Between 1988 and 1989, when AIDS cases increased by 18% among men, they jumped by 29% in women.[9]

Among young men aged 25 to 44, by 1988 AIDS had become the third leading cause of death, and by 1989 had arisen to the number two position. In 1990 AIDS was the leading cause of death among young men in Los Angeles, San Francisco, and New York City.[10] While there are currently believed to be one million HIV-infected persons in the U.S., this number rises to ten million in the world at large, with 30% of infections occurring in women. The vast majority of these are in Africa where up to 40% of women of childbearing age in certain urban areas are infected, and where one million children have already become AIDS orphans. By the year 2015, some 70 million persons are expected to be infected in Africa, accounting for 17% of the continent's population. African life expectancy will be reduced by 19 years, and AIDS will account for nearly 80% of the deaths of women in childbearing years, leaving some 16 million children orphaned.[11]

Fuller rightly points out that by virtue of its scale and by its anticipated permanence, AIDS is a new part of the human landscape that requires innovative responses from all sectors of the human community. Fuller interestingly suggests that AIDS is not simply a crisis of content but also a crisis of method: of switching, in Lonergan's words, from a classicist understanding to one that is more historical and dialogic. Fuller quotes Yves Congar:

> If the Church wishes to deal with the real questions of the modern world and to attempt to respond to them..., it must open as it were a new chapter of theologico-pastoral epistemology. Instead of using only revelation and tradition as starting points, as classical theology has generally done, it must start with facts and questions derived from the world and from history.[12]

Why is the HIV/AIDS epidemic different from any other epidemic in human experience?[13]

1.  The structure and the activity of the virus within the patient constitute HIV as one of the most complex disease-producing organisms yet known.
2.  AIDS is fatal.
3.  HIV continues to challenge leading experts in the field of virology.[14]
4.  Those living with HIV/AIDS have been highly stigmatized because of this illness, a factor that differentiates them from people with other illnesses, and greatly increases their burdens (and thus closely identifies them with the biblical images of the oppressed, the alien, and the stranger).
5.  The full clinical manifestations of AIDS are still becoming known, with the awareness that helping-drugs such as AZT slows the multiplication of HIV in people with mild symptoms of the disease, but then makes the disease much more painful and difficult in its later stages.
6.  HIV transmission often links intravenous drug use with sexual intercourse: i.e., use of alcohol, heroin, cocaine, or "crack" frequently is accompanied by reduced sexual inhibitions and heightened sexual interest. Nearly 30% of cumulative cases of AIDS are directly attributed to drug abuse, sex with an IV drug abuser, or vertical transmission by an infected mother to her fetus.

In light of our study in this book, it is of great interest to note that research related to this epidemic is casting new light upon certain aspects of sexual conduct: e.g., people engage in sexual intercourse and a variety of sexual expressions for different reasons and to meet many needs. Some people engage in sex for drugs; others use sex to secure basic human needs such as housing, income, security and love. People may seek sexual relationships as a coping mechanism to alleviate stress, loneliness, or to fulfill other felt needs; as an expression of love; as a way of seeking pleasure; in order to conceive a child. These are but some of the many reasons people express themselves sexually.

The first two chapters of this book explained how our bodies largely dictate how others see us, and how we see ourselves (sexuality-as-language). Our bodies are the primary modes through which we identify and know one another, communicate feelings, and invite or reject intimacy. Relationships involve bodily experiences. It is impossible to perceive each other or relate apart from our sexual identities.

This book has emphasized over and over again that sexuality is an all-embracing gift, part of God's creation. Sadly, many people view this gift with considerable ambivalence and to some, sex seems to become a liability. These responses may be manifested in ignorance of basic aspects of sexuality, anxieties regarding sexual expression, inability to enter into intimate relationships, and uncertainty about the limits of sexual expression. Ignorance about the body, including sexual expressions, may inhibit the capacity to find and enjoy intimacy. Since our capacity to know what we are feeling and to experience those feelings is rooted in bodily experiences, to be ambivalent about or alienated from our bodies is to be estranged from ourselves. Our sexuality is basic and affects our thoughts, feelings, and actions. People who are tossed about by such ambivalence are little prepared to confront the sexual dimensions of HIV/AIDS. Ambivalence and fear often exacerbate stresses common in our daily lives and thus create greater insecurity and discomfort regarding important matters of sexual behavior. HIV/AIDS is thus exposing aspects of human life, personal behaviors and relationships bearing on human sexuality that as individuals, religious communities, and society at large, we have been hesitant to acknowledge, let alone confront directly.

*The Many Faces of AIDS* importantly encourages the development of certain attitudes regarding HIV/AIDS:

1. To respond to this disease and suffering with compassion.
2. To deplore prejudice and discrimination and all forms of violence directed against persons with HIV/AIDS and members of high-risk groups.
3. To support public policies which reflect an integrated understanding of human sexuality.
4. To foster abstinence outside of marriage and fidelity within marriage; as well as the avoidance of intravenous drug abuse.
5. To critique "safe sex" campaigns which really do not take into account either the real values that are at stake or the fundamental good of the human person.
6. To support voluntary testing programs for HIV/AIDS, as long as there are provisions for counselling and adequate safeguards against breach of confidentiality and against discriminatory use of test results.[15]
7. To approach this whole question from a sound moral perspective, acting always out of a desire to promote people's well-being and not their condemnation.
8. To develop educational programs which advocate ethical values of chastity and monogamy and respect for the parents' rights as the primary educators of their children.
9. To combat the social, economic and psychological factors which reduce people's ability to act responsibly regarding sexuality in other areas of life.
10. To provide for adequate health care and health insurance for all those suffering from HIV/AIDS.
11. To take special care to provide the affirmation and spiritual support needed by persons with HIV/AIDS, their families and friends.

*Called to Compassion* reaffirms these basic attitudes when it articulates its intent: "(W)e issue five calls: to compassion, to integrity, to responsibility, to social justice, and to prayer and conversion. For, 'the joys and the hopes, the griefs and the anxieties of the people of this age, especially those who are poor or in any way afflicted, these too are the joys and the hopes, the griefs and the anxieties of the followers of Christ.'"[16]

## 2. ORIGIN AND DEFINITION

A decade before HIV/AIDS was detected in the United States (in mid-1981), the virus was present in Central Africa. It may have originated around Lake Victoria, bordered by Uganda, Tanzania, and Kenya. Although some scientists think the virus may have been present in the human population for centuries, others believe it has come more recently as an evolutionary descendant of a virus that has existed in monkeys for as many as fifty thousand years. One possible link to HIV/AIDS is the African green monkey. In these areas of Africa where many humans have developed HIV/AIDS or antibodies to HIV/AIDS, there has been considerable contact between people and the ubiquitous green monkeys. People have been scratched and bitten while chasing the monkeys away from garbage. The monkeys are also a food supply, often being eaten without being cooked. These close contacts may have been how the virus found its way into humans.

Once in humans, the virus mutated or changed into more deadly forms. Here it began its rapid spread among the human population through person to person contact. From Africa, scientists theorize the HIV/AIDS virus traveled to the United States by way of Haiti. Cultural exchanges between French-speaking Central African countries (e.g., Zaire) and Haiti may have brought the virus to this Caribbean island nation. Vacationers from the United States acquired the virus in Haiti through sexual activities and intravenous drug abuse and brought it back to the United States.[17]

The letters AIDS stand for *Acquired* (not inherited)[18] *Immune Deficiency Syndrome*. This syndrome is caused by a virus that destroys a person's defenses against infections. These defenses are known as the immune system. The HIV/AIDS infection known as Human Immunodeficiency Virus, or HIV (sometimes also referred to as the HTLV-III/LAV virus), can so weaken a person's immune system that he or she cannot fight off even mild infections and eventually becomes vulnerable to life-threatening infections and cancers. While HIV/AIDS is often referred to as a "disease," it is more accurately understood as a "syndrome" which destroys the body's immune system. The reason why HIV/AIDS is called a "syndrome" is because HIV/AIDS is not one disease; it is a combination of diseases.

The human body is equipped with white blood cells (specifically, T4 and T8 cells) which are known as lymphocytes, and which carry out the work of fighting off disease. Persons with HIV/AIDS have greatly depressed T4 and T8 counts and consequently have no success in overcoming infections. The devastating illnesses to which they are susceptible, including Pneumocystis Carinii Pneumonia (PCP) and Kaposi's Sarcoma (KS), take hold precisely because HIV/AIDS patients lack ordinary immunity.

In the past many have also used the term ARC (AIDS-Related Complex) to describe those persons whose symptoms, as a result of HIV infection, do not meet the Center for Disease Control's full criteria for AIDS: i.e., no tumors or specified opportunistic infections. ARC was never as well-defined as AIDS, but tended to include swollen lymph nodes, chronic diarrhea, weight loss, fevers and night sweats, oral yeast infections, easy bruising, and anemia. In addition, severe neurological symptoms may also have affected the ARC patient: e.g., pain, weakness, paralysis, incontinence, seizures, profound dementia, and coma. In the past few years, this term has fallen into disfavor because of medical disagreements regarding these symptoms and manifestations.

## 3. FACTS, SYMPTOMS AND TRANSMISSION

As *Called to Compassion* points out,[19] infection with HIV is followed by incubation and latency periods whose duration varies enormously from individual to individual. It is currently thought that 50% will develop full-blown AIDS within 10.8 years, 75% within 16 years and "almost 100% in 30 years."[20] Peter Duesberg, Professor of molecular and cell biology at the University of California in Berkeley, has caused great attention and controversy by maintaining that the human immunodeficiency virus — HIV — does not cause AIDS. Duesberg claims that most people who test positive for antibodies to HIV remain healthy on average at least ten (10) years, perhaps their entire lives. His explanation: AIDS in the United States and Europe is a collection of non-infectious deficiencies, most of which are caused by consumption of psychoactive drugs, which has escalated dramatically since the Vietnam War. The rest are a result of conventional clinical deficiencies, such as hemophilia. Virtually no research is done on the effects of long-term drug use, he claims, and complains that these studies are not being conducted because everyone has jumped on the $3 billion HIV bandwagon.[21]

Although people who are HIV infected do not manifest AIDS symptoms during the subclinical period, they are subject to serious emotional, social and physical problems. At the point when AIDS is diagnosed, a variety of symptoms emerge: prolonged fevers, rashes, swollen lymph glands, fungi around the nails, oral thrush, shingles, lymphoma, severe psoriasis, cryptococcal meningitis, cancers of the tongue, rectum and brain, and the illnesses classically associated with the disease, PCP and KS (lesions which spread over the body surfaces). These are opportunistic infections which, in various combinations, eventually prove fatal. Also, 75% of people with AIDS suffer significant brain damage often leading to dementia.[22]

While the progress of the HIV infection cannot be predicted in every case, there are identifiable stages:[23]

1.  HIV positive or antibody positive: The blood shows antibodies indicating exposure to HIV. At this "seropositive" stage, the individual may remain asymptomatic for 5 to 10 years, but he or she can transmit the virus to others.
2.  ARC: This includes symptoms such as chronic diarrhea, recurrent fevers, weight loss, and persistent swelling of the lymph nodes.
3.  AIDS: This refers to the most severe clinical manifestations of the HIV infection. It includes opportunistic infections, as well as PCP and neoplasms such as KS.

# The long road from HIV to AIDS

Who has AIDS? The definition has become a political as well as a medical question as people infected with the human immune deficiency virus, HIV, compete for treatment. For years, people weren't considered to have AIDS until they showed symptoms of certain infections and cancers that invade the body once the immune system breaks down. But after complaints that many ailing people were being excluded from the count, the Federal Centers for Disease Control has begun revising its definition to include every infected person whose number of T4 helper cells, an important measure of immune system strength, has fallen below 200 per cubic millimeter of blood; the normal level is around 1,000. It has been estimated that the broader definition, which is expected to go into effect next year, will add 160,000 people to the current caseload of 200,000 classified as having AIDS.

AZT, DDI and other drugs may prolong the lives of some of these patients. In the absence of treatment the path from HIV infection to AIDS commonly takes about 10 years, with death often following two years later. Though timing and other details vary widely, the following pattern is typical.

### Early stage: T4-cell count=1,000

5 Years

The HIV virus enters the bloodstream but antibodies cannot be detected for six weeks, or in unusual cases a year or more. Even after testing positive, many people show no symptoms, though some briefly develop a disorder similar to mononucleosis with fatigue, fever, swollen glands and possibly a rash. These initial symptoms disappear, usually in a few weeks. As the virus quietly multiplies, most people continue to feel fine, though some have chronically swollen lymph nodes.

### Middle stage: T4-cell count=500

5 Years

Though many people still have no symptoms, the number of T4 cells drops to about half the normal level. Treatment with AZT, DDI and other anti-viral drugs is recommended. As the infection progresses, skin tests show that another line of immunological defense, called cell-mediated immunity, is also disintegrating.

### Late stage: T4 cell-count=200

2 Years

As the number of T4 cells is halved again, many people initially remain asymptomatic, but the risk that bacteria, viruses, fungi and parasites will take advantages of weakened immunity increases dramatically. To prevent one of the most common opportunistic infections, pneumocystis carinii pneumonia, antibiotic treatment can begin. Early in this stage, some people suffer weight loss, diarrhea, lethargy and fevers. Also common are infections of the skin and mucous membranes, including a fungal infection called thrush, in which white spots and ulcers appear on the tongue and mouth, and chronic herpes simplex.

As the immune system collapse continues, the opportunistic diseases move deeper. The brain might be attacked by a parasitic infection called toxoplasmosis; the nervous system, liver, bones and skin by the cryptococcosis fungus. Cytomegalovirus can cause pneumonia, encephalitis and blindness. The list goes on and on.

The following Walter Reed Classification is also helpful:

Stage 0: A person has been infected but no antibodies have yet appeared. Persons at this stage can transmit the disease without knowing they are at risk. Typically, antibodies take from six weeks to a year to appear.

Stage 1: Antibodies appear, and the person would test positive for HIV.

Stage 2: Symptoms of the infection appear as swollen lymph nodes and other flu-like symptoms. This stage may last three to five years.

Stage 3: The white blood count drops below 400. This stage can last up to a year and a half.

Stage 4: A measurable loss of immune function detected by a failure to respond to specific proteins injected under the skin.

Stage 5: The white blood count drops below 200 and more viral infections set in that do not heal.

Stage 6: This is the stage of AIDS. The white blood count drops below 100 and opportunistic infections set in. Some of the most common and virulent ones are these: Pneumocystis carinii pneumonia which dries up the lungs to produce a hard, dry cough and breathlessness; Kaposi's sarcoma is a cancer of the nervous system which produces purple spots on the skin; toxoplasmosis is a brain infection causing dementia, seizures, and coma; cryptosporidiosis is severe diarrhea; cryptococcosis causes meningitis; histoplasmosis destroys the liver and bone marrow and causes chronic fevers; cytomegalovirus causes blindness and encephalitis. Once AIDS sets in, death comes within 18-36 months.

On the average, it takes 8-9 years to progress through these stages.

The HIV infection is very commonly transmitted through sexual intercourse with an infected partner; and the infection is also transmitted through the sharing of infected drug needles or syringes with an infected person. Because the virus is contained in some body fluids (mainly blood, semen and vaginal secretions), actions that involve the exchange of these fluids between people greatly increase the chances of passing the virus to another person. Women infected with the virus may also transmit it to their children during pregnancy or, later, during breast-feeding.

Because the virus can be transmitted by the transfusion of blood or certain blood products, hemophiliacs and other recipients of transfusions or blood products were at a very substantial risk of becoming infected. However, since 1985, donated blood has been screened by a new test that can identify blood containing antibodies to the virus.

The virus has also been found in saliva, tears, breast milk and urine. However, on the basis of current medical research, the chances of becoming infected with the virus by coming into contact with these body fluids and wastes are small, certainly far smaller than through the usual roots of sexual intimacy and intravenous drug abuse.

It is thus critical to remember that for the virus to be transmitted two essential components must be present: (a) An infected person; and (b) A vulnerability to receive the infection (e.g., an open wound or lesion). The Public Health Service to date has stated there is no evidence to suggest a risk of contracting the virus from day-to-day social or family contact with someone who has HIV/AIDS. A study of the families of 45 adults with AIDS found that none of their children became infected with the virus through contact with other family members or by sharing kitchen and bathroom facilities.[24] Regardless of whether the symptoms of AIDS are apparent, anyone who is infected with the virus must be presumed to be capable of transmitting the virus to someone else. Consequently, any sexual or drug behavior through which bodily fluids (mainly semen, urine, blood, feces, breast milk, vaginal secretions) are exchanged, and particularly come into contact with blood, can transmit the virus. Contact with blood can come by way of small cuts in the rectum, urethra, vagina, mouth/gums, fingers (other open wounds, abrasions, or blemishes). One exposure is potentially sufficient to transmit the virus. Multiple exposures to the virus are not required for transmission.

A major difficulty with the virus is that individuals infected with it can transmit the virus even if they do not develop AIDS. Persons infected by the disease may live as long as 15 to 20 years without showing any signs of its presence. The individual continues his or her normal sexual or drug behavior while spreading the disease. *This unknowing transmission of the disease is one of its more insidious aspects and has helped its great spread in the United States.* There is virtually no evidence that the virus can be transmitted by casual contact, i.e., touching or talking to a person with the virus is not a way of "catching" AIDS.

Anal intercourse seems to be the most prevalent means by which the virus is spread. During anal intercourse, delicate surface blood vessels may be damaged and the virus thus passes from semen to the bloodstream. For this reason, the individual who receives the semen probably is at greater risk of contracting the virus. Oral sex can also be hazardous, as can vaginal intercourse. HIV-carrying semen can find its way into a woman's bloodstream. And there is evidence suggesting that the virus can be transmitted from women to men. In addition, drug addicts who share needles or syringes with persons who carry the virus are at great risk of contracting the disease.

Basically, then, the HIV infection is spread through the exchange of body fluids in the following high-risk activities:

1. Sexual activity with someone who is HIV infected. This includes intercourse, oral sex, and anal sex. Having multiple partners, whether homosexual or heterosexual, greatly raises the risk. Although less risky, there is a possibility that deep kissing (sometimes called wet kissing or French kissing) in which saliva is exchanged can transmit the virus.
2. Intravenous (IV) drug abuse: Sharing needles and syringes with someone who is infected, where needles are not properly sterilized between uses and blood from one person is passed to another, using the same needle and syringe. Any skin piercing equipment that is not sterile could transmit the virus: e.g., ear piercing and tattooing needles.
3. Some blood transfusions with blood from an infected person before screening began in May 1985.
4. Maternal transmission from an infected mother to an unborn or newly born baby. As many as 50% of the babies of HIV infected mothers are born with the virus.

Is HIV/AIDS contagious? An answer requires an understanding of general principles that apply to all contagious diseases. In general, disease transmission requires a *vehicle* carrying a *significant number of germs* into a *susceptible person*. A vehicle can be as microscopic as an ounce of blood, such as in the case of some types of hepatitis. It can be urine or semen. It can be pus or feces or the objects contaminated with these.

There is no evidence which supports HIV/AIDS transmission by casual contact, by the airborne route, by objects handled by people with HIV/AIDS or by contaminated environmental surfaces. The medical profession uniformly agrees that one can engage in usual daily activities, such as working in a group setting, shaking hands, attending public events, eating in restaurants, and swimming in public pools, without any risk of acquiring HIV/AIDS. There is no known transmission of the virus from insects, such as mosquitoes, or from animal pets. Normal kissing (dry) is not a transmitter of the virus, provided that neither partner has open cuts or sores of the mouth, lips, or tongue. Although the degree of infectivity of saliva by the various routes of access into the body is not fully known, it is unlikely that the virus could be transmitted easily through normal kissing.

## 4. ETHICAL AND RELIGIOUS QUESTIONS

### A. *The Use of Prophylactics*

*The Many Faces of AIDS* (1987) in its section on "The Prevention of AIDS" (paragraphs 18-20) speaks about the use of prophylactics. Because this section raised such a degree of difficulty, it is quoted here at length:

> We recognize that public educational programs addressed to a wide audience will reflect the fact that some people will not act as they can and should; that they will not refrain from the type of sexual or drug-abuse behavior that can transmit AIDS. In such situations, educational efforts, if grounded in the broader moral vision outlined above, could include accurate information about prophylactic devices or other practices proposed by some medical experts as potential means of preventing AIDS. We are not promoting the use

of prophylactics, but merely providing information that is part of the factual picture. Such a factual presentation should indicate that abstinence outside of marriage and fidelity within marriage as well as the avoidance of intravenous drug abuse are the only morally correct and medically sure ways to prevent the spread of AIDS. So-called safe sex practices are at best only partially effective. They do not take into account either the real values that are at stake or the fundamental good of the human person.

With regard to educational programs for those who have already been exposed to the disease, the situation is somewhat different. For such individuals, without compromising the values outlined above, as a society, we have to face difficult and complex issues of public policy.

The teaching of classical theologians might provide assistance as we search for a way to bring into balance the need for a full and authentic understanding of human sexuality in our society and the issues of the common good associated with the spread of disease. As noted above, at the level of public programming, we must clearly articulate the meaning of a truly authentic human sexuality as well as communicate the relevant health information.

This last paragraph which refers to "the teaching of classical theologians" footnotes St. Augustine and St. Thomas.[25]

A great deal of debate surrounded this statement.[26]

*Called to Compassion* (1989) also treats the question of prophylactics and says in part:

The use of prophylactics to prevent the spread of HIV is technically unreliable. Moreover, advocating this approach means in effect promoting behavior which is morally unacceptable. Campaigns advocating "safe/safer" sex rest on false assumptions about sexuality and intercourse. Plainly they do nothing to correct the mistaken notion that non-marital sexual intercourse has the same value and validity as sexual intercourse within marriage.

We fault these programs for another reason as well. Recognizing that casual sex is a threat to health, they consistently advise the use of condoms in order to reduce the danger. This is poor and inadequate advice, given the failure rate of prophylactics and the high risk that an infected person who relies on them will eventually transmit the infection in this way. It is not condom use which is the solution to this health problem, but appropriate attitudes and corresponding behavior regarding human sexuality, integrity and dignity.[27]

The *difference* in the two approaches to the question of prophylactics is quite significant. *The Many Faces of AIDS*, in weighing the consequences of becoming infected by a life-threatening virus, judges that prophylactics (condoms) are the lesser of two evils. Fuller comments, "It has essentially made a proportionalist argument based on the relative weight it gives to two bad outcomes: HIV infection vs. condom use. This method weighs evils and finds it ethically appropriate to support the lesser one in order to avoid the greater."[28]

*Called to Compassion* rejects condom education because this is morally unacceptable for several reasons: this approach *in effect* promotes behavior which is morally unacceptable (the "safe/safer" campaigns); it does not recognize adequately the failure rate of prophylactics and the high risk that an infected person who relies on them will eventually transmit the infection; and condom education *de facto* does not promote appropriate attitudes regarding human sexuality, integrity and dignity.

It is important to note that *both* of these documents indicate that the "safe/safer sex" approach to preventing HIV/AIDS compromises human sexuality and leads to promiscuous sexual behavior. Both documents affirm that any person who is at risk of having been exposed to HIV or has been tested as positive for the virus must act always in a morally responsible way: i.e., should not act in such a way as to bring harm to another: this means not sharing needles used intravenously, and not engaging in sexual intercourse — either heterosexual or homosexual.[29] Because of the great amount of misunderstanding that arose regarding the lesser of two evils, it is critical to clarify this teaching. Traditional authors such as Noldin, Genicot, and Merkelbach taught that it is sometimes permissible to counsel the lesser evil. For instance, if one is about to steal $1,000 and I cannot otherwise prevent the theft, I could urge the person to take only $100. Or, if one is determined to murder someone and I am powerless to stop this action, I could persuade the individual to get drunk instead.

Traditional moralists defended this "method" because the object of the counsel was not evil but good: i.e., the lesser evil precisely as lesser. Two conditions were always given to justify this: (a) The person counseled is determined to commit and prepared for the commission of the greater evil; and (b) There is no other way of preventing the greater evil.

It is critical to understand this traditional teaching. The manualists indicated that it was sometimes permissible to "counsel" the lesser evil when a person is determined to commit an evil and cannot be reasonably prevented from doing so. Manualists sometimes give the example, "Don't kill him, just blacken an eye."

The reasoning behind this conclusion is not that eye-blackening is permissible and not morally wrong and may be indiscriminately approved. Rather, it is that in these circumstances, where it is the lesser of two evils and the person is determined to do the greater evil, it is counsel precisely *sub specie boni* (under the species of good): i.e., where an individual is determined to be irresponsible, it is good to narrow down that irresponsibility — the meaning of *sub specie boni*. In the Catholic moral tradition such counsel does not mean that the counselor becomes a "participant in the promotion" of irresponsibility.

It is clear in this traditional teaching, then, that such counseling is not the "normal" pastoral approach. The manualists indicated clearly that it was *sometimes* permissible to counsel the lesser evil. What are the criteria that would determine that "sometimes" is "this time"? The person is determined and prepared to do the greater evil: e.g., the spouse who is HIV positive having sexual intercourse with his wife, and there is no way of preventing this evil (e.g., convincing the husband to abstain from all sexual activity). Obviously, this teaching does not advocate the lesser evil but only tolerates it in certain circumstances when it is virtually impossible to convince an individual not to act in a way that would bring about a greater amount of harm.

Consequently, a counselor's or pastor's first responsibility in this regard is to advocate total abstinence when an individual is HIV positive. Only this approach safeguards the authentic meaning of sexuality as taught by the Church. While condoms are effective in reducing the possibility of transmitting HIV, condoms are not absolutely foolproof in this regard.[30] Contraceptive studies have indicated that for condom users, failure rates have ranged from roughly 5 to 15%.

A final, but important comment must be added here regarding the morality of promoting condom use to reduce the risk of HIV infection.[31] The term "safe sex" or "safer sex" gives the public the illusion that good use of condoms will protect them from HIV infection much of the time. However, the risk of HIV infection even with "good" condom use increases proportionately with each sexual act. Failure rates range from 17% to 65% per year (50-140 condoms/year). For an individual, one-time exposure to HIV through condom failure and bodily fluid contact is all that is needed to bring the virus into a person's system.

Condom manufacturers allow for the distribution of defective condoms. After distribution, if a batch is decidedly more defective than the allowable .4%, they are recalled. This may be too late for many. In November of 1990, 750,000 latex condoms were distributed to New York City residents. Weeks following distribution, they were recalled. Sottile-Malona cites sources at the Centers for Disease Control as indicating in this regard, "There are no wins for the players; only the owners (condom manufacturers) and promoters of sex anytime, any way, stand to gain economically and philosophically."[32]

When the condom is assigned an effectiveness rate in pregnancy prevention, that rate is based on couples randomly having intercourse throughout the menstrual cycle. Figures for effectiveness range from 95-80%. But through current Natural Family Planning research, we now know that at least 70% of the cycle is infertile and that conception is not possible during this time. Therefore, any measurement of a condom's effectiveness is only valid during the fertile time, and pregnancies occur when condoms fail during this "fertile window."

These types of serious considerations have critical ramifications when condoms are assigned effectiveness rates to prevent pregnancy. The HIV virus in an infected individual is present 100% of the time, and the risk for contracting HIV is many times greater than the possibility for pregnancy. The effectiveness of condoms to reduce the risk of HIV transmission and infection is not, then, as good as the public has been led to believe.

Consequently, distributing condoms in high schools and using teenagers as targets for this distribution is clearly unjust and unethical. Several reasons lead to this conclusion:[33]

1.  Free distribution of condoms in high schools is an affront to the authority of parents and erodes their role in regard to their children.
2.  It implies that condoms are a genuinely safe way of having sexual intercourse without risk of disease and that premarital sexual activity is acceptable behavior.
3.  The distribution of condoms quarrels with the strong messages being given about drugs. In the case of drugs, the message is: "Just say no!" In the case of sexual activity engaged in by unmarried adolescents, the message is: "Have safe, disease-free sex." In the case of drugs, the assumption is that youth is capable of rising to the challenge, of understanding the problem and of exercising self-control. In the case of morally reprehensible sexual activity, the assumption is that youth is not capable of rising to the challenge, of understanding the problem, and of exercising a humanizing self-control.

    Consequently, there is no real concern about a young person's growth in self-esteem, or growth in understanding and respecting the sacredness of sex and the importance of a genuine sense of responsibility in regard to sex. The implied message is that the parents, the school and the public authority do not really care about the personal well-being and integration of youth, but are only concerned about their not transmitting or contracting a disease.
4.  The very proposal to distribute condoms is itself a statement of moral values and touches on the question of what values and convictions we want to impart to our youth about the meaning of human sexuality and human integrity.

### B. Compassion

Walter J. Smith titles his excellent book on the HIV infection *AIDS: Living and Dying with Hope*.[34] Smith and so many other authors have emphasized that effective and consistent support for

# Disappointments in AIDS drug research

| Drug | Company | Problem |
| --- | --- | --- |
| L-697,661*<br>TIBO*<br>BIRG-587* | Merck & Co.<br>Johnson & Johnson<br>Boehringer Ingelhelm | The virus mutates and becomes resistant to drugs within weeks. |
| Soluble CD4 | Genentech | Ineffective and potentially toxic. |
| GLQ223 | Genelabs | Limited effectiveness found so far. |

# Drugs available against AIDS virus

| Drug | Company | Problem |
| --- | --- | --- |
| AZT | Burroughs Wellcome | Virus eventually resistant, sometimes within months. Drug can cause severe anemia. |
| DDI | Bristol-Myers | Works like AZT, but causes less viral resistance. Drug helps protect uninfected cells, but does not destroy virus in already infected cells. |
| DDC | Hoffmann-La Roche | Same type of drug as AZT and DDI, with less severe side effects. Likely will be approved early 1992. Already widely used in AIDS underground. |

NOTE: These three are similar drugs and likely work best used in combination. They are thought to extend lives of some patients by one to three years. But they do not rid the body of virus, and have limited effectiveness. Several other similar compounds — 3CT and D4T — are also being developed.

# Drugs in pipeline

| Drug | Company | Problem |
| --- | --- | --- |
| tat Inhibitor | Hoffmann-La Roche | May destroy the virus' ability to reproduce. No studies on effectiveness yet. Can cause kidney damage in animals. Likely 2 years away. |
| protease Inhibitor | Hoffmann-La Roche | In test tubes, stops enzymes from chopping HIV proteins to make new virus. Being tested in Europe. No proof of effectiveness yet. Likely 2 years away. |
| CD4-IgG | Genentech | By fusing the tiny protein with an antibody particle, researchers hope it will stay in the body long enough to soak up stray virus. No evidence of effectiveness yet. |
| Hypericin | VimRx | A plant extract that appears to damage the AIDS virus in test tubes. No evidence of effectiveness yet. |

*All are TIBO derivatives

From: *San Francisco Examiner*
2 February 1992
A-10

those suffering from the HIV infection must impart hope. It is demonstrable, e.g., that a lack of hope and compassion creates a situation where a person progresses more quickly from Stage 0-6 in the above-mentioned Walter Reed Classification. In this light, those suffering from the virus should not be labeled as *victim*, an ancient religious usage which referred to a living creature that was sacrificed. In practice, a victim was a disposable commodity: "During the period of the holocaust in World War II the thousands of Jewish people sent to their death in German concentration camps were described as victims of the Nazis. As victims, they were expendable... By definition, a victim has little hope. Victim implies passivity. Persons with AIDS, by rejecting the label victim, assert their prerogative to be treated as persons. They retain full possession of their human rights and dignity, and maintain control over their lives as long as they are alive."[35]

In order to avoid relating to a person with the HIV infection as victim, *Called to Compassion* makes a strong appeal for a compassion that is much more than sympathy.[36] It involves an experience of intimacy by which one participates in another's life. The Latin word *misericordia* expresses the basic idea: the compassionate person has a heart for those in misery. This is not simply the desire to be kind. The truly compassionate individual works at his or her own cost for the other's real good, helping to rescue them from danger as well as alleviate their suffering.

There are two biblical themes which highlight this concept of compassion: being a neighbor; and hospitality. Being a neighbor to the stranger is a central motif in the biblical tradition.[37] The Gospels give the stranger a specific identity: he or she is one who suffers most, one among the lowliest and most outcast of society. The stranger is not simply an individual, but one who represents a class of people who are pressed to the bottom layer of our society. This kind of stranger demands our attention and our compassion.[38]

The metaphor of hospitality was an image that played a central role in Jesus' teaching. Authentic hospitality invites us to supercede any differences that divide in order to reach the higher goals of recognition and acceptance.[39] Hospitality entails an attitude of openness and warmth freely given and comfortably received. Henri Nouwen explains hospitality in this way:

Hospitality wants to offer friendship without binding the guest and freedom without leaving him alone. Hospitality, therefore, means primarily the creation of a free space where the stranger can enter and become a friend instead of an enemy. Hospitality is not to change people, but to offer them space where change can take place..., to offer freedom not disturbed by dividing lines... Hospitality is not a subtle invitation to adopt the life style of the host, but the gift of chance for the guest to find his own.[40]

Because the HIV virus in the United States has primarily in the past affected stigmatized social groups, including homosexual men, IV drug users, and ethnic minorities, the negative impact of the disease has been severely compounded by a "secondary disease," namely, the fear of and prejudicial oppressive treatment toward marginalized groups. The language of plague and scourge has often been invoked toward those suffering with the HIV infection. Christians thus have a mandate of compassion to demonstrate neighborliness and hospitality toward these people.

*Called to Compassion* roots the biblical meaning of compassion in Jesus himself whose ministry contains so many examples.[41] With compassion, Jesus breaks through the barriers of sickness and sinfulness in order to encounter and heal the afflicted; and he tells us to do as he did, for "Whatever you did for the least brothers of mine, you did for me."[42] We need to keep in mind his warning on this matter: "When the Son of Man comes in his glory... all nations will be assembled before him... Then he will say to those on his left, 'Depart from me you accursed... For I was hungry and you gave me no food, I was thirsty and you gave me no drink, a stranger and you gave me no welcome, naked and you gave me no clothing, ill and in prison and you did not care for me... What you did not do for one of these least ones you did not do for me.' And these will go off to eternal punishment."[43]

*Called to Compassion* points specifically to the story of the good Samaritan which presents the call to compassion in concrete terms.[44] Pope John Paul II graphically demonstrated its meaning when in 1987 he embraced a young boy with AIDS at Mission Dolores Basilica in San Francisco. This was a way of saying that in each patient AIDS has a human face, a unique personal history. The Pope verbalized that message on Christmas Day 1988, in his *Urbi et*

*Orbi* blessing: "I think of them all, and to all of them I say, 'Do not lose hope.'" And he added that those with AIDS are "Called to face the challenge not only of their sickness, but also the mistrust of a fearful society that instinctively turns away from them." On 4 May 1989 he returned to this subject, declaring in a homily in Lusaka that the Church "proclaims a message of hope to those of you who suffer... to the sick and dying, especially those with AIDS and those who lack medical care."[45]

In his apostolic letter on "The Christian Meaning of Human Suffering" (1984),[46] Pope John Paul II called each of us to imitate the good Samaritan: "Man owes to suffering that unselfish love which stirs in his heart and actions. The person who is a 'neighbor' cannot indifferently pass by the suffering of another."[47]

In his 1987 visit to Mission Dolores Basilica, the Pope spoke of the meaning of compassion in the specific context of AIDS:

> (T)he love of God is so great that it goes beyond the limits of human language, beyond the grasp of artistic expression, beyond human understanding. And yet it is concretely embodied in God's son, Jesus Christ, and in his body the Church... God loves you all, without distinction, without limit. He loves those of you who are elderly, who feel the burden of the years. He loves those of you who are sick, those who are suffering from AIDS and from AIDS-related complex. He loves the relatives and friends of the sick and those who care for them. He loves us all with an unconditional and everlasting love.[48]

*Called to Compassion* thus concludes:

> Persons with AIDS are not distant, unfamiliar people, the objects of our mingled pity and aversion. We must keep them present to our consciousness as individuals and a community, and embrace them with unconditional love. The Gospel demands reverence for life in all circumstances. Compassionate love for persons infected with HIV is the only authentic Gospel response.[49]

## C. Responsibility

It is of critical importance in this epidemic that all persons exercise utmost integrity and responsibility. As we have seen, intravenous drug use plays a large role in the spread of HIV. Nearly 70% of the reported cases of heterosexually acquired AIDS in the U.S. have been associated with IV drug use; almost 75% of pediatric AIDS cases have been diagnosed in cities with high seroprevalence rates among IV drug users. These data, combined with the potential for the rapid spread of HIV infection among IV drug users through needle sharing, define a problem whose solution requires both immediate action and long-term research.

*Called to Compassion* points out that drugs and HIV are linked in several ways:

1.  Direct transmission of HIV occurs through the sharing of hypodermic needles, syringes and paraphernalia used in "shooting up" drugs.
2.  Sexual transmission occurs from infected IV drug users to their sexual partners.
3.  Perinatal transmission occurs when women who are IV drug users or the sexual partners of drug users become infected and transmit the virus to their infants during pregnancy, delivery or breast-feeding.[50]

We must also recognize the fact of increased sexual risk and needle-using behavior on the part of persons under the influence of drugs or alcohol. Even with good intentions, abusers may not live up to promises they have made to themselves and others. Those at risk because of their use of alcohol and drugs are called to *change their behavior*. They merit special attention because of their double burden of illness and addiction.

While drug abuse is a chronic, progressive, life-threatening disease, addicts can be freed from this form of enslavement. Participation in a treatment program is an interim step which allows substance abusers to receive comprehensive psychological help and counselling on how to avoid HIV. Drug dependency treatment must always be accompanied by education and counselling about the risk of infection and how to avoid it. Education for intravenous drug users who reject treatment should focus on the risk of repeated exposure to HIV and on the availability of help in conquering their addiction. In this whole area, education and treatment are of paramount importance.

*Called to Compassion* rejected the approach of the distribution of sterile needles to drug abusers who are seemingly beyond education and treatment. The document questioned this approach for both moral and practical reasons:

1. More drug use might result while fewer intravenous drug users might seek treatment.
2. Poor monitoring could lead to the increased spread of HIV infection through the use of contaminated needles.
3. Distribution of sterile needles and syringes would send the message that intravenous drug use can be made safe. But IV drug users mutilate and destroy their veins, introduce infection through contaminated skin, inject substances which often contain lethal impurities and risk death from overdoses.

Some writers have made reference to a "twin disease" of AIDS called AFRAIDS, Acute Fear Regarding AIDS. Some people have become paralyzed with fear as a result of misconceptions and myths about AIDS and the transmission of the virus. AFRAIDS can also lead to an indiscriminate fear of people infected with the virus, resulting in prejudice, discrimination, and ostracism. AFRAIDS is responsible for the violation of many human rights. Because of this acute fear, many people with AIDS have been forced out of jobs, housing, education, and even their own families. This unnecessary fear-based reaction deprives many people in our society of their basic moral and civil rights.

In this regard, HIV and AIDS have had a terrible impact on the homosexual community. The 1988 report of the Presidential Committee states, e.g., that "violence against those perceived to carry HIV... is a serious problem. The Commission has heard reports in which homosexual men in particular have been victims of random violent acts that are indicative of some persons in society who are not reacting rationally to the epidemic. This type of violence is unacceptable and should be condemned by all Americans" (9-103). *Called to Compassion* also emphatically condemns such violence as contrary to Gospel values. The Church teaches that all people, regardless of their sexual orientation, are created in God's image and possess a human dignity which must be respected and protected:

> Thus we affirmed in "To Live In Christ Jesus" (1976): "The Christian community should provide them [homosexual persons] with a special degree of pastoral understanding and care" (n 9). Specific guidelines regarding such pastoral support are found in our 1973 document "Principles to Guide Confessors in Questions of Homosexuality." It envisions a pastoral approach which urges homosexual persons to form chaste, stable relationships.[51]

## 5. HIV AND MARRIAGE

In the 9 January 1987 edition of *The New York Times* an article appeared entitled, "A Victim of AIDS is Denied A Wedding at St. Patrick's."[52] The main components of this report help focus this part of the discussion:[53]

1.  In 1986 David Hefner, a self-proclaimed homosexual, was diagnosed as having AIDS. In 1987 Mr. Hefner was a 38 year old Protestant who desired to validate a three year civil marriage with Maria Ribeiro, a 33 year old Catholic. The date of 14 February 1987 had been set for this validation at St. Patrick's Cathedral in NYC.
2.  The Rector of the cathedral would not allow this validation ceremony on various grounds based on his "own personal judgment": that people in a "life-threatening situation" such as AIDS would receive better pre-marriage counseling in their local parish rather than the cathedral; that Mr. Hefner's disease was "transmittable."

3. Evidence had been offered that Maria's blood was not infected by the AIDS virus by three negative tests.

4. On 12 January 1987 *The New York Times* and the *New York Daily News* reported that Cardinal O'Connor was reviewing the decision of the Rector of the cathedral. On the next day, *The New York Times* reported that "John Cardinal O'Connor yesterday reversed the decision of the Rector of the cathedral..."

Mr. Hefner was admitted to New York University Hospital on 5 January 1987 and died on 3 May 1987 of AIDS.

Commenting on this case some authors have concluded that AIDS prevents a person from physically consummating a marriage and this fact precludes the possibility of a valid marital union. Interpreting AIDS as a divine law prohibition to marriage, these authors reach the conclusion that a person with HIV can marry in the Church *only* because he or she is in danger of death; and the HIV carrier should be dissuaded from marriage since canon law allows the possibility to forbid marriage for a serious reason (c 1077).

### A. Church Law and Marriage

Canon 1058 states the principle of freedom regarding the basic fundamental human right of persons to enter marriage: "All persons who are not prohibited by law can contract marriage." Thomas P. Doyle in the CLSA commentary on the Code of Canon Law explains that sometimes prohibitions are placed on marriages in view of the effect this would have on "the spouses, the children, and the community." He further indicates that such prohibitions "are not an unjust denial of individual freedom but a limitation placed on the right to marry for the good of all concerned."[54]

Doyle notes that throughout history customary or legal structures have been provided "which in certain instances restrict the exercise of the right to marry,"[55] and indicates that these restrictions may arise from divine law or ecclesiastical law. Examples of divine law prohibitions include marriages between natural brothers and sisters, which are incestuous; prohibitions of ecclesiastical law include those which do not allow clerics in sacred orders to marry. Other "restrictions" which forbid a person to marry include instances where free marital consent cannot be given: e.g., the mentally insane, the intoxicated person, and the abducted person. Further restrictions would also include people who are unable to fulfill marital obligations: e.g., two females, two males, a certainly and absolutely impotent person.

Since canon law indicates that restrictions must be interpreted "strictly" and "literally," it is necessary that the law clearly state that a person with HIV/AIDS is prohibited from marriage: i.e., a legal prohibition cannot be presumed from a moral prohibition; it must be stated in the law. In the case of a person infected with HIV/AIDS, there is no legal prohibition. This is an important and pivotal point to keep in mind in forming any policy or guidelines on this issue. If one concludes a *moral* prohibition, it must be understood and applied as such. It should not be presented as a canonical prohibition and applied as such.

The canonical issue here, then, concerns a person's "right to marry." As is evident in canon 1058, this right is not an absolute one and is conditioned by a person's capacity to exercise the obligations concomitant with such a right. Canon law seeks to insure that a person's right to marry is not arbitrarily denied. In the case of a marriage of a person infected with HIV/AIDS, the exercise of the right to marry is relative to *moral* considerations. In the case of such persons, to insist on the right to marry as absolute and above *moral* considerations could well lead to the highest injury to other persons — their lives.[56]

## B. The Moral Issue

Consequently, the more compelling questions regarding marriage for a person with HIV/AIDS are moral rather than canonical. The moral and canonical questions are distinct and should be viewed and analyzed as such. The moral issues carry greater weight than the canonical ones, and indeed inform the canonical application of any questions. Therefore, even if a couple canonically *can* marry, given the life-threatening nature of AIDS and the moral issues involved, it is possible to conclude that a person in this situation *should not marry* in the Church. In other words, the moral issues take precedence over and inform the canonical ones.

According to canon 1057:1, "Marriage is brought about through the consent of the parties..." A marriage which is not consummated is still a marriage by canonical definition. It is not null. In some cases, a marriage without sexual intercourse *ab initio* can be sustained and a communion of life and love can be established. But this is another question. In other words, it is possible for some people to agree voluntarily and mutually to abstain from sexual intercourse and to have a relationship that can be recognized as marriage. It would take a certain level of love and commitment and it is likely that very few people would be able to do this. But such a marriage is still a possibility.

Canon law would thus admit of the possibility of a marriage in which the parties agree to abstain from sexual intercourse (*ratum et non-consummatum*). Such an arrangement is quite plausible in convalidating a marriage of a person with HIV/AIDS who would be considered in danger of death. It would doubtlessly be more difficult for an HIV carrier and a person who is neither infected with nor a carrier of the disease.

Would an agreement to abstain from sexual intercourse amount to an intention against children? Would such an intention allow for a denial of the Church wedding on the basis of the refusal on the part of the couple to intend what the Church intends when celebrating the sacrament?

The key issue here concerns whether the couple excludes children in their marriage "by a positive act of the will." It is one thing to exclude the possibility of children in a marriage because a couple does not want this responsibility, because they see children as a limitation of their lifestyle, or because having children is not part of their understanding of marriage. It is quite another thing to desire to have children but avoid having them so as not to spread a disease.

It is possible for a couple to marry with a mutual and voluntary agreement to abstain from sexual intercourse. The key question, however, concerns the party's capacity to consent to and assume the obligations of marriage under these conditions: e.g., are the persons in such a union capable of growing in love; do they have other means of expression and affectivity; can they communicate well? Such questions involve a great deal of discernment and discussion between the parties and also with the pastoral minister.

A person with HIV/AIDS should not consummate marriage on moral grounds, then, since HIV is clearly transmitted through sexual intercourse. If the couple freely agree to abstinence, such a decision does not constitute an impediment to marriage. Why? It is not impossible for a person with HIV/AIDS to consummate a marriage; it is irresponsible to do so. Hence, the impediment of impotency cannot be applied in such situations.

It is possible for a diocesan bishop to prohibit the marriage of a person with HIV/AIDS, but only for *moral* reasons: e.g., the health and life of the persons involved. This prohibition can only be imposed on a case-by-case basis.[57] Even if a prohibition is imposed and the two persons nonetheless marry in the Church, such a marriage would be presumed valid. Only the supreme authority in the Church can attach an invalidating clause to a prohibition.[58]

In counselling someone with HIV/AIDS regarding marriage, a pastoral minister should certainly discern a person's and a couple's capacity to make authentic discretionary judgments regarding the meaning of their marriage and the fatal nature of the disease. Canon 1095:2 clearly states that those "who suffer from grave lack of discretion of judgment concerning essential matrimonial rights and duties which are to be mutually given and accepted" are incapable of contracting marriage. This is the type of moral judgment that must be made on a case-by-case basis.

Appropriate counselling in this regard must include several components: assisting one to accept the critical nature of the disease; treating well the meaning of abstinence from sexual relations for the physical good of the couple themselves; the physical good of any potential child.

A marriage between a man and a woman is intended to be a union of support, psychic and physical, as well as moral and spiritual, with the possibility of the raising of a human family from the relationship itself (a communion of life and love). This *communio* is upheld not only in canon law but also in the teaching on marriage found in *Gaudium et Spes*, nn 50-52. A person with HIV/AIDS must be counseled to see this essential aspect of marriage in order to discern well his or her capacity to bring about a communion of life and love.

It is critical, then, that this whole question not be narrowed to a sexual one alone regarding the transmission of a fatal disease. It is important to appreciate the Church's teaching on marriage as a communion of life and love. The consequences that would fall upon a married couple who after marriage discerned the presence of HIV/AIDS, brings about tremendous psychological, physical and economic strain to the extent that such a relationship would indeed require the greatest amount of Christian charity to survive effectively.

If a person who knows that he or she has HIV/AIDS and marries while willfully concealing this fact from his or her spouse, then the marriage could be alleged invalid on the basis of deceit or fraud.[59] A few states presently require an AIDS test prior to marriage. However, the party is not required under these laws to reveal the outcome of the test and the fact that a person has AIDS does not prohibit a marriage. The point of these laws is to allow a person who is considering marriage to know if he or she has the disease or is a carrier, presumably so that this person can make a sound judgment about marriage.

The difficult legal question still outstanding concerns an individual's right to privacy. The fact that a person has tested positive is a private matter and often shared as privileged information sheltered under the umbrella of professional confidentiality. Unless a person shares this fact with a pastoral minister or in the context of marriage preparation, it would be a delicate matter to raise the question with the couple as a standard practice for premarital investigation.

It seems wise to have diocesan guidelines which categorically caution ministers and which give assistance in dealing with this question. The critical pastoral point remains that sexual intercourse in circumstances where the spread of HIV/AIDS is a possibility is indeed a life-threatening act. Potential spouses (or those already spouses) in this situation must be morally willing to limit the expressions of their sexuality by being encouraged to realize the moral obligation to respect present and potential human life. The responsibility not to endanger human life is a grave obligation in standard Catholic teaching and this responsibility must find consistent articulation in any attempts to deal pastorally and sensitively with a person with HIV/AIDS who desires to marry in the Catholic Church.

## 6. SOCIAL QUESTIONS

### A. *Voluntary Testing*

*Called to Compassion* notes that broadly based, routine voluntary testing and educational programs are needed as a matter of public policy. These voluntary programs should always guarantee anonymity and should be preceded and followed by necessary counselling for individuals diagnosed as HIV positive or negative. Counselling should supply information about the disease, the moral aspects involved, immediate emotional support and information about resources for continuing emotional and spiritual support. It should also underscore, sensitively but forthrightly, the grave moral responsibility of individuals with HIV to inform others who are at risk because of their condition.[60]

### B. *The Handicapped or Disabled Person*

*Called to Compassion* likewise points out that a growing body of legislation considers the individual with HIV a handicapped or disabled person. In 1978, in a statement on the handicapped, the bishops wrote, "Defense of the right to life... implies the defense of other rights which enable the handicapped individual to achieve the fullest measure of personal development of which he or she is capable."[61]

Discrimination against those suffering from HIV or AIDS is a deprivation of their civil liberties. The Church must be an advocate in this area, while also promulgating its own non-discrimination policies in employment, housing, delivery of medical and dental care, access to public accommodations, schools, nursing homes and emergency services.

### C. *Confidentiality*

*Called to Compassion* emphasizes that while the presumption should always favor confidentiality, there may be circumstances that warrant disclosure. In deciding for disclosure or confidentiality in a particular case, the following points are relevant:

1. The two main factors in favor of disclosure are (a) the need
   to prevent the infection of others and (b) the need to
   provide medical care to the person who is HIV positive or
   has AIDS. If disclosure in a particular case will reduce the
   danger of infection to others or increase the ability to treat
   the individual effectively, it may be the right course of
   action if no other effective action is possible.
2. Of primary importance in weighing the individual's interest
   in and right to confidentiality are (a) the ability to confine
   the disclosure to those who have the right to know, (b) the
   likelihood that recipients of the information will use it for
   proper purposes, and (c) the obligation to maintain patient
   confidentiality.

The final paragraph of *Called to Compassion* is a fitting conclusion to our discussion:

> HIV/AIDS brings with it new anguish and new terrors and anxiety,
> new trials of pain and endurance, new occasions for compassion.
> But it cannot change one enduring fact: God's love for us all. We
> proclaim anew this message: "God so loved the world that he gave
> his only Son, so that everyone who believes in him should not perish
> but might have eternal life."[62]

# FOOTNOTES

## Introduction

[1] Judith Viorst, "What Is This Thing Called Love?" Redbook Publishing Co.: *Redbook*, February 1975, 12.

[2] Lisa Sowle Cahill, *Between the Sexes*, Philadelphia: Fortress Press, 1985.

[3] Ibid., 150-151.

[4] Ibid., 152.

[5] See *Keeping Body and Soul Together*, The General Assembly Special Committee on Human Sexuality, Presbyterian Church, 203rd General Assembly, 1991, 147-148.

[6] See James B. Nelson, *Embodiment*, Minneapolis: Augsburg Publishing House, 1978.

[7] "Archbishop Quinn's talk at the Bishops' Meeting with the Pope," *Origins* 17 (1987), 258-260.

[8] *Gaudium et Spes*, nn 4-10.

[9] John Courtney Murray, "Natural Law and the Public Consensus" in *Natural Law and Modern Society*, ed., John Cogley, Cleveland: World Publishing Co., 1962, 66-67.

[10] *Gaudium et Spes*, n 11.

[11] *Gaudium et Spes*, n 4.

[12] Op. cit.

[13] Ibid., 4-5, 29-30, 33 and 77.

[14] John Paul II, *The Theology of Marriage and Celibacy*, Boston: Daughters of St. Paul, 1986, i-iv.

[15] See Lisa Sowle Cahill, *Women and Sexuality*, New York: Paulist Press, 1992, 71.

## Chapter One

[1] Dietrich von Hildebrand, *In Defense of Purity*, New York: Sheed and Ward, 1935, 12-14.

[2] 1 John 4:7-8. All translations throughout this book are from the Revised Standard Version.

[3] Matthew 22:30; Mark 12:25; Luke 20:35. For an excellent exegesis of these points, see John Paul II, *The Theology of Marriage and Celibacy*, Loften: St. Paul Editions, 1986.

[4] For a fuller development of this theme, see Jack Dominian, "Sexual Morality Today," *The Tablet* 242 (1988), 30-32; 57-58; 82-83; and 111-112.

[5] A. C. Kinsey, W. B. Pomeroy and C. E. Martin, *Sexual Behavior in the Human Male*, Philadelphia: W. B. Saunders Co., 1953, vii.

[6] Genesis 1:26-27. See National Conference of Catholic Bishops (N.C.C.B.), *Sharing the Light of Faith: National Catechetical Directory for Catholics of the United States*, Washington, D.C.: U.S.C.C. Office for Publishing and Promotion Services, 1979, n 85.

[7] For a fuller development of this theme, see U.S.C.C., *Human Sexuality*, Washington, D.C.: U.S.C.C. Office for Publishing and Promotion Services 1990, esp. 7-14.

[8] John C. Dwyer, *Human Sexuality: A Christian View*, Kansas City: Sheed and Ward, 1987. We will follow Dwyer's treatment in the next few pages.

[9] Lisa Sowle Cahill, *Women and Sexuality*, New York: Paulist Press, 1992.

[10] Ibid., 60.

[11] Ibid., 61-62.

[12] Ibid., 63-67.
[13] Abraham Maslow, *Motivation and Personality*, Chicago: University of Chicago Press, 1951.
[14] M. Scott Peck, M.D., *The Road Less Travelled*, New York: Simon and Schuster, 1978, 160-161.
[15] Erich Fromm, *Man For Himself*, New York: Rinehart Publishers, 1947.
[16] John C. Dwyer, op. cit., 52-54.
[17] Pope John Paul II, *Familiaris Consortio*, 22 November 1981.
[18] *Familiaris Consortio*, n 11.
[19] William H. Masters and Virginia E. Johnson, Little, Brown and Co.: *The Pleasure Bond*, 1970, 107-108.
[20] Congregation for Catholic Education, *Educational Guidance in Human Love*, 1 November 1983, n 4.
[21] U.S.C.C., *Human Sexuality*, n 9.
[22] See Patrick Carnes, *Out of the Shadows*, Minneapolis: CompCare Publications, 1983; and Stephen J. Rossetti, *Slayer of the Soul*, Mystic, Connecticut: Twenty-Third Publications, 1990.
[23] U.S.C.C., *Human Sexuality*, 13-14.
[24] Congregation for the Doctrine of the Faith, *Declaration on Certain Questions Concerning Sexual Ethics*, Washington, D.C.: U.S.C.C. Publications Office, 1976, n 1.
[25] N.C.C.B., *Sharing the Light of Faith: National Catechetical Directory for Catholics of the United States*, Washington, D.C.: U.S.C.C. Office for Publishing and Promotion Services, 1977, n 191.
[26] Congregation for Catholic Education, *Educational Guidance in Human Love*, 1983, n 4. Other pertinent documents in this regard are: John Paul II, *Familiaris Consortio*, op. cit.; the Holy See, *Charter of the Rights of the Family*, 22 October 1983; Congregation for the Doctrine of the Faith, *Instruction on Respect for Human Life in Its Origin* and *On the Dignity of Procreation: Replies to Certain Questions of the Day*, 22 February 1987; and Congregation for Catholic Education, *The Religious Dimension of Education in a Catholic School*, 7 April 1988.
[27] For a fuller description, see John A. Gallagher, *Time Past, Time Present: an Historical Study of Catholic Moral Theology*, New York: Paulist Press, 1990, esp. chs. 1-4.
[28] Vatican Council II, *Declaration on Religious Freedom*, in *The Documents of Vatican II*, ed., Walter M. Abbott, New York: Guild Press, 1966, n 3.
[29] See Michael K. Duffey, *Be Blessed in What You Do: The Unity of Christian Ethics and Spirituality*, New York: Paulist Press, 1988.
[30] Ibid., 15-16.
[31] 1 Corinthians 1:23-24.
[32] Thomas Merton, *A Thomas Merton Reader*, New York: Doubleday Image Books, 1974, 377-378.
[33] James Gustafson, *Christ and The Moral Life*, New York: Harper and Row, 1968, 183.
[34] Stanley Hauerwas, *The Peaceable Kingdom: A Primer in Christian Ethics*, Notre Dame: University of Notre Dame Press, 1983, 75-76.
[35] William E. May, "Is Pleasure Supreme?" *The Catholic World Report* 2 (1992), 12-17; citation at 15.
[36] Matthew 5:48.
[37] Michael K. Duffey, op. cit., 60.
[38] See Gerald D. Coleman, *Divorce and Remarriage in the Catholic Church*, New York: Paulist Press, 1988, esp. ch. 7.
[39] *Summa Theologiae*, II-II, 23, 8. See also Paul J. Wadell, *The Primacy of Love: An Introduction to the Ethics of Thomas Aquinas*, New York: Paulist Press, 1992.

⁴⁰ Duffey, op. cit., 102.

⁴¹ Bernard Haering, *Free and Faithful in Christ*, New York: Seabury Press, 1978, vol 1, 478-479.

⁴² United States Catholic Bishops, "Called to Compassion and Responsibility: A Response to the HIV/AIDS Crisis," *Origins* 19 (1989), 423-434, n 3.

⁴³ Ibid., n 4.

⁴⁴ Pope John Paul II, "Pope Addresses Vatican AIDS Conference," *Origins* 19 (1989), 434-436, n 5.

⁴⁵ *Human Sexuality*, 19.

⁴⁶ See U.S.C.C., *Sharing the Light of Faith: An Official Commentary*, Washington, D.C.: U.S.C.C. Office for Publishing and Promotion Services, 1981, n 105.

⁴⁷ *Human Sexuality*, 20.

⁴⁸ Ibid., 52.

⁴⁹ *Women and Sexuality, op. cit.*, 56.

⁵⁰ Jack Dominian, "Chastity," *The Tablet* 240 (1986), 7601.

⁵¹ Matthew Rzeczkowski, O.P., "Why Chastity?" *The Bible Today* 25 (1987), 305.

⁵² 1 Corinthians 6:19-20. See also William C. Spohn, "St. Paul on Apostolic Celibacy and the Body of Christ," *Studies in the Spirituality of Jesuits* 17 (1985), 1-30.

⁵³ Colossians 3:1.

⁵⁴ Colossians 3:2-3.

⁵⁵ *Summa Theologiae* II-II, 154, a 1, 12.

⁵⁶ John Paul II, "Apostolic Exhortation on Reconciliation and Penance," *Origins* 14 (1984), 433-458, n 17.

⁵⁷ See Timothy E. O'Connell, *Principles For A Catholic Morality*, New York: Harper and Row, Publishers, revised ed., 1990, 187-189. See also Albert DiIanni, "Judicial Terrorism: A Case of Intrinsic Evil," *America* 166 (1992), 407-410.

⁵⁸ We will follow here the treatment of this question given by Walter G. Jeffko in "Processive Relationalism and Ethical Absolutes" in *Readings in Moral Theology*, ed., Charles E. Curran and Richard A. McCormick, vol. 1, New York: Paulist Press, 1979, 199-214.

⁵⁹ Ibid., 209.

⁶⁰ John Mahoney, *The Making of Moral Theology*, Oxford: Clarendon Press, 1987, ch. 5.

⁶¹ St. Thomas, *II Sent. dist.* 36, q 1, a. 5 *ad* 5. The distinction between the end "at hand" and the end "at a distance," or the proximate and the remote ends, would be analyzed further to distinguish between the *finis operis*, the inherent purpose of the act, and the *finis operantis*, the purpose of the agent in performing the act.

⁶² To the question of how one was to satisfy oneself about the inherent morality of the object, or about the quality of the raw material available to one, Thomas replied that this was the work of reason invoking the law of nature and aided by divine law, enabling the human person to classify various objects, or types of action, as morally good, morally bad, or morally indifferent: "One object is reasonable and therefore good of its type, such as clothing the naked. Another is at variance with reason, such as taking other people's property, and therefore bad of its type. A third type is neither reasonable nor unreasonable, such as picking up a straw, etc., and this type is called indifferent." (*De malo*, q. 2, a. 5.)

⁶³ *Summa Theologiae* 1 q. 79, a. 12. See also Paul J. Wadell, *The Primacy of Love: An Introduction to the Ethics of Thomas Aquinas, op. cit.*

⁶⁴ John Mahoney, op. cit., 189-190.

⁶⁵ We will follow here the treatment of conscience given by Cardinal Joseph Ratzinger in a presentation on "Conscience and Truth" given to the bishops of the United States in a meeting in Dallas, Texas, in 1991. This talk will be published by the Pope John XXIII Center.

[66] *De Ethica situationis*, AAF 44 (1952), 270-278; 413-419; 48 (1956), 144-145. See also DS 3918-3921. See also "Undertakings and Promises: Sexual Ethics in the Life of the Church," Philip Turner, *Virginia Seminary Journal* XLIII (1991), 3-12.

[67] John Mahoney, op. cit., 218-219.

[68] *The Pastoral Constitution on the Church in the Modern World*, n 51.

[69] *Human Sexuality*, 23.

[70] William E. May, "Is Pleasure Supreme?" *The Catholic World Report* 2 (1992), 12-17; citation at 14.

[71] Heribert Jone, *Moral Theology*, Trans. Urban Adelman, Westminster, Maryland: The Newman Press, 1960, 46.

[72] For this treatment of parvity of matter, we will carefully follow Patrick J. Boyle's *Parvitas Materiae In Sexto in Contemporary Catholic Thought*, New York: University Press of America, 1987. See also Eduardus Genicot, *Theologiae Moralis Institutiones*, 6th edition, Vol. 1, Bruxellis: A. Dewit, 1909, 34.

[73] See Eduardus Genicot, *Theologiae Moralis Institutiones*, 6th edition, Vol. 1, Bruxellis: A. Dewit, 1909, 34.

[74] Heribert Jone, op. cit., 46-47.

[75] Congregation for the Doctrine of the Faith, *Declaration on Certain Questions Concerning Sexual Ethics*, n 59.

[76] *Ordinationes et Selectae Epistolae Praepositi Generalis Societatis Jesu*, Epp. NN. 115, p. 498, unpublished collection located in the Archivum Romanum Societatis Jesu, Romae, Borgo S. Spirito, C.P. 9048. Quoted in Karl-Heinz Kleber, *De Parvitate Materiae in Sexto, Studien zur Geschichte der Kath. Moral-theologie*, Heraus-Gegeban von Michael Muller no. 18, Regensburg: Verlag Friedrick Pustet, 1971, 172-174. "Some members in the Society teach that in venereal matters a small degree of pleasure deliberately sought is not to be considered a mortal sin because of the smallness of the matter. At the very worst this can be very prejudicial not only to the reputation of the Society, but also to the purity of life which the Society tries to bring about in its own members as well as among externs. Because of the possible dangers to which such teaching could lead and because of the moral impossibility of distinguishing on the practical level between light matter and serious matter, learned and respected fathers of the Society, with whom we have discussed the matter, judge the teaching to be altogether false, extremely dangerous and certainly contrary to purity. Thus, after having given the matter serious consideration, we are forced to decree that no one in the Society, either publicly or privately, can teach parvity of matter in the future, not only as true or probable but not even as tolerable for any reason whatsoever. They may not indicate that the teaching is pleasing to them or counsel anyone in this matter." Rome, 24 April, 1612, Claudius Acquaviva. As found in *Ordinatones et Selectae Epistolae Praepositi Generalis Societatis Jesu*, Vol. I, 289-290. Unpublished manuscript quoted in Karl-Heinz Kleber, op. cit., 173-174.

[77] Ibid., Ponte Jesuitico 657, 425. Cited in Boyle, op. cit., 14-15.

[78] H. Noldin and A. Schmitt, *Summa Theologiae Moralis: De Sexto Praecepto et De Usu Matrimonii*, Innsbruck: F. Rauch, 1934, 11-13.

[79] Joseph Fuchs, "The Absoluteness of Moral Terms," in *Readings in Moral Theology*, No. 1, ed., Charles E. Curran and Richard A. McCormick, New York: Paulist Press, 1979, 94-137.

[80] Ibid., 121.

[81] The so-called "physicalist" approach is said to consider only the biological structure of an act, a position based on the belief that in each act there is a God-given finality and structure which human beings must respect. An example of "physicalism" can be found in Gerald Kelly's 1957 volume *Medico-Moral Problems*, St. Louis: The Catholic

Hospital Association, in his explanation regarding sterility testing, 221.

[82] Boyle, op. cit., 95. For further details, see *Gaudium et Spes*, nn 27, 51, 79 and 80; Pius XII, "Address to the Italian Medical-Biological Union of St. Luke" in *Love and Sexuality*, ed., O. Lilbard, Wilmington: McGrath and Co., 1978, 91-92; John XXIII, *Mater et Magistra* in *Acta Apostolicae Sedis* 53 (1961), 194; Paul VI, "Address to the Society of Italian Catholic Jurists" in *Love and Sexuality*, op. cit., 390; Paul VI, *Humanae Vitae* in *AAS* 60 (1968), 14; and *Declaration on Certain Questions Concerning Sexual Ethics*, op. cit., 7-8.

[83] Boyle, op. cit., 102 and 105. Boyle also gives a good summary-statement regarding many contemporary moral theologians who disagree with the teaching on parvity of matter: "The intention of an act plays a very important part in determining... morality. However, this is not to imply that the intention of a particular act is the only determinant. Attention must also be given to moral norms and other aspects of life. The uniqueness of the moral agent, the moral situation, the comparison of present moral experience with past similar ones, and the various values and conflict must all enter into the determination of objective right and wrong. The methodology of this contemporary approach tries to make clear the different options which deserve preference after considering all the values at stake. It tries to uncover the means proportionate to the intended good and the evil inevitably caused without losing sight of the agent and his possibility for growth. Man's judgment is at the basis of this determination. It seeks to determine whether or not there exists a proportion between premoral evil (disvalue) that is present in any human action and the good (value) that the individual intends. If a proportion exists and the good intended outweighs the evil that is present, it is a morally good act. Thus, in considering the determinants of objective morality in contemporary moral theology, the judgment about the proportion and the good that an action achieves is the essential element. A morally evil action is one in which there is no value proportionate to the disvalue produced. Only when this judgment is made, can an action be called a moral evil. Consequently, the intrinsically evil acts as traditionally understood by the magisterium have no place in the contemporary approach to moral theology" (103-104). While Boyle's summary of some contemporary moral theologians is accurate and clear, it is critical to recall that the Church's teaching on parvity of matter in sexual acts is normative for all Catholics.

[84] Gerald Kelly, *Modern Youth and Chastity*, St. Louis: The Queen's Work, 1941.

[85] Ibid., ch. 10.

[86] See *Gaudium et Spes*, n 51.

[87] Joseph Fuchs, S.J., "The Absoluteness of Moral Terms" in *Readings in Moral Theology*, No. 1, ed., Charles E. Curran and Richard A. McCormick, New York: Paulist Press, 1979, 94-137.

[88] See Karl Rahner, "Zum Problem der Genetischen Manipulation," in *Sehriften zur Theologie* VIII, 303 ff.

[89] "The Absoluteness of Moral Terms," op. cit., 103.

[90] Ibid., 105.

[91] Ibid., 125-131. William E. May puts the same point this way: "Since the moral absolutes in question are negatives — do not kill the innocent, etc. — they are, at times, unpopular and seem to confirm the view that Church moral teaching is indeed rigoristic. Yet the handful of such absolutes — whose truth can be shown convincingly — is there to protect human persons and human dignity and to point out blind alleys. They protect human dignity because human rights and duties are correlative. If there are not absolute duties (specified by absolute norms), then there are no absolute rights. For instance, no one's "right to life" is absolute if others do not have an absolute obligation to refrain from killing him. The life of innocent human beings is not inviolable if there is no corresponding obligation never, under any circumstances whatsoever, to kill them." (See "Is Pleasure Supreme?" *The Catholic World Report* 2 (1992), 12-17; citation at 17.)

410                                              HUMAN SEXUALITY

[92] *Decree on Priestly Formation,* n 16.
[93] Bernard Haering, *Free and Faithful in Christ,* vol. 1, New York: The Seabury Press, 1978, 7-27.
[94] Genesis 1:27-28.
[95] See Exodus 6:10.
[96] Genesis 12:1.
[97] See 1 Samuel 8.
[98] Luke 1:50.
[99] Isaiah 40 ff.
[100] Matthew 4:17.
[101] Galatians 5:22.
[102] John 4:24.
[103] Galatians 5:22.
[104] Galatians 5:22-25.
[105] We will follow here the treatment by Stephen Sapp in *Sexuality, the Bible and Science,* Philadelphia: The Fortress Press, 1977.
[106] See Genesis 4:7.
[107] See Job 34:14-15; Psalm 104:29-30.
[108] See Genesis 9:1; 12:2; 17:2-6; 22:17. See also John Paul II, *The Theology of Marriage and Celibacy,* Boston: Daughters of St. Paul, 1986.
[109] *Women and Sexuality, op. cit.,* 27.
[110] See Genesis 2:23.
[111] Isaiah 54:5-6; 62:4-5; Jeremiah 2:2; 3:8, 20; Ezekiel 16:8, 23; Hosea 1-3; 11.
[112] Contrary to Deuteronomy 24:1-4.
[113] See also Jeremiah 31:31-34.
[114] Deuteronomy 25:11-12.
[115] Exodus 22:19; Leviticus 18:23; Deuteronomy 27:21.
[116] Deuteronomy 24:5; 20:7.
[117] Mark 1:15.
[118] Matthew 23:23.
[119] Matthew 5:20.
[120] Luke 6:45; Matthew 15:17-20.
[121] Leviticus 20:10.
[122] Galatians 5:6. See also Karol Wojtyla, *The Acting Person,* Dordrecht and Boston: D. Reidel Pub. Co., 1979.
[123] Romans 12:1; Philippians 1:20.

**Chapter Two**

[1] Bernard Haering, *Free and Faithful in Christ,* vol. 1, *The Truth Will Set You Free,* New York: The Seabury Press, 1979. See also Lisa Sowle Cahill, *Women and Sexuality,* New York: Paulist Press, 1992, 47-48; and Paul Ricoeur, "Wonder, Eroticism and Enigma," *Cross Currents* 14 (1964), 136-137.
[2] See Vincent J. Genovesi, *In Pursuit of Love: Catholic Morality and Human Sexuality,* Delaware: Michael Glazier, Inc., 1987, 140.
[3] Bernard Haering, op. cit., 504.
[4] Vincent J. Genovesi, op. cit., 140-141.
[5] John Paul II, *Reflections on Humanae Vitae: Conjugal Morality and Spirituality,* Boston: St. Paul Editions, 1984, n. 30.
[6] Op. cit., 141.
[7] On this point see James B. Nelson, *Embodiment: An Approach to Sexuality and Christian Theology,* Minneapolis: Augsburg Publishing House, 1978, esp. 118, 104-105.

8  Congregation for the Doctrine of the Faith, *Declaration on Certain Questions Concerning Sexual Ethics*, 29 December 1975, n 1.
9  Patrick Carnes, *Out of the Shadows*, Minneapolis: CompCare Publications, 1983. See also *Sex and Love Addicts Anonymous*, First Ed., *The Basic Text for The Augustine Fellowship*, Boston: Fellowship-Wide Services, Inc., 1986.
10 Matthew 5:27-28. See also John Paul II, "On Lust and Adultery," *L'Osservatore Romano*, n 18, 5 May 1980, 3-4.
11 Matthew 5:8.
12 See Congregation for the Doctrine of the Faith, *Declaration on Certain Questions Concerning Sexual Ethics*, nn 11-12.
13 Sigmund Freud, *Contributions to the Psychology of Love*, London: The Hogarth Press and the Institute of Psychoanalysis, 1953-1966, vol. XI, 180.
14 Rollo May, *Love and Will*, New York: Norton and Co., Inc., 1969, 91.
15 See *Celibacy for the Kingdom*, Howard Bleichner, Daniel Buechlein and Robert Leavitt, Baltimore: St. Mary's Seminary and University Press, 1990.
16 We will follow here the treatment of this subject by Stephen B. Levine, "The Origins of Sexual Identity: A Clinician's View" in *Sexuality and Medicine*, ed., Earl E. Shelp, Dordrecht: D. Reidel Publishing Co., vol. I, 1987, 39-54.
17 Simone de Beauvoir, *The Second Sex*, New York: W. B. Key, 1953, 41.
18 Levine, op. cit., 41.
19 Ibid., 42.
20 We will follow here the thought of John Money, "The Development of Sexual Orientation," in *The Harvard Medical School Mental Health Letter* 4 (1988), 4-6.
21 See Bernard Haering, *Free and Faithful in Christ*, vol. 2, New York: Crossroad Books, 1979, 493.
22 *Gaudium et Spes*, n. 49.
23 We will follow here Haering's treatment of this subject in chapter ten of *Free and Faithful in Christ*, "The Liberating Truth in Sexual Language," op. cit., 492-567.
24 James B. Nelson, *Embodiment*, Minneapolis: Augsburg Publishing House, 1978. We will follow here Nelson's treatment, especially in "Body Meanings: Sexuality and Communication," 25-36.
25 Vincent Genovesi, *In Pursuit of Love*, op. cit., 141.
26 See "Scientists Trace Aberrant Sexuality," *New York Times*, 23 January 1990, B7-B11.
27 John Money, *Lovemaps*, New York: Prometheus Books, 1990.
28 John C. Dwyer, *Human Sexuality*, Kansas City: Sheed and Ward, 1987, 59-61.
29 Leslie M. Lothstein, "Theories of Transsexualism," in *Sexuality and Medicine*, op. cit., 55-72. We will follow Lothstein's treatment here.
30 From Katchadourian and Lunde, *Fundamentals of Human Sexuality*, 3rd. ed., New York: Holt, Rinehart and Winston, 1980, 120-122.
31 John Money and Anka Ehrhardt, *Man and Woman/Boy and Girl*, Baltimore: Johns Hopkins University Press, 1973.
32 Cited in Lothstein, 59. See also "And the Two Shall Be One: Transsexuals and Marriage," *Ethics and Medics* 9 (1984), 1-2.
33 See "Transvestism" in Eugene Kennedy, *Sexual Counseling*, New York: Continuum, 1989, 148-153. We will follow here Kennedy's treatment of this subject.
34 Cited in Kennedy, 149.
35 Eugene Kennedy, op. cit., 152.
36 Stephen J. Rossetti, *Slayer of the Soul*, Mystic, Connecticut: Twenty-Third Publications, 1990.
37 Ibid., 19-43.

[38]  See John Money, "Paraphilias: Phenomenology and Classification," *American Journal of Psychotherapy* 38 (1984), 164-179.

[39]  M. Groth, W. Hobson, G. Gary, "The Child Molester: Clinical Observations," in *Social Work and Child Sexual Abuse*, eds., J. Conte and D. Shore, New York: Haworth, 1982.

[40]  F. Araji and V. Finkelhor, "Explanations of Pedophilia: Review of Empirical Research," *Bulletin of the American Academy of Psychiatry and Law*, 13 (1985), 17-37.

[41]  E. Litin, M. Giffin, and A. Johnson, "A Parental Influence In Unusual Sexual Behavior in Children," *Psychoanalytic Quarterly* 25 (1956), 37-55.

[42]  F. Berlin and G. Coyle, "Sexual Deviation Syndromes," *Johns Hopkins Medical Journal* 149 (1981), 119-125.

[43]  Anti-androgenic medication such as depo-provera (medroxy-progestrone acetate) lowers the testosterone levels in the human body and has been used with some success in sexually deviant men. The medication may raise their threshold for sexually acting out, increase their capacity for handling frustration, and decrease the frequency of erotic and compulsive sexual fantasizing. The effectiveness of such anti-androgenic medication provides additional support to the existence of hormone abnormalities in some types of child sexual molesters. Though sexual behavior can be influenced by changes in the male sex hormone, abnormal levels of this hormone cannot explain why certain individuals find children sexually arousing. Cyproterone acetate (Androcur) has been used with positive results but is not currently available in the United States.

[44]  Q. Regstein and P. Reich, "Pedophilia Occurring After the Onset of Cognitive Impairment," *Journal of Nervous and Mental Disease* 166 (1978), 794-798.

[45]  Lothstein, Cassens, and Ford in their "Electrical Activity Mapping and Neuropsychological Dysfunction in Deviant Sexual Behavior," *The Journal of Neuropsychiatry and Clinical Neurosciences* 49 (1990), using electrical activity mapping techniques and neuropsychological testing, found that the frontal and temporal parts of the brain are dysfunctional in pedophiles and in other paraphiles. Damage to the frontal part of the brain leads to disinhibition, poor judgment, anxiety, low frustration tolerance, and impulsivity. Damage to the temporal parts of the brain may lead to deviant fantasizing, compulsive thinking about sexuality, and hypersexuality. These findings suggest that pedophiles might have a brain disease which leads to deviant sexual behavior. Again, this type of research cannot yet answer why an individual's sexual pathology takes a specific form.

[46]  See, e.g., D. Richard Laws, ed., *Relapse, Prevention With Sex Offenders*, New York: The Guilford Press, 1989; Gerald O'Collins, *The Second Journey: Spiritual Awareness and the Mid-Life Crisis*, New York: Paulist Press, 1978; and Janice Keller Phelps and Alan E. Nourse, *The Hidden Addiction And How To Get Free*, Boston: Little, Brown and Co., 1986.

[47]  Patrick Carnes, *Out of the Shadows: Understanding Sexual Addiction*, Minneapolis: CompCare Publications, 1983. We will follow Carnes' treatment of sexual addiction in this section.

[48]  M. MacAuliffe and R. MacAuliffe, *The Essentials of Chemical Dependency*, Minneapolis: American Chemical Dependency Society, 1975.

[49]  See esp. 136-137 of Carnes.

## Chapter Three

[1]  John C. Dwyer, *Human Sexuality: A Christian View*, Kansas City: Sheed and Ward, 1987, 106-107.

[2]  Vincent J. Genovesi, *In Pursuit of Love*, Wilmington: Michael Glazier, 1987, esp. 192-203.

[3]  Ibid., 192.

[4] John T. Noonan, Jr., raises questions about this assertion, citing doubts from earlier times in *Contraception: A History of Its Treatment by the Catholic Theologians and Canonists*, New York: Mentor-Omega Books, 1967, Passim).

[5] This is resolution n 15, cited in John T. Noonan, Jr., ibid., 486-487.

[6] Cited in Odile M. Liebard, ed., *Official Catholic Teachings*, vol. 4, *Love and Sexuality*, Wilmington: McGrath Publishing Co., 1978, 23-70; quotation in the section "The Church's Teaching" (p 41).

[7] Ibid., 41-42.

[8] See esp. nn 47-52 of *Gaudium et Spes*. Here again, we will follow the presentation of these points as presented by Vincent Genovesi in *In Pursuit of Love*, 196-199.

[9] Vincent J. Genovesi, op. cit., 197. See also John T. Noonan, Jr., "Contraception and the Council," *Commonweal* 83 (1966), 657-659. In addition, see note 168 in Walter M. Abbott's text of *The Documents of Vatican II*, p 254.

[10] *The Digest* or *Pandects of Justinian*, Book I, t. 1, n. 1-4.

[11] In *IV Sent.* d. 33, q. 1, a, 1 ad 4.

[12] We will follow here the treatment of this subject given in *Absolutes in Moral Theology?*, Charles E. Curran, ed., Washington, Corpus Books, 1968, 116-119.

[13] In *V Ethic.*, lect. 12.

[14] For example, *Summa Theologiae* I-II, q. 90, a. 1, ob. 3; q. 96, a. 5, ob. 3; q. 97, a. 2; II-II, q. 57, a. 3, ob. 1 and in corp.

[15] *S.T.* I-II, q. 95, a. 4.

[16] *S.T.* II-II, q. 57, a.3.

[17] See, e.g., H. Noldin et. al., *Summa Theologiae Moralis: De Castitate*, 36th ed., Oeniponte: F. Rauch, 1958, 21-43.

[18] Charles E. Curran, "Absolute Norms and Medical Ethics" in *Absolutes in Moral Theology?*, op. cit., 119. See also "A Reformulation of Thomistic Natural Law Theory" by Germain Grisez in *Sexuality: Theological Voices*, ed., Kevin T. McMahon, Braintree: The Pope John Center, 1987, 3-37.

[19] Vincent J. Genovesi, op. cit., 198. See also *Health and Medicine in the Catholic Tradition*, Richard A. McCormick, New York: Crossroad, 1984, 96.

[20] Ibid., 199.

[21] In Abbott's edition, n 173, 256.

[22] Cited in Genovesi, op. cit., 200.

[23] See Odile M. Liebard, ed., *Official Catholic Teachings*, vol. 4, *Love and Sexuality*, Wilmington: McGrath Publishing Co., 1978, n 290, 290.

[24] Richard A. McCormick, "Notes on Moral Theology," *Theological Studies* 29 (1968), 726.

[25] *Humanae Vitae*, n 11.

[26] See John Mahoney, "The Impact of Humanae Vitae," *The Making of Moral Theology*, Oxford: Clarendon Press, 1987, 259-271.

[27] See *L'Osservatore Romano*, 6 August 1968, 1-2; and 15 August 1968, 1.

[28] Ibid., 8 August 1968, 1.

[29] Cited in John Mahoney, op. cit., 271. See also Leo Pyle, ed., *The Pill and Birth Regulation*, New York, Darton, Longman and Todd, 1964, 104.

[30] "The Moral Norms of Humanae Vitae," *Origins* 18 (1989), 630-632.

[31] See B. Sesboue, "A Propos de las Reception de Humanae Vitae," *Nouvelle Revue Theologique*, XCIII (1971), 36-362.) See also Gerald D. Coleman, "Marriage: The Vision of Humanae Vitae," *Thought* 58 (1983), 18-34.

[32] See John Mahoney, op. cit., 283-284.

[33] Cited in ibid., 284.

[34] Ibid., 285.

[35] Ibid., 286.
[36] Karl Rahner, "The Problem of Genetic Manipulation," *Theological Investigations* 9 (1972) 238-243; 251.
[37] See Mahoney, op. cit., 287.
[38] In 1978, e.g., Pope Paul said in a homily at St. Peter's in Rome on the Feast of Saints Peter and Paul that *Humanae Vitae* takes on a "new and more urgent relevance… because of the attacks inflicted by civil legislation on the indissoluble sanctity of the marriage bond."
[39] While the Catholic tradition has often been criticized for overly stressing procreation as the first goal of marital intercourse, there is some tendency today to make mutual fidelity the first goal. On the contrary, as we have seen, the value-emphasis of Pope Paul VI and *Gaudium et Spes* is that both meanings are of equal significance. The language of *Humanae Vitae* is also very striking when it describes conjugal love as *total*, as "a very special form of personal friendship," in which spouses "generously share everything." "Whoever truly loves his marriage partner loves not only for what he receives, but for the partner's self, rejoicing that he can enrich his partner with the gift of himself." (n 9) In addition, *Humanae Vitae* addresses the duty not of "procreation" but of "responsible parenthood."
[40] See William E. May, *Human Existence, Medicine, and Ethics,* Chicago: Franciscan Herald Press, 1977, 39-46.
[41] Andrew M. Greeley, William C. McCready, Kathleen McCourt, *Catholic Schools in a Declining Church,* National Opinion Research Center, Kansas City: Sheed and Ward, Inc., 1976. See also Andrew M. Greeley, *The American Catholic,* New York: Basic Books, 1977.
[42] Other trends in this thinking point out that a certain malaise had set in because *Humanae Vitae* was one man's (the Pope's) decision at a time when the Church and the Council had adopted a collegial mode of operation.
[43] See Michael Dummett, "The Documents of the Papal Commission on Birth Control," *New Blackfriars* L (1969), 241-250.
[44] *Humanae Vitae,* n 10. See also "A Symposium on Humanae Vitae and the Natural Law," *Louvain Studies* 2 (1969), 211-230; and J. Selling, "Moral Teaching, Traditional Teaching and Humanae Vitae," *Louvain Studies* 7 (1978), 24-44.
[45] See T. C. Potts, "The Arguments of Humanae Vitae," *The Month* XLI (1969), 144-145; and Germain F. Grisez, *Contraception and the Natural Law,* Milwaukee: Bruce Publishing Co., 1954, 76, 90-91.
[46] See numbers 4 and 8 of *Humanae Vitae.*
[47] See L. M. Weber, "Excursus on Humanae Vitae," *Commentary on the Documents of Vatican II,* ed., Herbert Vorgrimler, 5th ed., New York: Herder and Herder, 1969, 397-402.
[48] See L. Dupre, "Toward a Re-Examination of the Catholic Position on Birth Control," *Cross Currents* 14 (1964), 18-20. See also William May, op. cit., 79-86.
[49] St. Thomas had this same vision when he taught that each faculty exists for its own proper end; but each proper end in turn contributes to the unity of the whole person (*Summa Theologiae* I, 65, 3c); the human act thus bears an "incarnate significance"; the body and its operations are fundamentally linked to the self. This indestructibility of the union between love and life is the unchanging value enunciated in *Humanae Vitae.*
[50] *Declaration on Religious Freedom,* n 14.
[51] *Pastoral Constitution on the Church in the Modern World,* n 25.
[52] See Karl Rahner, "On the Theology of the Incarnation," *Theological Investigations,* Baltimore: Helicon Press, 1966, vol. 4, 107.
[53] In forming a good conscience, one should carefully consider the four basic points of (a) one's faith dimension; (b) the effect of one's action on oneself and on others; (c) the

context in which one finds oneself; and (d) the principles which apply in this context which for a Catholic must include the authentic teachings of the Church. In addition, as we saw earlier, there is the necessity to always sustain the critical link between *anamnesis* and *conscientia*.

54 See Josef Pieper, *Prudence*, trans., Richard and Clara Winston, New York: Pantheon Books, 1959.

55 Ladislas Orsy, *The Church: Learning and Teaching*, Wilmington, Delaware: Michael Glazier, 1987, 79-108; and Francis A. Sullivan, *Magisterium*, New York: Paulist Press, 1983, 153-173. See also Carlo Caffara, "Moral Conscience," *Living in Christ*, San Francisco: Ignatius Press, 1981, 107-127.

56 Yves Congar, *Vrai et Fausse Reforme Dans l'Eglise*, Paris: Editiones du Cerf, 1950 (2nd ed., 1968).

57 Joseph A. Komonchak, "The Right to Private and Public Dissent from Specific Pronouncement of the Ordinary Magisterium," *Eglise et Theologie* 9 (1978), 319-343.

58 See John Gallagher, "The Magisterium and Dissent on Moral Questions" in *The Basis for Christian Ethics*, New York: Paulist Press, 1985, esp. 221-237. See also Joseph A. Komonchak, "Ordinary Papal Magisterium and Religious Assent" in *Contraception: Authority and Dissent*, ed., Charles E. Curran, New York: Herder and Herder, 1969, 101-126.

59 United States Bishops, 15 November 1968, *Human Life In Our Day*, "Norms of Licit Theological Dissent." This section goes on to say: "When there is a question of theological dissent from non-infallible doctrine, we must recall that there is always a presumption in favor of the magisterium. Even non-infallible authentic doctrine, though it may admit of development or call for clarification or revision remains binding and carries with it a moral certitude, especially when it is addressed to the universal Church, without ambiguity, in response to urgent questions bound up with faith and crucial to morals. The expression of theological dissent from the magisterium is in order only if the reasons are serious and well-founded, if the manner of the dissent does not question or impugn the teaching authority of the Church and is such as not to give scandal... Even responsible dissent does not excuse one from faithful presentation of the authentic doctrine of the Church when one is performing a pastoral ministry in her name."

60 Congregation for the Doctrine of the Faith, *Instruction on the Ecclesial Vocation of the Theologian*, Vatican City: Libreria Editrice Vaticana, 1990.

61 Archbishop John R. Quinn, "Observations on Doctrinal Congregation's Instruction," *Origins* 20 (1990), 201-205 and Archbishop John R. Quinn, "Dissent: A Pastoral and Doctrinal Problem," *L'Osservatore Romano*, n 40, 1 October 1990, 12 and 14. For a differing interpretation, see Richard A. McCormick and Richard P. McBrien, "Theology As A Public Responsibility," *America* 165 (1991), 184-189, 203-206.

62 *Instruction on the Ecclesial Vocation of the Theologian*, n 23.

63 See Benedict M. Ashley and Kevin D. O'Rourke, *Health Care Ethics*, 2nd ed., St. Louis: Catholic Hospital Association, 1982, 66-69 and 74-76.

64 See Philip S. Keane, "The Objective Moral Order: Reflections on Recent Research," *Theological Studies* XLIV (1982), 260-278.

65 See J. O'Callaghan, "Reflection on Humanae Vitae," *Theology Digest* 16 (1968), 319-328; and Pope Paul VI, "The Ideal Concept of the Christian Life," *L'Osservatore Romano*, 15 August 1968.

66 See J. J. Mulligan, *The Pope and the Theologians*, Emmitsburg, Maryland: Mount St. Mary's Seminary Press, 1968, 91-103. This point was also emphasized in a letter from Cardinal Villot to Cardinal Terence Cooke: "...Couples must be assisted with Christian understanding and patient care, so that, with divine help, they may successfully face whatever difficulties may arise from physical, economic, psychological and social

conditions, or from trying circumstances" (n 348/856, 18 May 1978).

67 John C. Ford and Germain Grisez, "Contraception and the Infallibility of the Ordinary Magisterium," *Theological Studies* 39 (1978), 258-312; and Joseph A. Komonchak, "Humanae Vitae and its Reception: Ecclesiological Reflections," *Theological Studies* 39 (1978), 221-257.

68 John C. Ford and Gerald Kelly, *Contemporary Moral Theology 2: Marriage Questions*, Westminster, Maryland: Newman Press, 1964, 263-271. In using this expression, they did not intend to create a new category between infallibility and non-infallibility. Rather, by the words "at least definable doctrine" they intended to embrace the judgments of various groups of theologians. One group held that Pius XI defined the doctrine *ex cathedra* in *Casti Connubii*; a second group held that he only reaffirmed there a teaching already proposed infallibly by the ordinary magisterium; a third group made various comments which seemed compatible with the view that the received teaching could be defined.

69 In this presentation, we will follow closely the argument as presented by Ford and Grisez in their *Theological Studies* article.

70 Ford and Kelly, op. cit., 258.

71 John T. Noonan, Jr., *Contraception: A History of Its Treatment by the Catholic Theologians and Canonists*, Cambridge: Harvard University Press, 1965, 6.

72 Op. cit., 278.

73 Op. cit., 286.

74 Cited in "Contraception and the Infallibility of the Ordinary Magisterium," 302-303.

75 Op. cit., 306.

76 Pope Pius XII, *Humani generis, Acta Apostolica Sedis* 42 (1950), 568.

77 *DS* 3011, cited in Komonchak, 239. The direct force of this statement was *Tuas libenter*, in which Pius IX had taught that the submission of divine faith could not be limited simply to matters expressly defined in ecumenical councils or in papal decrees, "but must be extended also to those matters which are handed down by the ordinary magisterium of the whole Church throughout the world and are therefore unanimously and constantly considered by Catholic theologians to belong to the faith." (*DS* 3011)

78 Cited in Komonchak, 242.

79 Ibid., 243.

80 Ibid., 250. Komonchak reaches this conclusion in this fashion (249-250): "Apart from the Roman Catechism, none of the documents to which Pope Paul referred directly in these passages dates from before *Casti Connubii*, and none of them refers to the universal ordinary magisterium. It may be, of course, that Hans Kung was correct in maintaining that a belief that the condemnation of contraception was taught by the universal ordinary magisterium led Pope Paul to conclude that the teaching could not be changed. It may be true, but the Pope certainly does not say this in *Humanae Vitae* or (as far as I know) anywhere else; and his surprisingly modest references to previous magisterial pronouncements lend no support to Kung's theory.

"In the episcopal statements issued in response to *Humanae Vitae* I have found only eleven references to the Church's traditional condemnation. Three of these are rather general, the others more specific. Of the eleven references, nine are found in documents which Selling interprets as displaying a "clear acceptance" of *Humanae Vitae*; one (West Germany) appears in a document which "mitigates" the encyclical's teaching, and the other (Brazil) in a document Selling regards as "unclear." None of the eleven references invokes the thesis that the tradition is infallible. Many of the episcopal statements, of course, specifically say that *Humanae Vitae* is "authoritative," not infallible, teaching, and the frequent discussions of the rights and responsibilities of conscience do not favor the thesis."

[81] See L. Janssen's, "Moral Problems Involved in Responsible Parenthood," *Louvain Studies*, 1 (1966), 3-18.

**Chapter Four**

[1] Evelyn Eaton Whitehead and James D. Whitehead, *A Sense of Sexuality*, New York: Doubleday, 1989.
[2] Ibid., 29. We will follow here the treatment of this subject by the Whiteheads.
[3] Ibid., 32.
[4] See Morton Kelsey and Barbara Kelsey, *Sacrament of Sexuality: The Spirituality and Psychology of Sex*, New York: Amity House, 1986; Sam Keen, *The Passionate Life*, San Francisco: Harper and Row, 1983; and Lillian Rubin, *Intimate Strangers: Women and Men Together*, San Francisco: Harper and Row, 1983.
[5] Op. cit., 47.
[6] Romans 7:23-24.
[7] Op. cit., 48.
[8] Ibid., 48.
[9] Ibid., 50.
[10] Ibid., 50-51.
[11] Ibid., 51-52.
[12] See James Nelson, *Between Two Gardens: Reflections on Sexuality and Religious Experience*, New York: Pilgrim Press, 1983.
[13] Pope Paul VI, "The Family, A School of Holiness," *The Teachings of Pope Paul VI*, Washington, D.C.: United States Catholic Conference, 1971, 168, n 6.
[14] Pope John Paul II, "The Reality of Christian Marriage As Transfigured by the New Covenant," *L'Osservatore Romano*, 15 November 1982, 7, n 6.
[15] Lisa Sowle Cahill, *Between the Sexes: Foundations for a Christian Ethics of Sexuality*, Philadelphia: Fortress Press, 1985. See also her *Women and Sexuality*, New York: Paulist Press, 1992.
[16] Ibid. We will follow closely here Cahill's presentation, 91 ff.
[17] Ibid., 91.
[18] In outlining the various physiological factors, we will follow here mainly the presentation of Herant A. Katchadourian, Donald T. Lunde and Robert Trotter, *Fundamentals of Human Sexuality: Brief Edition*, 3rd ed., New York: Holt Rinehart and Winston, 1979. We will also depend heavily upon Earl E. Shelp, ed., *Sexuality and Medicine*, vols. I and II, Dordrecht: D. Reidel Publishing Co., 1987; Thomas J. O'Donnell, *Medicine and Christian Morality*, 2nd ed., New York: Alba House, 1991; and Susan Harlap, Kathryn Kost and Jacqueline Darroch Forrest, *Preventing Pregnancy, Protecting Health: A New Look at Birth Control Choices in the United States*, New York: The Alan Guttmacher Institute, 1991.
[19] Op. cit., 42.
[20] Ibid., 43.
[21] Ibid., 45.
[22] Ibid., 46.
[23] Ibid., 47.
[24] Reports of multiple orgasm in men have been rare, but there is recent evidence that men can learn to have multiple orgasms, the first one or several including all of the physiological reactions of orgasm except ejaculation.
[25] The first thrust during orgasm propels the semen out with some force. The fluid can sometimes be projected some distance.

[26] Physiologically a man cannot urinate with a fully erect penis because the urinary sphincter closes reflexively during full erection in order to prevent the mixing of urine and semen.

[27] See "Chemical May Draw Sperm to Egg," *New York Times*, 2 April 1991, C3. See also Meredith F. Small, "Sperm Wars," *Discover* 14 (July 1991), 48-53.

[28] See Tabitha M. Powledge, "Windows On the Womb," *Psychology Today* 4 (1983), 37-42.

[29] A phenomenon known as "sympathetic pregnancy" is sometimes seen in the husbands of pregnant women. These husbands become nauseated and vomit along with their wives. The cause of this condition is implied in its name.

[30] For a description of these various pregnancy tests, see Katchadourian, Lunde, and Trotter, op. cit., 101.

[31] In generally accepted medical terms, the ovum becomes an embryo one week after fertilization. The embryo becomes a fetus after the eighth week of pregnancy.

[32] In rare instances the tail fails to regress, and there are documented cases of human infants born with tails. The tails are usually removed surgically at an early age, but in one case recorded in the medical literature a twelve year old boy had a tail nine inches long.

[32] An overanxious woman, especially one who has not previously had a child, may misinterpret these first contractions and rush to the hospital only to be told that she is experiencing false labor.

[33] During this time the physician examines the mother and child carefully and sews up any tear that may have occurred in the perineum (the skin and deeper tissues between the openings of the vagina and anus). The episiotomy incision, if there has been one, is also sewn up at this time. An episiotomy is an incision of the perineum that is sometimes performed to ease the passage of the baby's head. These "stitches" may cause itching and discomfort for several days, but they usually heal with no complications.

[34] Susan Harlap, Kathryn Kost and Jacqueline Darroch Forrest, *Preventing Pregnancy, Protecting Health: A New Look at Birth Control Choices in the United States*, New York: The Alan Guttmacher Institute, 1991.

[35] Op. cit., 134.

[36] Katchadourian, Lunde and Trotter offer specific instructions on the proper use of the condom. Op. cit., 133-134.

[37] For an important discussion of the meaning of "contraceptive intention" in *Humanae Vitae*, see John Tuohey, "Methodology or Ideology: The Condom and a Consistent Sexual Ethic," *Louvain Studies* 15 (1990), 53-69.

[38] For a discussion of the serious side effects of the pill, see Katchadourian, Lunde and Trotter, op. cit., 126-127.

[39] Benedict M. Ashley and Kevin D. O'Rourke, *Health Care Ethics*, 2nd edition, St. Louis: The Catholic Health Association of the United States, 1982, 293. See Report of the British Bishops, "Use of the 'Morning-After Pill' in Cases of Rape," *Origins* 15 (1986), 634-638; and "Way is Cleared for DES Damage Claims," *The New York Times*, 5 April 1989, A17.

[40] "RU-486: The 'Abortion Pill,'" *Origins* 21 (1991), 28-33. We will follow here the presentation of Professor Herranz's article.

[41] Cardinal Alfonso Lopes Trujillo, president of the Pontifical Council for the Family issued the following letter to the Presidents of the Episcopal Conferences on 8 April 1991: "In the light of the mandate given by the Holy Father to the Pontifical Council for the Family... to support and coordinate initiatives for protecting human life from conception, we bring the following matter to your attention. A new serious threat to human life is the abortion pill RU-486. Therefore, we are enclosing a technically accurate and up-to-date study of this method of abortion prepared by Professor Gonzalo Herranz, Professor of Bioethics at the University of Navarra, Pamplona, Spain. The precise information in this report will be of use in the struggle to resist the introduction of the abortion pill RU-486 into your

country. It would also be useful to provide copies for pro-life leaders and groups, bioethics centers and Catholic medical organizations and hospitals." (Pontificium Consilium Pro Familia, n 285/89).

42 See n 22 of Professor Herranz's report.

43 Ibid., n 29.

44 Ibid., n 32. See also A. Lumann, G. Teutsch and D. Philibert, "RU-486," *Scientific American* 262 (1990), 42-48; Etienne-Emile Baulieu, "Contragestion and Other Clinical Applications of RU-486, and Antiprogesterone at the Receptor," *Science* 24 (1989), 1351-1357; "A French Doctor Defends RU-486, His Embattled 'Abortion Pill,'" *People Magazine* 33 (1990), 121-123; Carol Kahn, "A Drug That Prevents Life," 5 *Longevity* 14 (1990), 20-22; and "The Pill of Choice?" *Science* 245 (1989), 1319-1324.

45 See pp. 73-74 of Katchadourian, Lunde and Trotter, op. cit..

46 *Gaudium et Spes*, n 50.

47 Pope John Paul II, "Natural Family Planning," *Origins* 20 (1991), 507-508.

48 Ibid., n 5.

49 Pope John Paul II, *Familiaris Consortio*, n 32, *Origins* 11 (1981), 437-468.

50 See G. E. M. Anscombe, "You Can Have Sex Without Children: Christianity and the New Order," in *Ethics, Religion and Politics*, vol. 3, Minneapolis: University of Minnesota Press, 1981, 84. See also Bryan J. Shanley, "The Moral Difference Between Natural Family Planning and Contraception," *Linacre Quarterly* 39 (1987), 50-60. We will rely here in our treatment on Shanley's presentation.

51 G.E.M. Anscombe, *Contraception and Chastity*, London: The Catholic Truth Society, 1977, 17-18.

52 See J. Teichman, "Intention and Sex," in *Intention and Intentionality*, ed., C. Diamond and J. Teichman, Brighton: Harvester Press, 1979, 147-161.

53 Pope John Paul II, Karol Wojtyla, *Love and Responsibility*, translated., H. T. Willetts, New York: Farrar, Strauss, Giroux, 1981, 41.

54 Ibid., 228.

55 John Paul II, *Familiaris Consortio*, op. cit., n 32.

56 John Paul II, *Reflections on Humanae Vitae*, Boston: St. Paul Editions, 1984, 33-34.

57 Ibid., 64.

58 See Elsie B. Martinez, "The Ovulation Method of Family Planning," *America* 144 (1981), 277-279.

59 Thomas W. Hilgers, M.D., "The Ovulation Method: Ten Years of Research," *Linacre Quarterly* 35 (1978), 383-387. See also Vincent J. Genovesi, *In Pursuit of Love*, op. cit., 230-233.

60 See V.J. Genovesi, op. cit., 231-232.

61 See Benedict M. Ashley and Kevin D. O'Rourke, *Health Care Ethics: A Theological Analysis*, St. Louis: The Catholic Hospital Association, 1978, 278. See also Ronald Lawler, Joseph Boyle and William E. May, *Catholic Sexual Ethics*, Huntington: Our Sunday Visitor, 1985, 167-170.

## Chapter Five

1 Cited in Arno Karlen, *Sexuality and Homosexuality*, New York: W. W. Norton, Co., Inc., 1981, 255.

2 Congregation for the Doctrine of the Faith, *Letter to the Bishops of the Catholic Church on the Pastoral Care of Homosexual Persons*, 1 October 1986, printed in the U.S.A. by the Daughters of Saint Paul under the title *On the Pastoral Care of Homosexual Persons*, 1986.

3 Ibid., n 1.

[4] John Deedy interviews Reverend Richard A. McCormick, "Overview Exclusive," The Thomas More Association, 1991.

[5] James T. Hanigan, *Homosexuality: The Test Case for Christian Sexual Ethics*, New York: Paulist Press, 1988.

[6] John E. Fortunato, *Embracing the Exile*, New York: The Seabury Press, 1982, 17.

[7] Sigmund Freud, "Letter to an American Mother," (1935) reprinted in Ronald Bayer, *Homosexuality and American Psychiatry*, Princeton: Princeton University Press, 1987, 27.

[8] Sigmund Freud, quoted in *Die Zeit*, Vienna, 27 October 1903, 5. In 1930 Freud signed an appeal to the German Reichstag to repeal that part of the German penal code that since 1871 had made homosexual relations a crime. This petition stated, in part: "Homosexuality has been present throughout history and among all peoples... Their sexual orientation is just as inherent to them as that of heterosexuals. The state has no valid interest in attempting to motivate heterosexual intercourse or marriage on the part of homosexuals, for this would perforce lead to unhappiness for their partners, and it is quite likely that homosexuality would reappear in one of the ensuing generations... This law represents an extreme violation of human rights, because it denies homosexuals their very sexuality even though the interests of third parties are not encroached upon... Homosexuals have the same civil duties to fulfill as everyone else." Cited in Richard A. Isay, *Being Homosexual*, New York: Avon Books, 1989, 135-136.

[9] Isadore Rubin, "Homosexuality," Siecus: Discussion Guide, No. 2, New York: 1965, 1.

[10] Judd Marmon, ed., *Sexual Inversion*, New York: Basic Books, 1965, 4.

[11] John C. Dwyer, *Human Sexuality: A Christian View*, Kansas City: Sheed and Ward, 1987, 64.

[12] William F. Kraft, "Homosexuality and Religious Life," *Review for Religious* 40 (1981), 371.

[13] Warren T. Reich, ed., *Encyclopedia of Bioethics*, New York: The Free Press, vol. 2, 1978, 671. See also *Encyclopledia of Homosexuality*, ed., Wayne R. Dynes, Hamden: Garland Publishing, 1992.

[14] This "distinction" is a highly debated one among psychologists. Some schools of thought maintain that it is impossible for any person to have a profound sense of his or her own sexual orientation without having had some genital experience. This would be applicable to both the heterosexual and homosexual orientation. Still others claim that "actual sexual fulfillment of this desire" is not absolutely necessary for a self-awareness of one's sexual orientation.

[15] James D. Whitehead and Evelyn Eaton Whitehead, "Three Passages of Maturity" in *A Challenge to Love*, ed., Robert Nugent, New York: Crossroad, 1983, 174-188.

[16] Ibid., 175.

[17] Douglas C. Kimmel, "Adult Development and Aging: A Gay Perspective," *Journal of Social Issues* 34 (1978), 113-130.

[18] Cited in "Three Passages of Maturity." op. cit., 179.

[19] Ibid., 181.

[20] Ibid., 185.

[21] See Xavier John Seubert, "The Sacramentality of Metaphors: Reflections on Homosexuality," *Cross Currents* 18 (1991), 52-68.

[22] United States Catholic Conference, *Human Sexuality*, Washington, D.C.: United States Catholic Conference, Inc., 1990, 54.

[23] The U.S.C.C. document *Human Sexuality* states on page 56: "Educationally, homosexuality cannot and ought not to be skirted or ignored. The topic 'must be faced in all objectivity by the pupil and educator when the case presents itself.' First and foremost, we support modeling and teaching respect for every human person, regardless of sexual

orientation. Second, a parent or teacher must also present clearly and delicately the unambiguous moral norms of the Christian tradition regarding homosexual genital activity, appropriately geared to the age level and maturity of the learner. Finally, parents and other educators must remain open to the possibility that a particular person, whether adolescent or adult, may be struggling to accept his or her own homosexual orientation. The distinction between being homosexual and doing homosexual genital actions, while not always clear and convincing, is a helpful and important one when dealing with the complex issue of homosexuality, particularly in the educational and pastoral arena."

[24] See Robert T. Francoeur, *Becoming a Sexual Person*, New York: John Wiley and Sons, 1982, 513-516; and Michael R. Peterson, "Psychological Aspects of Human Sexual Behaviors," in *Human Sexuality and Personhood*, St. Louis: Pope John XXIII Medical-Moral Research and Education Center, 1981, 86-110; and James P. Hanigan, op. cit., 30.

[25] Judd Marmor, "Homosexuality," *Encyclopedia Americana*, vol. 14, 1990, 334. In the 1987 edition of the *New Catholic Encyclopedia*, John F. Harvey states that 4% of males are exclusively homosexual in behavior and 1% of females are exclusively homosexual in behavior (vol. 7, 116-117).

[26] J. Gordon Melton, *The Churches Speak Out: Homosexuality*, Detroit: Gale Research, Inc., 1991, 30.

[27] We will follow here Hanigan's treatment, 19-27.

[28] James P. Hanigan, op. cit., 20.

[29] Ibid., 20-21.

[30] See James P. Hanigan, *Martin Luther King, Jr. and the Foundations of Nonviolence*, Lanham: University Press of America, 1984, 162-163.

[31] James P. Hanigan, op. cit., 22-23. See also Edward A. Malloy, *Homosexuality and the Christian Way of Life*, Washington, D.C.: University Press of America, 1981, 106-136. Here Fr. Malloy indicates the variety of social patterns in the homosexual way of life.

[32] Arno Karlen, *Sexuality and Homosexuality*, New York: W. W. Norton Co., Inc., 1971. We will follow here the historical perspective in Karlen's work.

[33] Ibid., 7.

[34] Ibid., 26.

[35] Ibid., 33.

[36] Ibid. See also Robin Scroggs, *The New Testament and Homosexuality*, Philadelphia: Fortress Press, 1983, 17-65. Scroggs comes to the same general conclusions on this subject as does Karlen.

[37] Cited in Karlen, 38.

[38] Ibid., 38.

[39] Ibid., 122-123.

[40] Ibid., 125.

[41] Ibid., 126.

[42] Ibid.

[43] Ibid., 130.

[44] Ibid., 135.

[45] Ibid., 139.

[46] Ibid., 139.

[47] Ibid., 161.

[48] Ibid., 182.

[49] Ibid., 184.

[50] Cited in Karlen, 185-186.

[51] Cited in Karlen, 187.

[52] Cited in Karlen, 190.

[53] Cited in Karlen, 190-191.

[54] Cited in Karlen, 191.
[55] Cited in Karlen, 195.
[56] Karlen, 232.
[57] Ibid., 232.
[58] Ibid., 234.
[59] Cited in Karlen, 255.
[60] Cited in Karlen, 256.
[61] Sheldon Kranz, ed., *The H Persuasion*, New York: Definition Press, 1981.
[62] In the 1981 study *Sexual Preference: Its Development in Men and Women* by Bell, Weinberg and Hammersmith, exhaustive study demonstrated that no master factor was found for homosexuals: most homosexual people came from normal households and had conventional relationships with parents, siblings and (except where feminine males were concerned) peers. This conclusion had also been demonstrated in *Homosexualities: A Study of Diversity Among Men and Women* by Bell and Weinberg, New York: Simon and Schuster, 1978. See also Marshall Kirk and Hunter Madsen, *After the Ball*, New York: Doubleday, 1989.
[63] See Bruce Hilton, *Can Homophobia Be Cured: Wrestling with Questions That Challenge the Church*, Nashville: Abingdon Press, 1992. See also Craig O'Neill and Kathleen Ritter, *Coming Out Within*, San Francisco: Harper, 1992.
[64] See J. DeCecco, "Homosexuality's Brief Recovery: From Sickness to Health and Back Again," *The Journal of Sex Research* 23 (1987), 106-129; and W. Ricketts, "Biological Research On Homosexuality: Ansell's Cow or Occam's Razor?" *Journal of Homosexuality* 9, (1984), 65-93. We will rely here on the rather good analysis of the origins of homosexuality found in the *Minority Report of the Special Committee on Human Sexuality* that was prepared for the 203rd General Assembly of the Presbyterian Church in the United States in 1991.
[65] See J. Carrier, "Homosexual Behavior in Cross-Cultural Perspective" in J. Marmor, ed., *Homosexual Behavior: A Modern Appraisal*, New York: Basic Books, 1980, 100-122. See also B. Risman and P. Schwartz, "Sociological Research on Male and Female Homosexuality," *Annual Review of Sociology* 14 (1988), 125-147.
[66] D. Greenberg, *The Construction of Homosexuality*, Chicago: University of Chicago Press, 1988.
[67] The *Minority Report* of the Presbyterian Church points out on p 23 (footnote 5): "A number of factors plague all of the research into the causes of homosexuality. Perhaps the biggest problem is the diversity of persons to whom this description is applied. Persons describing themselves as homosexual range from the male who cannot remember a time when he was not 'different' and attracted to other men, to the female who embraces lesbianism as an adult after years of abusive relationships with men. Almost all of the existing research deals with very heterogeneous groups of people. Another major problem has been that almost all of the research has been with male homosexuals (gays); very little in comparison has been done with lesbians."
[68] For example, F. Kallman, "Comparative Twin Study on the Generic Aspects of Male Homosexuality," *Journal of Nervous and Mental Disease* 115 (1952), 137-159. See also *Twins and Homosexuality*, ed., Geoff Puterbaugh, Hamden: Garland Publishing, 1992.
[69] For example, R. Green in "The Imputability of (Homo)sexual Orientation: Behavioral Science in Vocations for a Constitutional (Legal) Analysis," *The Journal of Psychiatry and Law* 16 (1988), 537-575, concludes that the closer the genetic link between persons, the greater the likelihood of similar sexual orientation. However, B. Eckert, T. Bouchard, J. Bohlen and L. Heston in "Homosexuality in Monozygotic Twins Reared Apart," *British Journal of Psychiatry* 148 (1986), 421-425, produced evidence suggesting that

there is no genetic factor operative in lesbianism, even though genetics have some mixed role in male homosexuality.

[70] J. Money, "Genetic and Chromosomal Aspects of Homosexual Etiology" in J. Marmor, ed., *Homosexual Behavior: A Modern Reappraisal*, New York: Basic Books, 59-74; citation at 69-70. A September 1991 study was released by a biologist at San Diego's Salk Institute for Biological Studies which concludes that one tiny region in the brain of homosexual men was more like that in women than in heterosexual men: see "Are Gay Men Born That Way?" *Time* 138 (1991), 60-61. See also Marcia Barinaga, "Is Homosexuality Biological?" *Science* 253 (1991), 956-957. See also Michael Bailey and Richard Pillard, "Are Some People Born Gay?" *New York Times*, 17 December 1991, op. ed. and "Gay Men in Twin Study," ibid.

[71] See L. Ellis and A. Ames, "Neurohormonal Functioning and Sexual Orientation: A Theory of Homosexuality-Heterosexuality," *Psychological Bulletin* 101 (1987), 233-258.

[72] For example, R. Green, op. cit..

[73] See J. Lindesay, "Laterality Shift in Homosexual Men," *Neuropsychologia* 25 (1987), 965-969; and M. Annett, "Comments on Lindesay: Laterality Shift in Homosexual Men," *Neuropsychologia* 26 (1988), 341-343.

[74] See R. Green, op. cit.. However, the findings of D. Swaab and M. Hofmann in "Sexual Differentiation of the Human Hypothalamus: Ontogeny of the Sexually Dimorphic Nucleus of the Preoppic Area," *Developmental Brain Research* 44 (1988), 314-318 refuted the notion that the "sexually dimorphic nucleus of the hypothalamus" of male homosexual and heterosexual brains are structurally different.

[75] See, e.g., J. Harry, *Gay Children Grown Up: Gender Culture and Gender Deviants*, New York: Praeger Books, 1982.

[76] G. Rekers, S. Mead, A. Rosen and S. Brigham in "Family Correlates of Male Childhood Gender Disturbance," *The Journal of Genetic Psychology* 142 (1983), 31-42, report that "Significantly fewer male role models were found in the family backgrounds of the severely gender-disturbed boys" (p 31), and that there were more emotional problems in the families of the most disturbed boys.

[77] Cited in L. Ellis and A. Ames, op. cit. and R. Green, op. cit..

[78] The *Minority Report* of the Presbyterian Church, footnote 22 on p 26 cites John Money as explicitly concluding, "(T)here is no human evidence that prenatal hormonalization alone, independently of postnatal history, inexorably preordains... [homosexuality]. Rather, neonatal antecedents may facilitate a homosexual... orientation, provided the postnatal determinants in the social and communicational history are also facilitative." (In "Sin, Sickness, or Status? Homosexual Gender Identity and Psychoneuroendocrinology," *American Psychologists* 42 (1987), 384-399). This footnote in the *Minority Report* concludes, "In other words, prenatal influences may provide a 'push' in the direction of homosexuality, but there is no conclusive evidence that this push is powerful enough to be considered determinative, and there is no evidence that this push is present for all homosexuals."

[79] See, e.g., W. Ricketts, op. cit., 71-76 and R. Green, op. cit., 543-545.

[80] See, e.g., I. Bieber, H. Dain, P. Vince, M. Drellich, H. Grand, R. Gundlach, M. Kremer, A. Rifin, C. Wilber and T. Bieber, *Homosexuality: A Psychoanalytic Study*, New York: Basic Books, 1962. Different theorists emphasize either the boy-mother or boy-father relationship and postulate different dynamics at work.

[81] See C. Wolff, *Love Between Women*, New York: Harper and Row, 1971.

[82] See M. Siegelman, "Kinsey and Others Quote Empirical Input" in L. Diamant, ed., *Male and Female Homosexuality: Psychological Approaches*, Washington: Hemisphere Books, 1987, 33-80.

[83] For example, proponents of the prenatal hormone hypothesis would argue that all the research documenting problematic relations between pre-homosexual boys and their fathers, rather than proving that rejecting fathers cause homosexuality, instead reflects the tendencies for fathers to reject their gender-inappropriate sons.

[84] For example, A. Bell, M. Weinberg and S. Hammersmith, *Sexual Preference: Its Development in Men and Women*, Bloomington: Indiana University Press, 1981.

[85] See, e.g., M. Storms, "A Theory of Erotic Orientation Development," *Psychological Review* 88 (1981), 340-353.

[86] For an excellent overview of various theories regarding causes of homosexuality, see John F. Harvey, "Some Recent Theories Concerning the Origins of Homosexuality," *The Homosexual Person*, San Francisco: Ignatius Press, 1987, 37-63. See also John C. Dwyer, "The Causes of Homosexuality," *Human Sexuality: A Christian View*, op. cit., 67-69.

[87] See C. Socarides, *Homosexuality*, New York: Jasnon Aronson Publishers, 1978.

[88] See H. Adams and E. Sturgis, "Status of Behavioral Reorientation Techniques in the Modification of Homosexuality: A Review," *Psychological Bulletin* 84 (1977). 1171-1188; and W. Masters and V. Johnson, *Homosexuality In Perspective*, Boston: Little, Brown and Co., 1979.

[89] See E. Pattison and M. Pattison, "Ex-Gays: Religiously Mediated Change in Homosexuals," *American Journal of Psychiatry* 137 (1980), 1553-1562. See also Gerald D. Coleman, "Turning Gays 'Straight'?" *Church* 7 (1991), 44-46.

[90] R. Green, op. cit., 569.

[91] See J. Yamamoto, ed., *The Crisis of Homosexuality*, Wheaton: Christianity Today/Victor Books, 1990.

[92] See Vincent J. Genovesi, op. cit., 252.

[93] See James J. Gill, "Homosexuality Today," *Human Development* 3 (1980), 16-25. Also, Richard Woods, *Another Kind of Love*, Chicago: Thomas More Press, 1977.

[94] See, e.g., M. Saghir and E. Robbins, *Male and Female Homosexuality*, Baltimore: Williams and Wilkins Co., 1973; and Michael E. Cavanaugh, "Homosexuality," in *Make Your Tomorrows Better*. We will rely here on Cavanaugh's treatment.

[95] This point is also emphasized by Alan P. Bell and Martin S. Weinberg in *Homosexualities*, New York: Simon and Schuster, 1978.

[96] A. Kinsey, W. Pomeroy and C. Martin, *Sexual Behavior in the Human Male*, Philadelphia: W. D. Saunders, 1948, 639.

[97] For this assessment, we will rely on the excellent article by Eli Coleman, "Assessment of Sexual Orientation," *Journal of Homosexuality* 14 (1987), 9-24.

[98] See, e.g., M. Shively and J. DeCecco, "Components of Sexual Identity," *Journal of Homosexuality* 3 (1977), 41-48.

[99] F. Klein, "Are You Sure You're Homosexual? or Heterosexual? or Even Bisexual?" *Forum Magazine* 7 (1980), 41-45; F. Klein and T. Wolf, *Bisexualities: Theory and Research*, New York: Haworth Press, 1985; and F. Klein, B. Sepekoff and T. Wolf, "Sexual Orientation: A Multi-Variate Dynamic Process," *Journal of Homosexuality* 11 (1985), 35-49.

[100] A. Bell and M. Weinberg, *Homosexualities*, op. cit., 329. Eli Coleman also concludes his article by stating, "The labels homosexual, bisexual and heterosexual seem meaningless when one understands the complexity of sexual orientation. The words 'homosexual' and 'heterosexual' seem the most limiting. If labels are used, the phrases 'predominantly homosexual' or 'predominantly heterosexual' are probably more accurate..." (p 23).

[101] *Diagnostic and Statistical Manual*, 3rd ed., Washington, D.C.: American Psychiatric Association, 1980, 281.

[102] Ibid., 282.

[103] See John F. Harvey, "Changes in Nomenclature and Their Probable Effect" in J. R.

Cavanaugh, *Counseling the Homosexual*, Huntington: Our Sunday Visitor Press, 1977, 30-36; citation at 32.

[104] *Gaudium et Spes*, n 48.

[105] J. Hanigan, op. cit., 45.

[106] *Principles to Guide Confessors in Questions of Homosexuality*, Washington, D.C.: United States Catholic Conference, 1974.

[107] Congregation for the Doctrine of the Faith, *Persona Humana*, Washington, D.C.: United States Catholic Conference, 1976.

[108] U.S.C.B., *To Live in Christ Jesus*, Washington, D.C.: United States Catholic Conference, 1976.

[109] Ibid., 4. For other documents of the magisterium, see John Gallagher, *Homosexuality and the Magisterium: Documents from the Vatican and the U.S. Bishops, 1975-1985*, Maryland: New Ways Ministry, 1986.

[110] Edwin F. Healy, *Moral Guidance*, Chicago: Loyola University Press, 1942; revised by James F. Meara, 1960, 57.

[111] Ibid..

[112] James P. Hanigan, op. cit., 59.

[113] Ibid., 61.

[114] Congregation for the Doctrine of the Faith, *Letter to the Bishops of the Catholic Church on the Pastoral Care of Homosexual Persons*, Boston: Daughters of St. Paul, 1986.

[115] Archbishop John R. Quinn, "Toward an Understanding of the Letter 'On the Pastoral Care of Homosexual Persons,'" *America* 14 (1987), 92-95; 116.

[116] Ibid., 94. In a letter dated 28 January 1987, Cardinal Joseph Ratzinger wrote this to Archbishop Quinn (173/74): "...It had always, naturally, been our hope that the Bishops, upon receipt of the *Letter* addressed primarily to them, would welcome it as you have, drawing from it any pertinent guidelines for their local Church situation, and that they would recommend it to their clergy, religious and laity. May I express our gratitude to you then for your careful analysis and our hope that all the faithful entrusted to your care will profit from the clarity and pastoral sensitivity you have shown in this most sensitive matter." See also Gerald D. Coleman, "A Pastoral Reflection: The Letter on the Care of Homosexual Persons," *Church* 6 (1987), 34-37. In addition, see J. Gramick and Pat Furey, eds., *The Vatican and Homosexuality*, New York: Crossroad, 1988.

[117] *Letter to the Bishops...*, nn 6-7.

[118] See also Genesis 18:20-21.

[119] Victor Paul Furnish, "Homosexuality," in *The Moral Teaching of Paul*, Nashville: Abingdon Press, 1979, 52-82.

[120] Ibid., 56.

[121] We will rely heavily on Furnish for this biblical exegesis.

[122] See John W. Howe, *Sex: Should We Change the Rules?*, Florida: Creation House, 1991, 31.

[123] See V. Furnish, op. cit., 65-67.

[124] Dio Chrysostom, *Discourse* LXXVII/LXXVIII.36.

[125] Philo, *On Abraham* 135-136.

[126] Seneca, *Moral Epistles XLVII*, "On Master and Slave," 7.

[127] Robin Scroggs, *The New Testament and Homosexuality*, Philadelphia: Fortress Press, 1983.

[128] *Malakoi* denotes "men and boys who allow themselves to be misused homosexually" (*A Greek-English Lexicon of the New Testament and Other Early Christian Literature*, ed., W. F. Arndt and F. W. Gingrich; 2nd ed.; Chicago: University of Chicago Press, 1979, 488).

[129] V. Furnish, op. cit., 69.

[130] Richard B. Hays, "Relations Natural and Unnatural: A Response to John Boswell's Exegesis of Romans 1," *Journal of Religious Ethics* 14 (1986), 184-215. See also John Boswell, *Christianity, Social Tolerance, and Homosexuality,* Chicago: University of Chicago Press, 1980.

[131] R. Scroggs, op. cit., 113.

[132] Ibid., 127.

[133] I am grateful to Michael L. Barre, S.S., for his invaluable help with this scriptural section. Fr. Barre is currently the Editor of the *Catholic Biblical Quarterly Monograph Series.*

[134] See William A. Henry III, "To 'Out' or Not to 'Out'," *Time* 138 (1991), 17.

[135] *Encyclopedia of Homosexuality,* ed., Wayne R. Dynes, New York: Garland Publishing, Inc., 1990, vol 1, 323.

[136] "Some Considerations Considering the Catholic Response to Legislative Proposals on the Non-Discrimination of Homosexual Persons," Foreword. The first version read, "...legislation has been proposed in some American states which would make discrimination on the basis of sexual orientation illegal."

[137] Ibid.

[138] Ibid., n 6.

[139] Ibid., n 9.

[140] Ibid., n 15. The first version did not include the words "such things as..."

[141] Ibid., n 16. Most importantly, the first version did not contain the words "family life."

[142] This same point has been made numerous times in Church documents and most notably in the Holy See's 1983 *Charter of the Rights of the Family.* Pope John Paul II reiterated the family's centrality in society in *Familiaris Consortio* (1981) and the concern is sharply expressed in *Educational Guidance in Human Love,* the 1983 document from the Congregation for Catholic Education: "The family has an affective dignity which is suited to making acceptable without trauma the most delicate realities and to integrating them harmoniously in a balanced and rich personality." (n 48)

[143] *Letter to the Bishops of the Catholic Church on the Pastoral Care of Homosexual Persons,* 1 October, 1986, n 17.

[144] We will follow here the treatment on discrimination in the *Encyclopedia of Homosexuality,* op. cit., 320-321.

[145] Congregation for the Doctrine of the Faith, *Declaration on Certain Questions Concerning Sexual Ethics,* Washington, D.C.: U.S.C.C. Publications Office, 1976, n 1.

[146] Dietrich von Hildebrand, *In Defense of Purity,* New York: Sheed and Ward, 1935, 13-14.

[147] *Letter to the Bishops...,* op cit., n 10. See U.S.C.C., *Human Sexuality,* Washington, D.C., 1991, 54. The Considerations cite all of n 10.

[148] *Human Sexuality,* op. cit., 55-56.

[149] *Letter to the Bishops...,* op cit., n 3.

[150] The first version read, "As a rule, the majority of homosexually oriented persons who seek to lead chaste lives do not want or see no reason for their sexual orientation to become public knowledge." Also, the word "usually" does not appear in the first version before "arise."

[151] *Human Sexuality,* op. cit., 56.

[152] "Some Considerations...," n 11.

[153] Ibid., n 12. This adds, "Thus it is accepted that the state may restrict the exercise of rights, for example, in the case of contagious or mentally ill persons, in order to protect the common good."

[154] See *Encyclopedia of Homosexuality,* op. cit., 322. The *Encyclopedia* adds, "It is... a fact that homosexuals are overrepresented in many areas of employment relative to their numbers in the general population, and in these fields quotas would not benefit the gay community, but rather deprive its members of their hard-earned livelihood. Then too,

many homosexuals who are in no way obvious would never identify themselves as deserving preference under a quota system."

**Chapter Six**

[1] H. Katchadourian and D. Lunde and R. Trotter, *Human Sexuality*, New York: Holt, Rinehart and Winston, 1979, 137-138.

[2] Congregation for the Doctrine of the Faith, *Declaration on Certain Questions Concerning Sexual Ethics*, 29 December 1975, Washington, D.C.: United States Catholic Conference, 1976, n 7.

[3] *Gaudium et Spes*, 50-51.

[4] Matthew 19:4-6.

[5] 1 Corinthians 7:9.

[6] See Ephesians 5:25-32.

[7] 1 Corinthians 5:1; 6:9; 7:2; 10:8; Ephesians 5:5; 1 Timothy 1:10; Hebrews 13:4; and 1 Corinthians 6:12-20.

[8] See, e.g., Innocent IV, Letter *Sub Catholica Professione*, 6 March 1254, DS 835; Pius II, *Propos. damn in Ep. Cum Sicut Accepimus*, 14 November 1459, *DS* 1367; Decrees of the Holy Office, 24 September 1665, *DS* 2045; 2 March 1679, *DS* 2148. Pius XI, *Casti Connubii*, 31 December 1930: *AAS* 22 (1930), 558-559.

[9] *Declaration*, n 7.

[10] United States Catholic Conference, *Human Sexuality*, Washington, D.C.: United States Catholic Conference, Inc., 1991.

[11] Ibid., 33-35; 53-54; 58-62. See also Pope John Paul II, *Familiaris Consortio*, n 11.

[12] Ibid., 34.

[13] See M. Scott Peck, *The Road Less Travelled*, New York: Simon and Schuster, 1978, esp II.

[14] See William J. Bennett, "Sex and the Education of our Children," *America* 18 (1987), 120-125.

[15] See F. Harlap, K. Kost and J.D. Forrest, *Preventing Pregnancy, Protecting Health: A New Look at Birth Control Choices in the United States*, New York: The Alan Guttmacher Institute, 1991.

[16] Bishops' Committee for Pastoral Research and Practices, *Faithful to Each Other Forever: A Catholic Handbook of Pastoral Health for Marriage Preparation*, Washington, D.C.: U.S.C.C. Office for Publishing and Promotion Services, 1989, 71.

[17] Ibid., 71-77.

[18] See J. Dwyer, *Human Sexuality: A Christian View*, Kansas City: Sheed and Ward, 1987, 84-85.

[19] See J. Neely, *The Myth of Equality*, New York: Simon and Schuster, 1981. Neely comments, "Between the ages of 6 and 12, a girl learns a sense of her own worth to men from her father's image of her. At this time, above all, she needs his social companionship, a developed sense of sharing with a mature member of the opposite sex that she will emphasize and enjoy in her nature all the rest of her life... If the young girl is denied the esteems... that she seeks from her father, she begins, often prematurely, to seek it elsewhere... She will do this almost any way she can to discover her worth as a social self, which unfortunately often leads to time-honored means and to one of the greatest disasters of womanhood — to precarious, premature, promiscuous sexuality. She often invests her whole youthful, idealistic self in a man she thinks she loves, and when this fails..., she feels irrevocably damaged in her substance" (45).

[20] See, e.g., K. Lorenz, *On Aggression*, tr., M. Latzke, London: Methuen and Co., 1970.

[21] See John 15:13.

22 We follow here the treatment of Vincent J. Genovesi, *In Pursuit of Love*, Wilmington: Michael Glazier, Inc., 1987, 175-176.

23 Paul Ramsey, "A Christian Approach to the Question of Sexual Relations Outside of Marriage," *The Journal of Religion* 45 (1965), 100-118; citation at 113.

24 V. Genovesi, op. cit., 176,

25 Lisa Sowle Cahill, *Between The Sexes*, Philadelphia: Fortress Press, 1985, 143.

26 Pope Paul VI, *Humanae Vitae*, n 12.

27 *Gaudium et Spes*, n 51.

28 Cahill, op. cit., 149.

29 J. Neely, op. cit., 92.

30 Exodus 20:14 and Deuteronomy 5:8.

31 See John L. McKenzie, "Adultery" in *Dictionary of the Bible*, Milwaukee: Bruce Publishing Co., 1965. See also L. William Countryman, *Dirt, Greed, and Sex*, Philadelphia: Fortress Press, 1988.

32 Exodus 20:17 and Deuteronomy 5:21.

33 John Paul II, "Ethical, Anthropological Content of 'Do Not Commit Adultery!'" in *Blessed Are the Pure of Heart*, Boston: Daughters of St. Paul, 1983, 26-32.

34 Matthew 5:28.

35 John 8:11.

36 Mark 10:11-12 and Matthew 19:9.

37 Ephesians 5:25-33.

38 See, e.g., 1 Corinthians 6.

39 1 Corinthians 6:19 and 1Thessalonians 4:3-5.

40 See, e.g., 1 Thessalonians 4:4 and 1 Corinthians 6:9-10.

41 Hebrews 13:4.

42 We will follow here the treatment of this subject in R. Lawler, J. Boyle and W. May, *Catholic Sexual Ethics*, Huntington: Our Sunday Visitor, 1985, 149-150.

43 See Dietrich von Hildebrand, *Man and Woman*, Chicago: Franciscan Herald Press, 1965, 18.

44 See Gerald D. Coleman, S.S., "Living Together and Marriage," *Church* 6 (1990), 45-46.

45 For this statistical data, we will rely heavily upon *Keeping Body and Soul Together*, the Document for the 203rd General Assembly, Presbyterian Church of the United States, 1991, 84-87. See also "Majority Now Considers Premarital Sex Acceptable," *Emerging Trends* 8 (1985), 3; "More Today Than in 1985 Say Premarital Sex is Wrong," *Emerging Trends*, Princeton Religion Research Center 9 (1987), 2; "Sex Information and Education Council of the United States," *Sexuality and Man*, New York: Charles Scribner's Sons, 1970; J. F. Kantner and M. Zelnik, "Sexual Experience of Young Unmarried Women in the United States," *Family Planning Perspectives* 4 (1972), 9-18; R. C. Sorensen, *Adolescent Sexuality in Contemporary America*, New York: World Publishing Co., 1973; H. Katchadourian, D. Lunde and R. Trotter, *Fundamentals of Human Sexuality*, 2nd ed., New York: Holt, Rinehart and Winston, 1975, 565-566.

46 Elizabeth R. McAnarney and William R. Hendee, "Adolescent Pregnancy and Its Consequences," *Journal of the American Medical Association* 262 (1969), 74-77.

47 Ibid., 468-470.

48 Ibid., 76.

49 Dorothy Miller, "Poverty, Single Parenthood and Teen Pregnancy," Wichita State University, *Center for Women's Studies Newsletter* (Spring 1991), 2.

50 E. McAnarney and W. Hendee, op. cit., 76.

51 Robert Crooks and Karla Baur, *Our Sexuality*, 4th ed., Redwood City: Benjamin/Cummings Co., 1990, 466.

52 Cited in *Keeping Body and Soul Together*, op. cit., 86.

[53] Karen Lebacqz, "Love Your Enemy: Sex, Power, and Christian Ethics," *Society of Christian Ethics Annual* 5 (1970, 7.

[54] "Teenagers in Survey Condone Forced Sex," op. cit., 23.

[55] *Human Sexuality*, op. cit., 61.

[56] Richard A. McCormick, "Adolescent Affection: Toward a Sound Sexuality," *The Homiletic and Pastoral Review* 61 (1960), 244-261.

[57] Ibid., 245.

[58] Pope Pius XII, "Chastete-Amour Mariage," *AAS* 44 (1952), 275.

[59] Dietrich von Hildebrand, *Fundamental Moral Attitudes*, New York: Sheed and Ward, 1950, 11-14.

[60] "Adolescent Affection: Toward a Sound Sexuality," op. cit., 254.

[61] Ibid., 259-260.

[62] See John McLaughlin, *Love Before Marriage*, Washington, D.C.: Corpus Books, 1970.

[63] Edward Malloy, "Pre-Marital Sexuality in America," *The Priest* 37 (1981), 12-20; citation at 20.

[64] See Francis W. Nichols, "Sexuality Fully Human," *The Furrow* 34 (1983), 145-154. We will follow here closely Nichols' presentation.

**Chapter Seven**

[1] Congregation for the Doctrine of the Faith, *Declaration on Certain Questions Concerning Sexual Ethics*, 29 December 1975, n 9.

[2] United States Catholic Conference, *Human Sexuality*, Washington, D.C.: United States Catholic Conference, Inc., 1990, 62.

[3] *Declaration on Certain Questions Concerning Sexual Ethics*, n 9.

[4] See Congregation for Catholic Education, *Educational Guidance in Human Love*, 1 November 1983, n 99.

[5] U.S.C.C., *Human Sexuality*, op. cit., 63. The quotation cited is from the *Declaration on Certain Questions Concerning Sexual Ethics*, n 9. In a Lenten 1991 letter to his priests, Bishop Eldon Curtiss of the Diocese of Helena, Montana, counsels, "All of us, no matter what our sexual orientation, must work at sexual integration and mature control over situations that will lead us to erotic sexual behavior. We have to gradually control conscious sexual phantasies that lead to inordinate masturbatory patterns in our lives. This discipline is basic to a fully chaste life."

[6] See H. Katchadourian, D. Lunde and R. Trotter, *Human Sexuality*, Brief ed., New York: Holt, Rinehart and Winston, 1979, 191-204. We will rely heavily in this section on the treatment of the subject found here.

[7] Shere Hite, *The Hite Report*, New York: Dell Publishing Co., 1976, 79-80.

[8] Hite describes six basic types of female masturbation: stimulating the clitoral/vulva areas with one's hand while lying on one's back; stimulating one's clitoral/vulva area with one's hand while lying on one's stomach; pressing and thrusting one's clitoral/vulva area against a soft object; pressing one's thighs together rhythmically; water massage of one's clitoral/vulva area; and vaginal entry.

[9] See Winifred Gallagher, "The Etiology of Orgasm," *Discover* 6 (1986), 51-59.

[10] H. Katchadourian, D. Lunde and R. Trotter, op. cit., 195.

[11] Ibid., 195.

[12] A. C. Kinsey, et. al., *Sexual Behavior in the Human Male*, Philadelphia: Saunders Publishing Co., 1948, 502.

[13] Michael E. Cavanagh, "Putting Sex in Perspective," *Make Your Tomorrow Better*, New York: Paulist Press, 1980, 280-288.

[14] Cited in Katchadourian, Lunde and Trotter, op. cit., 202.

[15] Elaine C. Pierson and William D. D'Antonio, *Female and Male*, Philadelphia: J. D. Lippincott Co., 1974, 86.

[16] H. Katchadourian and D. Lunde, *Fundamentals of Human Sexuality*, 3rd ed., New York: Holt, Rinehart and Winston, 1980, 289.

[17] C. Henry Peshke, *Christian Ethics*, vol. II, Alcester: C. Goodliffe Neale, 1977, 401.

[18] For more detailed information on the statistics of autoerotic behavior, see A. Comfort, *The Anxiety Makers*, New York: Delta Publishing Co., 1967; E. H. Hare, "Masturbatory Insanity: The History of an Idea," *Journal of Mental Science*, 452 (1962), 2-25; and N. Friday, *Secret Garden*, New York: Pocket Books, 1974.

[19] We will follow here closely the presentation of this subject given by Vincent J. Genovesi, *In Pursuit of Love*, Wilmington: Michael Glazier, Inc., 1987, 307-318.

[20] 1 Thessalonians 4:3-4.

[21] 1 Corinthians 6:9-11.

[22] See Norbert C. Brockman, "Contemporary Attitudes on the Morality of Masturbation," *The American Ecclesiastical Review* 166 (1972), 597-614.

[23] R. Lawler, J. Boyle and W. May, *Catholic Sexual Ethics*, Huntington: Our Sunday Visitor, Inc., 1985, 187-195.

[24] Ibid., 188.

[25] Ibid.

[26] Congregation for the Doctrine of the Faith, *Declaration on Certain Questions Concerning Sexual Ethics*, 29 December 1975, n 9.

[27] R. Lawler, J. Boyle and W. May, op. cit., 190.

[28] N. Brockman, op. cit.

[29] Charles E. Curran, "Masturbation and Objectively Grave Matter" in *A New Look at Christian Morality*, Notre Dame: Fides Publishers, 1968, 200-221.

[30] Marcellino Zalba, *Theologiae Moralis Summa*, vol. II, Matriti: Biblioteca de Autures Cristianos, 1953, 366.

[31] Curran here quotes G. Prick and J. A. Calon, "Masturbation Among Boys" in *New Problems in Medical Ethics*, vol. I, 37.

[32] See, e.g., *Summa Theologiae* I-II, q 88, a. 2, corp.

[33] See, e.g., *Summa Theologiae* II-II, q 154, a 12 ad 1.

[34] As one example, see footnote 34 of Curran's article.

[35] *Declaration on Certain Questions Concerning Sexual Ethics*, op. cit., n 9.

[36] V. Genovesi, op. cit., 314.

[37] See Klaus Breuning, "Responsible Sexuality as an Educational Goal: Problems and Prospects" in *Sexuality in Contemporary Catholicism*, Concilium, eds., Franz Bockle and Jacques Marie Pohier, New York: The Seabury Press, 1976, 88-92.

[38] See the discussion of this point in Donald Goergen's *The Sexual Celibate*, New York: The Seabury Press, 1974, 199-200.

[39] V. Genovesi, op. cit., 316.

[40] Ibid., 317; the quotation is from Bernard J. Tyrrell, "The Sexual Celibate and Masturbation," *Review for Religious* 35 (1976), 404.

[41] For a fuller discussion of this point, see James B. Nelson, *Embodiment: An Approach to Sexuality and Christian Theology*, Minneapolis: Augsburg Publishing House, 1978, esp. 160-163.

[42] V. Genovesi, op. cit., 318.

[43] Bernard Haering, "Human Sexuality: The Sixth and Ninth Commandments," *Chicago Studies* 13 (1974), 311.

[44] *Declaration on Certain Questions Concerning Sexual Ethics*, op. cit., n 10.

[45] See John R. Connery, "Prudence and Morality," *Theological Studies* 13 (1952), 564-582; and Richard A. McCormick, "Adolescent Masturbation: A Pastoral Problem," *Homiletic*

*and Pastoral Review* 60 (1959-1960), 527-540.

[46] Connery and McCormick give very good advice for priests, counselors and confessors: There may be need for simply one conversation on this matter; do not prolong what is not necessary. In addition, there should never be an undue forcing of such a conversation, which at times perhaps is simply a need to satisfy the confessor's own interest and curiosity. One should never deal with the adolescent in such a way as to create suspicion: e.g., one talks to teenagers only about this problem. Finally, some priests are psychologically unfit for this level of pastoral work because they cannot speak matter-of-factly about sexual matters. It is thus important to know one's own abilities and have the comfort to refer persons to someone more comfortable and/or experienced.

[47] V. Genovesi, op. cit., 325.

[48] Congregation for Institutes of Consecrated Life and Societies of Apostolic Life, *Directives on Formation in Religious Institutes, Origins* 19 (1990), 678-699.

[49] James A. Coriden, Thomas J. Green and Donald E. Heintschel, eds., *The Code of Canon Law: A Text and Commentary*, New York: Paulist Press, 1985, 209-211.

[50] Bernard J. Tyrrell, "The Sexual Celibate and Masturbation," *Review for Religious* 35 (1976), 399-408.

[51] William F. Kraft, "A Psychospiritual View of Masturbation," *Human Development* 3 (1982), 39-45.

[52] Ibid., 41, 43 and 45. See also W. Kraft, *Sexual Dimensions of the Celibate Life*, Kansas: Andrews and McNeill, 1979.

[53] These "Presuppositions" are taken from *Ideal Characteristics of Candidates for and Those Ordained from St. Patrick's Seminary*, Menlo Park: St. Patrick's Seminary, 1990, 6-7.

[55] *Ideal Characteristics* goes on to say that for the homosexually oriented man (and the same would apply to a woman in her own context), the seminary situation can constitute a heavy burden because of his inclination to relationships with other men. To live in close proximity with males is as much a challenge to the developing celibate vocation of a homosexual as living with females is for the emerging vocation of a heterosexual. This is not to bar homosexually oriented men from the priesthood. It is to recognize that the priestly training formation process places a particular burden upon them which demands a greater discipline. Both heterosexuals and homosexuals share in different ways a second kind of difficulty in the seminary. They live in an environment in which the normal feminine presence is absent. Since celibacy implies an ability to relate in depth to women as well as men, this absence of a normal relationship to women often makes difficult proper development in this area of celibate life. Heterosexual seminarians striving to grow in a celibate vocation face a specific difficulty. The fact that some of the men they live with might be homosexual can place a strain on their developing celibate vocation. Their past history may not have equipped them to live in a healthy way in close proximity with those of a different sexual orientation. A few may become homophobic; others may experience uneasiness. All must be helped to attain a healthy Christian acceptance of homosexual persons.

## Chapter Eight

[1] See William F. Maestri, "The Stewardship of Life," *The Linacre Quarterly* 47 (1980), 166-170.

[2] Paul Ramsey, *Ethics at the Edges of Life*, New Haven: Yale University Press, 1978; citation at xiii.

[3] See Leonard J. Weber, "Practical Utopian, and Poor — Just Stewards," *Spirituality Today* 33 (1981), 329-339; and William Bryon, *Toward Stewardship*, New York: Paulist Press,

1975.

⁴ L. Weber, op. cit., 331. Fletcher's book *Situation Ethics* was published in Philadelphia: Westminster, 1966. The example is on p 115.

⁵ Thomas A. Shannon and Lisa Sowle Cahill, *Religion and Artificial Reproduction*, New York: Crossroad, 1988, 57.

⁶ See Lennart Nilsson, *A Child is Born*, New York: Delacorte Press, 1990; "How Life Begins," *Life* magazine, August 1990. See also Clifford Grobstein, *Science and the Unborn*, New York: Basic Books, Inc., 1988, esp. 24-26 and 70.

⁷ Congregation for the Doctrine of the Faith, *Instruction on Respect for Human Life in Its Origin and the Dignity of Procreation: Replies to Certain Questions of the Day*, 22 February 1987, San Francisco: Ignatius Press, 1987, n 1.

⁸ Ibid., n 2.

⁹ Ibid., n 4. On 26 July 1991 the House of Representatives, Washington, D. C., voted to lift a ban on the use of fetal tissue in federally funded research projects, but fell five votes short of the number to override a threatened veto by President Bush. The vote was 274-144 to authorize $4.4 billion for the National Institutes of Health (NIH). Administration officials have said that President Bush would veto the legislation if it did not continue the ban on fetal tissue research. Douglas Johnson, legislative director of the National Right to Life Committee, mourned passage of the legislation, saying that "It is unworthy of us, as a nation, to kill our unborn children and then cannibalize them for spare parts." This legislation would overturn a 3-year-old ban on the use of fetal tissue for most abortions in federally funded research. The only exceptions in the ban are on tissue from miscarriages and from abortions performed to save a mother's life. Researchers indicate they have had some success in using fetal tissue to treat Parkinson's and Alzheimer's disease, epilepsy, leukemia and diabetes and in research to prevent birth defects.

¹⁰ The *Instruction* also teaches that corpses, whether deliberately aborted or not, must be respected "just as the remains of other human beings"(n 4).

¹¹ *Instruction*, n 5. The *Instruction* refers to embryos obtained *in vitro* and not transferred to the mother as "spare" and "exposed to an absurd fate" (n 5).

¹² Ibid., n 6. The *Instruction* also condemns twin fission; cloning; parthenogenesis; and cryopreservation. It is significant to note that cattle embryos can be kept alive and growing outside the womb of the cow for up to six days by using tissue-cultured oviduct cells to provide nourishment. The technique, called embryo co-culture, was originally developed by the Agricultural Research Service (ARS), USDA. "This allows us to make sure that only embryos that survive the manipulations of genetic engineering will be implanted into surrogate mothers," says USDA animal physiologist, Caird Rexroad, Jr., of Beltsville, Md. In practice, single-celled embryos that have had a gene inserted are placed in cultures of cells from the female's oviduct. Scientists speculate that certain nutrients released from the cultured cells keep the embryos alive and developing outside the womb. The ARS research, which has been primarily in sheep, has had a 30 percent success rate of implanting embryos that have been cultured for three days in surrogate ewes. Rexroad says other laboratories are finding similar results with cattle embryos.

¹³ Ibid., Introduction to Chapter Two. It is important to note that scientists in South Korea are on the verge of a breakthrough in a procedure physicians have been dreaming about for some time: the freezing and storage of unfertilized eggs. Sperm and embryos are regularly frozen for later use, but not eggs, which quickly lose their viability when manipulated outside the body. Many scientists expect this procedure to be available within the next few years. See Philip Elmer-Dewitt, "Making Babies," *Time* 138 (1991).

¹⁴ Ibid., n 1.

¹⁵ Ibid., n 2.

¹⁶ Ibid., n 2. The document explicitly states that subjectively good intentions (e.g., to

overcome sterility) do not render heterologous artificial fertilization conformable to the objective properties of marriage.

[17] Ibid., n 4. The *Instruction* then refers to the one conceived or desired as equalling a "product of an intervention of medical or biological techniques," and "an object of scientific technology" (n 4).

[18] Ibid., n 5.

[19] Ibid.

[20] Ibid. The document then teaches that "technical" means which facilitate the conjugal act and help it reach its natural objectives, "can be morally acceptable" (n 6). But the technical means cannot replace the conjugal act: these are "morally illicit."

[21] Ibid., n 8.

[22] Ibid., n 8; the quotation here is from Pope John Paul II's *Familiaris Consortio*, 14: *AAF* 74 (1982), 97. The document then urges scientists to continue their work to remedy the situation of sterility.

[23] T. Shannon and L. S. Cahill, op. cit.

[24] C. Grobstein, op. cit.

[25] See Marilyn Wallace and Thomas W. Hilgers, ed., *The Gift of Life*, Omaha: Pope Paul VI Institute Press, 1990.

[26] Shannon and Cahill point out that a critical factor here is whether insurance, either private or public, is available for the procedure. For example, Traveler's, Aetna, and Blue Shield have "premium waivers that cover up to four treatments." Kaiser Permanente also supports some IVF costs.

[27] *Gaudium et Spes*, nn 49 and 51.

[28] *Humanae Vitae*, n 7.

[29] *Familiaris Consortio*, n 32.

[30] John T. Noonan, *Contraception: A History of Its Treatment by the Catholic Theologians and Canonists*, Cambridge: Harvard University Press, 1986. Shannon and Cahill point out that the 1983 Code of Canon Law stresses that the preeminent "acts" of marriage are the acts of consent and of consummation, even after the Church has accepted some fundamental changes in understanding of the relationship underlining these acts, and has come to see that it is not the acts that are the prism through which to comprehend a marital relationship, but the other way around (p 50). In other words, the overriding moral criterion should be that of interpersonal love: i.e., an affective, emotional attachment, primarily signifying a commitment to create with one's spouse a cooperative partnership in sexuality, parenthood, and in the domestic and social roles that pertain to the couple and the family. Shannon and Cahill thus conclude that within the trinity of love, sex, and procreation, it is love that is fundamental, most humanly distinctive, and thus most morally important: sex and procreation can be defined fully only within the interpersonal relationship of the persons.

[31] Shannon and Cahill point out here that Catholic teaching insists that there are three inseparable values: sex, love and conception; and these three goods or values must be present not only within the totality of a relationship but within "each and every act."

[32] Shannon and Cahill point out that this is important since it is the first time that a distinction is made regarding gravity among sexual sins. In addition, not only is a distinction made, but it is linked to the relationships in which the elicit acts are carried out.

[33] Thomas A. Shannon and Allan B. Wolter, "Reflections on the Moral Status of the Pre-Embryo," *Theological Studies* 51 (1990), 603-626. See also Edmund D. Pellegrino, John Collins Harvey and John T. Langan, eds., *Gift of Life: Catholic Scholars Respond to the Vatican Instruction*, Washington, D.C.: Georgetown University Press, 1990.

[34] Grobstein names it an "oversimplification" to merely say that "an individual" begins at conception.

[35] See Gerald Bishop and Michael Waldholz, *Genome*, New York: Simon and Schuster, 1991.

[36] As we have seen, blastocyst is the stage at which implantation into the uterine wall normally begins. The external cells, now designated trophoblast (feeding layer) are elements that actively penetrate the uterine wall.

[37] See Stephen G. Post, "Fetal Tissue Transplant: The Right to Question Progress," *America* 9 (1991), 34-36.

[38] This "conferral of status" is already occurring to some degree when IVF practitioners feel obliged to transfer to the uterus all available pre-embryos.

[39] Grobstein concludes that discard of pre-embryos under any circumstances should only be "a last resort" (p 74): pre-embryos sustain a profound value that attaches to all stages of humanity, whatever the stage of the life cycle. See Keith L. Moore, *Essentials of Human Embryology*, Philadelphia: Decker Publishing Co., 1988.

[40] Grobstein points out that in most instances the diagnostic capability exceeds the therapeutic one: i.e., defects revealed by these techniques, such as Downs' Syndrome, usually cannot be satisfactorily treated within the uterus. It is at this point that "the abortion controversy rages most seriously" (p 89).

[41] Current policy assumes that a pregnant woman is already maternal in motivation and attitude, in the sense of wishing to protect her offspring against harm, even at some sacrifice of self-interest. But it also assumes that coercion of an uncooperative woman on behalf of her offspring violates her reproductive privacy. Therefore, a pregnant alcoholic, or one addicted to heavy smoking or drugs, cannot be legally constrained or punished for behavior that places her embryo at risk. Nor, obviously, can her embryo be moved to other custody.

[42] See Stephen G. Post, "Fetal Tissue Transplant: The Right to Question Progress," *America* 8 (1991), 34-36; Leon Jaroff, "Giant Step for Gene Therapy," *Time* 7 (1990), 74-76.

[43] Grobstein also argues, however, that when the integrity of the embryo is no longer meaningful because it cannot or will not develop further, it is still a member of the human community and should be valued for the special contributions it can make to that community (p 106).

[44] Under the legal interpretation of *Roe vs. Wade* prior to this capability ("viability"), the life of the fetus is secondary to the mother's right to reproductive privacy, which includes the right to terminate pregnancy even though it means terminating the life of the fetus. After the fetus becomes viable, however, the state may assert a compelling interest to intervene. To be more specific, the status of the fetus beyond roughly thirty weeks must take into account that it is already essentially an infant if suitable external support is available.

[45] Thomas A. Shannon and Allan B. Wolter, op. cit.

[46] See Steven B. Oppenheimer and George Lefedre, Jr., *Introduction to Embryonic Development*, 2nd ed., Boston: Allyn and Bacon, 1984.

[47] Ibid., 87.

[48] Thus the process of fertilization generally takes between 12-24 hours to complete, with another 24-hour period required for the two haploid nuclei to fuse.

[49] About 30 hours after fertilization, there is a two-cell division; around 40-50 hours there is a division into four cells; and about 60 hours the eight-stage cell division is reached.

[50] Shannon and Wolter point out that it is critical to note here that from the blastocyst state to the completion of implantation the pre-embryo is capable of dividing into multiple entities. In a few documented cases these entities have, after division, recombined into one entity again. Nor must this particular zygote become a human: it can become a hydatidiform mole, a product of an abnormal fertilization which is formed of placental tissue.

[51] Shannon and Wolter, op. cit., 611.

[52] Ibid., 612.

[53] Ibid., 619-620.

[54] For background reading of these questions, see John Connery, *Abortion: The Development of the Roman Catholic Perspective*, Chicago: Loyola University Press, 1977; Vincent J. Genovesi, "Abortion: A Vipers' Tangle for Morality" in *In Pursuit of Love*, Huntington: Michael Glazier, Inc., 1987, 328-399; John T. Noonan, *A Private Choice*, New York: The Free Press, 1979; and Congregation for the Doctrine of the Faith, *Declaration on Abortion*, 1975.

[55] *Resolution on Abortion, Origins* 19 (1989), 395-396.

[56] See "Cardinal Bernardin's Call for a Consistent Ethic of Life" and "Religion and Politics: The Future Agenda," *Origins* 14 (1984), 322-328.

[57] For a useful discussion of the "Consistent Ethic of Life" and the Mario M. Cuomo debate on this issue, see Vincent J. Genovesi, *In Pursuit of Love*, Wilmington: Michael Glazier, Inc., 1987, 389-399. I am very grateful to Reverend Robert W. McElroy, Ph.D., S.T.D., for his invaluable assistance in analyzing the abortion question. Fr. McElroy is author of *The Search for an American Public Theology: The Contribution of John Courtney Murray*, New York: Paulist Press, 1989.

[58] Governor Cuomo's remarks were made in a speech at the University of Notre Dame on 13 September 1984; quoted by Charles M. Whelan, "Religious Beliefs and Public Morality," *America* 151 (1984), 159-163.

[59] Connecticut Mutual's Survey of American Values in the 1980's found that 65% of Americans consider abortion morally wrong. The percentage of women, minorities, and the poor opposed to abortion was higher than 65%. In the 1989 Newsweek/Gallup Poll, 88% of U.S. citizens favored informed consent for women seeking abortions; 75% favored parental consent laws for teenagers; 61% favored prohibition of public funding for abortions, except in life-threatening circumstances. In the 1989 *New York Times* poll, 60% favored laws mandating testing for fetal viability before abortion. Thus, the *status quo* in this country on abortion is not favored by the majority of Americans. Most U. S. citizens are morally "uneasy" with abortion.

[60] James R. Kelly, "Catholic Abortion Rates and the Abortion Controversy," *America* 10 (1989), 82-85.

[61] *Decree on the Ministry and Life of Priests*, n 4.

[62] Canon 915.

[63] J. Coriden, T. Green, and D. Heintschel, ed., *The Code of Canon Law: A Text and Commentary*, New York: Paulist Press, 1985, 653.

[64] John Paul II, "Letter on Combating Abortion and Euthanasia," *Origins* 21 (1991), 136.

[65] See Peter Chirico, "Moral Values and Political Responsibilities," *Chicago Studies* 24 (1985), 97-110. In this question of Catholic "disloyalty" it is important to recognize a hierarchy of certainty and importance in Church teaching, a hierarchy which the U.S. bishops themselves attach to the differing positions espoused in the pastoral letters on war and peace and the economy. For example, a Catholic is not "disloyal" to the Catholic tradition in supporting the MX missile, even though the bishops opposed the MX missile. It is always critical to understand the intrinsic importance of a teaching within the schema of the Catholic tradition [hence the significance of traditional theological NOTES]. Abortion, in this example, is much more a question of loyalty to the faith than the bishops' recommendation on acceptable unemployment levels, both because the correctness of the Church's position on abortion is more apparent to the magisterium than the correctness of the position on unemployment, and because the intrinsic importance of the issue of abortion is more significant than the unemployment level.

[66] The poetic statement of Don M. Gregory Dix in *The Shape of the Liturgy* (1945) is certainly applicable to this discussion: "*Do this in memory of me. — Was ever another*

command so obeyed? For century after century, spreading slowly to every continent and country and among every race on earth, this action has been done, in every conceivable human circumstance, for every conceivable human need — from infancy and before it, to extreme old age and after it, from the pinnacles of earthly greatness to the refuge of fugitives in the caves and dens of the earth. *Do this in memory of me.* We have found no better thing than this to do for kings at their crowning... or for the bride and bridegroom in a little country church; for the proclamation of a dogma or for a good crop of wheat; for a wisdom of the Parliament of a mighty nation or for a sick old woman afraid to die; for the famine of whole provinces or for the soul of a dead loved one; for the settlement of a strike or for a child for a barren woman; for the repentance of a sinner or for the wounded and prisoners of war. *Do this in memory of me.* This has been done while the lions roared in the nearby amphitheater, on the beach at Dunkirk, tremulously by an old priest on the 50th anniversary of his ordination, furtively by an exiled bishop who had hewn timber all day in a prison camp in Russia, gorgeously for the canonization of a saint — one could fill many pages with the reasons why we have done this, and not tell a hundredth part of them. And best of all, week by week and month by month, on a hundred thousand successive Sundays, faithfully, unfailing, across all the parishes of Christendom, pastors have obeyed this command just to *make* the *plebs sancta Dei* — the holy people of God."

[67] For a full discussion, see M. Wallace and T. W. Hilgers, eds., *The Gift of Life*, Omaha: Pope Paul VI Institute Press, 1990; and John Boyle, ed., *Creative Love*, Front Royal: Christendom Press, 1989.

[68] William E. May, "Begotten Not Made," *Perspectives in Bioethics*, Connecticut: Pope John Paul II Bioethics Center, 1983, 54.

[69] T. Shannon and L. Cahill, op. cit.

[70] They further argue that this "inseparability" does not need to be tied to specific sexual acts but rather to the marital relationship itself.

[71] See M. Wallace and T. Hilgers, op. cit., 9.

[72] Data taken from C. N. Frederick, J. D. Paulson and A. H. DeCherney, *Foundations of In Vitro Fertilization*, Washington, D.C.: Hemisphere Publishing Corp., 1987. As one example, Johns Hopkins Hospital in Baltimore requires the following indications for IVF-ET: tubal occlusion/failed reconstructive tubal surgery; endometriosis unresponsive to medical/surgical therapy; absent fallopian tubes; unexplained infertility; oligospermia; immunologic factor; and cervical factor. Couples requesting *in vitro* fertilization are required to obtain a psychologic evaluation prior to initiation of the IVF procedures. The purpose of this evaluation is to assess the psychological strengths and weaknesses of the marriage relative to the expected stress of IVF procedures as well as its result, which will be either a successful pregnancy or failure to achieve pregnancy.

[73] See T. O'Donnell, *Medicine and Christian Morality*, 2nd ed., New York: Alba House, 1991, 235-237.

[74] See C. Bennett, S. Seager, E. Vasher and E. McGuire, "Sexual Dysfunction and Electroejaculation in Men with Spinal Cord Injury: Review," *The Journal of Urology* 139 (1988), 453-457.

[75] T. O'Donnell, op. cit., 235.

[76] Presently, because of HIV-AIDS, some states have outlawed the use of fresh donor semen.

[77] If the sperm is provided by the husband, the insemination is called *homologous*; if the sperm is provided by a donor, the insemination is called *heterologous*.

[78] *Donum Vitae*, II-B-5.

[79] Ibid., II-B-5.

[80] National Conference of Catholic Bishops, *Statement on Tubal Ligation*, 3 July 1980.

[81] Ibid., n 1.
[82] Pope Paul VI, *Humanae Vitae* (1968), n 14.
[83] United States Catholic Conference, *Ethical and Religious Directives for Catholic Health Care Facilities*, 1971, Directive 20.
[84] Sacred Congregation for the Doctrine of the Faith, *Reply of the Sacred Congregation for the Doctrine of the Faith on Sterilization in Catholic Hospitals*, 13 March 1975; and N.C.C.B., *Commentary on Reply of the Sacred Congregation for the Doctrine of the Faith To National Conference of Catholic Bishops on Sterilization in Catholic Hospitals*, 15 September 1977.
[85] Repeat caesarian section is an obstetrical indication often cited as a reason for a tubal ligation at the time of delivery. Careful analysis is called for. The fact of a pregnancy existing in a patient who has previously undergone caesarian delivery does not, in itself, constitute a type of "pathological" condition, as necessitated in the Church's teaching (as indicated in the *Commentary*). A uterus previously operated upon, as in the case of caesarian section, bears a "scar" which it did not previously have. To this degree, the uterus would not be "normal." To the same degree, any organ with a "scar" that was created surgically could be considered "non-normal." Given this data, it is unreasonable to state that a repeat caesarian section automatically represents a pathological state and should be treated as such. This "non-normal" condition is complicated by reference to the type of uterine scar: whether it be vertical (midline) or horizontal (transverse) in the lower uterine segment. Most scars are of this latter type. In the midline type, most authorities advocate a repeat caesarian section; whereas in the transverse type, the patient is a more ready candidate for vaginal birth after caesarian (VBAC). Consequently, what was once thought of as a "pathological state" of the uterus is less significant in current thinking on this subject. In the United States in general, it is rare to have a repeat caesarian section constitute a pathological condition, making a future pregnancy truly dangerous. Very infrequently, an obstetrician may encounter a uterus so altered by previous surgery(ies) that it literally cannot be repaired. More commonly, but still relatively infrequent, an obstetrician may find that the uterus, while technically repairable, is of such a nature, due to past caesarian-induced "scarring," that it would not appear likely to sustain a subsequent gestation, if it were to occur. Such rare discoveries may necessitate the removal of the uterus, sometimes referred to as a caesarian hysterectomy. In the face of the possibility of such a cataclysmic uterine rupture, this life-threatening situation exists only if there is a subsequent pregnancy.

**Chapter Nine**

[1] U.S.C.C., Administrative Board, *The Many Faces of AIDS: A Gospel Response* in *Origins* 17 (1987), 482-489. This document treated nine basic topics: (1) Gospel values; (2) facts about AIDS; (3) societal responsibility; (4) health care professionals/institutions; (5) testing; (6) persons with AIDS; (7) public policy; (8) pastoral issues; and (9) prevention of AIDS.
[2] National Conference of Catholic Bishops, *Called to Compassion and Responsibility: A Response to the HIV/AIDS Crisis, Origins* 19 (1989), 422-434.
[3] This decision was made at the Spring meeting of the bishops in 1988 in Collegeville, Minnesota: see "AIDS Discussion at June Bishops' Meeting," *Origins* 17 (1988), 726; and "AIDS Statement: Proposal of Cardinal Bernardin Accepted," *Origins* 18 (1988), 118-120. The precise motion was: "That the president appoint an Ad Hoc Committee to prepare a new, updated statement on the AIDS crisis which will respond to the new facts, fears and efforts which have emerged in recent months. The committee, in preparing the new statement, will have the benefit of the extant Board statement on AIDS..., the

discussions which have taken place since its publication, dialogue with the Congregation for the Doctrine of the Faith, and participation by all the bishops in open, plenary session."

[4] Report of the Presidential Commission on the Human Immunodeficiency Virus Epidemic, Washington, D.C., June 1988.

[5] Jon D. Fuller, "AIDS and the Church: A Stimulus to Our Theologizing," Cambridge: Weston School of Theology, 1991.

[6] Ibid., 3.

[7] We will follow here closely the treatment of this subject in Fuller's lecture.

[8] Centers for Disease Control: "Mortality attributable to HIV infection/AIDS — United States, 1981-1990" in *Morbidity and Mortality Weekly Report* 40 (1991), 41-44.

[9] Centers for Disease Control: "AIDS in Women — United States", *Morbidity and Mortality Weekly Report* 39 (1990), 845-846.

[10] Fuller also points out (p 5) that it is critical to note the differential impact of HIV upon persons of color. A disproportionate share of the burden is being borne by women of color, especially by Black women, and by their children. By 1988, among children aged 1-4 in New York and New Jersey, AIDS was the number one cause of death among Hispanic children and number two among Black children. In the last decade in this country we have witnessed more than 100,000 deaths from AIDS; one-third of them occurred during 1990 alone.

[11] See footnotes 3-6 in Fuller, op. cit., for bibliographical material substantiating these statistics.

[12] Yves Congar, *Situation et taches presents de la theologies*, Paris: Les Editions du Cerf, 1967, as quoted in Fuller, op. cit., 7. Vatican II's *Gaudium et Spes* also teaches that "The human race has passed from a rather static concept of reality to a more dynamic, evolutionary one. In consequence, there has arisen a new series of problems, a series as important as can be, calling for new efforts of analysis and synthesis" (n 5).

[13] See the development of this question in *Keeping Body and Soul Together*, 203rd General Assembly, Presbyterian Church, 1991, 142-156.

[14] The etiologic agent that causes human immunodeficiency disease is known as the "human immunodeficiency virus" (HIV). HIV disease refers to a syndrome of medical diseases caused by a variety of pathogens (e.g., bacteria, and certain cancers and pulmonary diseases) that attack people living with AIDS whose immune systems have been weakened by HIV.

[15] See "*New York Times* Offers Unofficial Glimpse at Draft CDC Guidelines on AIDS Testing," *Hospital Ethics* 8 (1991), 9-10.

[16] *Called to Compassion*, n 8. The quotation is from *Gaudium et Spes*, n 1.

[17] See "The Sobering Geography of AIDS," *Science* 12 (1991), 372-373.

[18] See National Catholic Educational Association, *AIDS: A Catholic Educational Approach*, Washington, D.C.: N.C.E.A., 1988, esp. 6-10.

[19] *Called to Compassion*, n 6.

[20] Footnote 11 of *Called to Compassion* points out that researchers indicate that people who were over 40 years old when infected are 4-8 times as likely to develop AIDS within 7 years as people who were under 20. People who are older progress to AIDS at a significantly greater rate than teenagers or young adults. In addition, Richard T. Keeling, President of the American College Health Association, has said: "We are more disturbed than heartened. Because of patterns of sexual activity and drug abuse among college students, it is possible that there could be further significant spread of HIV in this population." Although researchers have learned a great deal about HIV spread, they are still struggling with some extremely important questions. For example, why are the patterns of AIDS virus infectivity so different in Africa and North America? In Africa, almost all of the cases occur in heterosexual people, affecting men and women equally;

in North America, the disease primarily strikes male homosexual people. Recent studies indicate that lack of circumcision alone increased the likelihood of AIDS infection some 5-to-8 fold, whereas a history of genital ulcers alone increased it 4-to-5 fold. See "Circumcision May Protect Against the AIDS Virus," *Science* 245 (1989), 470-471.

[21] See Steve Heimoff and Julia Sommer, "Is the HIV — AIDS Theory All Wrong?" *CalReport* 8 (1991), 6 and 18.

[22] An additional complication concerns the mysterious mutations of the AIDS virus. Up to now, researchers have encountered over 200. Although there is scientific controversy regarding these mutations, it is clear that the family of human retroviruses is on the increase.

[23] See The Walter Reed Classification System, taken from: Robert R. Redfield and Donald S. Burke, "HIV Infection: The Clinical Picture," *Scientific American*, 259 (October 1988), 94-96.

[24] See Gerald D. Coleman, *AIDS: Information Guide for Educators*, San Jose: Department of Education, 1988, 10-11.

[25] In *The Many Faces of AIDS*, this is footnote 7 and refers to Augustine's *De ordine* ii. 4. 12; and Thomas Aquinas' *De regimine principum* iv. 14 and *Summa theologiae* I-II. 96. 2; 101. 1 ad 2; II-II.10.11. Part of the "unofficial translation" of the *Summa* citation is, "Although God is omnipotent and good in the highest degree, nevertheless he permits certain evil things to develop in the universe, which he would be able to prevent except that, if these things were taken away greater goods would be eliminated and even greater evils would follow as a consequence. So also in human governance, those who govern rightly tolerate certain evils lest certain goods be impeded or also lest some greater evil be obtained..." This footnote also makes reference to various classic authors regarding the toleration of the lesser evil (Dugre and Zalba). Reference is also made to Pope Pius XII's *Ci riesce* of 6 December 1953.

[26] See, e.g., "National Federation of Catholic Physicians' Guilds Proposed Position Paper: Statement on Prevention of AIDS by Condoms," *Linacre Quarterly* 55 (1988), 12-15; and N.C.E.A., *AIDS: A Catholic Educational Approach*, op. cit.

[27] *Called to Compassion*, IV:3.

[28] J. Fuller, op. cit., 10.

[29] See Gerald D. Coleman, "Condoms and the Teaching on the Lesser of Two Evils," *Church* 9 (1990), 49-50.

[30] See "Can You Rely on Condoms," *Consumer Reports* 157 (1989), 135-140.

[31] See Beverly Sottile-Malona, "Condoms and AIDS," *America* 165 (1991), 317-319; and Archbishop John R. Quinn, "Distributing Condoms in High Schools," *America* 165 (1991), 320. We will follow here the presentation given by Sottile-Malona and Archbishop Quinn.

[32] Ibid., 317.

[33] See specifically the article by Archbishop Quinn.

[34] Walter J. Smith, *AIDS: Living and Dying with Hope*, New York: Paulist Press, 1988. See also C.H.A. of United States and the Conference of Major Religious Superiors of Men's Institutes of the U.S., *The Gospel Alive: Caring for Persons with AIDS and Related Illnesses*, St. Louis: The Catholic Health Association of the United States, 1988; and John E. Fortunato, *AIDS: The Spiritual Dilemma*, San Francisco: Harper and Row, 1987. See also Richard Dunphy, *AIDS: What the Church is Saying and Doing*, Liguori, Missouri: Liguori Publications, 1988.

[35] Ibid., 40.

[36] We will follow here the presentation of *Called to Compassion* in its section "A Call to Compassion" (II:1-3).

[37] See *Keeping Body and Soul Together*, op. cit., 151-153. See also Matthew 25:31 ff and

Luke 10:25-37.

[38] Parker J. Palmer, *The Company of Strangers: Christians and the Renewal of America's Public Life*, New York: Crossroad, 1983.

[39] See Leviticus 19:33-34 and 1 Peter 4:9.

[40] Henri J. N. Nouwen, *Reaching Out: The Three Movements of the Spiritual Life*, New York: Doubleday and Co., 1966, 51.

[41] For example, Jesus gives sight to the blind (Matthew 20:30-34; Mark 10:46-52; Luke 18:35-43) and makes the crippled walk (Matthew 9:2-7; Mark 2:3-5; Luke 5:18-24); he touches and heals lepers (Matthew 8:3; Mark 1:41; Luke 5:13); he shares a meal with people considered legally impure (Matthew 26:6; 9:10; 11:11; Mark 2:15-16; Luke 5:30); he shames the judges of the adulterous woman and forgives her sin (John 8:1-10).

[42] Matthew 25:40.

[43] Matthew 25:31-32, 41-46.

[44] Luke 10:30-37.

[45] Cited in *The New York Times*, 5 May 1989, A5.

[46] Pope John Paul II, "The Christian Meaning of Human Suffering," Washington, D.C.: U.S. Catholic Conference, 1984, n 29. The Pope emphasized this same point in speaking to the U.S. Catholic Health Care Leaders in 1987: "Besides your professional contribution and your human sensitivities toward all affected by this disease, you are called to show the love and compassion of Christ and his Church. As you courageously affirm and implement your moral obligation and social responsibility to help those who suffer, you are individually and collectively living out the parable of the good Samaritan..."

[47] This same point was made by the Pope in *Love and Responsibility*, New York: Farrar, 1981, 202: "Tenderness... springs from awareness of the inner state of another person (and indirectly of that person's external situation, which conditions his inner state) and whoever feels it actively seeks to communicate his feeling of close involvement with the other person and his situation. This closeness is the result of an emotional commitment. That sentiment enables us to feel close to another 'I'... Hence also the need actively to communicate the feeling of closeness, so that tenderness shows itself in certain outward actions which of their very nature reflect this inner approximation to another 'I.'"

[48] *The Pope Speaks*, 17 September 1987, 401-403.

[49] *Called to Compassion*, II:3.

[50] See Barbara G. Faltz and Joanna Rinaldi, *AIDS and Substance Abuse*, San Francisco: University of California at San Francisco, 1987.

[51] *Called to Compassion*, IV:1. In nn 9 and 11 of *Principles to Guide Confessors...* one reads, "The confessor should encourage the person to form stable relationships with persons of both sexes... Two other elements which should be stressed are regular access to spiritual direction and the formation of a stable relationship with at least one person. One of the greatest difficulties for the homosexual is the formation of such a friendship... If a homosexual has progressed under the direction of a confessor, but in the effort to develop a stable relationship with a given person has occasionally fallen into a sin of impurity, he should be absolved and instructed to take measures to avoid the elements which lead to sin without breaking off a friendship which has helped him grow as a person. If the relationship, however, has reached a stage where the homosexual is not able to avoid overt actions, he should be admonished to break off the relationship."

[52] For a full discussion of this issue, see Gerald D. Coleman, "Can a Person with AIDS Marry in the Catholic Church?" *The Jurist* 49 (1989), 258-266.

[53] Several articles have given attention to the question of whether a person with AIDS or an HIV carrier can marry in the Catholic Church: "An Opinion: Can An AIDS Victim Marry?" *Fellowship of Catholic Scholars Newsletter* 11 (1987), 6-11; William A.

Varvaro, "Canon 1058: Prohibition Against Marriage of AIDS Victims" in *Roman Replies* and *CLSA Advisory Opinions 1987*, ed., William A. Schumacher and J. James Cuneo, Washington: CLSA, 1987, 113-123; Pius Smart, "Another Opinion," ibid., 123-125. The question is further analyzed by William E. May, "The Question of the Use of Condoms by Spouses to Prevent Transmission of AIDS," *Fellowship of Catholic Scholars Newsletter* 12 (1988), 1-2.

[54] Thomas P. Doyle in *The Code of Canon Law: A Text and Commentary*, ed., James A. Coriden et. al., New York: Paulist Press, 1985, 743.

[55] Ibid.

[56] This point is underlined by C. Everett Koop: "Married people who are uninfected, faithful and don't shoot drugs are not at risk. But if they engage in risky behavior..., they can become infected with the AIDS virus and infect their partners. If you feel your spouse may be putting you at risk, talk to him or her. It's your life" (C. Everett Koop, M.D., *Understanding AIDS: A Message from the Surgeon General*, Washington, D.C.: U.S. Government Printing Office, 1988).

[57] Canon 1077.

[58] Canon 1077:2.

[59] Canon 1098.

[60] This latter point raises very significant issues: e.g., should physicians, dentists and those in health care who have tested positive for the virus be mandated to inform their patients.

[61] N.C.C.B., *Pastoral Statement of the U.S. Catholic Bishops on Handicapped People*, 15 November 1978, n 10.

[62] John 3:16.